STUDENTS
IN DISCORD

STUDENTS IN DISCORD

Adolescents with Emotional and Behavioral Disorders

C. Robin Boucher

The Greenwood Educators'
Reference Collection

GREENWOOD PRESS
Westport, Connecticut • London

Library of Congress Cataloging-in-Publication Data

Boucher, C. Robin.
  Students in discord : adolescents with emotional and behavioral
disorders / C. Robin Boucher.
      p.   cm.—(The Greenwood educators' reference collection,
ISSN 1056–2192)
  Includes bibliographical references and index.
  ISBN 0–313–30799–7 (alk. paper)
  1. Problem youth—Education—United States. 2. Learning disabled
youth—Education—United States. 3. Mentally handicapped youth—
Education—United States. 4. Conduct disorders in adolescence—
United States. 5. Behavior disorders in children—United States.
6. Behavior modification—United States. I. Title. II. Series.
LC4802.B68 1999
371.93—dc21   98–30492

British Library Cataloguing in Publication Data is available.

Library of Congress Catalog Card Number: 98–30492
ISBN: 0–313–30799–7
ISSN: 1056–2192

First published in 1999

Greenwood Press, 88 Post Road West, Westport, CT 06881
An imprint of Greenwood Publishing Group, Inc.

Printed in the United States of America

The paper used in this book complies with the
Permanent Paper Standard issued by the National
Information Standards Organization (Z39.48–1984).

10 9 8 7 6 5 4 3 2 1

Copyright Acknowledgments

The author and publisher gratefully acknowledge permission to quote from the following material:

From "Life's Just a Bowl of Chutney" by Phyllis C. Richman, Food Critic. *The Washington Post*, July
16, 1995: C5. Reprinted with permission of *The Washington Post*, 1150 15th Street, NW, Washington,
DC 20071.

Sound peeps from anywhere
From under a tree
From in a mouth
From an animal
When the phone rings
When you turn something on
From a yawn of boredom during school
From the footsteps of an angry man
From the quietest of creatures
To the loudness of man
From the music of a teenager
From the agony of pain
To snores of sleep
From the snaps of bubble gum
And the chews
From the sounds of nature
And the opposing ones
From the creak of a chair
To the whisper of gossip
From the sound of a band
To the sound of harmony
To the rips of a mistake
Yes, that is where sound comes from

Rick

Life is like a guitar
We all have potential to make music
But some guitars are naturally better than others
They're easier to play or they have a clearer sound
But it's not how nice the guitar is
It's how much one works and practices
That is what determines how the music will sound
Unfortunately, no matter how hard one may work
Sometimes he can't ever make beautiful music
Not because of him
But because of the guitar

Myra

Contents

Preface

Your world is you. I am my world.

Wallace Stevens

This book is dedicated first of all to public school students with emotional and behavioral disorders, who numbered 428,168 nationwide in the 1994-1995 school year according to the *Eighteenth Annual Report to Congress* (U.S. Department of Education 1996). They struggle to grow, to learn, to find meaning and a place in life, and to create order in the midst of their disorderly lives. The accord with others that most of us take for granted eludes them. For them, the challenge is to make sense of the forces within and around them. Unfortunately, discord is often their way of life.

This book is also dedicated to two particular students: Jason and Billy. Jason's life ended suddenly at age 18 because he could not cope with the forces in and around him. Billy's life continues, vastly improved. He walks with his head held high, and his gait is brisk and purposeful. He has a part-time job in computer sales and wants to apply that experience to a business career. He laughs a lot. He achieved honor roll grades in spring 1998, and he has been accepted at two universities. Billy faced his challenges and made sense of the forces within him and around him.

"Discordant" is often used to describe the behavior of these students. Kauffman (1993a) summarized these students well, noting that they arouse negative feelings and induce negative behavior in others; often are not popular with or leaders of their peers; and typically experience academic failure in addition to social rejection or alienation. Most adults avoid them, and their behavior persistently irritates those in authority. They seem to be asking for punishment; even in their own eyes they are failures. They obtain little gratification from life and repeatedly fall short of their own aspirations. Finally, they are disabled because of their behavior, which costs them many opportunities for gratifying social interaction and self-fulfillment, and their options are highly restricted.

These students need assistance to grow emotionally and socially and to acquire the skills necessary to move toward adult independence and competence.

They need to learn how to blend in with others, to learn how to improve what Goleman (1995) refers to as emotional literacy.

This book is dedicated also to the teachers of students with emotional and behavioral disorders. These teachers must deal with a heterogeneous population of students with both internalizing and externalizing problems. The mixture of presenting problems in any one student group can be overwhelming. These teachers must also develop a repertoire of skills to instruct their students in both academic and nonacademic areas.

Teachers of students with emotional and behavioral disorders often perceive themselves as only somewhat knowledgeable about the characteristics of these students. They frequently feel they lack knowledge of medical, behavioral, psychological, and educational approaches used to deal with this heterogeneous population, which is difficult to teach because of a complex combination of internalizing and externalizing problems (Cheney and Barringer 1995). In short, teachers of these students need information about the spectrum of emotional and behavioral disorders.

Finally, this book is dedicated to the parents of youngsters with emotional and behavioral disorders. There is a popular misconception that behind every disturbed youngster is at least one disturbed parent. Let it be understood here that not all disturbed children are created by disturbed parents. Some of these youngsters have competent parents who try everything imaginable to reach and teach their children. These problem youngsters may be the only troublesome offspring in a family that could be harmonious were it not for one discordant child.

Many parents of such youngsters suffer their own emotional upheavals while they try to understand why their children have these problems. Mothers and fathers who hear that parents cause their children's emotional and behavioral problems may suffer from long-term guilt and marital discord. It is understandable that parents of students with emotional and behavioral disorders are typically underrepresented at parent-teacher meetings and do not readily form parent support groups.

These parents, then, also need more information about emotional and behavioral disorders. First, they need to understand that many youngsters have constitutional and organic disorders, conditions that parents may have transmitted to their children, which manifest in emotional and behavioral problems. Second, these parents need to understand that life circumstances, which can be changed, may cause or aggravate disorders.

Above all, it is necessary to be objective about discordant youngsters. As parents live with and try to cope with these youngsters they deserve our understanding and commendation, not our censure for their struggles.

Introduction

A gap exists in the professional literature, particularly literature that blends theory and practical information, in relation to students with emotional and behavioral disorders. This book was designed to help bridge theoretical and practical information in the specific area of adolescent emotional and behavioral disorders.

This book's intended audience includes students preparing to become special education teachers, special and regular education teachers needing information about students in discord, and those who prepare and supervise these teachers. These professionals constitute a powerful group whose responsibility is to define, classify, and educate schoolchildren who have emotional and behavioral disorders. Other professionals, such as school psychologists, social workers, guidance counselors, and vocational counselors, as well as many others who work in public and private schools, clinics, detention centers, and assorted community agencies, may find this book helpful. Parents, too, may find that it contributes to a better understanding of their own youngsters.

The purpose of this book is to provide theoretical information, insights gained from actual cases of adolescents in discord, and some practical application. The intent is not to replace the current textbooks that provide important information concerning the vital statistics of this population, the federal regulations and guidelines, and the conceptual models that undergird treatments and services and represent the state of the art across the nation. Rather, the intent is to slice off a piece of the theoretical pie, specifically the one that deals with types and defining characteristics of emotional and behavioral disorders, and provide actual illustrations and suggested educational strategies that will stimulate a deeper understanding and increase the ability to educate.

The focus is on adolescents who are able to function in their communities and who are enrolled in public schools. These are the students who require instructional accommodations and intervention skills for inclusion in the mainstream setting. With a fuller understanding of these youngsters, the reader will be ready to pursue or further explore practical avenues toward inclusiveness.

FOUR SPECIFIC GOALS

One goal is to make it clear that most emotional and behavioral conditions are not unitary; they overlap. This is particularly true of children and adolescents, who are in a relatively rapid period of growth and development. Because our understanding of many emotional and behavioral disorders is in a fluid state, openness to evidence is more appropriate than rigid codes. Professionals use the word "interrelated" to describe this reality.

A second goal is to provide understanding about emotional and behavioral conditions that are just beginning to be understood in pre-adults. Historically, conditions such as depression, Tourette's syndrome, bipolar disorder, and narcissism have been viewed as predominantly adult disorders. Antisocial personality disorder, despite growing evidence of it among pre-adults, continues to be regarded as an adult phenomenon. Until very recently, diagnosis and classification of the psychological disorders of children have been a neglected and confused area of abnormal psychology. For example, the first *Diagnostic and Statistical Manual of Mental Disorders (DSM)*, published by the American Psychiatric Association in 1952, listed only two categories of children's disorders: childhood schizophrenia (now considered to be an inappropriate diagnosis) and a catch-all category labeled "adjustment reaction of childhood." Not until the 1987 version of the *Diagnostic and Statistical Manual* was there a generally accepted classification system for children's disorders.

The third goal of this book is to enhance understanding of the federal definitional guidelines for emotional disturbance (ED). This goal will be achieved by relating disorders to federal criteria throughout and by comparing the characteristics observed in the students whose cases are included with the characteristics defined in the federal guidelines.

The fourth goal of this book is to provide some educational strategies that will provide some guidelines. Emotional disturbance is a disability category that falls among the "soft" classifications. Unlike the "hard" disabilities, such as deafness or blindness for which there are objective signs of impairment, the soft categories, which also include learning disabilities, involve subjective identification criteria. The difficulty of identifying a disability correlates with the challenge of choosing appropriate educational strategies.

The educational programs for students with emotional and behavioral disorders should include a repertoire of change strategies representing various models, at least the behavioral, psychological, sociological, and environmental. A behavioral approach might involve a performance contract or systematic reinforcement; a psychological approach might involve relationship building or integration of the student's interests in activities; a sociological approach might involve the use of group dynamics to integrate the student, for example class meetings and cooperative learning activities; and an environmental approach might involve physical arrangement of the classroom to optimize learning. Any one approach might dominate at a particular time, as needed, but all models should be used in the long run.

Within the repertoire, change strategies should be able to address a variety of needs manifested by students with emotional and behavioral disorders. These students typically show needs for acceptance/approval, external control, internal control, appropriate engagement in activities, encouragement, consistency/routine, and attention. These students will manifest these needs, singly or in combination, at any one time, another reason for having a comprehensive repertoire of teaching strategies.

At this point, a caveat is in order. There has never been, and likely never will be, a manual for teaching all students with emotional and behavioral disorders. No cookbook could possibly address all the permutations and combinations of needs and strategies. There are, however, manuals, such as McCarney and McCain's 1995 manual, that purport to contain strategies for teaching the most commonly seen behavior problems identified by educators in the school environment. That particular manual claims that listed interventions should serve as a programming guide for any student in need of behavioral improvement. In effect, such a manual presumes that education begins with a list of interventions rather than with the student's needs. The reality is that effective, valid programming is needs-based.

Each student exhibits a constellation of needs and, consequently, a need for a constellation of teaching strategies. Therefore, the manifesting difficulties should be the paramount consideration in designing educational interventions. Indeed, the best guide to selecting any approach is the student, who shows us which approach is needed.

Hence, when reading the sections concerning educational strategies, the reader should keep in mind that the presented approaches are merely suggestions for particular disorders and that the suggestions are neither exhaustive nor limited to a particular disorder; they are intended to show a range of strategies that represent the behavioral, psychological, sociological, and environmental models. Also, the student's needs should be evaluated first, and then the array of possible strategies should be explored.

Finally, it is important to keep in mind that the aim of educational strategies for students with emotional and behavioral disorders should not simply be to stop undesirable behaviors. Horner and Carr (1997) noted that the goal of a comprehensive intervention is to produce rapid, durable, generalized reduction in problem behaviors while improving the individual's success. Neel and Cessna (1993) have pointed out that there is ample information in the literature about how to stop behavior, but only a few programs focus on instruction in new, desired behaviors. Too often programmatic progress is not evaluated in terms of students' movements toward social competency and maturity. For example, if a student deals poorly with frustration, the classroom might be engineered to eliminate frustrating events, which might decrease the number of outbursts resulting from frustration. However, the student also needs to learn how to deal more effectively with frustration, thereby building a generalizable social skill. Instruction, then, should be a planned response to various situations, rather than a highly controlled program designed to reward a limited set of social behaviors that apply only to instructional settings. Thus, the suggested educational strategies presented here are aimed at both decreasing undesirable behaviors and increasing desirable replacement ones.

In the balance, positive strategies should outweigh negative ones. It is not necessary to make students with emotional and behavioral disorders feel bad to engender appropriate behavior. Toward a positive approach, the following points are important: Regard each day as a new opportunity to learn and change; be easy on yourself; the goal is improvement, not perfection. Also, use a 10:1 rule: For every 10 reinforcers there may be one punisher.

Instruction should focus on *stimulus-based interventions*. These approaches focus on the events that precede behavior in contrast with the more conventional interventions that manipulate behavioral consequences and suggest follow-up strategies. Antecedent procedures are attractive because they can be nonintrusive; they manipulate conditions already in the environment rather than add new ones. They also have been effective in decreasing problem behavior (Munk and Repp 1994). Examples of stimulus-based strategies are student choice of task, task variation, pace of instruction, and decreased task difficulty.

THE PRIMARY AND SECONDARY SAMPLES

A primary sample of 13 middle school students appears throughout the book. These adolescents, who represent assorted emotional and behavioral disorders of the externalizing and internalizing types, are used to illustrate theoretical points. Anecdotal material, direct quotes from students and teachers, life facts, and some of the students' own writings are included. Primary case synopses are located in the appendix for reference. This practical content, interjected throughout, is offset in italicized print. The secondary sample (N = 44), all middle school and high school students, is used to illustrate various points of theory.

A list of the 13 students included in the primary sample has been provided; next to each name is an actual quote from that student. The synopses of their cases that appear in the appendix include positive and negative factors in their backgrounds that might contribute to emotional-behavioral disorders or that might favor normal development, signs of emotional-behavioral disorders, special education eligibility, and psychiatric and/or psychological diagnoses. The secondary sample appears on the page following the primary sample; these students are presented by first name in alphabetical order.

Kauffman (1993a, p. 7) described disturbed children and youths as those who "arouse negative feelings and induce negative behavior in others." Let this book arouse understanding. This is the place to engage in mental challenges and to acquire a mental set. This is the time to enjoy the luxury of learning without having to confront.

 With the idea that all the world is a stage, as Shakespeare said, let this book provide a stage upon which the players can strut and flaunt their stuff, informing us of who they are and what their emotions and behaviors mean as they receive their cues from theoretical points.

The Primary Sample

Name	Quote
Adam	*"I don't fit in."*
Andy	*"It's hard to concentrate."*
Billy	*"I wish my dad would run away from home."*
Chris	*"I feel like I'm in a pit. Every time I try to get out someone pushes me back in."*
Fred	*"I'm somewhere else."*
James	*"I'm deranged."*
Jesse	*"I'll wait 'til the movie comes out."*
Joel	*"I need action."*
Laura	*"I don't want to do this!"*
Michael	*"I don't need help."*
Olivia	*"I'm tired, I can't sleep."*
Rick	*"School has turned me into a wreck."*
Sara	*"I don't want to be treated special."*

The Secondary Sample

Names

Alan	JJ
Alicia	John
Andrew	John H
Bart	Juan Christian
BB	Judy
Billy H	Justin
Blythe	Karina
Brett	Laurel
Brian	Lisa
Brooke	Mark
Carrie	Mary
Chris B	Melissa
David	Myra
David O	Nathan
Delano	Ricky
Donnie	Rob
Eric	Robbie
Heather	Robby
Jed	Robert
Jeff	Sarah
Jennie	Sharon
Jennifer	Zach

1

Setting the Stage

Faith bleats to understand.

Emily Dickinson

It is common wisdom in education that practice should coexist with theory. When we have an idea, the proof of its fruitfulness is in the application. Conversely, practice that does not inform theory and build up the information base is worthless. Metaphorically, the fruit that does not seed more fruit-bearing parents has no perpetuity.

A melding of theory and practice is too often absent in education. Rather, there exists a schism. There has been a great deal of doing without knowing and knowing without doing.

When schools were first established in the United States, teachers learned their craft by working with other teachers. It was a learning-by-doing enterprise; neophytes were apprenticed to experienced teachers. At that time, supply and demand were in balance; the demand for and availability of teachers evened out. Each teacher who prepared an apprentice ensured replacement.

Compulsory schooling changed that situation. When schools were forced to accept more and more children, changes in teacher preparation became necessary. Sheer numbers threw supply and demand out of balance.

If the state mandated that a child attend school, the state also had to insist that the teacher in whose hands the child would be placed possessed at least a minimal level of competence. Teachers became, essentially, apprentices to the state, and state "certification" was born (Mayer 1964). Along with teacher certification came formalized teacher preparation outside the school and classroom. Teacher education was introduced to America in 1839 when the first normal school was established in Massachusetts to improve the quality of teachers (Howsam 1980).

Thus, 1839 could be regarded as the pivotal year in which the emphasis shifted from doing to knowing. Teachers no longer were expected to learn from doing, as apprentices to seasoned teachers. Instead, they became apprentices to standards set in state offices by "experts" in the field of education. These experts, in turn, decided what curriculum should guide teacher preparation programs. Many of the courses that were offered satisfied the instructors' interests rather than the teachers' job requirements (Smith 1980). Those courses represented theories espoused by experts, most of whom had never been in a classroom. Today the problem in teacher education has not been so much the establishment of training programs as the content of the training programs (Ysseldyke and Algozzine 1982).

Despite the proliferation of teacher preparation during this century, that preparation has been misleading. Undergraduates and graduate teachers in training often reveal their apprenhension of work in the real world; many become depressed by how little they know about teaching (Ysseldyke and Algozzine 1982). Teachers seem to be more painfully aware than any other professional group about the inadequacies and irrelevancies of their preparation, or the separation of knowledge and practice.

A schism in special education has paralled that in education generally. While the timeline, venue, and apprenticeship aspects differ, the evolution of a great divide between doing and knowing has been equally clear.

Preparation of special education teachers began where their students were most likely to be found: in institutions and training schools for the disabled. The Vineland Training School in New Jersey, for example, became active in training teachers, through a series of summer school programs, in 1903. The course of study, which began with five students, consisted of lectures and laboratory work (Johnstone 1909-1910).

The first model of teacher preparation in special education, then, involved no apprenticeship with an experienced teacher. Instead, there was learning by doing as one's personality and inclination dictated. The venue was the institution where the disabled population was found.

It has not been very long since such a model prevailed. My own preparation to teach students with emotional disturbances began in 1967 in a Boston College program of five graduate students, whose specialized instruction was controlled by the principal of the children's unit school of Waltham State Hospital, with internship at the hospital school for the duration of the program. Like the earlier general educational approach, lectures and practical work were integral with the institution where the disabled youngsters were situated.

In 1958 Congress enacted Public Law (PL) 85-926, which authorized grants to universities and colleges for training leadership personnel in mental retardation. In 1963 PL 88-164 amended PL 85-926 to include support for the training of personnel in other disability areas: for example, emotional disturbances. Thus began, as in general education, state standards for teacher preparation and a schism between theory and practice.

IMPACT OF THE SCHISM

Teacher burnout. The impact of the schism between theory and practice probably contributes to teacher burnout, which has been a problem in

U.S. education. In 1978, for example, it was estimated that of 250,000 teachers working in special education about 6 percent, or 15,000, left the field every year (Siantz and Moore 1978). By the late 1980s, this figure was estimated at 25,000, or 10 percent of the special education workforce (U.S. Dept. of Education 1991). By the 1989-1990 school year, the estimate had climbed to a need for 29,511 special education teachers (U.S. Dept. of Education 1993). Singer (1993) demonstrated, through longitudinal data, that of all special education teachers in Michigan public schools hired between 1972 and 1985, only about 34 percent reentered within five years of leaving, and only 58 percent stayed for more than seven years. Billingsley and Cross (1991) reported that 39 percent of those special education teachers sampled gave burnout as a reason for leaving special education. Lauritzen (1990), too, reported that 41 percent of current special educators perceived burnout to be a reason for attrition in their field.

These statistics reflect the emotional fallout of teaching students with disabilities; teachers feel apprehension, depression, and a general sense of unease and unreadiness. Many preparing teachers become depressed by how little they know about teaching, and others simply never enter the profession (Ysseldyke and Algozzine 1982). Those who do enter the profession realize quickly how far apart are their knowing and their doing. Teachers who face demanding students every day are painfully aware of the schism. In the 1980s teachers continued to assert that much of what they were taught in school was unrelated to what they actually must do (Ysseldyke and Algozzine 1982).

Teacher preparation. Many graduates of teacher preparation programs feel that the programs have not helped them. Teaching is complex and stressful, but teacher training is frequently simple and relatively stress free compared with the realities of the profession.

Teacher preparation programs too often are academically, rather than clinically, oriented (Ysseldyke and Algozzine 1982). In comparison with other professions, education has the lowest proportion of credit hours allocated to specifically professional aspects of teaching (Howsam 1980). The Florida Barbers' Board requires more hours of schooling than Florida requires of their secondary education majors (Smith and Street 1980).

There has been a move toward competency- or performance-based instruction. Unfortunately, our knowledge of what a teacher does is limited, which, in turn, hampers our efforts to identify teaching competencies. What is needed is an intensive, extensive collaboration between schools systems and institutions of higher learning to determine the most meaningful explication of competencies. Knowing and doing aspects of the profession must be joined. Until there is a meaningful blend of theoretical and practical information there will not be a well-prepared stable cadre of teaching professionals.

THEORETICAL LINK WITH CASES

This book is predicated on the assumption that readiness and coping are best addressed by integrating theoretical and practical information. In this book, theory is linked to practice by using actual cases of adolescents with emotional and behavioral disorders to articulate points of theory. The pertinent aspects of these youngsters' lives are detailed at important points to clarify and illustrate the knowledge base. The cases themselves may be tracked through the book. Case synopses for the primary sample are contained in the appendix, including outlines of medical, educational, psychological, and social information, information typically amassed for a comprehensive evaluation of students who are suspected of having a disability. Because most of the adolescents in the primary sample demonstrate problems that illustrate more than one condition, the reader can follow any cases of interest within and across conditions.

On the other hand, the secondary sample was chosen to illustrate specific points of theory with no attempt to subject it to further qualitative or quantitative analysis. As walk-on players, these students are more like character actors for specific conditions.

TEN PRACTICAL CHARACTERISTICS

A second major point in setting the stage for this book relates to the characteristics of the students. The author generated a list of 10 outstanding practical characteristics shown by secondary students in discord with whom she had worked over a 30-year period (see Table 1.1).

After the content of the cases is used to illustrate, clarify, and articulate points of theory, the field-generated characteristics are used to reanalyze the cases, characteristic by characteristic. Quantitative and qualitative analyses lead to

Table 1.1
Ten Outstanding Practical Characteristics of Students with Emotional and Behavioral Disorders

Characteristics
Low Self-Esteem
Narcissism
Misperception
Poor Body Awareness and Hygiene
Untrustworthiness
Physical Symptoms
Keen Sensitivity to Others
Depression
Mood Swings
Lack of Tolerance for Untroubled Kids

conclusions about what is significant to know about emotionally and behaviorally disordered adolescents. The practical characteristics actually   observed in the cases also are compared with the defining guidelines laid down in federal law, PL 101-476, the Individuals with Disabilities Act (IDEA), reauthorized as PL 105-17, the IDEA Improvement Act of 1997. (These conclusions are presented in Chapter 23.)

RESILIENT VS. VULNERABLE YOUNGSTERS
Another major stage-setting issue relates to the resiliency of children and their lack of resiliency. Resilient youngsters are those who, despite exposure to significant risk factors, show few or no signs of developmental impairment. Even when exposed to multiple risk factors at an early age, youngsters who subsequently show no severe psychological, learning, or behavioral disturbances merit the label *stress resistant* (Feldman and Elliott 1990).

It is easier to identify a resilient child than it is to understand why a child is resilient. Any explanation of stress resistance must include many factors: the pattern of stresses, individual differences caused by both constitutional and experiential factors, compensating experiences outside the home, the development of self-esteem, the scope and range of available opportunities and appropriate degree of environmental structure and control, the availability of personal bonds and intimate relationships, and the acquisition of coping skills (Rutter 1979). Many of these familiar factors are seen in stories about youngsters who have experienced a myriad bad experiences at home and in the neighborhood, including poverty, neglect, and abuse, but who have overcome them by bonding with one significant adult, for example, a teacher, a coach, or a guidance counselor.

On the other hand, youngsters who are not resilient are vulnerable to life's stressors. These are the students who show emotional and behavioral disorders.

These nonresilient youngsters are damaged by life's circumstances, including the circumstances of their own biological constitutions. They cannot seem to rise above their circumstances, and they create circumstances that interfere with their own, and others', lives. Packard summarized the resilience-vulnerability dichotomy:

My exploration has convinced me that youngsters are tougher and more adaptable than I had originally assumed. They can take quite a few hard knocks early in life, and even thrive from them, if certain other factors are present. At the same time we are seeing an increase in patterns of living and of child-raising that can often inflict lasting damage on children. (1983, p. xx)

Careful study of cases such as those presented in this book can help us develop an explanation for lack of resilience, particularly the "certain other factors" to which Packard alluded. Many factors presented in our primary and secondary cases suggest why some youngsters are unable to rise above their circumstances: familial mental illness, dysfunctional parenting, poor self-esteem, limited opportunities, lack of bonding, trauma, a learning disability, family stress, and internal biochemical imbalance. These and other daunting factors can mitigate against normal growth and development. Overall, the present cases suggest that resilience may be a multidimensional phenomenon involving internal and external factors.

Finally, youngsters who are resilient might also be called emotionally intelligent. As Goleman (1997), author of *Emotional Intelligence*, states, this critical gauge includes the ability to control impulses, soothe anxiety, calm anger, focus on goals, persevere in the face of setbacks, and empathize and interact with others harmoniously. Resilience seems to reflect an ability to live without discord, and vulnerability seems to reflect an inability to live without discord.

EXTERNALIZING VS. INTERNALIZING DISORDERS

Finally, this book comprehensively covers both externalizing and internalizing disorders. This feature reflects long overdue recognition of the range of skills needed to educate this heterogeneous population.

It has only been since about 1980 that research has focused on internalizing disorders that involve *acting in* problems, such as depression, social withdrawal, anxiety disorders, and childhood suicide and presuicidal behaviors. These are also referred to as problems of overcontrol, meaning that these youngsters are unable to express themselves, let go, or come out from behind their emotional masks. They expend a lot of mental energy holding their emotions in check.

Most attention, historically, has been given to externalizing disorders (Reynolds 1990a). These disorders involve *acting out* behavior, for example, noncompliance with authority. These youngsters have problems with undercontrol: They cannot delay their impulses, and they express themselves too readily. They expend a lot of mental energy on releasing their emotions on the environment. Over the years, students who act out have been the priority; quiet, withdrawn, anxious students have been underidentified.

The main reason for underidentification of internalizing disorders is that these students do not create the overt problems that demand immediate attention in the school. For example, Donnie, one of our secondary sample, reached the age of 18 without being identified for special education services despite chronic learning problems and one suicide attempt as a result of pervasive depression. A quiet, withdrawn student, he did not draw attention to himself. It is the squeaky wheel that gets the attention.

The subject of internalizing, or affective, disorders among adolescents has been especially shrouded in controversy because of the reputed difficulties of unraveling the problem of *adolescent turmoil* (Carlson and Strober 1983). It is often assumed that all adolescents experience affective disorders such as depression. Hopefully, this book will be edifying and help dispel myths.

Let us look at externalizing and internalizing disorders in more detail. First, externalizing students challenge teachers with a confrontational behavioral style. These are the kinds of behaviors that have been labeled antisocial, oppositional, and disruptive. Fighting with peers is an example. These students express themselves aggressively, are assertive to the point of being combative, and have no difficulty advocating their self-interest. As one teacher said, "They are always in your face."

For a student with an internalizing disorder, on the other hand, there is interference with self-expression, assertiveness, and self-advocacy. These students present intriguingly subtle problems involving thought disorders, anxieties, mood swings, dissociative reactions, fantasies, eating disorders, phobias, suicidal ideas, and other self-contained difficulties. In other words, these youngsters experience a great deal of internal distress. Their disorders represent underlying emotional tendencies and affective disturbances. Emotions are disorganized and disrupt personality development and functioning.

The emotions and behaviors of the acting-out student also have a serious impact on development and functioning. Their emotions may involve internal distress but in different ways. For example, the academic achievement of students with externalizing disorders is typically significantly lower than that of their internalizing peers. Some of the behavioral problems of acting-out students may result from low frustration tolerance in the face of academic demands (Cheney and Barringer 1995).

There also may be combinations of externalizing and internalizing disorders. Many antisocial youngsters are depressed, even suicidal, and many have thought disorders. In the primary sample featured here, the lines of demarcation between internalizing and externalizing disorders are blurred. Most of these youngsters show signs of both types of disorders.

This interrelation may predict diverse outcomes. Youngsters with both types of disorders may be at highest risk for chronic, serious mental health impairment. For example, the complexity of interrelatedness is evident in youngsters who have attention deficit disorders, either with hyperactivity (ADHD) or without hyperactivity (ADD). Studies of ADD and ADHD show that ADHDs are more impulsive and aggressive, and demonstrate more signs of conduct disorder than ADDs, who appear to be more lethargic and sluggish and who are more likely to receive an internalizing diagnosis, particularly anxiety disorder (Cole and Zahn-Waxler 1992).

SUMMARY

In conclusion, this book concerns adolescents who are in discord as a result of internalizing and/or externalizing problems. They are presented in a context that integrates theory and practical illustrations, with explication of their vulnerability and the multidimensionality of their disorders.

2

Primary and Secondary Samples

This chapter focuses on three issues related to the primary and secondary student samples: the rationale for focusing on adolescents, including developmental guidelines, sample attributes, and the methods employed in developing this book.

RATIONALE FOR FOCUSING ON ADOLESCENTS

Background. The word *adolescence* is derived from the Latin verb adolescere, which means "to grow up." As Muus (1988) defines it, adolescence is a period between puberty and maturity, a period marked by the appearance of secondary sexual characteristics, physiological changes that ready the individual for procreation. A definition that focuses on social-emotional aspects is offered by Sebald (1968): Adolescence in the social-psychological sense refers to the experience of passing through the unstructured and ill-defined phase that lies between childhood and adulthood. Adolescence is a phase that is different from the one before and the one after. It is a stage of life that is distinct from both childhood and adulthood.

What makes this phase different? For one thing, unique internal and external forces operate simultaneously. Internal work needs to be accomplished: physical and sexual maturation, acquisition of skills to become independent, autonomy from parents, and clarification of social interconnectedness with same- and opposite-sex peers. External forces operate, imposing specific expectations on the adolescent that shape some of the internal tasks. These forces, primarily social influences, "are pivotal in human adolescence because society shapes the expression of biological imperatives to a remarkable degree" (Elliott and Feldman 1990, p. 1).

These unique internal and external forces create special conflicts. The conflict between internal and external forces is exemplified by the external pull to acquire formal education and the internal drive to assume adult roles; society encourages extended education, which conflicts with readiness to procreate and desire to enter the workplace.

Adolescence has become a particularly stressful phase of life. There are many pressures to grow up fast, experiment with dangerous lifestyles and substances, and take risks. The rise of teenage pregnancies, the numbers of adolescents charged with crimes as adults, and the rising death rate among adolescents owing to suicide, drugs, crime, and violence attest to a major crisis. Adolescence has become a test of survival rather than just another, albeit rocky, developmental stage, and signs of emotional and behavioral disorders become acute and dramatic during this time. Children, generally, have different developmental issues than adults:

Adolescence is, among other things, an organized set of expectations closely tied to the structure of adult society. It stands out from the other stages of human development as a period of preparation rather than fulfillment. Infancy is cherished in its own right; childhood and adulthood are seen as noble enterprises; and old age, we believe, is rightly brandy, not vinegar. But adolescence is a phase of imminence that is not quite imminent enough, of emergent adult biology that is not yet completely coordinated with adult roles, of hopes that are not yet seasoned by contact with adult reality, and of peer culture and society that mimic those of adults but are without adult ambitions or responsibilities. Adolescents are in a state of preparing themselves for adulthood by experimenting, studying, resisting, or playing. (Modell and Goodman 1990, p. 93)

Those attempting to articulate the distinct needs of adolescents often must confront negative images. "To a degree possibly never experienced before, the present image adults hold of youth is one of discontent and alienation" (Garrison 1973, p. 64). Many adults stereotype adolescents, and many of the stereotypes are charged with fear. Frequently, adults are more willing to stereotype adolescents than other adults.

This stereotyping is aggravated by age segregation. In the United States today adolescence is characterized by marked age segregation; in fact, adolescents often have little regular interaction with adults. "Peer interactions and peer pressures are particularly prominent" (Elliott and Feldman 1990, p. 3). Compared with adolescents in other cultures and at other times, American adolescents currently have an unequaled freedom of self-determination in many areas of their lives; for example, their academic efforts, their choice of friends, their sexual behavior, and their use of illegal substances. Indeed, there seems to be an adolescent ghetto.

While every generation of adolescents undergoes similar biological changes, every generation faces social problems that differ from those of previous generations. As a society, we are in a period of rapid change. Parents are uncertain about what and how to teach their children, and adolescents are troubled about what choices to make, what models to emulate, and what to think and believe (Garrison 1973). The complexity of our society today has presented adolescents with problems unknown to past generations, and we can expect more complexity and more problems in future generations.

Finally, some professionals have defined adolescence in terms of chronological age subdivisions. The modern period of adolescence extends over so many years that it can be subdivided into early, middle, and late substages. Early adolescence has been defined as ages 12 to 14, a period of profound physical and social changes that occur with puberty and an intensifying of interactions with the opposite sex; middle adolescence as ages 15 and 16, a time of increasing independence; and late adolescence, ages 17 to 19, a period of identity firming and consolidation. These demarcations have been institutionalized into American educational structures: junior high school, middle school, high school, and college (Elliott and Feldman 1990). (See Table 2.1.)

ADOLESCENT DEVELOPMENT: THE NORMAL COURSE

In adolescence a number of factors indicate that development is proceeding on course. Even allowing for individual differences, there are physical, psychological, cognitive, social, sexual, and educational and occupational signs that the youngster is evolving normally.

Physical development. Normal physical development involves changes. Changes in early adolescence include marked and sizable growth spurts, even while the individual still looks, acts, and thinks like a child. At this time, parents may comment that the young boy of last summer has suddenly become the gangly adolescent; his nose or lower jaw may be noticeably large; his arms and legs are relatively long; and his hands and feet look too large for his body. One 13-year-old girl commented when looking at a photograph of herself, "I look like I've got frying pans growing off my arms."

With increased secretion of hormones, the growth spurt begins. Height may increase by as much as five inches, and weight may increase by 20 pounds, in a year. During early adolescence differential growth and change rates are also normal. In any middle school one can expect to see students of very different heights and weights. Glands at the surface of the skin also begin to secrete more sweat and oil, resulting in more intense body odor and acne, the bane of many adolescents.

Puberty, alas, has been reached. Sexual maturity is reality; both genders have developed their primary sex characteristics. Boys can reproduce when they produce live sperm, and girls can reproduce as soon as they ovulate.

Secondary sex characteristics, the much heralded indicators of gender, accompany puberty. The boy's voice deepens, and his external reproductive organs grow. The girl's breasts enlarge, and her proportions begin to look more rounded. Both genders develop pubic and underarm hair, and the male develops facial hair. Some boys are sensitive about dressing out for physical education during this phase because they do not yet have pubic hair and the other boys do.

Table 2.1
The Challenges of Adolescence

Early Adolescence (12-14)

Struggle with sense of identity
Moodiness
Improved ability to use speech for self-expression
Close friendships gain importance
Less attention shown to parents; occasional rudeness
Realization that parents are not perfect; identification of parental faults
Search for people to love other than parents
Tendency to return to childish behavior, fought off by excessive activity
Peer group influences interests and clothing styles

Middle Adolescence (15-16)

Self-involvement, alternating between unrealistically high expectations
        and poor self-concept
Complaints that parents interfere with independence
Extremely concerned with appearance and own body
Feelings of strangeness about self and body
Lowered opinion of parents; withdrawal of emotions from them
Effort to make new friends
Strong emphasis on new peer group; group identity involves selectivity,
        superiority, and competitiveness
Periods of sadness as the psychological loss of parents occurs
Examination of inner experiences; may include writing a diary

Late Adolescence (17-19)

Firmer identity
Ability to delay gratification
Ability to link ideas and to express ideas in words
More developed sense of humor
Stable interests
Greater emotional stability
Ability to make independent decisions
Ability to compromise
Pride in own work
Self-reliance
Greater concern for others

Girls, too, may be shy about undressing in front of peers because their breasts are still buds compared to those of the girls who need to wear brassieres.

By middle adolescence, then, physical changes have already begun. The adolescent typically is drawn to the opposite sex. Yesterday's boy who mocked kissing as "boy biting girl" is today's boy whose palms sweat at the sight of an appealing girl.

Physical maturity is essentially complete during late adolescence. Concerns about education, occupation, romantic relationships and long-term commitments, and the future become important. Normally, the changes are less obvious, and the youngster is more able to deal with what is ahead rather than the uncertainties of the present. By now the physical changes are less dramatic.

Psychological development. During normal development the adolescent is driven to replace attachments. This process, essential in establishing identity (Erikson 1968), is necessary for consolidating a sense of self (Howard 1960). This phase is characterized by an essential conflict between independence and dependence. The adolescent, typically, is ambivalent about accepting responsibility and demonstrating independence, which represents a certain amount of risk. At this time, too, the adolescent may show moodiness and a mixture of independent rebellion along with conformity. Confusion may be evident about what he or she wants from day to day.

This process makes both parent and child nervous. Engaged in a struggle called "dual ambivalence" (Stone and Church 1968), they seek simultaneously to approach and avoid aspects of their relationship that involve assertiveness and support. Parents want to be needed, and children want to be loved and nurtured, yet each is nervous about too much of a good thing. Adolescence also is a source of normal anxiety:

With the onset of adolescence comes another potential source of anxiety. For the first time the individual is perceived by the world as a sexual being. This can be a troublesome point: Am I attractive? Am I sexually desirable? Why are my friends growing so much faster than I? Why do I have such a small penis? Will my breasts ever fill out? Many more insecurities arise. Peer relationships reinforce the cultural ideals for physical desirability (it should be emphasized that these ideals, however important, are completely arbitrary), and the individual soon develops an attitude about how well he or she meets these ideals. (Simon and Gagnon 1972, p. 457)

Cognitive development. According to Piagetian theory, adolescence marks entry into the highest stage of cognitive development, the period of formal operations. Unlike children, adolescents often display the ability to solve problems in a systematic way. They are now able to think of several alternative solutions to problems, and they can test alternative solutions in a rational, orderly manner. Thinking also becomes abstract in contrast to the concrete thinking of younger children.

Adolescents also are beginning to distinguish between what is real and what is possible, between what is and what might be. Imagination is used not only for fantasy and play but for solving problems mentally because they can manipulate symbols, which enables them to think about their own thoughts and play with ideas. Horror movies, which in the past triggered nightmares, are sought out and enjoyed during this period of development. While young children are readily scared and amazed, adolescents readily critique horror and science fiction films for their historical inaccuracies and technological inadequacies and look for hidden meanings and implicit messages. Reality takes over from magical and irrational thinking (Deutsch 1967).

The tendency to think abstractly is made manifest during this stage in academic and personal areas. For example, there are significant changes in self-perception during adolescence. A nine-year-old will normally describe himself in concrete terms, listing physical attributes such as hair color and interests, while a 17-year-old will normally describe himself in terms of human qualities, personal attributes, religious values, and ambiguities. One adolescent described herself as follows:

I am a human being. I am a girl. I am an individual. I don't know who I am. I am an indecisive person. I am an ambitious person. I am a very curious person. I am a confused person. I am a pseudoliberal. I am an atheist. I am not a classifiable person. (Harris and Liebert 1984, p. 469)

With abstract thinking comes the ability to build theories, and often the adolescent is full of them. He may tell his teachers what is the right religion; he may tell his parents what the correct child-rearing practice is; and he may tell his little sister that she knows nothing about life compared to his exalted understanding. It is the dawn of ideology.

Various aspects of adolescent cognitive development differentiate. For example, during early and middle adolescence, while the ability to process information evolves, "puberty noise" interferes with thinking (Pishkin 1967). During the late adolescent phase, when the physical changes have become less dramatic, the ability to commit to ideals emerges (Adelson 1975), with less interfering static. At this time, too, adolescents typically can use universal moral principles to guide their behavior, and there is an increasing tendency to think of issues in terms of fairness rather than of practicality (Adelson and O'Neill 1966).

Social development. Social development at this time involves a struggle to shift primary allegiance from parents to peers. Not only is it time to shift from one reference group to another, it is time to become a model for younger people. The adolescent's identity becomes firmer; his ideas become more his own or more like those of his friends rather than those of his family.

In the struggle to gain independence, it is normal for adolescents to have conflicts with their parents. Disenchantment with parental values and attitudes is a common way for young people to begin to express their independence. Some adolescents may engage in open revolt against parental demands and restrictions and refuse to comply with parental expectations, a characteristic that troubles many parents.

On the other hand, adolescents typically conform readily to peer group standards. Early adolescence, particularly, is characterized by intense peer conformity. Numerous studies have shown that youngsters are more likely to conform to group pressures in early adolescence than at earlier or later ages. This is one reason why many secondary educators are turning to peer mediation for conflict resolution.

Few adolescents have just a single close friend (Harris and Liebert 1984). Adolescent subcultures, made up of individuals of the same ages who share knowledge, values, and experiences, thrive. In any one school there may be academic, delinquent, and fun subcultures thriving simultaneously. It is normal to be part of some subculture, regardless of socioeconomic class or ethnic group. In some ethnic groups, especially Asian, Afro-American, and Hispanic, gangs thrive. Most adolescents are members of groups, either informal cliques or more formal clubs or gangs. These peer groups provide support even though they may represent petty, intolerant, or even cruel attitudes and behaviors, for example Skinheads and neo-Nazis. Some extreme groups reject outsiders who are different in race, religion, social class, abilities, or appearance (including dress). Adolescents are able to derive a sense of identity from the particular group to which they belong, their "in" group. Intolerance for the "out" group is normal at this stage.

Adolescents, of course, do not describe their groupings as "subcultures"; they describe their associates as friends. The number of friends varies. Among adolescent boys affiliations are normally among large, nonexclusive groups, while among young adolescent girls there is a tendency to have a few close friends and exclude outsiders. In late adolescence a sorority, or clique, pattern among girls normally develops.

There is a tendency to solidify identity by choosing friends who are similar to oneself in attitudes and preferences; in academic achievement; in tastes for music, clothing, recreation activity, and athletic ability; and in extracurricular pursuits. Also, attitudes concerning smoking, drug use, and sexual behavior are likely to be shared. These attitudes and preferences, furthermore, seem to become more alike over time because of bonding.

Aside from quantity and quality issues, what distinguishes adolescent friendships from those of childhood is closeness and intimacy with the opposite gender. As the adolescent develops closer same-sex friendships, those with the opposite sex are also developing. However, adolescents of opposite genders may be uneven in their ability to develop opposite-gender friendships, attesting to some lag between the genders in social development.

SOCIAL DEVELOPMENT EXAMPLE. *Heather, at 18, is proud of herself for the number of friendships she has developed with boys. Her boyfriend, with whom she has had a close, sexual relationship for about six months, however, is jealous of Heather's male friends. Jeff does not understand Heather's desire to spend time with male friends and is convinced that she is sleeping with them. As those boys are older than Jeff, he assumes that Heather has been lured into the arms of older men. In fact, Heather has not been sexually active with other boys. Jeff has been unable to develop platonic relationships with girls.*

Sexual development. Sexuality is critical for adolescent identity and more important than most parents may want to acknowledge. Since the late 1960s adolescents have been sexually active in greater numbers and at younger ages. There is dissonance between parents' hopes that kids are the same as ever and statistics that document the numbers of 12-year-old boys and girls "doing it" (Winn 1984).

Sex is part of adolescent socialization. It is real, and it is very much with us. As anthropologists have made clear, sex-role patterns must be learned during adolescence in preparation for parenthood and adult relationships. Behavioral scientists put great stock in the idea that social processes shape sexual behavior.

In addition to having to learn appropriate sexual behavior, there are pressures concerning safe sex, sexual identity, and changing sexual attitudes. Sexual orientation, which may be heterosexual, homosexual, or bisexual, is consolidated in adolescence. The threat of AIDS and other sexually transmitted diseases, as well as the struggle of individuals to understand their own and others' sexual behaviors and preferences, has added to an already stressful area of adolescent development. No longer does adolescent sexuality simply involve matters of deciding when, why, how, and with whom to be sexual.

SEXUAL DEVELOPMENT EXAMPLE 1. *As of April 1998, Billy is within two months of graduating from high school. Since ninth grade he has made enormous progress academically and emotionally. He has come to grips with his learning disability, as well. While Billy is eager to be more independent and to try living without his parents, he knows there's a lot "out there" waiting for him. When asked about dating and girls, Billy just shook his head and said, "There are other priorities." Now is not the time.*

One complication of sexual behavior is pregnancy. Adolescent pregnancy has always been with us, and in fact was the norm when wives often were adolescents with husbands who were older and established. Today teenagers of both genders often become parents without first becoming spouses. In the United States the birthrate among adolescents is one of the highest in the Western world. Many teenage fathers do not actively parent their children, and many babies are being raised by mothers who do not have good prospects for jobs, education, or adult relationships.

SEXUAL DEVELOPMENT EXAMPLE 2. *Heather is pregnant. She has doubts about her boyfriend's parenting ability, but she has no doubts about becoming a mother. However, she does not use the word "parent." Heather has not completed high school, plans to live with her mother after the baby arrives, and has no prospects for a job. Furthermore, Heather suffers from depression and needs a great deal of psychotherapeutic support.*

Educational/occupational development. In an early theory about identity formation, the division of labor between the sexes assumed that males typically are directed toward career and ideological commitments and females toward marriage and childrearing (Erikson 1968). Studies that supported this theory showed that vocational concerns seem to play a greater role in male identity formation (Bell 1969) and affiliation concerns in female identity (Douvan and Adelson 1966). The educational and occupational challenges facing adolescents continue to show a divergence. Since the 1980s the challenge for women has become integrating work and family roles; the challenge for men remains career development (Grotevant and Cooper 1986).

In the course of normal development adolescents, then, must come to grips with their identity in regard to the world of education and occupation. This is an area that relates integrally with other developmental issues. For example, if an adolescent female becomes pregnant, she has to face the issues of completing school and finding employment. Even without any complication, the adolescent normally deals with occupational goals in many areas: high school course selection, part-time job choices, and leisure and recreation pursuits, to mention just a few.

Overall, then, adolescence is a pivotal point in the development of adjustment. Larson and Ham (1993) found early adolescence to be a critical point in developing a positive or negative adjustment to daily life. The adolescent subjects in Larson and Ham's study carried electronic pagers for a week, recording their feelings when paged every two hours during each day. There were more reports of bad moods among the seventh- to ninth-graders than among the fifth- and sixth-graders. Events seemed to hit the adolescents harder, particularly illness in the family, an argument with a close friend, or change of school. Furthermore, the adolescents seemed to be more sensitive to negative events and transitions than the preadolescents. Adolescence appears to be a critical time for establishing one's response style and emotional outlook on life.

For adolescents with emotional and behavioral disorders, there are added challenges. They must adjust to a combination of challenges commensurate with their developmental stage and in accordance with their special needs. For example, adolescents with emotional and behavioral disorders are at great risk for rejection by their peers during this time. Their adjustment requires straddling a wavy line between being and becoming.

SAMPLE ATTRIBUTES

Sample similarities. The primary and secondary samples used in this study are similar in six ways.

First, at the time of data collection, the students were eligible for special education services in the area of emotional disturbance.

Second, both genders are represented. The attempt was made to select cases based on illustrative value, not gender. The primary sample, which represents younger adolescents, contains 10 males and 3 females, or a ratio of about 3:1. The secondary sample, which represents the entire range of adolescence, contains 28 males and 16 females, or a ratio of about 2:1. The ratio of males to females for the combined primary and secondary samples is 38 males to 19 females, or 2:1, or 67 percent males, 33 percent females. Among the emotional disturbance (ED) population, boys typically outnumber girls. For example, Kauffman (1993a) and Landrum et al. (1995) documented a male-female ratio of 4:1. The ratios for our primary and secondary samples, then, are similar in terms of males outnumbering females.

Third, at the time of data collection, students were enrolled in general education programs at least part of the time, with special education support. They may have come from or gone to clinical or more restrictive settings, or they may have been enrolled in alternative secondary programs, but all were found in mainstream schools at some point.

Fourth, the cases represent a variety of emotional and behavioral disorders: personality disorders, disruptive behavior disorders, eating disorders, mood disorders, anxiety disorders, and developmental disorders. All of the present sample, primary and secondary, had been diagnosed as having one or more emotional or behavioral disorders by school and nonschool professionals. Also within this variety are students with learning disabilities and communication disorders.

Therefore, these cases do not represent only those who are found eligible for special education services in ED. The assumption is that emotional and behavioral disorders are commonly observed in children and youth receiving special education regardless of categorical designations (Kauffman 1993a). The featured students represent, then, an assortment of externalizing and internalizing disorders and combinations thereof, and they do not represent only those students categorized for special education purposes as emotionally or behaviorally disordered.

Fifth, the primary sample is small (N = 13), but because of the aforementioned four factors it is rich in examples. It enables the reader to track the content of the lives of these students and to think in depth about theories of emotional and behavioral disorders. These students also help clarify the idea that emotional and behavioral disorders frequently overlap. (Interrelatedness will be discussed in Chapters 23 and 26.) Hence, the primary sample is considered to be representative and useful for linking theoretical and practical information.

The secondary sample also is small (N = 44). These students not only exemplify particular disorders but illuminate the unique manifestations of these conditions.

Sixth, the demographics of the sample, overall, are representative. The students come from a variety of social and economic backgrounds. They represent intact, split, and blended families; highly educated and relatively uneducated parents; and wealthy and poor families. Some of the students have siblings, some do not.

Demographics. The demographics of Fairfax County, Virginia, render the primary sample and the bulk of the secondary sample representative in terms of national sampling. Fairfax County, ranked twelfth in size in the United States, contains 13 percent of Virginia's public school students. As part of the Washington, DC, metropolitan area, this county, comprising 399 square miles, ranges across urban, suburban, and rural landscapes. Its student body, estimated at 149,830 for the 1997-1998 school year, is enrolled in 234 schools and centers, including 20 high schools. Fairfax County of the 1990s has been compared to Los Angeles County of the 1980s. In fact, as of the 1995-1996 school year, the student population represented 158 nations and 100 different languages. Its median income is high, but Fairfax County's residents, numbering 913,012 as of September 1997, are diverse economically.

Cultural and racial diversity are also reflected in the combined primary and secondary samples. The specific   mixture is as follows. Of the 57 students in the total sample, 47 are Caucasian (82 percent); 5 are Hispanic (9 percent); 3 are African-American (5 percent); 1 is native American (2 percent); and 1 is Asian (2 percent). Thus, the majority are Caucasian, and the rest   represent   an assortment of other reference   groups. Whatever reference   groupings   the students represent is   by   happenstance.   Cases were selected in terms   of availability and suitability for practical purposes.

Except for age and gender, the students are not identifiable in the text in terms of demographic features. With such a small sample, specific demographic analysis would be meaningless and would detract from the main purpose of this book.

Sample differences. The primary and secondary samples differ in four ways.

First, the primary sample comprises middle school students; the secondary sample comprises both middle and high school students.

Second, while the primary sample contains case content in depth, with case synopses that summarize life content, the secondary sample serves to illustrate particular points of theory.

Third, the ages of the primary sample were roughly (at the time of information gathering) 13 to 15; the ages of the secondary sample, roughly 13 to 21.   Overall, the age spectrum of the combined samples provides a good perspective of adolescence, from early to late adolescence.

Fourth, while the gender ratios in both primary and secondary samples are similar in terms of males outnumbering females, the primary sample, which comprises younger students with a male-female ratio of about 3:1, and the secondary sample, which includes some older students with a male-female ratio of about 2:1, mirrors the findings that the gender ratio among adolescents with emotional and behavioral disorders approaches parity with age (Barber et al. 1992).

METHODS EMPLOYED

Sampling. The primary sampling occurred between 1992 and 1997, and most of the secondary sampling occurred in that period as well as from 1974 to 1976. Case information about educational and psychological evaluations and social case histories, including medical and developmental information, anecdotal material, student writings, and observations, were obtained during those direct service periods.

Last names have been withheld to protect the identity of students and families. Also, to ensure confidentiality, no references to parent occupations or other revealing details about families have been provided.

The following seven steps were used to select and organize the material for this book.

Step 1. The first step involved selecting the specific emotional and behavioral disorders to be covered and determining how to organize them. Two criteria were established: importance and relevance.

Importance was determined by two means. First, the current national literature was examined, primarily special education textbooks and professional journals in psychiatry, special education, education, and psychology. Disorders that were mentioned frequently in the literature on adolescence were selected.

While the selected disorders represent important emotional and behavioral problems, typically they are not given specific labels such as "bipolar disorder" or "post-traumatic stress disorder" by their school systems. In accordance with federal regulations governing special education, school officials routinely determine eligibility on the basis of criteria relating to such areas as academic, interpersonal, physical, and intellectual functioning. In other words, school officials determine eligibility for special education in ED by considering factors that interfere with educational functioning, not clinical diagnoses. After all, special education eligibility occurs in a school context. Furthermore, even the reports of school psychologists typically do not offer diagnostic labels; these reports attest to social, intellectual, and psychological functioning without applying clinical labels.

Relevance was the other criterion used in choosing the disorders. Importance determined the roster; relevance narrowed the list. The resulting list reflects the probability that teachers will encounter students with these disorders. By this criterion, rare conditions such as multiple-personality disorder or schizophrenia were excluded, and conditions most likely to be seen in schools were included.

Once the disorders had been targeted in terms of importance and relevance, they were organized into categories. Various classification schemes were consulted. The American Psychiatric Association (APA) system, reflected in the series, *Diagnostic and Statistical Manual of Mental Disorders,* particularly DSM-IV (1994), was the primary reference. The final categorization and organization most nearly reflects the APA schema.

Step 2. A list of ten practical characteristics of adolescents with emotional and behavioral disorders was generated. (See Chapter 1 listing.)

Step 3. The third step involved selecting cases to illustrate the chosen disorders. Selection criteria included clearness of match between disorders and manifest behaviors as well as quality of notes and observations.

Step 4. The cases were sorted into their respective disorders according to diagnoses by clinicians, psychologists, and psychiatrists, or, in the case of the few secondary sample cases representing an earlier period, notes regarding diagnostic patterns.

Step 5. Primary sample cases were organized in terms of pertinent background factors. Primary sample case synopses were written, and secondary sample cases were outlined. Also, working files and notes were collated relative to particular disorders. The content of the overall sample, thus, was readied for integration with theoretical discussions.

Step 6. The targeted disorders were researched thoroughly. As the discussions proceeded, case content was integrated with theoretical points. Further, practical information was separated from theoretical by highlighting the practical in italics.

Step 7. As presented in Chapter 23, a comparison was made of the federal ED criteria and the ten targeted practical characteristics of the primary sample. Quantitative and a qualitative analyses are applied to the cases.

RATIONALE FOR THE METHODOLOGY

Research using large samples typically generates data suitable for number crunching. Research with large samples is important for many reasons, one of which is to test questions raised by small-group, qualitative research methods. Large-group research has nearly eclipsed small-group and single-subject research and other qualitative methods. While the individual has remained of paramount importance in clinical science, until recently this science lacked adequate methods to study behavior change in individuals. Applied behavior analysis, while slow to develop, has shown enormous value in defining change variables. Other qualitative methods have been even slower to establish themselves. In the shadow of large-group research, qualitative research has struggled for a foothold.

Some researchers do not recognize the value of small-group, qualitative research. Some experts in applied research still maintain that idiographic study has little place in the confirmatory aspects of scientific activity that looks for laws applying to individuals generally (see Hersen and Barlow 1976). As psychology has come into its own through methods that suggest traits and behaviors of people in general, it is difficult for some professionals to share the spotlight with methods that suggest traits and behaviors of individuals.

Nevertheless, idiographic study has a distinct place. The foundation of psychology, in fact, was built on single cases. Clinicians carefully documented the procedures used in casework and communicated them. Hypotheses sprang from the cases, and the layering of casework ultimately built theories. Bolger (1965) articulated the case study method, which was the sole method of clinical investigation through the first half of this century (Hersen and Barlow 1976). It is the basis for the single-case experimental design.

In reality, both large-group and single-case experimental design, as well as small-sample, idiographic studies, have a place in research. Both contribute to understanding by approaching problems from different vantage points.

Single-case experimentation and large-group studies typically involve manipulation of variables, their special vantage point. In other words, these methods involve attempts to change people. Whether using one individual or one large group at a time, treating or employing one or more variable(s) at a time, the focus is on manipulation. Interventions are used, and variables are controlled or allowed to proceed normally. The numbers are crunched or the data patterns are analyzed, and implications are described in terms of whether or not change has occurred.

The special vantage point of idiographic methodology, on the other hand, is not one of manipulation. Rather, it focuses on in-depth analysis. This method may reveal change and patterns, with even some quantification, but it does not attempt to create change by direct intervention. An often used qualitative method is *content analysis*, which attempts to flush out patterns, typically with predetermined questions and guidelines.

Both large-sample and single-subject experimental design, as well as small-sample, idiographic studies, have one thing in common that merits their being considered research efforts. All these methods begin with questions or hypotheses. Curiosity drives all of these researchers to find answers to nagging questions. Because questions drive research, then, the choice of method should be determined by the questions.

The choice of the idiographic method for present purposes grew out of questions raised by many educators related to current theories about internalizing and externalizing disorders. One particular question nagged: Who are adolescents in discord, and how might a teacher recognize and deal with these students?

The aforementioned question, it was decided, could best be addressed by researching current information about targeted emotional and behavioral disorders and by analyzing case content in order to relate that practical information to theory.

Two other features of qualitative research bear mentioning. One is that such research raises questions that large-sample research can use to reach generalizations. Qualitative research, then, serves as a testing ground for usable questions. Another feature worth noting is that idiographic research stimulates practical exploration. Readers, it is hoped, will be stimulated to look for further examples of the disorders presented in this book. One value of this book, then, is that it offers readers theories to explore practically.

ADDITIONAL APPROACHES

Additional approaches deserve mention. At the conclusion of each chapter, concerning a particular emotional or behavioral disorder, there is a summary in terms of the relevant federal ED criteria. Thus, each discussion of a particular disorder refers not only to clinical diagnosis but also to special education eligibility criteria in the ED area.

Also, at the conclusion of each chapter, there is a section devoted to practical guidelines where strategies for educating these such students are suggested.

3

Overview:
Personality Disorders

I study your face intently but its secret eludes me.
Denise Levertov

PERSONALITY: THE QUALITY OF BEING A PERSON

Before discussing personality disorders it is appropriate to define personality and what an adequate personality is. Defining the normal helps to define the abnormal.

"Personality," the totality of predisposing behavioral tendencies, is defined variously by different authors. It is a distinctive set of personal characteristics that affect behavior; it is a characteristic way of responding (Sarason and Sarason 1993). Indeed, it is not what you say, but how you say it. Further, it is an umbrella term that subsumes "temperament," tendencies that are related to constitutional factors, and "traits," which are circumscribed aspects of personality (Graham 1991). Personality is something we all have; it is the quality of being a person (Morris 1973). Personality also has been defined as the total of a person's ways of behaving and "all that one is" (Landau, Epstein, and Stone 1972, p. 41); in other words, it is our total pattern of behaviors, traits, and temperament.

Inasmuch as personality is an encompassing term, it nearly defies explanation. While personality constitutes some measurable characteristics, such as physique, talents, and abilities, there are also inner dimensions, such as drives, emotions, impulses, and unconscious motivations. Baller and Charles describe an individual's personality: "He is that unique combination of all the characteristics that are outwardly evident, and he is at the same time all that is concealed in his inner and relatively private experience" (1968, p. 397).

PERSONALITY: NATURAL AND NURTURED

Our personalities are both born and made. There is considerable evidence that many characteristics of adult personality are present in infancy; however, evidence also suggests that the interrelationships between the individual and the environment are important in personality formation. Parent-child relationships significantly affect personality development, as do the developing child's interactions with societal forces. A lifestyle emerges from the interaction of the child, with all that he or she brought into this world, and his or her environment. Fromm concluded, "Man's main task in life is to give birth to himself, to become what he potentially is" (1947, p. 237).

THE ADEQUATE PERSONALITY

Sontag (1972) provides a classic definition of the adequate personality. In this view, the adequate personality enables the individual; specifically, it allows a reasonable degree of freedom from anxiety, an effective use of basic abilities, and constructive, nondestructive participation in society. The adequate personality, then, appears to be one that grows and develops without interfering emotions, that progresses and reaches potential unfettered, and that participates in social experiences in a cooperative, nonconflictual manner.

The adequate personality varies among individuals. Children show wide variation in behavioral styles during development. Some are cheerful and resilient; others have enduring tendencies to show anxiety or to dissolve into tears when facing stress. Normally, personalities are varied along a continuum from easy to difficult, warm to cold, open to closed.

Finally, the adequate personality adapts to situations, showing resiliency. An individual with an adequate personality does not behave similarly in all situations. Personality styles can be maladaptive if individuals are unable to modify their behaviors when the environment undergoes significant changes that demand different approaches.

PERSONALITY DEVELOPMENT AND ASSESSMENT

Clearly, personality development is an important topic, but it has not received the research attention it deserves. Some professionals have been discouraged from pursuing this topic because it is difficult to study in a scientifically respectable way (White 1975). In recent years, few have been willing to pursue personality development in the way that it demands. Murphy (1956) focused on one child between the ages of two and five in order to document normal personality development. Erikson (1950) documented the relation between child-rearing practices and the growth of personality and character. In this rare effort, Erikson clarified the complexity of the human personality.

In recent years, personality assessment has occurred in abbreviated efforts. For example, we hear frequently about tests of personality, measures that purport to collect information about the adjustment, motives, interests, and attitudes of students. Personality testing may include short checklists with questions designed to determine energy level, ability to make friends, irritability, and ease of embarrassment. School psychologists can conduct personality evaluation of students over a two- or three-hour testing period.

In their function as gatekeepers, those whose psychological evaluations are heavily relied upon in determining eligibility for special education   services, school psychologists typically evaluate assorted personality factors. Their reports attest to such personality factors as anxiety, self-esteem, depression, adaptive behavior, cooperation, and competition. The school psychologist, then, is responsible for measuring and describing the inner and outer dimensions of a student's personality.

Teachers provide further documentation of a student's personality by describing academic achievement and abilities, classroom behavior, interpersonal relations, and other factors that describe the student's functioning. In this narrative of a student's total functioning, usually for the purposes of referral for special education purposes or child study, the teacher is describing the student's personality from an educator's vantage point.

PERSONALITY DISORDER: INTRACTABLE FUNGUS

As discussed previously, the adequate personality is flexible and adaptive. The inadequate personality, on the other hand, represents the opposite scenario. "If personality characteristics are not flexible enough to allow an individual to respond adaptively to at least an ordinary variety of situations, a disorder may be present" (Sarason and Sarason 1993, p. 250).

Implicit in a personality disorder is, then, impaired functioning. When personality styles become pathological, they can impair a person's functioning and can lead to anxiety, distress, and unhappiness. Those with personality disorders show rigid patterns of behavior. These personalities, which are self-defeating, deeply ingrained, and highly resistant to change, severely limit an individual's approach to stress-producing situations because the characteristic style of thinking and behaving allows for only a narrow range of responses.

Because of this deeply ingrained rigidity, individuals with personality disorders do not see a need to change. Rather, they see their traits as natural parts of themselves. Consequently, they are unlikely to seek help (Nevid, Rathus, and Greene 1994). As Rule remarks:

A personality disorder, once established in the mind, clings like an intractable fungus. It becomes part of the thought processes, and trying to remove it would be akin to cutting down a tree to eliminate a fungus. It is better to be "crazy" because crazy can be cured. Personality disorders die with the host, entangled for life in the brain's functioning. (1992, p. 521)

A personality disorder, thus, is an   ingrained disorder. It *is* the individual's personality, and it is not temporary.   Such disorders affect all aspects of a person's life. The individual is unable to be free of anxiety, is unable to use basic abilities effectively, and is antisocial or destructive to other individuals or to society.   Students who, over a long period of time, become easily distressed about schoolwork, who have rigid behaviors, who do not make friends, and who have poor impulse control (which often leads to aggression) may have inadequate, disordered personalities.

A CLINICAL DEFINITION OF PERSONALITY DISORDERS

The American Psychiatric Association's *DSM-IV* (1994) provides a clinical definition of personality disorders. The general diagnostic criteria for a personality disorder include the following:

A.   An enduring pattern of inner experience and behavior that deviates markedly from the expectations of the individual's culture. This pattern is manifested in two (or more) of the following areas:

     1.   Cognition (i.e., ways of perceiving and interpreting self, other people, and events)

     2.   Affectivity (i.e., the range, intensity, lability, and appropriateness of emotional response)

     3.   Interpersonal functioning

     4.   Impulse control

B.   The enduring pattern is inflexible and pervasive across a broad range of personal and social situations.

C.   The enduring pattern leads to clinically significant distress or impairment in social, occupational, or other important areas of functioning.

D.   The pattern is stable and of long duration, and its onset can be traced back at least to adolescence or early adulthood.

E.   The enduring pattern is not better accounted for as a manifestation or consequence of another mental disorder.

F.   The enduring pattern is not due to the direct physiological effects of a substance (e.g., a drug of abuse, a medication) or a general medical condition (e.g., head trauma).

CAUSE

In each of the chapters devoted to separate personality disorders, specific issues of cause will be addressed. For now, suffice it to say, "No one knows for certain where personality disorders come from. Most psychiatrists agree, however, that they are not present at birth but, rather, take root in the first few years of life" (Rule 1992, p. 521).

TYPES OF PERSONALITY DISORDERS

Major personality disorders are classified into three general types. The first, odd or eccentric behavior, includes individuals with paranoid, schizoid, and schizotypal personality disorders. The second group includes people who appear anxious or fearful (e.g., avoidant, dependent, passive-aggressive, and obsessive-compulsive types). The third group comprises those whose behavior is dramatic, emotional, or erratic, e.g., antisocial, histrionic, borderline, and narcissistic types.

Anxiety disorders are dealt with in Chapters 15-18, specifically school phobia, obsessive-compulsive disorder, and post-traumatic stress disorder, and odd or eccentric types are not included in the book because of the infrequency of their manifestation in public schools. In this book Chapter 4 deals with the borderline type, Chapter 5 with the antisocial type, and Chapter 6 with narcissism.

CLASSIFICATION ISSUES

Personality disorders pose problems for those who construct classification systems, as well as those who write textbooks and those who teach abnormal psychology. While these disorders seem important, and while their existence can easily be recognized even by nonprofessional observers, little is known about their origins and development. With the exception of the antisocial personality disorder and, recently, the borderline personality disorder, little research has been done on these problems.

A particular classification issue is "obsessive-compulsive personality disorder" versus "obsessive-compulsive disorder." Obsessive-compulsive personality disorder (OCPD) is included among the personality disorders. *DSM-IV* (1994) classifies obsessive-compulsive, antisocial, and borderline personality disorders together and classifies obsessive-compulsive disorder (OCD) as an anxiety disorder. Nevid, Rathus, and Greene (1994) add that borderline and antisocial personality disorders represent two of a subtype disorder with overly dramatic, emotional, or erratic behavioral features, while obsessive-compulsive disorder, even when classified as a personality disorder, involves significant anxiety features.

Besides the shared feature of anxiety, another way to look at the difference beween OCD and OCPD is that the former, as an anxiety disorder, is distressing to the individual, who cannot stop behaving that way. On the other hand, individuals with OCPD usually show behavior that is rigid and maladaptive, but they believe that the behavior is under their own control (Sarason and Sarason 1993).

Finally, classification of personality disorders is problematic because they yield the least reliable diagnoses of any APA (*DSM*) classification. One difficulty in deciding on the appropriateness of a diagnosis is the unclear boundary that exists between those personality characteristics within normal limits and those that represent disordered behavior (Sarason and Sarason 1993). Recall the discussion of the wide latitude that represents adequate personality. For children, especially, such diagnosis is elusive because children are in the formative phase of life.

A case in the annals of crime illustrates that point. Rule summarized the case of Patricia Taylor, who was responsible for several murders and caused great pain for the people who loved her. Patricia reached adulthood, and prison, without a precise diagnosis of her pathology.

There may never be definitive answers to these questions. Unlike many felons, Pat Taylor apparently never did undergo psychological testing. Aside from the diagnosis of Dr. [name], the psychiatrist who examined her after she slashed her wrists and ran wildly through the woods, no psychiatric or psychological reports exist in her court records. It was unlikely that Pat was ever insane. Often hysterical, yes. From the time she was a tiny girl, she whipped herself into emotional tizzies to have her own way. No one ever put limits on her behavior. When Patty cried, the adults in her life gave in. She grew up believing that that was the way the world operated. (1992, p. 519)

While Patricia Taylor never had an official diagnosis, she exhibited signs of several personality disorders. Her criminal acts, for which she showed no remorse, suggest an antisocial personality; her belief that she was special, her self-absorption, her jealousy, and the rages when she did not get what she wanted, suggest a narcissistic personality disorder; her intense moods, unstable personal relationships, chronic anger, self-multilation, dependence, and excesses suggest a borderline personality disorder; and her seductive behavior, need for immediate gratification and constant reassurance, rapidly changing moods, shallow emotions, and need to be the center of attention suggest a histrionic personality disorder. If she was not crazy, Pat quite likely suffered from a melange of personality disorders (Rule 1992). Although no psychiatrist or psychologist would probably deny that this woman has a major personality disorder, the precise diagnosis remains unknown.

Other issues of overlapping conditions in relation to the problems of diagnosing personality disorders are presented in Chapter 26.

PERSONALITY DISORDERS IN CHILDREN

The psychiatric profession has reservations about using the concept of personality disorder in children, believing that it cannot be applied appropriately to individuals younger than 16 or 17 years of age. Such disorders as borderline personality disorder, narcissistic personality disorder, and obsessive-compulsive personality disorder may be used in those unusual circumstances in which the maladaptive personality traits appear to be stable. Thus, diagnosis of personality disorder implies a chronic disability, and clinicians are reluctant to apply to a child what might be regarded as a damning label (Graham 1991).

However, some children show early signs of enduring inadequate personality characteristics. For example, borderline personality disorder can be a stable personality in adolescents. Still, we must be cautious about applying a personality disorder label. "Commonly, [children] are described as showing unusual patterns of personality development without a firm diagnostic statement being made" (Graham 1991, p. 232).

4

Borderline Personality Disorder

What passionate outcry of a soul in pain.
Henry Wadsworth Longfellow

THIS STUDENT IS ODD

In common parlance, the word "borderline" implies an indefinite line between two qualities or conditions. In reference to personal qualities, the implication is that one cannot be described in a definite manner. In psychology, the understanding is that a borderline condition is one that does not fit readily into existing categories. If an individual does not fit readily into a diagnostic category but, instead, is on the cusp between two disorders, there is an element of oddness, or poorness of fit.

Indeed, some adolescents with severe disturbance lie in the fuzzy area between psychosis and milder forms of pathology. They represent borderline personality disorder (BPD).

Poorness of fit has been seen in terms of special education classification. Over the years, students with borderline qualities have been classified variously. It is not uncommon to see a history that includes eligibility for special education services in such areas as learning disabilities and emotional disturbance. Additionally, these students may have been diagnosed as having attentional disorders or other psychiatric problems. Blythe's school system, for example, determined that she was learning disabled (for reading and written language difficulties), emotionally disabled, and speech impaired in both expressive and receptive areas; and the psychiatrists concluded that she suffered not only from BPD but also from manic-depression, attention-deficit disorder (ADD), and depression.

The oddness that has been described is both general and specific. Generally, "some of the children who have been described as borderline have a quality of changing shape, a fluidity" (Pine 1982, p. 867). Waller (1994) refers to affective instability. Broadly, the disorder is elusive, inconsistent, and contradictory in nature (Kreisman 1989).

Specifically, "kooky" moods have been described; peculiar thoughts and reasoning have been noted; odd body movements have been observed; and peculiar mixtures of openness and guardedness have been seen. Such mixtures make relationships difficult. "For the borderline, much of life is a relentless emotional roller coaster with no apparent destination" (Kreisman 1989, p. 8).

HISTORICAL PERSPECTIVE

The term borderline was first used when clinicians were unsure of a correct diagnosis. Frequently, the term was used to describe a mild form of schizophrenia. When the client showed a mixture of neurotic and psychotic symptoms, a probable diagnosis was borderline personality disorder (Beck and Freeman 1990).

While the term was first used in the 1930s, the borderline condition was not clearly defined until the 1970s. "As more and more people began to seek therapy for a unique set of life problems, the parameters of the disorder crystallized" (Kreisman 1989, p. 5). BPD was included in the American Psychiatric Association's *DSM-III* (1980), and it was officially recognized as a diagnosis in that year. Since then, the borderline category has been used widely.

While BPD is now recognized as a true category of pathology, there is still debate. One argument is that borderlines represent a boundary area between personality disorders and mood disorders. Indeed, it has been estimated that about half of those with BPD could be diagnosed as having a mood disorder. However, Benjamin and Wonderlich (1994) noted that BPDs have less self-control than adolescents with mood disorders. The validity of a separate BPD category appears to hold sway.

The growing number of character disorders, in general, and borderline personality disorder, in particular, may be a reflection of our contemporary society. Lasch (1978) offers the following quote from Durkheim: "Personality is the individual socialized." In other words, the society is reproduced in its individual personalities. The American society has become fragmented and polarized; societal forces have made relationships difficult to achieve and maintain; gender roles have shifted; and child-rearing patterns have been complicated by child abuse and neglect, divorce, the increase of infant day care, and geographical mobility (Kreisman 1989). All of these modern factors have created a climate that may foster BPD.

SOME SPECIFIC THEORIES AND FACTS

Cause. Theories about possible causes of borderline personality disorder range from nature to nurture and combinations of both. Most of the theories focus on nurture (i.e., a disturbed early relationship between a preborderline child and the parents). The various nurture subtheories focus particularly on poor attachment, inadequate attention to the child's feelings resulting in a poor sense of self, parental abuse, and family stressors, such as divorce and alcoholism.

Nurturing gone wrong in BPD cases also includes childhood sexual abuse, early separation and loss, and high paternal control in cases of male BPD. Nature theories include genetic vulnerability. Still other theories posit a combination of factors related to nature and nurture. The best conclusion at this point is that the cause of BPD likely is multifaceted, and that the disorder probably develops through a combination of neurobiological, early developmental, and later socializing factors (see Sarason and Sarason 1993).

Prevalence. One estimate is that 20 percent of psychiatric patients are given this diagnosis and that it occurs in from 3 to 5 percent of the general population.

Gender. About two-thirds of those with BPD are female, according to Sarason and Sarason (1993).

DEFINITION OF BORDERLINE PERSONALITY DISORDER

Beck and Freeman (1990) offer one definition of BPD that includes four markers: poorly integrated identity, primitive defenses, relatively firm self-object boundaries (compared to those of a psychotic), and reasonably intact reality testing (also compared to a psychotic). Added to these basic defining points are the most striking features: intense emotional reactions, changeable moods, and great variety of symptoms.

Specific indicators (Beck and Freeman 1990; Waller 1994) are as follows:

o   Diverse assortment of problems and symptoms that may shift

o   Unusual symptoms or unusual combinations of symptoms

o   Intense emotional reactions out of proportion to situation; poor anger control

o   Self-punitive or self-destructive behavior

o   Impulsive, poorly planned behavior that may later be recognized as foolish

o   Brief periods of psychotic symptoms

o   Confusion regarding goals, priorities, and feelings

o   Feelings of emptiness or void

o   Lack of stable intimate relationships; relationship difficulty

o   Tendency to either idealize or denigrate others

o   Tendency to confuse intimacy and sexuality

o   Affective instability

Altogether, these descriptors point to a serious disorder. In fact, BPD is classified as a major personality disorder involving dramatic, emotional, or erratic behavior; intense, unstable moods and relationships; chronic anger; and substance abuse.

According to the *DSM-IV* (1994) BPD is a pervasive pattern of instability of interpersonal relationships, self-image, and affects, and marked impulsivity beginning by early adulthood and present in a variety of contexts, as indicated by five (or more) of nine criteria.

Kreisman (1989) uses eight of those criteria. The first criterion refers to unstable and intense interpersonal relationships, with marked shifts in attitudes toward others (from idealization to devaluation or from clinging dependency to isolation and avoidance), and prominent patterns of manipulation of others. Kreisman calls this criterion "the relentless search for Mr./Ms. Right" (1989, p. 27).

A related issue is social perception. Benjamin and Wonderlich (1994), who noted that those with BPD differ from bipolar and unipolar subjects in particular social perceptions, found that BPDs view relationships with their mothers, hospital staff, and other patients with more hostility than mood-disordered patients. BPDs see themselves as attacked by other patients and as part of hostile and noncohesive families. Sarason and Sarason (1993) point out that intense clinging dependency and manipulation characterize the interpersonal relationships of BPD patients and make interaction with them very difficult. Hostility enters on the heels of denial of dependency; as part of vehement denial, BPDs devalue the strengths and personal significance of others. Often, this takes the form of extreme anger when others set limits for relationships, or when separations are about to occur. Social perception is pervasively dysfunctional.

SOCIAL PERCEPTION EXAMPLES 1 AND 2. *Alicia's attitudes about people shift regularly from dependency to avoidance. Despite her guidance counselor's attempts to counsel her, Alicia shows up at appointed times for a while, then disappears; Alicia works well with the counselor one day and is angry the next. The counselor feels that Alicia depends upon others to solve all her problems, and that when the counselor does all that is humanly and professionally possible, Alicia rejects her. Alicia seems to be angry that the counselor cannot fix all of her problems.*

Blythe's conversations typically show abrupt shifts of topic and tone. During an interview with a psychologist, for example, Blythe was cooperative in talking about how well she was doing. When the psychologist opened the subject of interpersonal relationships, Blythe's tone of voice changed, she became belligerent, and she was visibly agitated. Her cooperation was quickly replaced with swearing and verbal confrontation.

This dysfunctional social perception involves either/or thinking. For example, the idea that a counselor can either fix a problem or not, or that someone is totally trustworthy or not. The borderline personality shows a distinctly black and white style of thinking.

What underlies this thinking style may be a struggle between dependence and independence; the dysfunctional social perception may be symbolic of an emotional tug-of-war. Kreisman (1989) concluded that the borderline's unstable relationships are related to intolerance of separation and fear of intimacy. The continual tug-of-war between the desire to be taken care of, on the one hand, and the fear of engulfment, on the other, results in shifting relationships. Their strong need for a relationship leads borderline persons to fear that the people on whom they are dependent will abandon them (Sarason and Sarason 1993). Consequently, those with BPD often make unrealistic demands of others and appear to others as spoiled (Kreisman 1989).

SOCIAL PERCEPTION EXAMPLE 3. *Karina was born in El Salvador and lived with grandparents and great-grandparents because her parents left her for the U.S. when she was about three years old. By the age of nine she had been reunited with her parents in the U.S., but there was ensuing abuse by the father, mother, and brother, and further relocation to other relatives. Child Protective Services subsequently placed Karina in a foster home, and eventually she was adopted by those parents. When she was 15 years old, her adoptive mother was diagnosed with breast and uterine cancer, which precipitated great emotional upset in Karina, who already had difficulty dealing with separations and losses. By the later adolescent years, Karina could not tolerate even overnight separations from her adoptive mother.*

On the issue of indulgence, Rule, in describing the case of Patricia Taylor, referred to her childhood indulgence, "[A]ll around them lay the evidence of the destruction of a family, caused not by the neglect of a child, but by the utter, complete, almost mindless, indulgence of a child" (1992, p. 524). Taylor's grandmother put the problem succinctly: "I can't understand why anyone in this whole wide world would think Pat got whatever she wanted; she never got *anything* she wanted" (Rule 1992, p. 520). Indeed, nothing Patricia attained was enough to fill up the emptiness in her life, and she did everything and anything she could to try to plug the holes. She manipulated in an attempt to fill the void.

Part of this clinical criterion for BPD, then, is manipulation. Alicia and Robby, both diagnosed with BPD, show manipulative qualities.

SOCIAL PERCEPTION EXAMPLES 4 AND 5. *Alicia drew a lot of attention from her teachers with her story of impending homelessness. She said that she likely would end up at a homeless shelter where she could have none of her belongings and no place to do her homework in quiet. The school staff immed-*

iately began to check out alternative housing arrangements for Alicia, a task not made easier by the fact that Alicia was 18 years old. When Alicia next came to school, which was many days following her tale of desperation, she rejected the resources that had been found for her and seemed indifferent to the issue she had presented so dramatically.

Robby seems to know that he can get away with some behaviors for which other kids his age are punished. For example, one day, playing around with his dad's motorcycle, he did a "wheelie," ran into his dad's truck, and caused extensive damage. He said that his dad would not yell at him because it would cause Robby to think about suicide.

The second criterion relates to an impulsive character. Kreisman (1989) has noted impulsiveness in areas that are potentially self-destructive: chemical abuse, sexual promiscuity, gambling, shoplifting, excessive spending, overeating, anorexia nervosa, or bulimia. He describes a borderline's behaviors as sudden and contradictory, resulting from strong, momentary feelings, "perceptions that represent isolated, unconnected snapshots of experience" (Kreisman 1989, p. 29). Kernberg (1985) also describes perverse sexual trends, "impulse neurosis" and addictions, and "lower level" character disorder featuring chaotic and impulsive functioning. Like the generation of the 1960s, the borderline lives for now. Excess is characteristic.

IMPULSIVE CHARACTER EXAMPLES. *Robby was caught using and distributing marijuana on school grounds soon after two of his friends were shot at a high school football game. Robby said that he was upset after this incident. Two other friends had been killed in a shooting two months previously. Robby felt as if all his friends were dying.*

Blythe is extremely impulsive. She has few resources for coping with stress, typically acts before thinking, and often shows faulty judgment. At home, her behavior frequently shows lack of sensitivity to the amount of work she causes others. She leaves gum on her bed headboard or on walls; leaves towels on the floor (five used each morning to dry her hair); and she moves through the kitchen like a tornado, spilling liquids and leaving them to dry, walking over things and grinding them into the carpet, and writing telephone numbers on walls.

Karina, too, is impulsive. She has a history of frantic eating. When first adopted she ate rapidly, almost frantically, for fear that the food would not last.

Both Alicia and Blythe are extremely overweight. Blythe is 100 pounds above her optimal weight; at one point she weighed 267 pounds, a lot for a young woman of average height.

The third criterion relates to mood shifts. While these affective shifts usually last just a few hours and rarely more than a few days (Kreisman 1989), they are abrupt and radical.

MOOD SHIFT EXAMPLE. *Blythe's emotional lability is seen in shifts between sociability and gregariousness to anger and depression. Her mother describes Blythe as a "constant challenge" because of fluctuating moods. During one conversation, in which she became animated about her interest in cars, she suddenly dropped her head, looked down, and declared that she did not want to talk about cars because that subject made her angry. It was a jolt to those who had been interacting pleasantly about a topic that seemed to engage Blythe's attention.*

The fourth criterion relates to inappropriate, intense anger, or the lack of anger control. Recurrent fights may be involved.

ANGER EXAMPLES. *In Alicia's family there is a long history of intense sibling rivalry. Alicia usually is in the center of this conflict. Violent scenes have occurred that are disproportionate to the incidents. For example, Alicia threatened her older sister with a carving knife when her sister borrowed an item of clothing without asking Alicia. Also, she has been oppositional and aggressive following her mother's simple requests to do household chores.*

Blythe has been bothered by uncontrollable rage reactions for at least twelve years, or since she was ten years old. At these times, she sweats and becomes tremulous and flushed. These reactions have become more violent and difficult to control. She describes her rage as a feeling that starts in her stomach and moves toward her mouth, building up in strength as it moves. Frequently, these reactions lead to an overwhelming need for sleep. Blythe will drop to the floor in a deep sleep. Numerous psychiatric and neurological evaluations have revealed no epileptic disorder or other physical explanation. Antidepressant and mood altering medications have been ineffective. No drug abuse is known, and Blythe does not use alcohol. She is constantly in marked conflict with her brother and has frequent disputes with her father. Blythe has said that when people tell her what to do she wants to put a gun to their heads.

Robby cannot desist from annoying his peers. He continuously starts fights by verbally taunting peers. For example, Robby teases peers that they are too "chicken" to try drugs.

Karina is argumentative and violent. She likes to have the last word in arguments. Numerous violent episodes have occurred. When first adopted, she had frequent temper tantrums, bit, yelled, kicked, and screamed. She would play roughly with her adoptive father, and more than once bit him on the leg. She blows up when disciplined, or she becomes oppositional when directed to do something like clean her room, despite the fact that she is usually a tidy person. When her adoptive parents denied her use of the car (at age 16), she became quite violent, breaking her mother's eyeglasses and a telephone. During violent episodes, she has destroyed her own possessions.

The fifth criterion relates to pleas for help. Recurrent suicidal threats, gestures, or behavior, and self-mutilating behaviors are characteristic. "Self-destructive behaviors have been called the behavioral specialty of those with borderline personality disorder" (Sarason and Sarason 1993, p. 261). Kreisman adds, "Self-mutilation, except when clearly associated with psychosis, is the hallmark of BPD" (1989, p. 33). Borderline students frequently overdose, mutilate themselves, cut their wrists, or bang their heads. In recent years, severe bulimia has become a common self-destructive tactic.

This self-abuse has been explained in terms of early experiences. Benjamin and Wonderlich (1994) comment that borderline individuals seem to internalize hostile, abandoning relationships, which leads to self-attack and self-abandonment. Furthermore, reports of physical and sexual abuse occur with high frequency, great severity, and for long periods, in addition to high rates of early separation and loss of parents as well as a high degree of paternal control, among borderlines (Paris, Zweig-Frank, and Guzder 1994). These findings may help explain the development of BPD.

Whatever the cause, BPDs seem to feel uncomfortable in their own bodies. Rule commented about Patricia Taylor's history of injuries. Not only was Taylor addicted to drugs, "Pat never seemed comfortable in her own skin. Indeed, she attempted to literally destroy her own body." Furthermore: "Perhaps because her world did not give her everything she ever wanted, Pat could not stand being herself" (Rule 1992, p. 523).

PLEA FOR HELP EXAMPLES. *Robby has a long history of suicide threats. He claims to have played Russian Roulette with a loaded gun while on drugs.*

Blythe has shown suicidal behavior, as when during one especially depressing time she walked into the kitchen and said to her mother, "See this bottle? It's empty." She had consumed a bottle of prescription valium.

Karina also has shown self-destructive behavior: She has made numerous incisions on her arm and has attempted suicide several times between the ages of 12 and 15 by overdosing on aspirin and other pills.

Delano, at 14, takes razor blades and carves symbols and words on his forearm.

Some youngsters with BPD may hide their self-abuse.

SELF-ABUSE EXAMPLE.   *Judy, at 15, frequently scratches her wrists, abdomen, and waist. Deep fingernail marks are covered by clothing.*

The sixth criterion relates to marked and persistent identity disturbance. There may be uncertainty in at least two of the following areas: self-image, sexual orientation, long-term goals or career choice, type of friends, and values (Kreisman 1989).

IDENTITY DISTURBANCE EXAMPLES.   *Robby's choice of friends is consistent in terms of type but inconsistent in terms of his values. Robby expresses understanding that friends should bring out the best in someone rather than the worst, but he is unable to choose friends who match his ideals. Instead, Robby's friends typically have been hospitalized for drug abuse and/or emotional problems.*

Blythe's aspirations are more like fantasies than goals.   She has no concrete career goals or realistic ideas about reaching such goals. A couple of months prior to her twenty-first birthday Blythe told her mother that she wanted to become either a bank president or a doctor. At that moment, Blythe still needed two credits to complete high school, had just been fired from her job, and had taken no steps to find another job or to enroll in school. About a year later, after dropping out of an alternative high school, Blythe announced that she was not interested in a medical career because she could not deal with the sight of blood or stressful situations. Rather, she had become very interested in cars and knew a lot about them. When probed about her specific interest, she indicated that mechanics or sales were totally out of the question; she could not work on cars and did not want to deal with people. Instead, she wanted to detail cars or move them around storage lots. Essentially, Blythe likes to feel and touch cars. As for what she might do to become employed in the automobile industry, Blythe avers that she does not want to think about that. "I just want to deal with one day at a time," she said. Even suggesting avenues of exploration upsets Blythe. On a day that Blythe is willing to talk about taking steps toward finding a job in the automobile industry, her feelings still interfere. She argues that women who work at car dealerships are invariably petite, gorgeous, thin, and shapely. She admits to being overweight, but exaggerates her condition as "obese and ugly." Blythe believes that she will never get a job at a dealership. She imagines the job interview, where she gives "100 percent of myself" and then is told that they do not have a place for her.   She believes that she will be rejected on the basis of looks.   The fantasy interview ends with Blythe either yelling obscenities at the interviewer or breaking down, "crying my heart out."

When she is reminded that she has no training or experience to work with cars, and when she is offered the opportunity to meet with a high school automobile body and mechanics teacher about an apprenticeship, she cannot listen. "You just don't understand," she complains, "I have this passion and have had since I was ten years old. I just want to be around cars." Despite this passion, and despite her lament that she would be rejected for a job because of appearance, Blythe had two large tattoos put on each upper arm: one picturing a ferocious bulldog, with bright green eyes and red collar, the other part of a woman's face peering out from behind a tangle of leaves and vines. Just two days later, after spending $200 for the tattoos, Blythe regretted it. She got the tattoos, she said, because she was "pissed off" that her world studies course had been cancelled. She was angry at everyone. She is unwilling to consider what the tattoos mean in terms of employability, and the process of reaching her goal continues to elude her. Similarly, Blythe's poor school attendance, coupled with refusal to keep psychiatric appointments and unwillingness to take prescribed medications, contrast with her expressed intention of finishing school and becoming employed at something of interest.

The seventh criterion relates to chronic feelings of emptiness or boredom. "In many ways, the borderline seeks out a new relationship or experience not for its positive aspects but to escape the feeling of emptiness" (Kreisman 1989, p. 39). Borderline students cannot bear being alone. Mood swings, dramatic stories, and self-expression may provide anxiety-relieving ways to fill up holes. Hypochondriasis may develop to relieve anxiety by garnering attention. Sexual activity, too, may help relieve tension.

FEELINGS OF BOREDOM EXAMPLES. *Robby's on-and-off relationship with his girlfriend reflects his mood swings. Not only does Robby want to control this relationship, but he seems to search for ways to change it in order to relieve boredom. When the relationship stabilizes and becomes calm, Robby soon stirs things up.*

Alicia's dramatic stories seem to provide new experiences in terms of others' reactions. On one of many occasions, she went to the school clinic complaining of severe abdominal pain. Despite Alicia's chronic physical complaints, and not wanting to err on the tragic side, school authorities called the medics to dispatch Alicia to the local hospital emergency room. The hospital staff found nothing wrong. Alicia had, in effect, mobilized staffs at two locations to deal with a false alarm.

Blythe often feels lonely and isolated. She has told so many tall tales to fill the void that people have begun to call her "the girl who cried wolf." At age 20, one of her goals was to be an actress. She oozes drama; she is dramatic in dress, make-up and behavior. Her skin is pale and creates a stark contrast with ruby red lipstick. She wears flashy jewelry, notably a pair of gold hoop earrings two inches in diameter with her name spanning the gap, joined by a pendant at her neck with her name in large gold letters. Further, Blythe is unable to modulate her voice. It varies unpredictably from quiet to loud, as if to control the conversation, and keeps the listener off balance. Blythe's persona is, altogether, theatrical, as if she is playing a part that she has created and scripted. Blythe also likes to talk about her body, recounting how she nearly died from a brain tumor caused by an imbalance in spinal fluid following an extreme weight gain. The story, essentially untrue, is a metaphor for her emotional imbalance.

Karina has been described as dramatic and rebellious. Rather than talking with her parents to make a point, she will stay away from home overnight. Despite the fact that she fears separations, she will make a statement by running away. Karina's rebellion is manifest in her intense dislike for binding routines. Further, she indulges in sexual activity when feeling lonely and anxious. During one such slump, she conceived.

The eighth criterion relates to the efforts made to avoid real or imagined abandonment. A borderline student often experiences temporary aloneness as perpetual isolation, cannot tolerate solitude, and craves the physical presence of others. This feeling of isolation relates to Kernberg's (1985) description of chronic, diffuse, free-floating anxiety, which is characteristic of the borderline personality.

ISOLATION EXAMPLES. *Alicia craves attention and constantly seeks it. Even though she frequently rejects the help that others offer, she persistently seeks their company. While she has been resistant to talk with teachers and counselors about her concerns, claiming that such talk will not help, she is a hovering presence when in their classrooms and offices. Furthermore, Alicia seems to need to fill up her days with exposure to people. Even though she complains about situations in all settings, her days are long and filled with people, from school to part-time job to home.*

Karina fears abandonment. This fear is an outcome of early years spent living with grandparents and various relatives as well as the deaths of a grandfather and great-grandparents when she was still in El Salvador. Karina's emotional upheaval has been extreme. She has a tendency toward undifferentiated, pervasive, generalized anxiety, manifest in recurrent nightmares.

WHAT IT MEANS TO HAVE BPD
Aside from meeting certain clinical criteria, a BPD adolescent is unique in four important ways. First, to be borderline means to have a primary developmental defect that began early in life. This disorder is neither a regression, assuming that normal development was under way, nor a transition phase toward

psychosis. The borderline, rather, tends to remain unstable as a result of arrested or aberrant development. According to Kreisman, BDP is "a cluster of longstanding, ingrained traits that are prominent in an individual's character" (1989, p. 20). Furthermore, these traits are rigid and result in maladaptive patterns of perceiving, behaving, and relating to others.

Second, as an outcome of developmental arrest or aberrance, students with borderline personalities seem to have made a partial commitment to the reality of the world outside themselves. However, their psychological incorporation of that world is noticeably incomplete, and the result is a disturbed sense of reality and a failure to develop constructive anxiety to deal with situations defensively. Unpleasant feelings may readily escalate to panic instead of helping the youngster generate defensive maneuvers. Many of these students are unable to modulate anxiety with self-mediated strategies; they bypass anxiety on the way to panic. According to Pine,

[T]hese children lack the basic stabilizers of functioning that other children acquire: a reliable anchor in external reality and in patterned object relations that give the children shape, and an array of intrapsychic defenses reliably set into motion when anxiety is aroused. (1982, p. 866)

A third important point about the BPD is that the disorder persists; it is chronic and characteristic. It endures over time and is ingrained in the individual's character. Beck and Freeman (1990) have concluded that BPD is an enduring pattern of perceiving, relating to, and thinking about the environment and oneself in which there are problems in a variety of areas including interpersonal behavior, mood, and self-image.

Children with BPD grow up to be odd adults, borderline, schizoid, or worse. They have a personality disorder that does not go away.

Part of the characteristic picture are two enduring processes: one cognitive, one behavioral. According to Kroll (1988), who described these two aspects, there is first a particular cognitive style that is marked by poorly focused thinking, self-rumination, transient dissociative states, disorganization under stress, and the use of impulsive action to short-circuit unpleasant mental states. Along with this style is an emotional intensity that is overwhelming for the student.

COGNITIVE AND BEHAVIORAL STYLE EXAMPLE. *Blythe has returned to school to complete the graduation requirements before turning 22, which is just four months away. She admits to feeling stressed about the work. Her cognitive style works against academic success. In biology, especially, she is feeling overwhelmed. When she does not understand something, she does not know what to do. She described a situation in which she took lots of notes even though she failed to understand what she was writing, as if her hand was moving independently of her mind, and she was able to make a sensible oral report to the class at the conclusion of one activity. Blythe said that intelligent, meaningful words came out of her mouth, surprising her. Later, she was unable to explain any part of the content that she had reported about in class. Her thinking, it seems, is disorganized. She does not know how to begin to work with ideas in order to commit them to long-term memory. "My mind," she says, "is mush," particularly when she has cramps, which was true on the day she had difficulty dealing with the biology material. However, when the cramps abated, Blythe did not seem any more able to develop strategies for organizing her thinking and learning.*

The fourth point relates to treatment. BPD is an extremely difficult condition to treat, educationally or therapeutically. Because it is a personality predisposition, the condition *is* the personality, or what the personality has become by dint of arrested or aberrant development. It is not merely a set of symptoms or defenses that relate to some inner conflict. The expression, "What you see is what you get," takes on special meaning with BPD.

TWO KINDS OF BORDERLINES

Two kinds of children fall under the classification of BPD. One kind is the child whose ego organization shifts. "They fluctuate back and forth from a reality-oriented, though often painfully troubled, world to a world of idiosyncratic fantasy" (Pine 1982, p. 867).

EGO ORGANIZATION FLUCTUATION EXAMPLE. *Jennifer periodically goes into what she calls her "freaky" moods: states of rage, of incredible access to normally unconscious memories, of perceptual confusion about her physical surroundings, and of distorted fantasies about her body and physical appearance. These moods alternate with rational functioning characterized by sensitivity, appropriate contact with reality, and cooperation with teachers, despite emotional pain. It becomes clear to those who work with this 16-year-old that what triggers her "freaky" moods are her own thoughts and feelings. She carries her pathology with her; it is her character, her core personality.*

A second kind of BPD involves destructive behavior (toward self or others), sometimes with extreme uncontrollability, hallucinations, and inappropriate affect. Yet when put into a highly structured, stable setting (for example, a hospital program), those with such destructive tendencies make rapid gains. These youngsters typically come from traumatizing environments (violent, psychotic, and generally neglectful or abusive settings) that lead to *reactive disorganization* (Pine 1982, p. 870).

DESTRUCTIVE BEHAVIOR EXAMPLES. *Blythe's family background contains abuse, notably her father's violent temper. Often his interactions with Blythe are violent. On one occasion she pressed charges against him for pushing her head through a wall. However, a witness testified that Blythe provoked the incident. Also, Blythe often takes belongings of family members, shows no remorse and lies about her involvement. When confronted, she screams. Consequently, family members put locks on their bedroom doors.*

Recall the early abuse that Karina suffered at the hands of immediate family members.

These youngsters often relate well to kind adults, as well as to situations with firm behavioral controls and clear boundaries. Pine (1982) described a 10-year-old girl who was hospitalized after she announced that she would leap out a window, and then tried to do so. Prior to this, she had stayed out of school without her mother's knowledge, spending the time crying in a hallway. There was a question about her thought processes and capacity for self-control. When hospitalized, she became charming and actively wooed adults for attention. Her adjustment in the hospital was so good, in fact, that there did not seem to be good reason to keep her there. However, any move toward discharge precipitated self-destructive behavior.

STRUCTURED SETTING EXAMPLE. *Robby exemplifies the kind of BPD that turns around in a structured setting. Robby's family environment is fraught with emotional instability, and his capacity for self-control is limited. He admitted himself to a hospital psychiatric program when the going got rough. One particularly rough period occurred when he was 15 years old. Within a one-month period, he was threatened by peers, was involved in two car accidents, received all "F's" on his report card, and his girlfriend was admitted to a psychiatric hospital. Robby liked the hospital he was in and threatened to kill himself if he was sent home. Nevertheless, he was discharged when it appeared that he would be safe.*

THE NEED FOR STRUCTURE

Robby exemplifies, then, the BPD type that shows a failure of psychic integration, of adequate self-control, even of realistic thought processes. He is able to achieve some integration in a highly structured setting where his fragile defenses can be supported and where he can use relationships for nurturance and to support his defenses and reality testing.

Another example is Blythe's dependency on her special education support system. Her emotional disturbance and learning disability teachers provided the only consistency and structure in her life.

Two aspects of this type of borderline personality interrelate. One serious aspect of this type of BPD is that when situations are not optimally structured, these individuals are at risk. Robby's pattern is to threaten suicide. Another aspect of this type of BPD involves control. These borderlines attempt to control situations in order to achieve some order. Karina evidences this pattern. As her mother said, Karina tries to be "in command" as much as possible. These students' attempts to control situations demonstrate their need for structure.

SPLITTING

   Splitting is another behavior pattern that characterizes BPD. It, too, illustrates the BPD's intolerance for inconsistency and ambiguity. The borderline student cannot tolerate the normal inconsistencies of life or understand the mixture of good and bad qualities in others. "At any particular moment, one is either 'good' or 'evil'; there is no in-between, no gray area" (Kreisman 1989, p. 10). Splitting is the borderline's primary defense mechanism, a "rigid separation of positive and negative thoughts and feelings about oneself and others, that is, the inability to synthesize these feelings" (Kreisman 1989, p. 10). Splitting is their way of warding off anxiety and dealing with ambiguity.

SPLITTING EXAMPLE 1. *Karina evidences a form of splitting. Her thinking is inflexible, she cannot adapt her attitude, and she cannot assume another's perspective. Role-playing, consequently, is an impossible mental feat. She is very narcissistic, self-centered, and unable to consider anyone's needs but her own.*

   Practically speaking, borderlines split other people, individually or in groups, into separate pieces or sides as a function of their own needs. This divide-and-conquer strategy enables the borderline personality to deal with contradictory feelings and images; thoughts and feelings are selected to serve the need of the moment.
   The result is not peace and calm, however. What typically happens is that the "frays in the personality fabric become full-fledged rips; the sense of his own identity and the identities of others shifts even more dramatically and frequently" (Kreisman 1989, p. 11). The borderline student may choose a thought to match the moment's need, but at a price: coherent self-identity.

SPLITTING EXAMPLE 2. *16-year-old Brooke's BPD pattern involves manipulation. She splits staff at her high school, working different angles with adults, creating disagreement and discord among them. She may flip back and forth in terms of allegiances and may pit one teacher against the other. She is manipulative at home, too, claiming that the school authorities support her arguments. In turn, Brooke tells teachers stories about her home situation that invariably prove to be false. For example, she has manipulated teachers into believing that she is no longer using drugs, all the while actively dealing. When teachers confront her with contradictory information, Brooke's refrain is, "Why won't you believe me?" Her manipulation is infectious. Consequently, it is difficult to deal with Brooke in a group. Any confrontation with her is likely to provoke peers to defend her, even if it is not the same peers every time. Brooke has a strong personality, and she preys on weaker personalities. She needs reinforcement, and she pursues it by fooling a lot of people a lot of the time.*

A well-developed personality like Brooke's, with no diverting inner conflict and anxiety to raise doubts, can easily dominate personalities that experience those niggling little "neurotic" concerns. As with many such students, Brooke calls the shots and manipulates weaker peers into positions that meet her needs. The pattern is well developed; it is Brooke's character.

As mentioned earlier, it is characteristic of the borderline personality to split because of inability to deal with ambiguity. Alicia shows splitting of this nature.

SPLITTING EXAMPLE 3. *Alicia, at 18, has a certificate of independence from her mother. Therefore, she is legally entitled to represent herself at her IEP (individualized education plan) conference. When an IEP conference was held to discuss adding support service for her emotional problems, Alicia cooperated well, asked few questions, and agreed to the drafted needs and goals. However, immediately after signing that she had participated in the conference and agreed to its outcome, which placed her in ED resource where she could share problems and seek solutions, she went directly to the school's main office to complain that she had been "railroaded" into something and did not understand why.*

BPD AND THE FEDERAL DEFINITION OF ED

Adolescents with BPD are clearly in discord. Their cognitive styles and behavior patterns indicate that they experience great difficulties and need the support of special education in order to progress educationally. Specifically, the adolescent with BPD clearly needs the structure of nurturance and reason within a context of clear communication. Yet confronting borderline behavior and participating in its reeducation and treatment is difficult, for, as Kreisman (1989) writes of BPD students, their explosions of anger, rapid mood swings, suspiciousness, impulsive actions, unpredictable outbursts, self-destructive actions, and inconsistent communications are upsetting to everyone around them.

Among the ED criteria contained in the Individuals with Disabilities Education Act (IDEA) are several that relate particularly to BPD. One is *an inability to learn that cannot be explained by intellectual, sensory, or health factors*. BPD has no known medical condition to explain its genesis or manifestation. It is apparent in the cases described in this chapter that the educational progress of these students is significantly hindered by a constellation of emotional and behavioral problems. They are overwhelmed by self-defeating behaviors and interfering thoughts and feelings.

Another part of the ED definition that relates to BPD is *an inability to build or maintain satisfactory interpersonal relationships with peers and teachers.*

We have seen, again and again, examples of unstable relationships characterized by manipulation and intense anger. Who can relate to a student who vacillates between acceptance or dependence and rejection and uses people for whatever need dominates the moment? Who wants to be in a relationship in which the other person wants to exert total control?

Inappropriate types of behavior or feelings under normal circumstances characterize an adolescent with a borderline personality disorder. These students show impulsive and hostile behavior, with intense emotions that are disproportionate to specific situations. What is normal for them is extremely upsetting to others.

Finally, among adolescents with BPD we often see *a general pervasive mood of unhappiness or depression*. Moodiness is frequently seen. These students may entertain thoughts of suicide, and they may engage in self-destructive thoughts and behaviors. Karina, for example, has had bouts of severe depression, one of which resulted in hospitalization.

SUGGESTED EDUCATIONAL STRATEGIES

Students with borderline personality disorder need to learn to deal with their anger and to cope with less intensity and less impulsivity. Additionally, they need structure in order to dispell confusion, realistic feedback to learn rational social perceptions and flexible thinking, and opportunities to develop independence and responsibility. Specifically, they need strategies that relate to external control, internal control, appropriate engagement, encouragement, acceptance/approval, consistency/routine, and attention. These students, then, need the entire spectrum of strategies.

The following effective strategies are suggested.

1.   Ask the student to explain the rules of a specific situation; for example, before sending the student to the auditorium for a special program, ask him or her to review the rules and the kind of behaviors that are expected.

2.   Provide additional structure and guidance during transitional periods; warn the student about any upcoming changes.

3.   Provide a secure, consistent, predictable routine.

4.   Reinforce specific behaviors one at a time and remind the student that you like him or her even if a particular behavior is inappropriate and needs to be changed.

5.   Use group activities that build trust. An example is cooperative learning.

6.   Be sensitive to the student's need for constructive criticism. Emphasize positives in feedback.

7.   Give specific praise rather than broad praise, for example, "I like the way you included humor in your speech," not "great speech."

8.   Go after the student with tenacity when work is not turned in; show a personal touch.

9.   Do not accept inadequate explanations or excuses for late work. High expectations show care.

10.   Give the student an outline or itinerary for the period's or day's activities.

11.   Activate the student's current knowledge about a new concept so he or she can make a bridge from old knowledge to new. For example, use semantic mapping, which may involve free association of ideas followed by categorizing responses. This readies the student for new information.

12.   Use an aide to sit next to the student in order to prompt him or her when something important is mentioned that should be recorded.

13.   Speak with the student prior to class to increase his or her comfort level. Remind the student about your availability beyond class time.

14.   Accommodate the student's unique, perhaps even unconventional, style by allowing options to complete assignments and projects.

15.   Model patience and understanding. This student will probably balk at requests to be patient or understanding and is more likely to see these qualities in you and want to emulate them rather than to respond as such on demand.

16.   Give realistic options and choices.

17.   Conduct all disciplinary feedback with the student in private.

18.   Provide a flexible range of consequences rather than one rigid response for every transgression. For incomplete homework, an appropriate response might be to stay after school to finish it, to hold a conference with teacher and parent to develop a plan, to issue a reminder or warning, or to ask the student to hand in work before the close of the school day.

19.   Provide logical consequences to teach the reality of the social order and to show that the rules do not stem from the authority figure but from social reality.

20.   Give the student a real and legitimate means of control, influence, responsibility, and power.

21.   Try alternative strategies before seeking others' help. This shows the student that you have the authority and power to deal with him or her.

22.   Give the student responsibility to keep track of his or her own behavior. For example, have the student maintain a notebook for self-control. Coach the student to use it when he or she feels the need to lash out verbally or physically. Review the entries daily and discuss how he or she felt at those moments. Praise the student for jotting down the incidents rather than losing control.

23.   Schedule activities that the student likes after those he or she does not like. This will give the student something to look forward to, will focus the student on the difficult tasks with fresh energy, and will give the student less reason to complain and seek refuge outside the classroom.

24.   Avoid power struggles. Do not get hung up on small issues. Provide choices so that the student will feel empowered yet leave the adult's options structured.

25.   Teach the student to read his or her own internal signals so that he or she knows when he or she is angry, afraid, or frustrated.

26.   Once the student is able to identify his or her own feelings, discuss some possible coping means. For example, the student could make a chart of targeted strategies to keep in a notebook. of targeted strategies. The student might check off each strategy when it is used. Meet with the student periodically to review situations and attempted strategies and to re-design strategies in light of outcomes.

27.   Maintain maximum supervision of the student. Gradually decrease supervision over time as the student demonstrates self-control.

28.   Treat the student with respect. Talk in an objective manner at all times. Remember that a student does not have to feel bad in order to behave well.

29.   Be careful to avoid embarrassing the student by giving him or her orders or demands in front of others.

30.   Do not force the student to interact with others.

31.   Empower the student to voice opinions in situations in order to avoid becoming angry or upset.

5

Antisocial Personality Tendency

Though I've made a mess of my life, I never stew about
the things I have done.

Gary Gilmore

THE ANTISOCIAL PERSONALITY

First, *antisocial personality disorder* (APD) is the term applied to an inadequate
personality that chronically disregards and violates the rights of others. Not only
do they persistently violate the rights of others, they also often break the law
(Nevid, Rathus, and Greene 1994).

Second, APD is not a condition of childhood. As defined by the
American Psychiatric Association's *DSM-IV* (1994), APD is recognized as an
adult disorder. To be diagnosed as having APD, an individual must be at least
18 years of age.

While people with antisocial personalities typically engage in many
antisocial acts during the course of their lives, it is the gestalt of APD that defines
it as a disorder of personality and character. In other words, what constitutes an
antisocial personality is not so much the particular acts as the distinctive,
deeply ingrained approach to life (Sarason and Sarason 1993), or character.

As a character disorder, what distinguishes APD is the individual's low
level of anxiety and lack of guilt. Guilt requires that one consider the
consequences of behavior. Consequences do not influence the behavior of
individuals with APD; they persist in their misdeeds despite feedback or
punishment from others, and they seldom seem to feel remorse.

Although APDs seem to worry less than other people, they experience
all of the common somatic indicators of anxiety (high heart rate, shortness of
breath, tense muscles). If we divide anxiety into its cognitive part, worry, and its
physiological components, particularly the body's responses to fear, antisocial
individuals seem to lack the cognitive component of anxiety (Sarason and
Sarason 1993).

In common parlance, the terms *psychopath* and *sociopath* are used when
referring to antisocial personalities. These terms describe people whose behavior
is amoral, asocial, and impulsive; they lack remorse and shame. The stereotype is

that of a violent career criminal like Gary Gilmore, whose life was chronicled by Norman Mailer in *Executioner's Song* (1979) Gilmore was unable to follow rules at home or at school. He began abusing alcohol and drugs during adolescence, and he was repeatedly in trouble with the law for crimes that included armed robbery and murder. He never showed any remorse for his crimes and never held a job or maintained a steady relationship. He was intentionally abusive and cruel. Some antisocial personalities, however, may be charming and seem unlikely to engage in violent behavior. Theodore Bundy, a serial murderer who also was executed, was one of those who could con, lie, and charm his victims without experiencing guilt. For both men, there was a characteristic self-centeredness and insensitivity to others' needs.

An individual with APD is likely to commit acts of violence, but not all criminals have APD. Criminal behavior, while antisocial, does not in itself justify a diagnosis of antisocial personality disorder. Conversely, fewer than half of the people with antisocial personalities run afoul of the law (Nevid, Rathus, and Greene 1994).

There are six specific signs of an antisocial personality disorder: (1) failure to conform to social norms with respect to lawful behaviors as indicated by repeatedly performing acts that are grounds for arrest; (2) deceitfulness, as indicated by repeated lying, use of aliases, or conning others for personal profit or pleasure; (3) impulsivity or failure to plan ahead; (4) irritability and aggressiveness, as indicated by repeated physical fights or assaults; (5) reckless disregard for the safety of self or others consistent with irresponsibility, as indicated by repeated failure to sustain work behavior or honor financial obligations; and (6) lack of remorse, as indicated by being indifferent to or rationalizing having hurt, mistreated, or stolen from another.

The profile of adult APD, then, involves failure to conform to social norms, outright lawlessness, violence, chronic unemployment, marital problems, substance abuse, a history of alcoholism, and disregard for the truth. Sarason and Sarason (1993) add that, by early adulthood, the following features are apparent: failure to plan ahead, mistreatment or neglect of one's children, and sexual promiscuity.

The adult who is diagnosed with APD probably exhibited a conduct disorder prior to the age of 15, featuring truancy or school suspension; arrest; running away from home; lying; sexual activity; use of liquor, tobacco, or other nonprescribed drugs unusually early compared to peers; stealing; vandalism; fighting; and violating rules at home or at school. A history of continuous, serious, and chronic misconduct is characteristic of this disorder.

This is not the profile of an individual who is likely to respond to clinical treatment. Antisocial personalities do not see themselves as the cause of their problems but, rather, see the tough spots they find themselves in as caused by flaws in other people (Sarason and Sarason 1993). The adage, "the best defense is a good offense," comes to mind.

SOME FACTS ABOUT APD

Gender. Men are more likely than women to suffer from antisocial personality disorder. There may be as many as five males with APD for every APD woman.

Prevalence. The prevalence of APD has been rising for both genders in recent years, more sharply in women. Also, it is more prevalent among the lower socioeconomic classes, partly because antisocial personalities tend to drift downward occupationally (Nevid, Rathus, and Greene 1994). These behaviors, which carry strong social sanctions and the possibility of legal proceedings, are low-rate problems. Commonly, antisocial children also present other, high-rate behavior problems, such as physical aggression, verbal abusiveness, noncompliance, and poor social interactional skills.

Ethnicity. There appears to be no connection between ethnicity and APD.

Sociological factors. Criminal and aggressive behavior has multiple causes and represents many personality types, not only APD; criminal or aggressive behavior could be related to any of a variety of circumstances and conditions, even certain forms of brain impairment (Sarason and Sarason 1993). Although infamous crimes have been committed by people who apparently fit the diagnosis of APD, some people become criminals or delinquents simply because they are reared in environments or subcultures that encourage and reward such behavior, and where antisocial personalities serve as role models for children. There appears to be a strong link between the presence of antisocial personality in one or both parents and similar behavior in their children (Graham 1991). McManus (1989) documented a significantly overrepresented diagnosis of APD among parents of children with a combination of attention-deficit and conduct disorders, both of which are disruptive disorders if not overtly antisocial.

APD researchers have been hampered by the fact that it is easier to identify antisocial personalities among individuals who have been convicted of crimes than among the general population. Consequently, the group on which research is based may not be typical of all people with an antisocial personality. Sarason and Sarason tell of one researcher who dealt with this methodological dilemma in an interesting way: inserting the following ad in a Boston counterculture newspaper:

Wanted: charming, aggressive, carefree people who are impulsively irresponsible but are good at handling people and at looking after number one. Send name, address, phone, and short biography proving how interesting you are to.... (1993, p. 268)

The ad drew 73 responses, of which about two-thirds were from males. In the backgrounds of one-third of the respondents who met the criteria for a diagnosis of APD were broken homes (21.4 percent), suicide attempts (28.6 percent), juvenile incarceration (10.7 percent), and adult arrest (64.3 percent). The main difference between this sample and prison samples was that those who answered the ad had been able to avoid convictions after arrests or detention.

Cause. There is increasing evidence that heredity may play a role in antisocial behavior. A Swedish study revealed that adopted children who were separated at birth from their APD parents showed more antisocial behavior later in life than control subjects (Sarason and Sarason 1993). Aggression, too, has been related to low levels of serotonin, a neurotransmitter, and researchers are investigating the connection between brain activity, particularly slow alpha waves, and antisocial behavior. (See the discussion in Chapter 7 of similar issues among those with disruptive behavior disorders.)

PRECURSORS OF APD

Predictors of antisocial personality disorder can be seen during childhood, early adolescence, and middle adolescence. Aggressive children gravitate toward one another and coalesce into cliques well before adolescence. In turn, early adolescent behavior that is characterized by one or more of the following is likely to persist into late adolescence and adulthood: early onset and high rate of aggression, aggression in several forms (for example, hitting, lying, stealing), and antisocial behavior in more than one setting (Snyder and Huntley 1990).

Antisocial behavior puts an adolescent at risk for adult problems such as psychiatric impairment and low educational attainment. In fact, one-third to one-half of referrals to psychiatric settings come from the population noted for antisocial behavior (Snyder and Huntley 1990). Aggression is substantially stable over time and is clinically more reliable as a predictor of later problems than other adolescent behavior patterns (Lochman 1984).

Specialists in violence and victimization have concluded that children headed for an antisocial personality disorder show no loyalty, no ethics, and no ability to connect with an adult. Also, those children already show a resistance to help. Therapists can succeed only if the children with whom they work are capable of learning to trust others. Some clinicians believe that most delinquents do not benefit from therapy because they often are not in treatment long enough and often are very manipulative.

According to some experts, for therapy to have a lasting effect, it must be redefined as an ongoing effort by a team of specialists. The behaviors of antisocial youngsters need to be modified by turning daily activities into therapeutic experiences. Psychologists, social workers, parents, teachers, recreation workers, and other team members can teach communication skills during meals, change attitudes through positive learning experiences, and use conflict on the basketball court as teachable moments. Some psychiatrists argue that we need to abandon the notion that therapy for these youngsters is a fifty-minute hour where someone sits and discusses his childhood. Instead, the therapist must become a guide to help the youngster feel the world that is being relearned. The scars never go away, but a therapist can help antisocial youngsters restructure their responses to hurt feelings.

TENDENCY OR INTENTIONALITY

As APD is recognized only as an adult disorder, the present focus is on a pre-adult tendency toward APD. Pre-adults may show distinct signs of early onset APD, either in combination with other disorders or as a separate disorder. Adolescents have not lived long enough for us to be sure that they are functioning characteristically in opposition to society. At this stage, we can only verify that they show a tendency toward an antisocial personality disorder.

Psychologist Charlotte Buhler describes intentionality as what individuals do and say by their own initiative, not solely as a reaction to environmental events. Buhler (1933; 1959) proposed that individual personalities have an "inner coherence" that unifies them. This inner coherence also may be defined as independent expectations that motivate the individual.

Buhler studied many biographies in order to articulate this inner coherence and concluded that successful and mentally healthy individuals possess this unifying personality trait and that even those who are unsuccessful or unhealthy have some expectations. In other words, all individuals develop intentionality to some extent.

As Buhler's theory developed, psychological stages of self-determination were described. According to this schema, the period between 15 and 25 years of age involves a tentative and preparatory phase of self-determination of life goals, a beginning of awareness of life as a whole. This period is notable for the adolescent's first attempts to find direction, purpose, and meaning for life as well as first concepts of the different fulfillments that life might offer. Because the individual's actions are predicated upon internal tendencies, and are not simply reactions to external events, individual initiative is seen as a factor that determines a selective and directive thrust into the world (Buhler 1968).

A logical step is to merge the aforementioned indicators of APD with individual biographical material. We can look at the lives of adolescents who show spontaneous, self-generated antisocial behaviors. In the process, we may speculate about the probable development of APD from the pattern of behaviors. This approach is supported by the American Psychiatric Association's *DSM-IV* (1994), which points out that child or adolescent antisocial behavior may be a focus of clinical attention caused by isolated antisocial acts that may not yet have formed a pattern of antisocial behavior. Thus, it is important to look at the tendency toward antisocial behavior even if there is no diagnosable pattern.

The following script represents one teacher's interview during crisis counseling with Bart, a 15-year-old boy in his high school's self-contained program for students with emotional disabilities. This script introduces the specific criteria that will be presented in relation to antisocial personality tendency.

Teacher: *You've been fighting in class a lot, haven't you?*

Bart: *Yeah, sure, but that's part of the game.*

Teacher:	*Have any other students tried to push you around?*
Bart:	*Yeah, a couple of them. But I set them right.*
Teacher:	*How did you set them right?*
Bart:	*I kicked their butts.*
Teacher:	*I bet you can take care of yourself real well. Have you been in many fights?*
Bart:	*Yeah, kids know not to mess with me. In the 'hood [neighborhood] you got to know how to fight to survive.*
Teacher:	*How many fights do you think you've had?*
Bart:	*Maybe about one every month, and I've been in fights ever since I can remember, like since I was 10.*
Teacher:	*Let's see, so that's got to be about 50 or 60, right?*
Bart:	*I guess so. Maybe more.*
Teacher:	*Have you ever been hurt, had to go to the hospital?*
Bart:	*No, but I did a number on a few bad boys.*
Teacher:	*Did you ever put one of them in the hospital?*
Bart:	*Yeah, there was one dude that I cut up real good, but he really asked for it.*
Teacher:	*O.K., how about drugs and alcohol?*
Bart:	*Yeah, I've done a lot of that. There's a lot of stuff on the street, easy to get.*
Teacher:	*Does it make you feel more angry, nasty?*
Bart:	*Yeah, sometimes. I start a lot of fights when I'm high.*
Teacher:	*Have you ever been in a gang? How did you learn to defend yourself so well?*
Bart:	*In my 'hood, you got to learn to fight to survive. Yeah, I hang out with a gang lots o' times. The kids in this school don't hang with me. They live in different 'hoods.*

THE CRITERIA

The first criterion relates to failure to conform to social norms with respect to lawful behaviors as indicated by repeatedly performing acts that are grounds for arrest. Implied is that the youngster might meet this criterion even if not apprehended for unlawful behavior.

FAILURE TO CONFORM EXAMPLE 1. *Laura has engaged in shoplifting, vandalism, and neighborhood pranks for years. Usually, she steals small items from drug stores. Her vandalism has included spray painting a neighbor's van and destroying the Christmas lights on neighboring houses. One prank that she enjoyed was to invite a friend to spend the night at her house and call repeatedly for pizza delivery to a neighboring house.*

The second criterion relates to deceitfulness, as indicated by repeated lying, use of aliases, or conning others for personal profit or pleasure.

DECEITFULNESS EXAMPLE 1. *Laura lies to her parents constantly. She might forge a parent note so that a friend may take the school bus to her house, and then tells her mother that the friend has permission to visit. She lies to both teachers and parents about taking her medication at school. Laura has also decided that she would like to change her name.*

The third criterion relates to impulsivity or the failure to plan ahead.

IMPULSIVITY EXAMPLE 1. *Laura typically acts before thinking about the consequences of her actions. For example, she met a friend in the rest room at her school to gossip between classes one day and persuaded her friend that it would be fun to stay there instead of going to class. Laura did not consider that the consequence for this behavior was detention.*

The fourth criterion relates to irritability and aggressiveness, as indicated by repeated physical fights or assaults.

IRRITABILITY AND AGGRESSIVENESS EXAMPLE. *Laura frequently becomes irritated by events in her home and uses physical aggression against her younger brother. She also has threatened her mother verbally and pushed her on more than one occasion.*

The fifth criterion relates to reckless disregard for the safety of self or others.

RECKLESS DISREGARD EXAMPLE 1. *Laura likes to take risks. It is fun, it is adventure. One day she and a friend told their parents that they were staying after school to catch up on work. Instead, the girls went to a nearby shopping center and shoplifted. When they returned to school, Laura thought it would be fun to stand on the median strip of the busy road in front of the school to wave at motorists, pretending that she needed help. She did not consider the possibility that an accident might result.*

The sixth criterion relates to consistent irresponsibility, as indicated by repeated failure to sustain consistent work behavior or honor financial obligations.

IRRESPONSIBILITY EXAMPLE 1. *When it comes to sustaining effort at school or honoring financial obligations, Laura is deficient. Inconsistency and irresponsibility are her style. She may work hard at something for a few days, only to abandon it abruptly in favor of something more interesting. For example, while she said that she was interested in writing a short story about a Civil War character, getting off to a creative, effortful start, she dropped the project after a few days. As for financial responsibility, when Laura owes someone money it is quickly forgotten, as if she were entitled to keep the money. When her mother confronted her about money missing from her purse, while Laura did not deny taking it, she did not offer to repay it.*

The seventh criterion relates to a lack of remorse, as indicated by being indifferent to, or rationalizing, having hurt, mistreated, or stolen from another person.

LACK OF REMORSE EXAMPLE 1. *Laura seems to lack a conscience. It does not bother her that she stole money from her mother. She rationalizes that she deserves the money and earned it by doing household chores. When she was finally caught for shoplifting, she reasoned that stores expect to be "ripped off" and that they raise prices of items to compensate.*

Laura shows an important APD tendency: aggression toward people and animals. She bullies her little brother into giving her money; she threatened her mother and older brother with a knife; and she is cruel to peers and to animals. She once dangled a sick pet mouse out a window by its tail to prevent her mother from treating the pet. Her destruction of property, theft and deceitfulness, and serious violation of rules, such as opening a neighbor's mail, also point to a tendency toward APD.

Altogether, Laura shows signs of a budding antisocial personality disorder. Assorted behaviors at home, in the community, and at school point to a pattern of behaviors that are internally generated; they are not responses to events in her life. In short, she shows a tendency toward APD.

Eric, too, shows a tendency toward APD. His pattern, unlike Laura's, occurs exclusively at home. Like Laura's, his behavior pattern does not appear to be shaped by external events; his behavior, particularly the antisocial behavior, seems to be self-determined and, notably, highly self-selective.

Let us look at Eric in terms of the seven criteria for APD. The criteria for Eric have been slightly reworded to fit his home situation.

The first criterion relates to nonconformity to home norms with respect to rule-governed behaviors, indicated by repeated actions that are grounds for discipline

FAILURE TO CONFORM EXAMPLE 2. *Eric strives to be in control and is resistant to external control. If his parents try to discipline him, he becomes oppositional and shows passive-aggressive tendencies. If his parents tell him that the family has plans, Eric can be expected to do something to disrupt them. For example, one Christmas reservations were made for a family ski trip. At the last minute, Eric refused to go. He stayed, instead, with his grandparents, and his parents were unable to recoup Eric's air fare. He ruined a Thanksgiving holiday by threatening to commit suicide. If he does not want to clean his room he will choose to miss a reward. Eric says that he will only do something if he agrees with it.*

The second criterion relates to deceitfulness, as indicated by repeated lying or conning others for personal profit or pleasure.

DECEITFULNESS EXAMPLE 2. *When Eric was a young child he would refuse to attend birthday parties unless he could be first and win all the games. His parents could entice him to attend a birthday party only if he was given a bigger present than the one he was giving the birthday child. When he began school and had homework to do, Eric would hide his work and show his parents only his good papers. He frequently steals things around the house. If he takes something from a sealed box he will stuff the box with paper and then reseal it. Eric is fixated on the game "Dungeons and Dragons," which involves role-taking, weapons, and fantasy. Adolescents have been known to get so involved in the fantasy world that they create when playing it that they neglect other aspects of their lives. In his passion to play D&D Eric has stolen money from his stepmother to order new games through the mail. By eighth grade his parents, in consultation with mental health professionals, banned the game because it   might stimulate violent behavior, but Eric showed aggression even during periods when he was cut off from the game. Other antisocial home behavior includes stealing food and candy from his stepsister, taking outgoing checks from the family mailbox, and stealing his stepmother's jewelry.*

Criterion three relates to impulsivity. The impulsivity of a youngster with a tendency toward APD is not merely inability to plan ahead; it is highly spontaneous behavior that is prompted by a sudden urge, is not governed by reason, and is sometimes even contrary to reason. Often, impulsivity is defined as the inability to think before acting. For a student with a tendency toward

APD, there is a qualitative difference. While the impulsive student may not think of the consequence of his action, a student with antisocial tendency seems to take the consequence into his plan, intentionally setting himself up to avert the outcome, even if it is a positive one. In short, this youngster seems to plan his own consequence. The outcome may seem to spite himself, however, the key is that he is in control.

IMPULSIVITY EXAMPLE 2. *Eric's desire for control is evident in his response to parental requests. He would rather not get a reward for cleaning his room if cleaning it means doing what his parent wants. For him, the urge to be in control outweighs the benefit of the reward.*

Criterion four relates to irritability and aggressiveness, as indicated by repeated physical fights or assaults.

AGGRESSIVENESS EXAMPLE. *Eric shows extreme aggressiveness. One day his stepmother asked him to leave his backpack by the front door when he returned from school. He took all the clothes out of the hall closet and then used the closet pole to try to knock her down the stairs. He later said that he had wanted to "bash mom's head in." He has also kicked his stepsister. On another occasion, Eric was told that he could not go to his room to play until he had completed a chore. He shoved and kicked his stepmother. Eric told a psychologist that he is easily angered.*

Criterion five relates to reckless disregard for the safety of self or others.

RECKLESS DISREGARD EXAMPLE 2. *Eric keeps a stash of knives in his room, including a razor blade and an exacto knife. The parents are concerned for their safety, so they have installed locks on their bedroom door and that of Eric's stepsister.*

Criterion six relates to consistent irresponsibility, as indicated by repeated failure to sustain consistent work behavior.

IRRESPONSIBILITY EXAMPLE 2. *Eric begins activities but tends to stop them midstream. For example, he started taking horseback riding and ice skating lessons, at his request, only to stop when he learned that practice, i.e., effort, was required.*

Criterion seven relates to lack of remorse, as indicated by being indifferent to or rationalizing having hurt or mistreated another.

LACK OF REMORSE EXAMPLE 2. *Eric shows no remorse when caught stealing. He rationalizes that it is all right to hurt someone if the goal is important enough. In other words, the end justifies the means.*

Overall, Eric seems to show a tendency toward APD. He shows a pattern of spontaneous oppositional behavior that is evident at home. Although he is cooperative at school, Eric is actively, chronically oppositional at home. He appears to select his battles carefully and controllably. It is as if he is playing a game with his family. This pattern of spontaneous opposition at home is long-standing. Based on Eric's history, the pattern seems likely to continue.

Laura and Eric provide a glimpse of what it means to have a tendency toward an antisocial personality disorder. Laura's antisocial character appears to be fairly well defined already in every setting, whereas Eric's antisocial personality tendency appears to be well defined in only one setting. Because both students are still in the formative period, only time will tell if they will meet the criteria for an antisocial personality disorder when they become adults.

APD AND THE FEDERAL DEFINITION OF ED

The Individuals with Disabilities Education Act (IDEA) specifies criteria for ED that may exclude students from this category if they manifest an antisocial personality tendency. The word antisocial, whether associated with personality or behavior, connotes social maladjustment. By federal criteria, students must be excluded from the ED category *unless it is determined that they are emotionally disturbed.* The unlawful, deceitful, impulsive, aggressive, irresponsible, remorseless, nonconforming, and risk-taking behaviors of students with a tendency toward an antisocial personality disorder suggest a social maladjustment. Therefore, it would be necessary to exclude them from consideration, according to the law, unless they are also emotionally disturbed.

Indeed, as will become clear by the conclusion of this book, Laura is emotionally disturbed. Chapter 23 contains a summary of the federal and practical characteristics (the 10 targeted characteristics presented in Chapter 1) considered to reach the conclusion that Laura is a very disturbed student. Laura shows an abundance of ED characteristics, and she meets federal criteria, specifically because she has *an inability to build or maintain satisfactory interpersonal relationships with peers and teachers*. Because of her deceitfuness, aggressiveness, and disregard for others' safety she is not a good candidate for healthy relationships. In Laura's case the school system determined that she met the federal ED criteria and could not be excluded from ED because of social maladjustment because she also is emotionally disturbed as a result of difficult relationships.

Eric, too, has been found eligible for special education services as a student with an emotional disability. Despite his obvious antisocial personality tendency, Eric has been deeply *depressed* since his mother's death. His anger has been channeled into antisocial behaviors that seriously affect his family, if not his school life. Eric was determined by his school system to meet the federal criteria for ED as a result of depression.

Both Laura and Eric show *an inability to learn that cannot be explained by intellectual, health, or sensory factors.* Eric is more compliant at school than at home, but he is reticent to participate actively during instructional activities and does not achieve commensurate with his ability. Laura is too impulsive and irresponsible to succeed at school. Her aggressive, reckless, deceitful, and nonconforming antics draw her far away from academic concerns.

SUGGESTED EDUCATIONAL STRATEGIES

These students need to learn to conform to rules, to plan and think ahead, and to be responsible. In order for them to be part of a safe environment and to learn remorse, situations must be structured so that they cannot destroy the environment or do something that requires remorse. Suggested strategies fall into the areas of external and internal controls as well as appropriate engagement.

1. Seek feedback from the student. This strategy not only gives information about what the student understands and has attended to but gives him or her power in the situation to direct or redirect instruction and goals.

2. Periodically have the student restate aloud classroom rules. This provides evidence of his or her knowledge of them.

3. Teach the student to divide large tasks into small, manageable parts and to decide on the order in which to do them. By enabling the student's decision making, investment in his or her own learning is ensured.

4. As many APD students are unable to delay gratification, and are now-oriented, help the student make a bridge to the future by estimating time required for tasks. The student might also record the time a task is started and completed, showing how long the task took. The student might also record times in a log for reference and participate in planning a period's or day's activities to include work and relaxation or positive reinforcement times.

5. Provide a consistent, predictable routine with flexibility that is negotiable. Maintain consistency in rules and general expectations of conduct and procedure.

6. Use group pressure. For example, "Robert, none of us can hear the movie until you're with us."

7. Use "I" messages rather than "you" ones. For example, "I expect those math problems to be done by 11:15." Adolescents who have trouble with authority figures are more responsive to indirect commands.

8. Reward the student for compliance. Also, be specific about appropriate behavior. For example, praise the student for following your direction to throw his gum away, not for "being a good person."

9. Make sure the student is capable of performing tasks. Many stu-

dents act out to avoid difficult work.

   10.   Establish a private nonverbal cue to redirect behavior. APD students are likely to show their antisocial tendencies when targeted in a group by verbal redirections. Nonverbal cues are less likely to   evoke   arguments   and   other show-off,   defiant   behaviors. Also, conduct disciplinary feedback privately so the student can save face.

   11.   Provide opportunities to be a leader. Students with APD can be socialized to promote social order when they have a vested interest in creating and sustaining it.

   12.   Use logical consequences to teach the social order and to show that the rules are not arbitrary but represent the larger social world. Also, when setting up classroom rules, draw parallels with rules outside the classroom and school. Review these parallels at all points that rules need clarification.

   13.   Develop a personal relationship to enhance persuasion power.

   14.   Give the student the power to choose his or her assignments, the order for doing them, and the method of doing them. The issue should always be not if he or she will work but on what, how, and when.

   15.   Try alternative strategies in the classroom. To relinquish power to staff outside the classroom shows the student that you do not have the authority or power to deal with him or her. This provides the student with a sense of security and safety from his or her own negative impulses.

   16.   Limit the student's opportunity to engage in activities in which he or she will not follow directions (for example, field trips).

   17.   Be mobile in order to be   near the student often. Vigilance and awareness are also important.

6

Narcissism

The shattered water made a misty din.
Robert Frost

A THEME OF SELF-INDULGENCE

Some say that narcissism, frequently seen in adolescents with emotional and behavioral disorders, is increasing. In his forty years as a therapist, Lowen (1985) has seen a change from the *neuroses* of earlier times, represented by incapacitating guilts, anxieties, phobias, and obsessions, to complaints of inner emptiness, frustration, and unfulfillment.

This inner void often does not match an outwardly full, active life. For example, an individual may spend years striving for power and wealth only to discover that something is missing. The split between external and internal lives has been cited as explanation for the split beween adult and child rates of maturing in modern society. One professor of media and culture commented that children are growing up too fast because adults are growing up too slowly. Adults want to be kids instead of taking on adult roles. In an effort to market themselves, adults are too busy polishing their youthful images to nurture children. Self-sacrifice is no longer the norm among adults.

One of the first writers to recognize this problem was Ginott, who advised parents not to emulate the language and conduct of their children. He quotes Belinda, age 16, describing her mother:

My mother tries hard to be a teenager. She dresses in mini-skirts, wears beads, and talks hip. When my friends come visiting, she asks them to "ooze her some skin" [shake hands] and tell her some "groovy" news. It makes me sick to see her act so foolish. My friends pretend that she is one of us, but they laugh at her behind her back, and they make fun of me. (1969, p. 33)

In trying to emulate youth, adults lie to themselves. The physical image, essentially, is a lie. Most of us were not suave or sexy in our youth. It is a lie to try to remake ourselves in a false image.

When lack of "realness" is evident in parents who abuse and neglect their children, narcissism is more than unfortunate; it is shocking. In recent years, there have been terrible stories of manipulation and control that override humanizing emotions. For example, the attitude that one would rather die than yield power to another is tragically illustrated in the North Carolina case of Susie Leary, who destroyed herself and her two children in a car explosion rather than surrender custody to the children's father.

Another example of a narcissistic mother's willingness to sacrifice her own children to get what she wanted is the case of Diane Downs, who tried to murder her three children, as documented in the book and film, *Small Sacrifices*. Downs' case shows the extent to which a narcissist will go to lay a clear path to matrimony when a lover does not want to become a parent.

In the belief that individual narcissism parallels that of the culture, some theorize that there is a culture of indulgence in America's homes and schools. Damon (1995), for example, points to one theme that dominates today's culture: the ascendancy of self, clearly a narcissistic theme. This theme relates to Lowen's (1985) premise that society is fostering empty humans. Youth are not being expected to get outside themselves to consider the problems and needs of others; instead, they are encouraged to lose themselves in toys and video games or to to wander the malls in search of image-enhancing peers, clothing, and objects. In essence, they are encouraged to indulge themselves.

NARCISSUS THE HEARTBREAKER

In ancient Greek mythology, the beautiful lad Narcissus was a heartbreaker. He scorned the love of a sweet and beautiful nymph, Echo, who had been deprived of speech because she always wanted to have the last word. Hera, queen of the goddesses, stopped Echo's chatter by condemning her to repeat others' last words. Echo fell in love with Narcissus, but she could not express her ardor for him. Narcissus, who believed that no female deserved him, broke Echo's heart, and subsequently she wasted away hiding in canyons and caves, leaving only her voice to call out from hidden places.

Narcissus continued to break hearts until one young woman angrily pleaded with the gods to make him suffer, to feel her unrequited love. Soon after, while bending over a pond to drink, Narcissus saw his own reflection and fell in love with it. When he reached out to touch the image, it vanished. Again and again he tried, to no avail. Narcissus cried, and his tears made ripples in the pond. He stayed at the pond, feeling sad and growing weaker until he died of languor, unable to leave his own reflection. He turned into a flower, the narcissus that grows at the edges of springs.

The story of Narcissus, who was concerned with his appearance and stroking his ego through numerous female conquests, has been incorporated into psychiatry to describe an inability to love and the denial of the inner being in favor of appearance (Lowen 1985). As such, narcissism is understood to be a disturbance in self-regard; the narcissist's interactions with others involve an unusual degree of self-reference, an overwhelming need to be loved and admired, and an inflated self-concept that needs tribute from others (Kernberg 1985).

Sometimes narcissists are confused with borderline personalities, but narcissists generally are better able to organize their thoughts and actions (Nevid, Rathus, and Greene 1994).

DEVELOPMENTAL CONSIDERATIONS

Modern psychology, particularly psychoanalysis, has incorporated the myth of Narcissus to describe two processes. One is a normal stage in early development. There are many references in child development literature to *primary narcissism,* a phase characterized by self-absorption that occurs during the first year of life. Normally a child passes through, and out of, this self-centered stage and develops the ability to love another.

The second psychological process that incorporates the myth of Narcissus is an abnormal one. Here the child fails to evolve out of primary narcissism. The infantile narcissism persists, with overconnectedness to self and underconnectedness to others. In this abnormal process, a personality disorder develops.

The individual with a narcissistic personality disorder develops an inflated or grandiose sense of self. While a certain degree of narcissism or self-aggrandisement may represent a healthy defense against criticism and failure, excessive narcissistic qualities can become unhealthy, especially when cravings for reassurance and adulation are insatiable. As narcissism increases, the importance of anything and anyone outside the person diminishes (Malmquist 1972). In effect, the importance of the self grows larger and the importance of everything and everyone else grows smaller.

In this unhealthy process of self-aggrandizement, narcissistsshow extremely negative reactions to criticism, an overblown sense of importance, and belief that their problems are unique and special. They brag about their accomplishments and expect others to shower them with praise. Narcissists often are preoccupied with fantasies of unlimited success, power, brilliance, or beauty; a sense of entitlement because they have special qualities, even when their accomplishments are quite ordinary; and a need for constant attention and admiration.

Narcissists also are driven by ambition. The narcissist typically lacks empathy, is self-absorbed, and is obsessed with feelings of envy for those who achieve greater success. Insatiable ambition may prompt them to devote themselves tirelessly to work, driven to succeed, not so much for money as for the adulation that attends success (Nevid, Rathus, and Greene 1994).

SELF-ABSORPTION EXAMPLE. *Sarah is acutely self-absorbed and seems to feel entitled to special treatment. She exemplifies "narcissistic injury." For example, she felt "dethroned" when her parents gave attention to her siblings, and betrayed by parental demands for limits and consequences for her behavior. Intense anger typically ensues when normal limits and consequences are imposed on her. Narcissistic injury is also suggested by Sarah's demand for attention. If she does not get it, Sarah's reaction is to rebel.*

As part of the abnormal psychological process of narcissism, there is a focus on the body. Physical appearance is important to the narcissist because appearance is used to attract and then to control. Psychoanalyst Melanie Klein believes that a narcissistic personality develops as a means for dealing with anxiety; the narcissist's misguided efforts to control others dispells anxiety (Klein 1975).

IMPORTANCE OF APPEARANCE EXAMPLE. *Sarah's most intense episodes of feeling unloved by her parents are accompanied by intense sexual activity. She is proud of her physical prowess and uses it to get what she wants from her boyfriend when she cannot get what she wants from her mother and father.*

The developmental process of the narcissist is unfocused. It has not been easy to understand the onset of abnormal narcissism in children. Adults who lie, contrive, manipulate, seduce, and betray are relatively easy to spot, but the developmental process in children is ongoing and subtle, particularly in the early years. Children may get their way because parents want to avoid scenes and tantrums. Parents may dread the children's sharp tongues or may fear their wrath and give in to behavior they know is wrong. Consequently, these children may grow up believing that they can get what they want when they want it. Their needs become the center of their lives, and other people are seen as having only one purpose: to satisfy the children's needs or to be sacrificed if they interfere with their goals.

By adolescence, the narcissist's relationships typically are stunted. Rather than normal relationships, characterized by zones of caring between both parties and by issues and concerns that relate to both, these youngsters have relationships that serve one primary purpose: self-aggrandizement. Instead of caring about another's feelings and interests, even putting them first, interpersonal exploitation prevails. The narcissist is incapable of having a mature relationship.

NARCISSISTIC RELATIONSHIP EXAMPLE. *Alan, at 17, should have at least one friend in school or in his community, but this is not the case. While he is attached to his resource teacher, whom Alan's mother describes as her son's friend, it is a curious attachment. This adult provides Alan with unconditional concern and care, which a peer likely would be unable to do. Alan begins each session with this teacher on his own terms. He enters the room talking about his latest obsession. He may be smiling, suggesting a greeting, but there are no opening pleasantries, and there is no reciprocity in deciding what will be discussed. When the teacher tries to focus Alan on an issue, he evades and perseveres with his own issues, which typically involve concerns about his car,*

his computer, the stupidity of school and other students, and his father's
unfairness.

NARCISSISM AS A PERSONALITY DISORDER

As a personality disorder, narcissism involves two key elements: (1) an exaggerated sense of self-importance and denial of feelings, and (2) a serious impact on self and others. In exaggerating one's own importance, the individual believes that his problems are unique and comprehensible only by "special" people (Campbell 1989).

As to denial of feelings, because this personality disturbance involves an exaggerated investment in one's image, the self is expended (Lowen 1985). There is more concern about how one appears to others than about one's own feelings. Consequently, denial is a big part of the problem; the narcissist denies any feelings that contradict his desired image.

Finally, narcissism affects the self and others so significantly and pervasively that it develops into a disordered personality. Lowen (1985) offers numerous criteria for recognizing and understanding narcissism as a personality disorder. Some key criteria, suggested in the previous discussion, are presented below. Illustrations from our primary and secondary samples accompany the criteria.

The first criterion relates to a preoccupation with self to the exclusion of all others. Narcissists have a shallow emotional life. They are preoccupied with themselves and lack empathy, the ability to recognize how others feel. They are missing this essential ingredient for relationships; unable to feel what others feel, they cannot forge connections. Other people serve one function: They reflect the narcissist's image. The "looking-glass self" is a sociological concept that explains how individuals acquire a sense of identity partially by incorporating information from generalized others throughout life. The narcissistic process, on the other hand, involves incorporating information primarily from self-feedback. One's own image is the source of identity rather than objective others. Interpersonal relationships are invariably strained by narcissists' demands and by their lack of empathy with, and concern for, other people (Nevid, Rathus, and Greene 1994).

PREOCCUPATION WITH SELF EXAMPLES. *In her self-absorption Laura betrays friends if it suits her purpose. For example, when she had the opportunity to attend a party given by an admired classmate, Laura ignored her best friend, who suddenly became too fat in her eyes because the friend was not invited. Mary no longer reflected the image to which Laura aspired. Laura lacked empathy; she could not see anyone's needs or feelings unless they matched hers. She walked away from another friend who became pregnant. Laura's goals involve college and great success, and becoming a teenage mother does not match that self-image.*

Jesse's narcissism is evident in his perception of himself as the center of all events. He blames himself not only for actions under his control but for events that are out of his control. This is not simply a matter of low self-esteem; Jesse is so self-absorbed that he cannot perceive others as separate entities. He chooses friends who are, like him, disabled in some way. When asked about his friends, he cannot identify an attribute that is different from him, no matter how trivial. It is incomprehensible to Jesse that anyone can have a different opinion of world events or a different philosophy from his.

Adam rages when criticized. His overblown sense of his own importance not only makes it difficult for him to understand how anyone could find fault with him, but he believes most of the time that he is without fault. Even in the face of undeniable fault, he becomes angry. Correction by a teacher is a tricky matter. Providing correction for a math problem or a misspelled word must be handled quietly and unobtrusively. For Adam's more outrageous faults, such as standing on a chair and yelling, it is harder to provide unobtrusive, subtle feedback. The more obvious the feedback, the angrier Adam becomes. When he was in elementary school Adam bit a teacher who dared to correct him. To perceive events differently from how Adam sees them is, in his view, to betray him. He has carved out a very narrow path and finds himself walking it alone most of the time. He is overconnected to himself and underconnected to others. He is like Narcissus, wasting away beside the pond.

The second criterion relates to being without a sense of limits or acting out of impulse. Narcissistic students, without a good sense of boundaries, often do what feels good at the moment. Without concern for the boundaries of propriety, explicit rules, or implicit social code their behavior often is not rule- or code-governed. There may be a need for attention and admiration that may manifest itself in exhibitionistic tendencies (Campbell 1989).

IMPULSIVE BEHAVIOR EXAMPLE. *In eleventh grade during the midyear examination in advanced computer science, a class of eight students, Alan took off his shoe and sock and began to trim a toenail with his teeth.*

The third criterion relates to minimizing feelings. Narcissus, unable to grasp his own image in the pond, despaired and died of his own anguish. The narcissistic youngster denies his or her essential reality and strives to grasp the illusion of the perfect self. At the same time, self-denial involves downplaying his or her own feelings and behavior and playing up others' behavior.

SELF-DENIAL EXAMPLE. *Alan nearly ran into a school monitor with his car in the parking lot one afternoon when he tried to leave school early. The principal relieved him of the privilege of bringing his car to campus, and Alan could not understand that his lack of self-control was the reason. He raged about how the problem was the principal's, and he accused the monitor of being suicidal by getting in the car's way. When asked how he felt about losing his privilege, and about what he needed to do in order to prove to the principal that he was capable of driving safely, Alan became quiet. He was, it turned out, not pausing to reason; it was a calm before another storm. Subsequently, he raged again, contending that the principal was punishing him when it was the monitor's fault for not getting out of the way of his car.*

The fourth criterion relates to ruthless, exploitative, sadistic, or destructive behavior. Students who are narcissistic often are cruel to others. They use people to reach their own goals, and they can be perverse. They destroy others in order to build up their own images. Kernberg (1985) describes narcissistic exploitation as parasitic, for the process involves dependency on others to feed their needs. This cruelty, perversity, and destruction can be dangerous. Narcissists exploit others and disregard their rights and feelings (Campbell 1989), as if they have a right to exploit without guilt (Kernberg 1985).

DESTRUCTIVE BEHAVIOR EXAMPLE. *Laura's sense of herself is built on the destruction of others. Her towering self-image is constructed out of the pieces she has taken from others. A psychiatrist commented to Laura's mother that, perhaps, Laura does not have a conscience. Indeed, as her image has been shored up by so many others' broken parts, it seems at times as if Laura has no moral core. For example, she physically assaulted her younger brother because he would not turn over his allowance to her, and she exploited this brother's naivete, taking his money with false promises to use it for charitable purposes.*

The fifth criterion relates to lying. Adolescents who deny unacceptable feelings or psychological problems often fake it to look good. Lying to themselves and to others may become a personality style. This relates to Campbell's (1989) description of belief in entitlement to special favors with no reciprocal responsibility. In effect, narcissistst feel they can take what they want.

LYING EXAMPLE. *Alan's psychological evaluation yielded a significantly high score on the Minnesota Multiphasic Personality Inventory lie scale, which measures consistency of responses and defensiveness. He showed a "fake good" configuration, which usually is obtained by adolescents who try to deny unacceptable feelings or psychological problems. In effect, Alan lies to himself in order to appear good to others. His personality is basically a pretense.*

The sixth criterion relates to striving for power and control. The narcissist acts without feeling. Actions that do not have underpinnings of feeling are simply seductive and manipulative, and the narcissist is readily able to seduce and manipulate. Striving for power and control also is easy without feeling to rankle the ego. Indeed, acting without feeling is the core disturbance in the narcissistic personality (Lowen 1985).

Enthralled with themselves, narcissists want to control. Their needs take precedence, and in a position of control their needs can be fed constantly. Campbell (1989) refers to their fantasies of unlimited power or brilliance.

CONTROL EXAMPLE. *Laura's mother fears her daughter's wrath, and she looks the other way many times when Laura exceeds her limits. Laura has physically assaulted her mother when she has not gotten what she wants, and she is proud of her prowess. Laura has reached a position of control in her family. Her needs and desires take precedence over those of all other family members; her mother commented that she spends over half her time dealing with Laura's needs, with the other half divided among all other family members and herself. Laura's resource teacher, too, has spent an inordinate amount of time on this one student: reminding her to take her medication, taking her to the cafeteria manager to replace a lost meal card, collecting overdue library books from her locker, amassing past-due assignments, looking for a lost wrist watch, and on and on. In Laura's life there are many loose ends. Laura also indulges in fantasies of power. She dreams of becoming a wealthy, successful writer with power to buy anything she wants.*

Kernberg (1985) offers two additional criteria to define narcissism: idealization and distrust. *Narcissitic idealization* involves idealizing some people from whom the individual expects nourishment, contrasted with depreciation of and contempt for those from whom he or she does not expect anything (Kernberg 1985).

IDEALIZATION EXAMPLE. *Alan seems to idealize his resource teacher. He seeks her out constantly to "fix" things for him: unfair assignments, problems with peers, consequences for behaviors. As she is the only one who listens to his endless talk, Alan believes that she can perform miracles and provide damage control. Contrarily, Alan denigrates those who do not feed into his self-image. If they do not nourish this self-concept they are not worthy of his regard. He treats his classmates as less than human because they do not elevate him to the status he believes that he deserves. One day in computer class Alan asked the teacher teacher if he could see his resource teacher for help. He went to her room, screaming that he needed her assistance. She tried to calm him down and get his story, which basically involved Alan's perception that a group of students was excluding him from the opportunity to repair a computer. Alan believed that this was a job for which only he was eminently skilled. Despite coaching on cooperative strategies, Alan tried to force himself on the group that was working on the impaired computer when he returned to class. Alan was excessively persis-*

tent about joining the group, to the point of physically climbing over other students and furniture to do so. Finally, when Alan would not follow the teacher's direction to work at a computer alone, his resource teacher offered him a choice: work alone or go back to her office. Alan chose the latter, and there he continued to scream and complain that the other students had excluded "an expert." Alan could not understand that the other students did not exclude him because of his expertise but because of his contemptible, insulting verbal behavior. He could not fathom the idea that no matter what one's skills they are useless unless one is able to get along with others. Certainly, calling fellow students "idiots" does not gain entry into a group.

Distrust. Narcissists also distrust other people (Kernberg 1985). While narcissists depend upon others' tribute and adoration, they are unable to trust others.

DISTRUST EXAMPLE. *Alan has been scheduled for several short meetings each week with his resource teacher; however, he drops by her office many more times. It would seem that he has become dependent on her. After all, Alan has no friends, and no other teacher has been willing or able to give him the attention he demands. These resource sessions afford Alan the opportunity to vent and pace, enabling him to return to classes less agitated, even if he has not been invested in a change process. On several occasions, when he decided it was time to return to class but his resource teacher had not yet written a pass, he pointed to the pad of paper, raised his voice, and said angrily, "Now, write a damned pass so I can go to class!" It was as if he did not trust that she would do it, although she had done it routinely over many months. The anger seemed to leak out, uncontained by any positive feeling of acceptance, as if all the teacher's care and patience had been for naught.*

NARCISSISM AND SCHIZOID PERSONALITY

The absence of feeling seen in a narcissistic personality disorder may relate to a schizoid personality, where an absence of feeling also is seen. There may be an overlap between the two disorders in some individuals. While the narcissist's thinking may not depart from reality, as does the schizophrenic's, they may look at others as images rather than as real, feeling beings. Like Narcissus, this individual may regard others as mere reflections. "Thus, they can be aware of everything you do but still not see the essential you" (Lowen 1985, p. 129).

There is, it seems, a split in the narcissist's personality. Again, it is not a break with reality. The narcissist is not crazy at the surface, which he manages well enough, but there may be a degree of insanity in the depths of his personality (Kernberg 1985).

SCHIZOID ASPECT EXAMPLE. *Alan looks at others but does not see them. Eyes made even larger by thick eyeglasses appear ready and able to absorb the world, but, instead, they are vigilantly capturing images that match his own. He talks at his resource teacher, for example. She merely exists to receive his messages and to reflect back. He becomes angry when interrupted or disputed. He does not care to know how she feels or thinks; anything she says merely intrudes upon his train of thought. He enters the room talking, and leaves talking, about his concerns. It does not matter if his resource teacher has another student with her. Alan will stand outside the room staring through the glass window, smiling, trying to catch her eye. He runs up to her in crowded hallways, stands close, smiles, and begins talking engagingly, as if he has the most interesting and important ideas. This teacher had a bad fall, breaking three front teeth and suffering bad facial abrasions and swelling. When Alan walked into the room, seeing her for the first time in this condition, he laughed and said, "What truck hit you?" He tried to change the subject when the teacher tried to tell him about her accident. Alan's lack of feeling also was evident when he heard about the South Carolina mother who pushed her car into a lake with her two young sons strapped inside. His comment was, "What a waste of a perfectly good Mazda." (Alan's car is a Mazda.)*

Despite shared features, narcissistic and schizoid personalities also differ. For example, while the schizoid's body may be frozen with terror, the narcissist is relatively unaffected by the experience of horror. Narcissists are unaffected by horror because they deny their feelings.

On the other hand, a person can be subject simultaneously to both schizoid and narcissistic processes. It is a matter of clinical judgment (Lowen 1985).

What may have contributed to Alan's schizoid aspect is his anger. As previously indicated, Alan thinks a lot about fairness issues. Given his father's punitive tactics, Alan has reason to grieve. The narcissist may feel powerless to express anger directly at the significant person or persons who hold the power. In Alan's case, it is a controlling father, who can withhold money, car keys, and computer access. In Laura's case, it is her authoritarian father, so Laura expresses anger toward her mother and siblings. In Adam's case, teachers are on the receiving end of his anger, not his parents, who are embroiled in a protracted custody battle for control of Adam. If children were allowed to voice their anger at their parents whenever they felt they had a legitimate grievance, we would see far fewer narcissistic personalities (Lowen 1985). Giving a child this right would show a real respect for the child's feelings and selfhood.

FAIRNESS EXAMPLE. *Alan earns good grades in subjects that his father devalues: English and history. Earning low grades in mathematics and science courses, which are valued by his father, and for which Alan has the strongest aptitude, seems to be Alan's way of punishing his father, who uses highly puni-*

tive disciplinary strategies. For example, the father keeps a ledger of Alan's misbehaviors, and Alan is fined for each infraction. Failure to use the correct implement at the dinner table costs $1, failure to say "fine, thank you" when an adult asks how he is, even if Alan's response is appropriate in another form, results in a fine of $2.

Descriptions of the schizoid personality also refer to a split between overt behavior and thoughts. There is a narcissistic split between the quality of work that individuals perform and what goes on inside them (Lowen 1985). Features of narcissism and a split personality may coexist in the form of a mismatch between what the individual thinks and does.

MISMATCH EXAMPLE. *Alan describes himself as a "damned good mechanic," "inquisitive with a desire to learn," and "completely lazy." Despite his desire to learn, Alan produces nearly nothing in school. His written work typically is submitted late, is fraught with spelling and grammatical errors, and contains tasteless vocabulary. Alan believes that because he is learning, production is irrelevant. Therein lies a rub between his internal and external worlds.*

Some individuals are unable to gulate their own behavior and emotions appropriately relative to external events. Those whose self-regulatory systems are impaired may behave in both narcissistic and schizoid ways. They may deny their feelings by focusing on others' behaviors or extraneous factors, or they may spend a lot of time acting out their feelings, as if to get rid of them. Or they may react to so many events, with equal intensity, that it is unclear what matters to them. Such a pattern can make it very difficult to diagnose the youth and offer the appropriate interventions.

INAPPROPRIATE BEHAVIOR EXAMPLE. *Alan's behavioral and emotional difficulties have eluded precise diagnosis since he was first taken to specialists at the age of two years. Even prior to that time, he warranted careful observation. His neonatal assessment showed below average functioning, and he remained in the hospital for observation. Developmental milestones in language were delayed, and he began receiving speech therapy at two years. At three years, preschool was recommended to facilitate social development, and he was found eligible for special services due to developmental delays, specifically deficits in auditory processing and in fine motor skills. Noted, too, was echolalia with a high-pitched, sing-song voice. Hyperactivity was suspected at age four, and a neurological evaluation at that time was significant for soft signs. There appeared at age seven to be immature motor and motor control systems, typically seen in children with attention deficit disorders. Alan's ability to perform consistently seemed to be compromised by extreme overactivity, impulsivity, distractibility, and oppositionality. At age nine, Alan was found eligible for special education ser-*

vices for learning disabilities because of a discrepancy between ability and achievement in reading and written language, with processing difficulties in the auditory and visual-motor coordination areas. At age 10, he was placed in a school-based gifted and talented program, which was combined with LD resource service. By the time Alan was 15 years old the hyperactivity and attentional problems were still present, but odd, disruptive behaviors had emerged. He resisted teachers' guidance and was socially isolated. Alan seemed to be easily distracted not only by irrelevant stimuli but by his own thoughts. When the school psychologist asked him to accompany her to the testing room he complied but groaned and made faces. While walking toward her office, Alan jumped in front of her, waved his arms, and ran ahead. During the testing he was agitated, frequently out of his chair and pacing. He explored, made irrelevant comments about the furniture and events outside the window, spun around in a swivel chair, and ignored requests to stop. The psychologist had to physically stop the spinning chair. Firm limits, discussions, and warnings seemed only moderately effective in managing specific behaviors. Alan would briefly show appropriate behavior and effort and then resume his irrelevant activities and commentary. Frequently, he wandered off the topics or inappropriately elaborated, digressing in great detail on irrelevant details. At one point he commented that he was "overheating his brain." Also, he perseverated on topics, such as his interest in computers, or on something that had upset him or made him angry that day. Frequently, too, his comments were critical and aggressive. At one point, he stuck his fist close to the examiner's face and stated that he felt like punching; "I hate all shrinks," he said. The psychologist concluded that behavioral and emotional interference was compromising Alan's abilities; data suggested emotional disturbance. Feelings of anger, rejection, and loneliness were present, along with a negative attitude toward the environment. Coupled with these feelings were seen personality factors of immaturity and extreme narcissistic characteristics. Alan's apparent method of coping with his world was to deny his feelings and to use rationalization and externalization as defenses. He seemed to be struggling to control himself from expressing anger aggressively. Alan's experience of reality seemed to be distorted by his emotions, particularly his anger and negativistic orientation to his surroundings. He evidenced a great deal of suspiciousness and mistrust, and there were indications that his self-concept and concepts of others were based more on imaginary than real attributes or actions. Serious thinking problems were evident: discontinuous ideas, faulty conceptualization, poor judgment, and a tendency to impulsively reverse judgments.

SOME FACTS

Cause. Theorists relate narcissism most often to a psychodynamic model, notably early rejection by the primary parent. This theory accounts for the inability of the child to form an object relation to the parent in the first year of life, to the other parent and siblings later, and to those in the outside world still later. Without rewarding, focused attention from others, the infant cannot develop a normal sense of self and others. Bowlby's (1969) ideas concur. In his developmental theory the peak of primary narcissism coincides with the critical phase of attachment.

Prevalence. The prevalence of narcissism has not been well articulated, partly because this personality disorder has been viewed as a crucial variable in depression. Specifically, one hypothesis is that the child's self-image becomes devalued due to early deprivation, neglect, or loss. Repeated rebuffs or losses reaffirm to the child that a significantobject does not value him.

The outlook. Narcissism appears to be a personality disorder with serious implications. The combination of distrust of others, alternating with idealization of others, desire for control, destructive tendencies, lack of boundaries, deception (of self and others), minimizing of feelings, and preoccupation with self does not augur well for a youngster's future. Adolescents who are deeply self-absorbed, yet who have no insight into their own psychological makeup, probably will continue to behave impulsively and destructively in their quest for power and control.

The narcissistic pattern also suggests that these youngsters are not amenable to psychodynamic approaches, which depend on relationships to achieve change. As Alan's case suggests, a nurturing relationship may simply encourage narcissistic adolescents to use mental health professionals as they see fit and when they see need. In fact, Alan's parents preferred that Alan see his resource teacher when he needed help, and they left it up to Alan to decide when and if he wanted to see a psychiatrist. His parents believe that their child's problem can be treated by an intellectual approach. For example, Alan's mother hoped that he would benefit from a psychology course; she said it might help Alan to "gain insight." Instead, about one week into the course Alan commented that he had learned that his parents were crazy.

Without extensive help, the narcissist's future will probably be conflictual and unsuccessful. These students need a comprehensive treatment program that reeducates their emotions and behaviors. We can see in Alan's case that despite some exceptional intellectual abilities, he does not achieve commensurately. In all probability, his adult life will be dysfunctional in all areas: education, occupation, psychological, and social. It is unlikely that he will participate in an appropriate mental health program inasmuch as Alan and his parents do not believe that he has an emotional problem. In fact, Alan's parents did not permit the school to conduct a triennial evaluation during his senior year. Continued eligibility would have entitled Alan to community mental health services following high school.

NARCISSISM AND THE FEDERAL DEFINITION OF ED

Looking at the Individuals with Disabilities Education Act (IDEA) criteria for ED, the student who is narcissistic, first, shows an *inability to build or maintain satisfactory interpersonal relationships with peers and teachers.* Students with an emotional void do not connect readily with others. Self-absorbed by their own needs and lacking empathy, along with failure to see others as separate personalities, narcissists are poor candidates for friendship and mutually supportive relationships. Too, narcissists devalue other people, to the extent of perversity or cruelty, or they attribute overimportance to some people. Poorly socialized, Alan would begin conversations in the middle of his train of thought or simply blurt out his thoughts without conventional conversational openings or niceties. This lack of socialization impeded relationship building.

The student with a narcissistic personality also shows *inappropriate types of behavior or feelings under normal circumstances*. Without a sense of limits, and focused on his or her own needs and perceptions, the narcissist probably feels and behaves inappropriately. If the narcissist does what feels good at the moment, there is a good chance that behavior will not match the circumstance. Recall Alan's reaction to his consequence for dangerous driving: The adult was at fault for getting in the way of his car.

Also, this student exhibits an *inability to learn that cannot be explained by intellectual, sensory, or health factors*. The narcissistic student's emotional disorder interferes with learning. The student is otherwise capable of achieving academically, for there is no known medical, sensory, or health reason for the lack of progress. At times this student appears to be retarded socially, unable to attach to others and to understand social rules. However, there is a strong ability to plan behavior to meet his or her own needs.

SUGGESTED EDUCATIONAL STRATEGIES

The educational strategies indicated for the student with a narcissistic personality disorder should address issues of inattention, lack of self-control, self-absorption, lack of boundaries, needs for socialization and power and control, and distrust.

1.   Instruct the student in appropriate ways to start a conversation and to ask for help, to ask questions, or to seek permission.

2.   Acknowledge publicly and privately the student's unique contributions.

3.   Provide the student with opportunities to "shine." Increase ways for the student to be noticed for appropriate behavior.

4.   Use cooperative learning to build trust, mutuality, and interdependence, as well as appreciation of group members' contributions based upon different skills.

5.   Ensure that the target student has the skills to contribute to these activities.

6.   Redirect the need for power and control by involving the student in planning and setting up activities, and increase choice opportunities. Give the student the chance to choose a group activity and the group members.

7.   Impose logical consequences for inappropriate behavior to teach the social order.

8.   Limit power plays by ignoring minor misbehavior. Pick the battles with care.

9.   Arrange space so that power interactions can be easily and quickly terminated.

10.   Coach the student about rules prior to his or her engagement in new situations.

11.   Use active listening exercises starting with a one-on-one format and building to a small-group discussion. The rule is that each student must repeat what another says to the speaker's satisfaction before each listener may speak.

12.   Increase shared tasks and group activities, especially cooperatively structured ones.

13.   Set expectations and rules at the outset so that limits are clear.

14.   Use class meetings to review rules and expectations and to discuss personal boundaries and preferences for interactions. The adult should participate in expressing personal limits.

15.   Teach the student to recognize the appropriate times to speak (for example, when the teacher has finished speaking).

16.   Provide a full schedule of structured activities. Prevent lag time during which the student could bother other students.

17.   Seat the student away from those students he or she is most likely to bother.

18.   Make certain that the student's feelings are considered when it is necessary to deal with his or her interruptions or intrusions. Handle comments in such a way as to not diminish the student's enthusiasm for participation.

19.   Assess the appropriateness of the social situation in relation to the student's ability to function successfully.

20.   During class meetings or counseling sessions discuss specific behaviors and how they make others feel.

21.   Provide feedback on the student's strengths and weaknesses so that he or she can solidify a sense of his or her own personality and boundaries.

22.   Verbally label the student's behavior in order to reinforce the

student's boundaries.

23.   Provide the student with a specific description of appropriate behavior. For example, if a student sits at his or her desk inappropriately, describe the appropriate positions: facing forward, feet on floor, back straight. These positions could be modeled as well. Have the student provide input about when the proper positioning is unnecessary and acceptable.

24.   Provide activities that are interesting to the student.

25.   Teach the student to take turns and share. Reinforce the student for taking turns. Coach him or her in how to take turns. Begin by having him or her work with one peer in order to model taking turns. Gradually increase group size over time. Initially allow the student to have many turns and enough materials to satisfy immediate needs, and gradually require sharing and taking turns. Provide special activities for the entire class contingent upon their sharing and taking turns. The target student should be clearly led to the conclusion that his or her input and behavior helped the group receive a reward.

26.   Ensure that the student understands that interacting with peers is contingent upon appropriate behavior. Use group games to teach appropriate interacting, suggesting activities, sharing materials, problem solving, taking turns, and following rules. However, ensure that the activities are not so stimulating that successful peer interactions are made difficult.

27.   Match the student with a peer, with whom he or she will hopefully interact successfully, in terms of similar interests, background, and classes. Do not force the student to interact with anyone with whom he or she is uncomfortable.

28.   Give the student the responsibility of helping peer(s), first in a one-on-one situation, later in larger groups.

29.   Allow the student to be present during group activities without requiring active participation. Require more involvement over time as he or she becomes more active in group situations.

30.   Make certain that the student is productive and accurate in performing individual assignments before placing him or her in a group activity.

31.   Go over group rules and expectations at the start of each group activity.

32.   Remove the student from the group if his or her behavior is inappropriate and before the group process deteriorates to the point where reentry would be a problem. Allow the student to leave a group activity when he or she can no longer be successful.

33.   Place the student initially in group activities he or she prefers.

Gradually require participation in less desirable ones.

34.   Provide the student with alternative ways to perform an assignment, whether individually or in a group.

35.   Schedule group activities when the student is most likely to be successful (e.g., after the first individual assignment of the day has been completed in order to establish productive behavior).

36.   Program alternative individual activities if the student is unlikely to be successful (e.g., if the schedule has changed or if holidays or special events have stimulated the student excessively).

37.   Teach the student acceptable ways to communicate displeasure, anger, frustration, and other negative, interfering emotions.

38.   Ensure that the student is allowed to voice an opinion in a situation in order to avoid becoming angry or upset.

39.   Coach the student in ways of handling situations successfully without conflict.

40.   Create peer models by reinforcing those students who make their comments brief or speak at appropriate times.

41.   Interact with the student frequently to reduce his or her need to interrupt.

42.   Reinforce the student's raising his or her hand in order to be recognized.

7

Overview:
Disruptive Behavior Disorders

Disordered behaviors conflict with established social standards and values; they are contrary to the established order. When behavior goes against the social grain, it defies the rules and disturbs the social order.

A behavior disorder also is an externalizing problem because youngsters with behavior disorders act out against the social order; their behaviors have an externalizing effect. Although externalizing disorders may also have internalizing aspects, their primary feature is their negative impact on the environment.

Behavior disorders are manifest in varied forms. Because sufficient data have been published on the frequent co-occurrence of attention-deficit disorder with hyperactivity (ADHD), conduct disorder (CD), and oppositional-defiant disorder (ODD), the supradomain *disruptive behavior disorders* is justified. The abundant data concerning co-occurrence of these three disorders include the following examples. Livingston, Dykman, and Ackerman (1990) found that the majority of children with attention deficits have oppositional disorders. McMahon and Wells (1989) noted that conduct disorders in children represent a broad range of acting out behaviors, from yelling to whining to stealing, and that youngsters displaying them have been labeled oppositional, antisocial, conduct disordered, and socially aggressive. Abundant data support the reference to ADHD, ODD, and CD as disruptive behavior disorders, collectively.

SPECIFIC OVERLAPPING CONSIDERATIONS

Let us look at specific points of overlap among these three disruptive behavior disorders. These considerations are important for understanding this cluster as well as the specific conditions presented in Chapters 8 and 9.

Noncompliance. One descriptor of this cluster is noncompliance. It has long been assumed that youngsters with ODD and CD are noncompliant, but only relatively recently has ADHD been characterized by noncompliance. Barkley (1989) noted that, although the notion is not yet widespread, many have come to accept the idea that difficulty with adhering to rules and instructions may also be a primary deficit of ADHD children.

When any student has difficulty adhering to rules and instructions, particularly difficulty with sustained responding to teacher expectations, the outcome is similar: disruption of the educational flow. One high school teacher commented:

A rose is a rose is a rose. If a student cannot follow directions and do what is expected I don't care if he has an attention deficit, a conduct disorder, or whatever. He's still defiant, and he still disrupts my class. (Author's personal communication 1994)

Internalizing components. All three of the targeted disruptive behavior disorders have overlapping emotional and behavioral components. While this cluster has strong externalizing aspects, internalizing aspects are also manifest. For example, students with disruptive behavior disorders often are identified as emotionally disturbed. Hendren (1991), for example, noted that students diagnosed as conduct disordered may have other emotional disorders such as depression or psychosis. (See Chapter 26 for other points of interrelatedness.)

Externalizing features. Those suffering from disruptive behavior disorders typically show impatience and physical and/or verbal aggressiveness. ADHD is increasingly recognized as a persistent condition that carries strong risk for escalating difficulties, primarily in the externalizing spectrum. As oppositional-defiant and conduct disorders also involve primary externalizing difficulties, particularly aggression, all three disorders are associated with aggression.

Arousal dysfunction. It has been theorized that disruptive behavior disorders and attention-deficit disorder (ADD) share a pervasive arousal problem. Arousal refers to activation, drive, and awakeness; it relates to a state of consciousness and alertness.

Some background will clarify. Early in this century, it was observed that such emotional states as distress, anxiety, and rage influence bodily functions, including heart rate, hypertension, and the digestive process. Since that time, there has been a growing interest in the response of the autonomic nervous system to stress.

Focused research began with biobehavioral studies of animals (e.g., studies among primates of cardiovascular reactions induced by social challenges). Manuck and his colleagues (1992) found that the most aggressive animals were the ones that are most reactive to (aroused by) stress. Human experiments have shown similar results. One human learning situation demonstrated intense physiological reactivity among boys who were disruptive and aggressive (Harden et al. 1995).

Observations of physiologic reactivity under conditions of fear and stress led Gray (1987) to propose the existence of an arousal-based behavioral control system. That is, instead of expecting autonomic responses to external situations, the expectancy was that some individuals may have low reactivity, or arousal, that predisposes them to certain behaviors.

Subsequent studies reported impaired electrodermal activity arousal among individuals with antisocial personality (Raine 1994) and antisocial traits (Fowles 1993). Damasio, Tranel, and Damasio (1991) associated poor electrodermal reactivity with diminished perception of the emotional significance in social stimuli. Specifically, they found impairment in processing empathic information. They concluded that the inability to empathize with other people may underlie the indifference that characterizes certain psychopathies, which include disruptive behavior disorders.

Other studies have focused on the relation between emotion and hormonal levels. For example, research has shown that children with co-occurring anxiety and conduct disorder suffer great emotional distress and have high levels of stress hormone (McBurnett et al. 1991; Walker et al. 1991).

Assuming a biological basis for an arousal dysfunction, one theory about the shared arousal problem among disruptive behavior disorders relates to learning. Volavka defined the arousal hypothesis as follows: "The *arousal* hypothesis argues that the avoidance of aggressive behavior must be learned and that a low level of arousal inhibits the learning process" (1995, p. 116). His explanation of this hypothesis is as follows:

Pavlovian literature indicates that low arousal inhibits conditioning. Therefore, if the learning of socialized behavior (and law abidance) is accomplished via conditioning, one would expect children with habitually low levels of arousal to have more difficulty learning socialized behavior and to be more likely to break laws when they grow up. (Volavka 1995, p. 169)

In practical terms, students with disruptive behavior disorders have a predisposition that makes it difficult for them to learn the expected behaviors. In this light, the student with ADHD, constantly moving to search for stimulation, and the indifferent, insensitive student with a conduct disorder are comparable.

Certain research findings make sense in this light. For example, Egan (1991) discovered that, in early childhood, the ODD child might be fussy, colicky, or difficult to quiet and soothe, showing dysfunctional arousal. Earls (1994) concluded that both ODD and CD share insensitivity to others, or, by implication, low arousal in situations calling for sensitivity.

Further perspective on this issue is provided by Klove (1989), who examined the evidence for the hypoarousal hypothesis in attention-deficit disorders. ADHD has long been recognized as a dysfunction of the brain's attention system, specifically the brain-stem center that coordinates other areas of the brain to regulate and adjust input and output. It has been established that the arousal mechanism in these youngsters is suppressed, which is why stimulant medication is effective. The most likely explanation for decreased hyperactivity after administration of stimulant drugs is that an underactive central nervous system caused the hyperactivity. In other words, stimulant medication was needed to arouse attention.

Additional studies of psychopathic behavioral styles have shown that certain behavioral styles are associated with violent crime (Hare 1991; Volavka 1995), specifically impulsivity and a need for stimulation and a tendency to boredom. Both of these behavioral styles have been associated with low arousal.

Other arousal research has focused on patterns of brain-wave activity. For example, some researchers have shown a relation between one type of electrical brain activity, slow alpha waves, and antisocial behavior. In normal individuals, alpha-wave frequency is known to decrease with relaxation and drowsiness and to increase with tension, but some antisocial individuals have shown slower than normal alpha- wave levels during all conditions. This may mean that sensory inputs that would be disturbing to most people would not be strong enough to excite antisocial individuals and that such people may crave increased stimulation and may therefore seek out unusual forms of excitement (Sarason and Sarason 1993).

A related issue involves the neurobiology of violence. For exmple, electroencephalogram (EEG) slowing, a slow resting heart rate, and low spontaneous fluctuations of skin conductance were shown in a sample of adolescents who later became criminals.

Also, impaired cortical functioning has been related to disruptive behavior disorders, specifically disinhibition, which includes impulsiveness, inability to delay gratification, and antisocial behavior. One study concluded that an inhibitory deficit may be a risk factor in the development of conduct disorder (Harden et al. 1995). Generally, evidence of arousal-mediated impairments of inhibitory mechanisms underlying learning, socialization, and conscience have provided the foundation for theories of criminality (Eysenck 1977).

Further research is needed to clarify the specific arousal patterns among students with disruptive behavior disorders. The neurobiology of aggression and violence and the hypoarousal hypothesis are ripe areas for continued research, which might contribute greatly to our understanding and to the educational and clinical approaches used with students who have disruptive behavior disorders.

Educational placement. Students with disruptive behavior disorders are likely to be found in general education classrooms. There are no existing special education categories that cover ADHD, CD, or and ODD. While, as mentioned earlier, some of these students may be found eligible for special education services in the area of emotional disturbance (ED), others will not be considered eligible for such support because they are assumed to be socially maladjusted. (See Chapter 25 for a comprehensive discussion about emotional disturbance with or without social maladjustment.)

Thus, educational programming for disruptive students is inadequately differentiated, and appropriate education may elude them. Joel, Robbie, and Rob, who are featured in Chapters 8 and 9, did not fit readily into existing special education programs. Joel experienced varying eligibility for programs for students with emotional and learning disabilities, but the type of ED program that would have been appropriate, theoretically, was filled with street-wise, drug-involved or severely depressed, withdrawn students. Joel's parents chose to place him in a small military academy where, they hoped, he would get both attention and discipline. Rob, too, needed something more than his school system could provide. He qualified for ED and learning disabilities services, but his noncompliance showed a need for a program with a heavy behavioral emphasis and a reeducation approach that would focus on accountability and building of values. Rob's parents, exasperated with his noncompliant behavior at home and at school, finally placed him in a private boarding school for troubled youth. Robbie could not succeed even in a public day school for students with emotional disabilities. His extremely hostile, aggressive, destructive behaviors eventually took him to court, and he became part of the juvenile justice system.

Students with disruptive behavior disorders arouse negative reactions among adults. Consequently, rather than provide instructional accommodations, many teachers favor excluding them from regular classrooms. Some experts argue that by denying special education eligibility to disruptive students, school administrators may more readily suspend or expel them. On the other hand, when disruptive students are found eligible for special education, it may be for the wrong reason: to limit the student's participation in general education as much as possible.

Continuum of severity. Students with disruptive behavior disorders show gradations of disruptiveness. The ODD student typically picks his battles with familiar peers and adults; there is no random aggression or damage. Students with ADHD typically do not look for trouble outside of familiar situations; they search for action, not trouble, although trouble may find them. The student with a conduct disorder, who seems to be angry at the world, is the most likely of the three types to initiate fights, be cruel to animals and people, and steal. Of the three disruptive behavior disorders, students with ADHD are least harmful, those with conduct disorder the most dangerous, and students with oppositional-defiant disorder seem to fall somewhere between ADHD and CD.

However, this is not to ignore the possibility of serious problems along the continuum, particularly when any of these three disorders co-occur. For example, children with CD and ADHD seem to have a worse outcome than those with CD alone (Routh and Daugherty 1992). It is understood that the more externalizing and internalizing problems students exhibit the more trouble they are for themselves and for others.

Far-reaching problems. The problems of students with disruptive behavior disorders affect many areas of life. They do not fit into peer groups well, or they may fit in for the wrong reasons; they contribute to family conflict and stress; and they may have low self-esteem because of social rejection. These students typically show significant impairment in social and academic areas. Their behavior interferes significantly with personal and educational progress.

These far-reaching problems call for multidimensional education models: teaching approaches that use behavioral, psychological, environmental, and sociological interventions. Many disruptive students also require medication.

According to Volavka, who focuses on our understanding of the problem of disruptive behavior, rather than on how it should be handled,

A principal problem shared by studies is that sociologists, developmental specialists, child psychiatrists, and psychophysiologists do not join forces to study the same subjects. Unless they do so, it will be difficult to determine how the various minitheories relate to each other; a more comprehensive theory of the development of violent behavior will remain out of reach. (1995, p. 171)

Gender and prevalence. Boys are most often mentioned in descriptions of students with disruptive behavior disorders. Although it is difficult to estimate prevalence because of underreporting of crimes among youths and varying definitions of problems, one estimate is that boys outnumber girls under age 18 by a 9:2 ratio (Hendren 1991). Other reasons for the difficulty in estimating prevalence are the lack of an accepted definition and the lack of standardized measures for identification.

Outlook. Because these disorders persist, the outlook is not optimistic. Fergusson, Horwood, and Lynskey (1995) point to the stability of child conduct disorder and oppositional-defiant behaviors in youngsters between seven and 15 years of age. They documented a strong continuity of problem behaviors; only 14 percent showed remission within two years. Earls, who found considerable overlap between oppositional-defiant and conduct disorders, noted that "most adults who have had a conduct disorder in childhood continue to show significant indications of social dysfunction" (1994, p. 323). As for ADHD, there are indicators that not all ADHD students outgrow their problems. All three disruptive behavior disorders are serious, persistent problems.

Long-standing problems. Disruptive behavior disorders not only permeate the present and reach into the future, but they seem to begin early in life. The overactive, temperamental infant often becomes the hyperactive, noncompliant preschooler (Barkley 1978). As many as from 60 to 70 percent of children later diagnosed as ADD were identifiable by their symptoms during the preschool years (Barkley 1981). Parents of these students report problem behaviors beginning in the preschool years. One theory of ODD is that it is persistence of maladaptive efforts to deal with the conflict between the child's wish for autonomy and separation, on the one hand, and for dependency, on the other. Viewed this way, oppositional-defiant disorder is a separation disorder.

NONOVERLAPPING CONSIDERATIONS

ADHD, ODD, and CD separate in noteworthy ways. For one thing, there has been a heavier research emphasis on attention-deficit disorders, with particular focus on both externalizing and internalizing concerns. On the other hand, it seems that oppositional-defiant and conduct disorders have been lumped together as social maladjustment subtypes, with scant attention paid to overlap with other externalizing conditions or with internalizing conditions.

A socioeconomic differential may also be operating. Diagnosis of ADHD is not typically done by public schools. It falls on parents to take their youngsters to pediatricians or mental health professionals for evaluation of attention problems. Despite similarly disruptive behaviors, students in higher economic strata may be labeled ADD or ADHD, while lower-strata students may simply be described as disruptive or socially maladjusted.

Another point of dissimilarity is that some of the signs of ADHD are different from oppositional-defiant and conduct disorders. As Chapter 8 will show, students with ADHD exhibit a unique pattern of restlessness, inattentiveness, excitability, overactivity, impulsivity, fidgetiness, disruptiveness, and distractibility.

As Chapter 9 will show, students with oppositional-defiant and conduct disorders typically are argumentative; actively defy adult rules or directives; deliberately annoy; blame others for their own misbehavior; are touchy, angry, and resentful; and are spiteful and vindictive. Students with conduct disorders act flagrantly against the rights and feelings of others; theirs is the most outrageous disruptiveness known to schools. These are the students who "rape, pillage, and plunder" the social landscape. Students with oppositional-defiant and conduct disorders may not be hyperactive, but their presence certainly is as acutely felt.

ACUTELY FELT, FAIRLY DEALT?

As noted in the discussion of similarities among disruptive behavior disorders, these students arouse negative reactions in adults that may lead to their exclusion from the classroom or school. To be fair to general educators, who must directly confront disruptive behavior disorders, educational programs have not kept pace with the problems. There may be no appropriate alternative program, or alternative programs may be the first to be cut when school system budgets are pared. Students with disruptive behavior disorders have not been dealt a fair hand, and school administrators may feel acute frustration about what to do with them.

Classroom teachers, too, often feel frustrated. There may not be appropriate special education programs, and placement changes take time. A lot of damage can take place in classrooms before an appropriate educational setting is found for a disruptive student.

Many students have disruptive behavior disorders, yet there is a disparity between educational programming and special needs. In describing educational interventions for students with attention-deficit disorder Fiore, Becker, and Nero (1993) summarized behavior therapy and cognitive-behavior therapy interventions. These are not interventions that classroom teachers can readily use. Practical guidelines for teaching students with ADD/ADHD (see, for example, Burcham, Carlson, and Milich 1993) may provide isolated, albeit worthwhile, examples. Without systematic programming for these students, we cannot develop a consistent understanding of practices that work with particular types of students (for example, ADD with and without hyperactivity).

　　While reading the next two chapters keep in mind that students with disruptive disorders have not merited a niche within special education that will address their special needs. Part of this problem relates to the issues covered in Chapter 25 related to exclusion of students with social maladjustment from the ED category. Part of this problem relates to political and economic pressures to restrain school district special education budgets and to screen students out of special education if they are disruptive. Too often, disruptive students are removed before the appropriate questions can be asked about why they behave as they do.

8

Attention-Deficit Disorder with Hyperactivity

Nature without check with original energy
Walt Whitman

Attention-deficit disorder with hyperactivity (ADHD) is one of the most commonly diagnosed and heavily researched childhood disorders. Thousands of studies spanning the fields of medicine, psychology, and education have appeared on this topic (Reid et al. 1994). These studies, which have clarified the picture, have led to the following five noteworthy points.

First, many students with attention-deficit disorders have been identified under disability categories and are receiving special education services. The majority of students with ADHD have been identified as having behavioral disorders (Barkley et al. 1990; Wender 1975), followed by learning disabilities (Reid et al. 1994). Dykman and Ackerman (1993) identified behavioral subtypes of attention-deficit disorders and concluded that those with ADHD may be at risk for oppositional and conduct disorders. Eligibility for special education services in the emotional disturbance (ED) category may also occur because of emotional difficulties; difficulties in psychosocial functioning in late adolescence may be an especially salient feature of hyperactive children (Slomkowski, Klein, and Mannuzza 1995). Evidence for co-occurring emotional problems is less consistent for girls with ADHD, but it becomes significant as they approach adolescence (McKinney, Montague, and Hocutt 1993). Those with attention-deficit disorder (ADD) may be at risk for anxiety and depression (Dykman and Ackerman 1993). Too, adjustment problems for students with ADD or ADHD are likely to continue into adulthood as a result of diminished self-esteem (Slomkowski, Klein, and Mannuzza 1995).

Second, despite possible identification under a disability classification, the majority of students with ADHD spend most, or all, of their school time in the general education classroom (Reid et al. 1994). Given an incidence estimate of from 1 to 6 percent of the student population (Lambert, Sandoval, and Sassone 1978), a general education secondary teacher with a 25-year career and an average of 125 students per year can expect to teach from 31 to 188 students with ADD or

ADHD, or from one to eight students per year.

Third, ADHD frequently is associated with academic underachievement (Slomkowski, Klein, and Mannuzza 1995; Wenar 1990). Failing grades, grade retention, dropping out, and other school-related problems are associated with this population. Students with ADHD are more likely than the average to underachieve and drop out of school (Burt 1994).

Fourth, ADHD involves a complex of cognitive-behavioral problems: restlessness, inattentiveness, excitability, overactivity, impulsiveness, fidgetiness, distractibility, and disruptiveness. The complexity of ADHD is reflected in the divergent diagnoses: as a psychiatric disorder, as a nonspecific conduct disorder, and as a nonpathological personality style.

Fifth, while the majority of students appear to outgrow the core symptoms of ADHD, a minority do not. Longitudinal research attests to the likelihood that adjustment problems will continue into adulthood. Life-span problems in social, family, legal, psychological, substance abuse, and relationship areas have been well documented (Burt 1994).

SOME FACTS ABOUT ADHD

Demographics. There is disagreement about the relation between ADHD and socioeconomic status. One report indicates a high incidence of attention disorders among children in lower socioeconomic areas (Goldstein and Goldstein 1990), while another (Graham 1991) finds no association between socioeconomic status and ADHD.

Prevalence. Approximately 3 percent of the childhood population may have ADHD, but prevalence figures differ widely. In the United Kingdom, the incidence has been reported at 0.06 percent; in the United States, on the other hand, incidence has been estimated at from 1 to 5 percent of the school-age population. Variations in reported incidence could be due to differences in adult perceptions of behavior, social and cultural factors, differences in clinic referral rates, and differences in diagnostic practices (Graham 1991). Prevalence may reflect the tempo of our society. As that tempo increases, so does the incidence of attention disorders. On the other hand, more public awareness of attention-deficit disorders may be translating into increased referrals and accurate identification.

Onset. Youngsters with ADHD first are identified as deviant between the ages of three and seven, but signs are typically first noticed during the early elementary school years, usually in the first two grade levels.

Gender. Students with ADHD are predominantly male. Research shows varying ratios of males to females: from 3-4:1 (Graham 1991), 5-9:1 (Ross and Ross 1982), and 2-10:1 with an average of 6:1 (Barkley 1989). The invariant finding is that boys outnumber girls.

CHANGING VIEWS OF ADHD

Since ancient Greek physicians prescribed opium for restless infants, there have been varied perspectives on children with attention and hyperactivity problems. Some physicians and others in the past have perceived patterns of underaroused attention and overaroused behavior to relate to brain injury, some to a defect in moral control, some to health problems such as encephalitis, and some to head trauma.

During most of the twentieth century, the prevailing assumption has been that attention disorders have an underlying neurological or genetic basis. Neurologically, the frontal lobes, basal ganglia, and brain stem, as well as one of the major neurotransmitter systems, have been implicated. Some evidence points specifically to the brain's right hemisphere (Riccio et al. 1993). Different subtypes of attention deficit disorders may relate to different neural substrates of varying severity, occurring in variable constellations, yet sharing a common response to psychostimulants (Voeller 1991). Genetically, one fact is that from 20 to 30 percent of parents and siblings share the disorder. Also, there is concordance in identical twins (Barkley 1989).

UNDERSTANDING INATTENTION

In order to understand inattention, it is important to clarify attention. Attention is a complex cognitive ability, a multidimensional construct that can refer to problems with alertness, arousal, selectivity, sustained attention, distractibility, or span of apprehension, among others (Barkley 1989). The following five points are basic.

First, a student who has difficulty completing two simultaneous tasks, such as listening to the teacher and taking notes, has a problem with *divided attention*.

Second, a student who is described as a daydreamer, and who often is preoccupied with activities other than the task assigned by the teacher, has a problem with *focused attention*.

Third, a student who is easily distracted by extraneous events, such as minor noises in the classroom, has a problem with *selective attention*, or prioritizing focus. For example, if the teacher is standing in front of the classroom and speaking, the student may be unable to identify this as the most important event at the time and, instead, may pay attention to the student sitting next to him or her.

Fourth, a student who is unable to remain on task for a sufficient amount of time to complete it has a problem with *sustained attention*, or *persistence*. This issue has also been referred to as lack of task vigilance. The student who lacks task vigilance finds it difficult to sustain attention in the face of dull, boring, and repetitive tasks.

Intertwined with this difficulty is a deficiency in inhibiting behavior, or impulsivity, which is also multidimensional. Impulsivity, or *disinhibition*, may be another facet of poor sustained attention; both require persistence (Barkley 1989).

Fifth, a student who is unable to perform such tasks as listening for the next spelling word presented by the teacher during a test would be considered to have a problem with *readiness to respond*. Such readiness relates closely to vigilance, which requires the student to hang on through repetitive, unappealing situations.

DEFINING CHARACTERISTICS
The four commonly accepted criteria for an attention disorder are inattention and distractibility, behavioral overarousal, attention underarousal, and gratification delay difficulty. These four components attest to ADHD's multidimensionality.

One standard for comparison in *inattention* and *distractibility* is that the average five-year-old should be able to focus for 15 minutes on an independent activity without direct supervision and without a stimulus that is constantly changing (such as television). From that point on, a child's attention span continues to increase with age. By first grade we expect children to be able to sit and work for an hour at a time. (Recall the average age of onset for ADHD and relate it to this expectation.)

In terms of *behavioral overarousal*, students with ADHD tend to be excessively restless and overactive, behaviorally and emotionally. Difficulty in controlling bodily movements is especially trying in situations in which they are expected to sit still for long periods of time. The speed and intensity with which they go to the extreme of their emotion is much greater than that of their same-age peers (Goldstein and Goldstein 1990). Thus, while the student with ADHD may become quickly upset about something, he or she will also forget it just as quickly and move on to something else. This is frustrating and confusing to many adults. Often, adults say that these students lack a sense of guilt. In truth, these students wear their emotions on their sleeves and are able to dust off their feelings and carry on while the rest of us are focusing on our feelings and their behaviors.

Also, characteristic of these students is impulsivity, which relates to *attentional underarousal*. Students with attention deficits do not appear to think before they act. Their external behavior is aroused before their internal mental function. As a result, they find it difficult to weigh the consequences of their actions before they act and do not reasonably consider the consequences of their past behavior (Goldstein and Goldstein 1990). They are likely to go on to another behavior while their thought processes struggle to keep up. They may be able to explain the rules and consequences, but they are unable to control themselves because overt behavior occurs before the consequences are considered. These students are not intentionally oppositional; their behavior is at odds with their thoughts. In short, their behavior is propelled by a need for information. The behavior of students with ADHD may be summed up in the words of "Dennis the Menace": "By the time I think about what I am gonna do I already DID it!"

Because these students have difficulty with *gratification delay*, long-term goals are difficult for them. Behavior management techniques appeal to teachers of students with ADHD because of the difficulty these students show in waiting for payoffs. The teacher may reason that these students need to learn systematically how to work toward long-term goals. Often, behavioral systems are designed with frequent pay-offs as the students progress toward long-term goals, rather than one reward when the goal is reached. In theory, short-term goal setting and payoffs should work.

Rewards, however, are not always effective in changing the behavior of these students. Often, once the reward and the accompanying structure of the behavioral-change program are removed, the student with ADHD regresses and again exhibits the behavior that was the target of change (Goldstein and Goldstein 1990).

These students often do not respond better to negative reinforcement. One explanation is that they have had more experience with removal of aversive stimuli rather than with presentation of positive ones. For example, the child may have experienced denial of privileges for not doing chores. He has, thus, learned that if he does not do his chores he will not be able to do something that he likes. Thus, his attitude will likely be oriented toward avoiding the negative consequence rather than earning the positive one. This is not simply a matter of splitting behavioral analysis hairs; children with ADHD may learn to be motivated by negative reinforcement. However, many students with ADHD do learn under a condition of positive reinforcement. This is the most powerful and encouraging condition, particularly for students who have both behavioral and emotional problems.

It is clear, overall, that the student's learning history must be taken into account. A behavioral plan will succeed or fail contingent upon the student's experience with positive and negative reinforcement.

BEHAVIORAL PLAN EXAMPLE. *Joel, who has been diagnosed with ADHD, was put on a weekly system whereby he was required to present each academic teacher with a sheet on which one target behavior was to be rated. Each day Joel was responsible for presenting the sheet to his teachers so that they could initial if and only if Joel had shown the target behavior "mind my own business." At the end of each week Joel's resource teacher reviewed the sheet. If Joel met the criterion for that week, he was given a reward such as one period to do beading, color intricate pictures, or play a game. If he met the criterion for four consecutive weeks, a bigger payoff was possible, such as a pack of baseball cards along with a certificate of achievement. Joel met his short-term goals consistently over a four-month period, with rising criteria for mastery. He completed seventh grade having met his long-term goal. It looked as if the behavioral system had worked.*

However, when Joel began eighth grade he did not mind his own business. It seemed futile to resume a behavioral system. During the intervening summer Joel's parents had continued to discipline him as they had for many years, i.e., by removing toys and privileges when Joel misbehaved. When school resumed it was clear that a new strategy was needed. First, Joel was reminded that high school loomed and that he would be expected to be more independent. He was told that instead of a contract he would be monitored through teacher rating sheets made up of his individualized education plan (IEP) short-term objectives. Further, he was told that if he failed to reach a satisfactory rating for any objective, then a sheet similar to the one used during seventh grade would be designed for him and the old system would resume. The new system seemed to work and, while not all of Joel's distracting, meddlesome, and bothersome behaviors were extinguished, there appeared to be more conscious self-control and ability to get back on track with reminders.

Joel not only needed an approach that capitalized on his past learning but a combination of behaviorally and cognitively oriented approaches. The first step was to make him more aware of his behaviors through continuous feedback. The second step required that he think about the behaviors that his teachers were rating. Additionally, he was counseled about better ways to satisfy his needs, how to think before acting, and self-advocacy. This combination of interventions was successful.

The success of a combined behavioral and cognitive approach attests to the very nature of ADHD. There is, in part, a cognitive basis for ADHD, and there are inappropriate behaviors, but the most powerful approach focuses on both social behavior and the student's thought processes. Approaches that combine proactive and reactive methods seem to have a greater chance of success than approaches that focus only on behavior or cognition.

TYPICAL MANIFESTATIONS IN THE CLASSROOM

Typical manifestations of ADHD can be seen in the classroom. Ten of the conventional diagnostic criteria for ADHD are listed below. As can be seen, these criteria expand on those previously presented. Teacher comments about Joel are italicized.

1. The student fidgets with hands or feet or squirms in his or her seat.

Joel just can't seem to sit still during assemblies.

Quiet reading time? Forget it! He looks like a snake trying to shed its skin.

He's always moving something: his hands, his feet, or his mouth.

2. The student has difficulty remaining seated when required to do so.

Joel's supposed to stay at one lunch table, but he finds his way to others.

3. The student is easily distracted by extraneous stimuli.

Joel is easily distracted and distracts others. He is drawn even to the flies that are trapped inside the windows; he wants to let them out during instructional time.

He seems to seek distractions, anything to relieve him of the stress of concentrating.

4. The student has difficulty following through on instructions from others.

Joel often turns in assignments late.

He doesn't follow directions for projects.

Joel procrastinates. He does a good job on assignments when he doesn't wait until the last minute.

Joel couldn't follow through on what he was directed to do, probably because he missed something when he wasn't paying attention.

5. The student has difficulty sustaining attention in tasks or play activities.

He has a real problem sticking to the research during library time. He really needs individual attention in that type of situation.

Joel can stick with an activity if he's really interested in it or if the room is very quiet. Otherwise, he has trouble staying on task.

6. The student often shifts from one uncompleted activity to another.

He works at inappropriate times. While we are having a class discussion or I am teaching, Joel will be doing that night's homework. Consequently, he misses the instruction for one assignment and doesn't do the homework satisfactorily because he couldn't concentrate well while instruction was going on.

7. The student often talks excessively.

A conversation with him is really just a one-sided affair.

Joel talks too much in class. He distracts other students with his chatter.

8. The student often interrupts or intrudes on others.

Classmates frequently ask to change their seats so that Joel can't bother them.

Joel minds other students' business too much. He butts in.

He will try to interrupt another student even when the other student is operating a shop power tool.

9. The student often loses things necessary for tasks or activities.

Joel never seems to have a pen or pencil for class.

He missed five homework assignments this quarter because he couldn't find them.

10. The student often engages in physically dangerous activities without considering possible consequences.

He tries to dribble a basketball all over the court without looking to see where other players are. One day he rammed into another boy.

Joel seems to be accident prone. He is constantly bumping into things and getting scrapes and bruises. It is as if he acts before thinking.

ADHD AND THE FEDERAL DEFINITION OF ED

The Department of Education's position is that attention-deficit disorder does not need to be added to the Individuals with Disabilities Education Act (IDEA) as a separate disability category because students with this disorder, who require special education and related services, can meet the eligibility criteria for services under other IDEA provisions.

These students may qualify for ED provisions when they show *an inability to learn that cannot be explained by intellectual, sensory, or health factors.* Joel, for example, is a healthy boy who rarely misses school because of illness; he is average in intelligence; and his vision and hearing are normal. A youngster who has marked inattention and lack of persistent task involvement is not likely to cope readily with instructional demands.

INABILITY TO LEARN EXAMPLE. *Elementary school years were not too bad for Joel in terms of learning. During those years he was able to move around during the day because there was an emphasis on hands-on projects and activities involving movement. Middle school also afforded Joel opportunities for movement because of group projects, hands-on activities, an industrial arts course, and transition times between the seven periods. While Joel's grades during elementary and middle school years did not match his potential, he was able to achieve in the "B" to "D" range, mathematics being consistently low. High school, on the other hand, was a disaster. By the third quarter of ninth grade, Joel was failing several academic courses. There was less emphasis on hands-on activities and movement, and he had to cope with block scheduling, which is an ADHD student's worst nightmare when the blocks are academic ones.*

Not only academic learning is impacted by ADHD. This student may be unable to focus in order to learn strategies for coping socially. A combination of overactive, poorly modulated behavior does not augur well for social harmony.

SOCIAL LEARNING EXAMPLE. *Joel is so active and talkative that he has difficulty settling down. This has affected his learning of social skills. He has been mentally unavailable to acquire the skills needed to cope with stress, changes, and others' expectations. He is, essentially, in social discord.*

A student who has ADHD is at risk for emotional disturbance because of *an inability to build or maintain satisfactory interpersonal relationships with peers and teachers.* Students who drive teachers crazy with their restlessness, disorganization, impulsivity, and distractibility may also be bothersome to peers, who may not want to work with them or even sit near them. Because of his annoying behaviors Joel does not evoke many good feelings from peers or teachers. Generally, students with ADHD are overly reactive; they typically express their emotions quickly and intensely. This is annoying to both peers and teachers.

EMOTIONAL EXTREMES EXAMPLE. *Joel shows emotional extremes. For example, he will whine about a minor disappointment but seem to have forgotten the matter five minutes later. Too, he has an explosive temper, but these flare-ups are short-lived and soon forgotten. Peers and teachers, however, have trouble forgetting.*

Students with ADHD also show *inappropriate types of behavior or feelings under normal circumstances.* Researchers have reported consistently high rates of co-occurrence between attention deficit disorders and disruptive behavior disorders marked by aggression, oppositional-defiant behavior, and conduct problems. Dykman and Ackerman (1993) concluded that most ADHDs would meet the criteria for oppositional-defiant disorder (ODD). Furthermore, Barkley (1981) found that 80 percent of parents of hyperactive children provided ratings suggesting that their children were having serious problems playing with peers, compared with 7 percent of nonhyperactive controls. Whalen et al. (1979) also found that hyperactive youngsters showed greater negative verbalizations and physical aggression compared with nonhyperactive peers.

Overall, students with ADHD appear to be less accepted and more rejected in social situations than nonhyperactive peers. These students are unable to cope with the frustration of peer rejection. A vicious cycle typically ensues. The student with ADHD frequently responds to rejection by inappropriate behavior, which, in turn, leads to more social rejection, which leads to more inappropriate behavior.

The critical issue is that the student with ADHD cannot readily adapt behavior to meet situational demands. A repertoire of social skills is needed, and, here, the student with ADHD is at a disadvantage. This student, typically, lacks cooperative working skills and the social skills to resolve conflicts.

SOCIAL SKILLS EXAMPLE. *Joel's lack of a social skills repertoire became acutely apparent when he aided and abetted serious, illegal behavior on the part of his only friend, David. When Joel saw that David had set a toilet seat afire in the boys' lavatory, Joel did not report the incident. When David set off a smoke bomb in a school trash can, Joel served as look-out. When David set off the school fire alarm, resulting in evacuation of the building, Joel remained silent. He did not tell anyone about the incidents until other students named him. The police interrogated Joel at length before he would admit to any involvement. Joel remained loyal to David despite the prospect of severe consequences. Joel's choice of friend matched his own self-esteem; David, a loner with antisocial tendencies, was the only student who would befriend him.*

A student who can regulate his own feelings is likely to adapt to social situations. Students with ADHD often show difficulty in maintaining emotional equilibrium, which correlates with poor behavioral modulation.

BEHAVIORAL MODULATION EXAMPLE. *Joel has difficulty regulating his affect. He experiences frequent emotional peaks and valleys. Consequently, his feelings steer his behavior in directions that do not match situations. He keeps his feelings to himself and avoids strong emotional stimuli. He seems to be uncomfortable with interpersonal closeness, probably due to an inability to match his feelings to situations.*

Despite an understanding that students with ADHD have social problems, these difficulties often are overlooked when considering a diagnosis of ADHD (Goldstein and Goldstein 1990) but should be included (Pelham and Bender 1982). Peer interaction problems are as useful in distinguishing children with ADHD from normal children as are attention span, impulsivity, and hyperactivity.
Among students with ADHD there is often a *pervasive mood of unhappiness or depression.*

MOOD OF UNHAPPINESS EXAMPLE. *Joel feels socially inadequate due to frequent rejection, and his self-image suffers from comparison with taller peers. As he moves into tenth grade he remains shorter than most female classmates. Too, Joel is often discouraged. He feels that he should be able to succeed in school, and he does not understand how to do better. His outlook is depressive. He feels alone and pessimistic about social interactions. He feels sad when rejected by other students and is easily stressed by interpersonal conflict. Robert, age 13, has ADHD and shows high levels of anxiety and depression as well as low self-esteem. When tested by the school psychologist, he offered responses such as: "I feel alone even when others are with me" and "a lot of people are against me." He is very angry at his mother, who abused him when he was three years old and then abandoned the family. With a strong need for approval and affection Robert has regressed to using baby talk and crawling under tables. It appears that he continues to experience grief related to separation from his mother. ADHD is apparent in his hyperactivity, impulsivity, and aggressive outbursts. He slams doors and stomps his feet a lot. Impulsivity is evident when he plays with candles and matches. He also has destroyed property. Oppositionality is shown in his argumentativeness; he often protests at home about how he is treated unfairly compared to his older brothers. Robert is caught in a cycle: He behaves impulsively and then regrets his behavior, which contributes to feelings of sadness and isolation. In turn, his depression leads him to act out in ways that relieve his sadness. And the cycle continues.*

Finally, students with ADHD show a complex of behaviors and emotions, some of which may overlap with the federal criteria for ED. In light of this complexity, some professionals have proposed that there be three subtypes of attention disorders. Shaywitz and Shaywitz (1988), for example, proposed the following breakdown: (a) attention-deficit disorder without hyperactivity (ADD/WO), (b) attention-deficit disorder with hyperactivity (ADDH), and (c) attention-deficit disorder with any comorbid diagnosis, with emphasis on aggressive disorders (ADDPlus). Subtype (b) is most relevant to disruptive behavior disorders, and subtype (c) is most relevant to issues of emotional and behavioral disorders, or combined externalizing and internalizing disorders. Type (c), also, supports inclusion of ADHD in a discussion of emotional and behavioral disorders. Research support for subtyping attention-deficit disorder is provided by Marshall et al. (1997), who found that math achievement scores for students with ADD were significantly lower than those for students with ADHD, further supporting previous research suggesting that ADD may represent a distinct subtype of attention-deficit disorder, specifically that inattention interferes with the ability to master abstract symbol systems, especially basic arithmetic skills.

SUGGESTED EDUCATIONAL STRATEGIES

For students with ADHD, a multidimensional perspective is helpful in selecting interventions. Specifically, an appropriate multidimensional intervention involves four elements: medical management, psychological support, educational management, and behavior modification (Pfiffner and Barkley 1990), with management the key. Goldstein and Goldstein (1990) have noted that disorders of attention and arousal cannot be cured and must be managed throughout childhood.

Researchers have focused on strategies designed to increase certain desired behaviors and/or to decrease other, undesired behaviors, assuming that academic productivity will improve as a byproduct of improved attending behaviors. Less research has been focused directly on instruction and learning (Fiore, Becker, and Nero 1993), but there is increasing recognition of a need to focus on instructional interventions for these students.

That recognition is reflected in research. For example, Conte and his colleagues (1987) found that students with ADHD benefited most from learning tasks that were presented at varying speeds: activities that are broken into segments that are alternately fast, slow, and moderate in pacing. Other research (e.g., Zentall and Gohs 1984) showed that students with hyperactivity took significantly longer to complete tasks when initial information was detailed rather than global. Finally, Zentall and Meyer (1987) showed that students with hyperactivity performed significantly better under an active-response condition, where they could do something during instruction.

When a student with ADHD disrupts classes (for example, drifting in after the bell rings), talks while the teacher is giving directions, or does his homework while a videotape is being shown, the usual response is to discipline, usually with a counterforce at least equal to the offense committed, despite the variety of options available in schools for coping with such disruptive behavior (Diamond 1992). The teacher may refer the student to the office for tardiness, request that he or she be detained after school, or at least mark the student tardy in the record book. The teacher also may reprimand the student for excessive talking or take books from him or her while the videotape is playing.

Students with ADHD, however, do not respond well to such tactics. Instead, these students generally find ways to counteract disciplinary measures. They may bother students sitting next to them instead of attending to the videotape. Or they miss the lesson altogether by spending time in the office, which is not a bad outcome for a student who does not want to be in the classroom.

Diamond offers an alternative approach, assuming that the standard operating procedure is ineffective:

But what happens if we don't give the anticipated response? What if we do not perpetuate the cycle? We do need to respond in some way to unacceptable behavior; yet our response does not have to be the one the student elicits repeatedly and predictably. . .in school. In fact, the usual responses have not solved the problem, or the behavior would not still be present. Thus dancing to that old tune holds little promise for change. Just trying new responses is a useful intervention in itself. It offers the possibility that an approach can be found that will help the student to learn new, more productive behaviors. (1992, p. 154)

Diamond suggests that the student's tardiness, for example, be met with humor. Instead of a routine referral to the office or a reminder that X number of tardies translates to detention or a lowered grade, a response such as, "I see the matinee crowd has arrived," might capture the student's attention and elicit a thoughtful response.

Or the teacher might offer to talk with the student after class. Instructive would be a problem-solving conversation in which teacher and student collaboratively design a project focusing on timely arrival to class. Both parties become invested. The conference also might include the teacher's sharing of how late arrival makes him or her feel.

TARDINESS EXAMPLE. *JJ, age 16, has ADHD. He is consistently late to physical education class. With a class of 35 students, his teacher does not have time to deal with him when JJ arrives late. After months of exasperation, and after penalizing JJ for tardiness, which resulted in grades of "D" and "F," the teacher decided that another approach was needed. After all, JJ was a gifted athlete, and low grades in a course that he liked and for which he had strong potential for success, made no sense.*

The P.E. teacher made an appointment to meet with JJ after class one day. During the meeting the teacher made it clear that he believed JJ capable of outstanding performance in his class. He expressed concern about JJ's achievement, saying: "I hate to put a low grade on your report card when I know how well you can do. I'd really like to be able to mark you on your skills as an athlete."

Subsequently, JJ began to arrive on time to P.E. class. Evidently, a little care and concern on the teacher's part worked to turn things around. The teacher opted for a personal exchange rather than a power struggle.

A multidimensional approach should also encompass strategies related to predominant needs for acceptance/approval, external control, and appropriate engagement. First, these students benefit from behavior management strategies such as positive reinforcement when they stay on task and when they do not hassle or show disrespect toward peers. Approval also is communicated by giving them leadership roles that elicit peer respect, and acceptance is promoted by preparing the peer group to include and help the student, and by providing feedback that combines both strengths and weaknesses. Another acceptance strategy is to seek ways to interact in a positive, personal way following necessary reprimands. This is difficult when the student has been very annoying, but contact needs to be reestablished after punishing events. This strategy communicates to the student the message, "I like you even if I don't like some of your behaviors."

External control strategies include ensuring that the student knows the rules; developing a behavior charting system to increase awareness of his or her own behavior; standing near him or her during critical activities (for example, when he or she is likely to talk), providing him with short-term objectives and a progress chart to show the student that he or she is meeting those objectives, and structuring cooperative activities where students monitor one another, thereby building in peer pressure.

Appropriate engagement, the ADHD student's most obvious need, can be addressed in many ways. Some include the following.

1.   Interact often with the student in order to maintain his or her attention; ask questions and ask for opinions.

2.   Ask the student to restate directions or classroom rules.

3.   Help the student divide large tasks into small, manageable parts and to decide on the order in which to do them.

4.   Plan activities that flow from formal to informal, focused to unfocused, or structured to unstructured.

5.   Reduce lag time by providing sufficient activities to maintain engagement.

6.   Encourage the student to take notes, even when he or she understands what is being discussed.

7.   Seat the student away from distracting noises.

8.   Present the broad idea at the start of the activity so that the student will have a central theme to which details can be attached. This helps with notetaking and focusing. Also, ensure that the subject matter is meaningful to the student.

9.   Use hand or body movements to emphasize points or to add interest.

10.   Use physical objects such as props related to content.

11.   Decrease the selective attentional requirements (i.e., details and descriptions). They disrupt the listening comprehension of ADHDs. Focus on the essential content. Use global cues such as "It looks like" rather than "It has the following parts."

12.   Give the student frequent opportunities to leave his or her seat for appropriate reasons: getting materials, running errands, and so on.

13.   Stand near the student and gently refocus him or her by touching his or her shoulder.

14.   Separate the student from any peer who stimulates inappropriate behavior or disengagement.

15.   Use modeling by reinforcing those students who show on-task behavior.

16.   A peer tutor can help the student maintain attention.

17.   Maintain visibility to and from the student at all times.

18.   Recognize the student when his or her hand is raised; give a private signal that help will be given as soon as possible.

19.   Place the student in a carrel, or use a divider, in order to reduce

distracting stimuli.

20.   Administer tests in a quiet, nondistracting setting.   Ideally this setting should be away from the classroom.

21.   Teach the student to question any directions explanations, or instructions he or she does not understand.

22.   As ADHD students have been found to be more talkative than classmates when they initiate conversations, and less talkative when asked to respond, give them ample response opportunities.

23.   Add visual cues to auditory cues in order to enhance recall.

24.   Help the student establish and maintain routine locations for books, notebooks, supplies, and materials.

25.   Have the student highlight important features: the directions on tests, the function signs on math problems, and so on. Be careful as this may interfere with complex or new task performance.

26.   Provide opportunities for active responding (e.g., simple motor responses instead of oral responses).

27.   As ADHDs typically are very sensitive to rewards, partial rewards are less effective than continuous rewards. Token economies, however, may be substituted for continuous rewards.

28.   If using reprimands, short ones are more effective than long ones. (Be careful not to reinforce inadvertently an undesirable behavior.)

29.   Response cost programs, a combination of positive reinforcement and punishment, can improve attention, on-task behavior, and task completion.

30.   Teach gratification delay by systematically observing and counting appropriate behaviors and rewarding at a later, convenient time. Inform the student in advance what behavior is targeted and what the reward will be and when it will occur.

31.   Post daily schedules and assignments. Set specific times for tasks.

32.   Alert the student to schedule changes.

33.   Inject the student's name into the instructional flow.

34.   Provide regularly scheduled and frequent breaks.

35.   Evaluate the appropriateness of tasks to determine if they   are   too easy, if they are too difficult, and if the length of time scheduled to complete them is appropriate.

36.   As often as possible use one-to-one, small-group, and independent

formats rather than whole-class instruction. Logan, Bakeman, and Keefe (1997) believe that the independent format is especially effective because of peer modeling (i.e., disabled students see peers engaged and imitate them).

37.   Post for all students and tape to the ADHD student's desktop strategies to use while awaiting teacher assistance; e.g., try the problem again, go on to the next problem, review the sample problem, wait quietly.

Engagement can also be facilitated by self-management. McDougall and Brady (1998), confirmed prior findings that self-management increases academic productivity and engagement during independent practice. Their research specifically showed the effectiveness of fading the cue to self-monitor once math fluency reached high levels. The implication was that initial academic improvements through use of self-graphing can be enhanced, and maintained at high levels, when students continue to self-graph without prompting. Self-management might include having the student chart the length of time he or she is able to stay engaged. This can be integral in a performance contract. A timer is helpful when the student needs to aim to work for increasingly longer periods.

Three other strategies for facilitating engagement deserve mention. Engagement can be promoted by having the student paraphrase what people tell him to be sure he understands (for example, "So, Mrs. Smith, you want me to do the first 10 problems on this worksheet, right?"). Also, calling on students randomly means they must pay attention because they cannot predict when their turn will come. Finally, when reading, the student can be taught to skim the material first so that familiarity can be established before actual focused reading takes place.

Within a multidimensional approach, three other strategies have been found to be effective: modeling and self-verbalization, relaxation training, and increased stimulation. *Self-verbalization/modeling* involves steps: The adult performs a task while speaking aloud; the student then does the task while the adult gives instructions; the student does the task while whispering and then only while moving his lips; finally, the student does the task while self-instructing only by thinking about the instructions. Modeling enters in when the adult models the questions that need to be asked at each step of the self-verbalization procedure. Positive reinforcement can be used, also, to reinforce attention, reducing the amount as soon as the desired behavior is evident. When the correct behavior is not evident, the adult can again model it while speaking aloud. With adolescents, the initial steps of this approach are best accomplished in a quiet, private setting.

Relaxation training and strenuous exercise reduce tension, improve cognitive performance, and reduce impulsivity in students with ADHD. Exercises that are commonly used in physical education classes may be incorporated in the classroom and used before or after instructional activities. In-seat relaxation exercises such as shoulder and neck shrugs, arm stretching, and cross-torso twists are also effective, as are isometric exercises.

One game that is effective for relaxation and appropriate engagement is "Bop It." The Bop It toy provides auditory, rhythmic commands to slap, pull, or twist the toy, and it commands when to pass the toy to the next player. This game, which can be played while sitting or standing, best in a circle, requires attention and turn-taking. It can be done for one round of passes or multiple rounds.

Increased stimulation optimizes classroom learning and lessens the need for the student to produce his own stimulation through overactivity. Zentall (1977) theorized that environmental stimulation decreases (rather than increases) hyperactivity owing to the student's inadequate stimulus filters, which cause a flood of unfocused responses. By this reasoning, students with ADHD increase their activity, verbalizations, and body movements to seek optimal stimulation. This theory is supported by the fact that both sensory-deprived individuals and hyperactives show poor concentration, disorganized thoughts, and poor visual-motor skills, and the fact that stimulant drugs (e.g., Ritalin) have successfully "calmed" hyperactives, rather than making them more active, by maintaining an adequate arousal level.

A balance must be struck, however. Prevent the student from becoming overly stimulated by an activity, particularly in physical activities and games, and reduce the emphasis on competition, which tend to excite the student.

Specific classroom strategies intended to provide stimulation include the following. They all relate to task presentation in the most attractive, appealing, and interesting manner possible. At the same time, these strategies should be well structured so that the student will not become overly stimulated.

1. Provide color and pattern in the form of bright pictures and posters; use pictures, diagrams, an overhead projector, and a chalkboard to provide added information.

2. Use small groups because there is higher stimulation in small-group settings, with less waiting for attention.

3. Allow the student to pace himself or herself. Self-regulated working without waiting periods enables the student to control the amount of stimulation. This strategy engages his or her mind. As the mental process guides behavior, self-regulated thinking is more likely to result in self-regulated, modulated behavior.

4. Structure several short work periods rather than one long one. The student with ADHD responds better to variety; monotony deadens his or her attention.

5. Alternate types of work and use a multisensory approach.

6. Speak in varied tone, pitch, volume, and inflection to emphasize points and to add interest.

7. Use novel settings for tests, films, and games. For example, alter

the classroom physical arrangement or move the class to another location.

8.   Mix   rates of presentation.

Additionally, the strategy of self-monitoring, as a means of providing stimulation, merits discussion. Carr and Punzo (1993) found that adolescent students made gains in academic accuracy, productivity, and on-task behavior after recording their own daily academic scores on charts at the end of each class period. The students seemed to be aware of their improvement through this nonintrusive method. The intervention was easy to learn (one 15-minute session) and use, and the students did not need to be prompted to self-monitor.

As well, social strategies are very important for students with ADHD. School strategies for students with ADHD often neglect the need to improve peer relationships (Anhalt, McNeil, and Bahl 1998). Rather, many strategies to improve social functioning are clinic-based and focus on teaching social skills apart from the natural peer groups. Consequently, knowledge about appropriate and inappropriate behaviors may increase, but the learned skills are not consistently performed in the school settings.

One school-based strategy to improve social functioning is a whole-classroom reinforcement system. This technique prevents peers from feeling that it is unfair to reward one or a few students for complying with rules all students should follow. Group meetings can also provide an important social opportunity for students with ADHD. Structured group discussion of feelings and behavior, which has been used with students as young as early childhood, can be applied in classroom or counseling settings. This method promotes positive learning and relinquishing of ineffective attitudes and behaviors using common concerns. During these meetings, students can be encouraged to assume different roles: talker, listener, and observer. The counselor or teacher might begin by saying that he or she wants to learn more about students their age. The talker would have two minutes to say, for example, what he or she likes and dislikes about school; the listener would ask questions and try to repeat what was said (an active listening strategy that promotes engagement); and the observer watches and later makes suggestions to the listener, then joins the discussion. Afterward, the adult expands, summarizes, clarifies, and restates feelings. A second session might focus on talk about behavior, students might be asked to tell about what they did to cause feelings in others. Throughout, the talker-listener-observer format is used so that each student can receive feedback. Classroom observations following the use of this procedure have demonstrated that students became more interested and attentive and expressed enjoyment of the sessions.

Finally, it is recommended that interventions for students with ADHD occur in the natural classroom setting, as suggested earlier when referring to the lack of generalizability with clinic-based interventions. It is also recommended that behaviors be targeted that will facilitate academic progress, that targeted behaviors receive quick and frequent responses, and that interventions continue as long as maintenance of targeted behaviors is desired (Barkley 1994).

9

Oppositional-Defiant
and Conduct Disorders

A soft answer turneth away wrath;
But a grievous word stirreth up anger.
                    The Bible, Book of Proverbs

In this chapter the two extremely disruptive behavior disorders, oppositional-defiant disorder (ODD) and conduct disorder (CD), are discussed. It will become clear that students with these disorders typically do not elicit soft answers but, rather, generate and stir up a great deal of anger and wrath.

DEVELOPMENTAL AND CONTEXTUAL PERSPECTIVES

Most children show contrary, if not antisocial, behavior at some time. Occasional lying, stealing, and bullying are within the normal range of child behaviors. Extremely antisocial behavior, on the other hand, is abnormal. Consequently, chronic conduct disturbance is the most common reason for referral of children and adolescents for psychiatric evaluation.

Among antisocial youngsters there are three subgroups who violate social norms so chronically as to merit psychiatric evaluation. The largest group represents misconduct that is relatively minor and nonrepetitive. The second subgroup consistently violates age-expected norms by cutting school, running away, and conflicting with authorities. The smallest subgroup consists of youngsters who show repetitive criminal activity, some of which may be violent (McManus 1989).

According to contextual theory, individual actions are decisively influenced by early experiences, and no behavior can be understood or treated without knowledge of those experiences (Carr 1994). Research shows that students with extremely disruptive behaviors are likely to be found in particular school and family contexts. Rutter and his colleagues (1979) found that such students are less likely to be seen in schools where staff are committed to educational values, set and mark homework consistently, and concentrate on rewarding good rather than punishing bad behaviors, and where values are clear, expectations are consistent, and there is a positive climate. These schools show lower rates of truancy and other forms of delinquency among their students.

As for families, extremely disruptive behaviors seem to occur more commonly among working-class than middle-class youngsters, perhaps due to differences in family size, rates of overcrowding, and levels of child supervision. Middle-class children are more likely to engage legal services and be warned and cautioned by police for minor crimes (Graham 1991). In other words, delinquency among youths varies according to socioeconomic status.

Implicit in contextual theory is that youngsters who show extremely disruptive behavior disorders are not a homogeneous group. They differ in the extent and severity of antisocial behavior. Adolescents with extreme behavior disorders are often more different from one another than they are similar because the factors impacting their behaviors are varied, multiple, and produce an array of clinical outcomes.

BACKGROUND: OPPOSITIONAL-DEFIANT DISORDER

Fuzzy diagnosis. ODD is a relatively new diagnosis in the classification system for children's disorders. However, not all professionals consider it to be a bona fide disorder; many clinicians consider it an unattractive and upsetting phase that is experienced by some children on their way to a normal maturity (Costello and Costello 1992). Some professionals refer to these students as under- or un-socialized, and the courts often refer to them as socially maladjusted. There is, then, a fuzziness of diagnosis, which feeds into issues of eligibility for special education services. For present purposes, ODD is considered to be an extreme behavioral disturbance that interferes significantly with educational progress.

The American Psychiatric Association's *DSM IV* (1994) defines ODD by four criteria. These follow, with illustrative material.

The first criterion relates to a pattern of negativistic, hostile, and defiant behavior that lasts at least six months. During that time, four or more of the following behaviors must be seen frequently: loses temper, argues with adults, actively defies or refuses to comply with adult requests or rules, deliberately annoys people, blames others for mistakes or misbehavior, is touchy or easily annoyed by others, is angry and resentful, is spiteful or vindictive.

Costello and Costello (1992) note that these behaviors are most often expressed at home. Egan (1991) points out that the symptoms are usually exaggerated manifestations of child-rearing problems common to most parents. For example, expectations to keep a tidy room and to take baths are grist for the youngster's opposition and defiance.

However, the symptoms may also be expressed at school. Students with ODD frequently procrastinate. They often forget to bring school work or assignments home, or they say they did not heard irections. They may turn in school work late. Parents then take their youngsters to hearing specialists with the complaint that their children fail to pick up essential information. Really, the behavior is a sign of what Egan (1991) calls *passive aggressiveness*. These youngsters seem to be very angry and direct their anger away from themselves. Teachers and parents frequently complain that these youngsters defy them in subtly aggressive ways.

The second criterion relates to a significant impairment in social, emotional, and academic functioning. Noncompliance, argumentativeness, anger, and other features interfere with peer and adult relationships. Similarly, academic functioning is impeded by social and emotional issues that infuse negativity into school situations.

The third criterion relates to the fact that behavior does not occur exclusively during the course of a psychotic or mood disorder. Behavior may develop into a mood disorder (Goldstein and Goldstein 1990).

The fourth criterion relates to the fact that ODD does not meet the criteria for a conduct disorder. ODD involves negative, hostile, and defiant behavior, along with a pattern of resistance to authority and displaced anger, without the more serious violations of the basic rights of others that are seen in conduct disorder (CD). While a CD student may break the law and violate others' rights randomly, the ODD student is oppositional and defiant toward those with whom he is familiar. It is as if familiarity breeds contempt. Also, the ODD antisocial behavior pattern is not as extreme as that of CD.

ODD EXAMPLE. *Rob's psychological evaluation showed extreme emotional vulnerability, intense anger, low frustration tolerance, poor judgment and reasoning, and poor reality testing. His attitude toward school is antagonistic, particularly toward authority figures, whom he perceives as threatening, demeaning, and unyielding.*

Rob met once or twice weekly with his resource teacher for half of ninth grade before he laid his contempt and negativity on the table. When he became surprised that this teacher would not buy into his arguments about the ineptness of certain classroom teachers and his particular war plan to take revenge on one teacher whom he regarded as incompetent and unfair, it became clear that Rob was only interested in using the situation to vent feelings of arrogance and superiority. To Rob, life is fraught with unfairness, and his job is to make things right.

During twelfth grade Rob continued to plot revenge against authorities. While it was he who stole an SAT booklet, a crime to which he eventually confessed when his accomplice's story unraveled, Rob railed against the school authorities whom he perceived to be incompetent in their handling of the incident and its fall-out.

Onset. ODD seems to begin by eight years of age. By adolescence ODD likely is in full bloom.

Prevalence. Prevalence is difficult to estimate. For one thing, it is unclear if ODD is a temperamental issue or a disorder (Earls 1994). If we accept the McMahon and Wells (1989) position that CD subsumes ODD, we could assume, until further research clarifies, that the best estimate is that 9 percent of male children and 2 percent of female children have conduct disorders (Hendren 1991), or from 3 to 4 percent (McMahon and Wells 1989). Egan (1991), too, offers a figure of 6 percent ODD among 11-year-old children.

ODD CRITERIA ILLUSTRATED

Let us look at each of the aforementioned ODD criteria illustrated by observations of of two students, Rob and Nathan.

Students with ODD have short fuses. Teachers describe them as walking a thin line between simmering and bubbling anger.

SHORT TEMPER EXAMPLES. *Rob's fuse is easily lit. Most of the time, he assumes a defensive posture; he defines the adage "A best defense is an offense." Teachers tiptoe around him lest he ignite. He seems to personalize everything, as if each teacher has him in mind when making a rule, giving a direction, or making a point. Rob often misperceives events and cannot put his own behavior in perspective. For example, one day while listening to a science classmate make a presentation, Rob rested his chin on his hands, holding a pencil. Suddenly, the pencil slipped and rammed into the roof of his mouth. Rob saw some blood and panicked. Immediately, he went up to the teacher to ask to go to the water fountain, explaining what had happened. The teacher, seeing no gushing blood and believing that it was no emergency, asked Rob to sit down and wait, for she wanted the presenting student to have the opportunity to finish. Rob grew restive and fumed. The teacher, he thought, did not care about his needs. Rather than wait, he left the room. He did not know that the teacher was not only recording her evaluations of the presenter but was writing a pass for Rob to see the school nurse. Later, when Rob was told that he had left the room without permission, he responded, angrily and with expletives, that he had had an emergency. While he had a defensible position, Rob's verbal behavior did not help his case.*

Nathan, age 14, was found eligible for ED services due to oppositional-defiant behavior and quickly evoked feelings of anxiety and threat. Specifically, Nathan often loses his temper; he is unable to express feelings in a controlled manner.

Students with ODD can be maddeningly argumentative. Typically, they believe that their positions are eminently defensible; they assume an "I'm right, you're all wrong" attitude. Their thinking seems to be all black and white. This youngster's arguments are persistent, chronic, and pervasive.

ARGUING WITH ADULTS EXAMPLES. *Rob is very combative with adults, often arguing minor points. For example, during history class one day the teacher announced that the class would spend the period in the library doing research. She announced, further, that students were expected to sit at library tables in groups of three or less. When the class arrived at the library, Rob looked straight at the teacher and then sat at a table where three students already sat. Shortly, the teacher walked up to Rob and quietly reminded him of the direction. For the next five minutes Rob argued with the teacher about the unfairness and meaninglessness of her direction. The teacher, weary of the argument, finally said that she expected Rob to follow directions, and walked away. Immediately, Rob arose and walked from table to table, asking each student for an opinion about the direction, which he wrote on a piece of paper. Then Rob went up to the teacher, thrust the paper at her, and said, "See, the class doesn't think your direction makes sense." Clearly, Rob was unable to accept the teacher's direction, he made a big case out of his disagreement, and he wasted half the period building his case.*

Nathan, too, is argumentative. His eighth-grade resource teacher commented, "Don't argue with Nathan; be very upfront with him." His mother added, "Don't push Nathan into a corner." An appropriate warning for adults would be: "Don't let Nathan push you into a corner." For example, on the first day of ninth grade Nathan tried to start an argument with his Spanish teacher when she attempted to provide examples of Spanish words that have different connotations than their English counterparts. When she referred to the English word, "gang," Nathan asked why she did not like gangs. This exchange could have escalated into a confrontation, but the teacher wisely treated Nathan's question in a straightforward manner, devoid of emotion and argument, and as a sincere expression of interest in cultural differences. She did not let Nathan control the situation.

In many circles, defiance and noncompliance are called insubordination, which disrupts the flow of instructional activities and is often cited by teachers as a major behavior problem that is "contagious." How teachers handle noncompliance either makes or breaks a situation. If handled well, the teacher may feel confident and in control; if handled poorly, the teacher may feel that all is lost because the student is in control.

NONCOMPLIANCE EXAMPLE. *Teachers complain that Rob breaks minor rules regularly. Chewing gum is one minor rule that Rob chooses to ignore. He has an argument ready if caught chewing: It keeps his mouth busy so that he will not get into trouble. His teachers have chosen to ignore this behavior overtly and to record the incidents as examples of insubordination without confronting Rob. However, when Rob began to chew tobacco in school, teachers could not ignore this behavior any more than they could ignore the tobacco that was spit into a potato chip bag in his desk.*

Students with ODD press on others' nerve endings. They rankle and irritate, and many teachers speak of them as thorns in their sides. These students deliberately annoy other people.

ANNOYING OTHERS EXAMPLE. *Often Rob deliberately annoys classmates and adults. For example, he calls out in class a lot. While his answers may be correct, the shouting is annoying. He also calls out to other students and makes snide remarks about teachers. Further, Rob entertains his friends in class by verbally jousting with classmates about ideas, and he centers attention on himself by challenging teachers' ideas. Teachers often feel annoyed because Rob's issues are either matters of attitude and belief or are either-or positions when, really, a lot of grey area exists. For example, Rob is being raised as a fundamentalist Christian. He believes that his is the only true faith and denigrates all other religions. In history class the teacher has tried to represent all major religions fairly, teaching that belief is more a matter of faith than of fact. Rob has offered to bring in his list of Biblical facts. Also, he has not taken well to the term, "before the Christian era," or BCE, preferring the term "before Christ," or BC. In fact, the teacher has used the two terms interchangeably, but this has not satisfied Rob, who continues to argue about it. In his view, not only is the teacher wrong but he has the responsibility to correct her. With deliberation, and at every opportunity, he annoys the history teacher with reminders of his position. Rob, truly, is on a crusade, but it does not seem to have much to do with religion.*

Rob was being counseled by his resource teacher about the inappropriateness of his confrontational style. After listening to an explanation about how his behavior will call more attention to him than to his history teacher's rules or credibility, his response was, "Are you saying I'm insane and a pervert?" As his resource teacher's words were twisted, so can conventional rules be twisted by a student who is defiant and oppositional. A defiant defense, it seems, is to turn the tables.

BLAMING OTHERS EXAMPLES. *Rob blames his science teacher for his own misbehavior. A typical sequence of events is as follows. Rob leaves his seat with laboratory equipment in hand. Seated on the heater by the window he refuses to comply with Ms. S's direction to return to his lab table. Rob is told again to return to his seat. While ambling back to the lab table he is heard by students and teacher referring to Ms. S as a "bitch." Later, when asked about the incident Rob (1) denies that he made the remark and (2) blames Ms. S for singling him out. He claims that Ms. S needs to set standards for the whole class. Furthermore, Rob asserts, he has done his best to ignore Ms. S's inconsistencies and lack of knowledge about science.*
    Even one's strengths can be perverted for an oppositional cause. In English class one day, the teacher directed the class to read 20 pages of the novel

under study. Rob responded that he could not be expected to read that many pages because he has a learning disability. The teacher did not know what to say as she did not have a solid fact to dispute Rob's claim. In fact, as she later learned, Rob's educational evaluation had showed that his reading comprehension was about five grade levels above expectancy. Rob turned a strength into a weakness in order to make a case for opposing a direction. The ploy worked until the teacher was informed about his actual reading skills.

Nathan cannot accept responsibility for his own behavior. Time and again, Nathan blames someone else for his own behavior. Even when he admits to misbehavior, Nathan argues that "everyone does it," or "I'm not the only one."

Not only is there blaming; there may be an added layer of self-righteousness. Rather than simply rationalizing his behavior, the defiant student may also claim to have been victimized. To the teacher of such student this can be deeply frustrating. It is the ultimate twisted defense.

SELF-RIGHTEOUSNESS EXAMPLE. *During a disciplinary conference for seven incidents involving tardiness, chewing tobacco in classes, forgery of a parent's note regarding an absence, insolence with teachers, and failure to serve a detention, Rob had assorted excuses, rationalized his behavior, and portrayed himself as a victim. He claimed that his science teacher was "childish" and unfair with him, which gave him the right to talk rudely to her and   refuse to follow directions. In twelfth grade Rob blamed school staff for not securing SAT booklets in order to excuse his theft. When the school took him to court to recoup cost, Rob was determined to win the case based upon his victimization.*

A student who is touchy or easily annoyed has a short fuse. This is also a student who one day may not react to a situation, only to erupt another day. The ODD student intimidates with threat of an explosion and unpredictability. This attribute can be unsettling for teachers, who must juggle the needs of many students and on whom most students depend for peace and stability.

TOUCHINESS EXAMPLE. *In Rob's case, any criticism is likely to evoke an overreaction, and any reprimand likely will result in testiness. He often becomes verbally aggressive in response to perceived threats to his self-perception. He believes that he is smarter than his teachers and most of his peers. He wants to be in complete control and anything less is unsatisfactory. Hence, Rob is touchy about feedback that conflicts with his self-image and need for control.*

The student with ODD is often angry and resentful.

ANGER EXAMPLE. *Rob's intense anger toward adults, particularly, interferes with his academic progress. He is unable to set aside negative emotions so that he can be objective; his emotions spill over into his school work. For example, Rob did not like an English 9 assignment to review a movie. He thought the movie was stupid, and he resented having to spend time writing about it. Consequently, Rob's composition oozed with resentment, as shown by the following excerpt.*

Nothing was humorous or even slightly interesting. In fact, it was downright boring. My general thought of this movie was that it was: annoying, boring, stupid, and it stunk.

By definition, a student who is defiant and oppositional is confrontational. These students are at war with their parents, teachers, and some of their peers. A student with ODD often is spiteful and vindictive.

VINDICTIVENESS EXAMPLE. *Outside of school Rob has shown a thirst for revenge. His written description of a fun time at the beach shows his attitude about getting even in order to win, and about aggression:*

One day I was playing soccer with my team at the beach. We were playing a tournament. The last game of the tournament we were up 2-0, then the other team scored on a corner kick, so it was 2-1. A couple of minutes later they had a fast break, I came out to stop them. I drilled the player into the dirt but he still scored. The important thing is I hurt him. The next goal belonged to us. Then, with less than a minute to go they had a free kick, but I blocked it. Anyway, I had fun at the beach and I was glad we won the whole thing. I will remember it for a long time.

Likely, Rob will remember that his aggression was the turning point in the game; bad behavior justified by a good outcome. A bad offense is twisted into a good defense.

WHAT IT MEANS TO HAVE A CONDUCT DISORDER

Conduct disorder is associated with a greater probability of police contacts and school suspensions than ODD (Earls 1994). The student with ODD may simmer in anger and show passive-aggressive behavior, but the student with CD acts out his or her anger in violent ways. CD is not a subtle disorder.

Fifteen criteria are used to define conduct disorder (Earls 1994; *DSM IV* 1994). These criteria, with illustrative material, follow. The CD student (1) bullies, threatens, or intimidates others; (2) initiates physical fights; and (3) has used a weapon. In short, this student is violent.

VIOLENCE EXAMPLE. *Robbie, age 14, has a long history of dangerous behavior, beginning when he was about nine years old. About that time he went to live with his maternal grandmother because his father was imprisoned for attempted murder, and Robbie's mother thought she could only handle two small daughters. Robbie is a bully at his special school for middle school students with emotional and behavioral disorders. He pushes smaller and younger boys around, and he intimidates teachers. He frequently shoves peers against lockers and bats them with his hands. He makes many statements about how ugly a teacher is, how he is going to "get" a peer, and the like. He often starts fights, typically over petty matters. If he does not like the way another student looks at him, that is reason enough to strike the student.*

The CD student (4) has been verbally or physically cruel to people, and (5) has been physically cruel to animals.

CRUELTY EXAMPLE. *Robbie's school maintains a lot of animals: floppy-eared rabbits, salt water fish, a tarantula, some hamsters, and a white mouse. He is the only student at this school who has been barred from animal care, which is a chore that most of the students enjoy. On one occasion Robbie tried to flush a hamster down a toilet. His cruelty to people was evident when one student's mother died. Robbie told the grieving student, "Your mama was a 'ho' [whore] anyway."*

The CD student (6) has stolen while confronting a victim.

STEALING EXAMPLE. *Routinely, Robbie steals other students' lunch money. He threatens them with bodily harm if they do not give him money.*

The CD student (7) has forced someone into sexual activity.

FORCED SEXUAL ACTIVITY EXAMPLE. *While Robbie has not been apprehended for rape or sexual assault, word on the street is that he has indulged in physical pleasures despite some resistance from the females. Other students describe how Robbie prides himself on "getting it on" with numerous girls even if they do not want sex. His attitude seems to be that when he wants it, he gets it. Female students fear him.*

The CD student (8) has deliberately destroyed others' property.

DESTRUCTION OF PROPERTY EXAMPLE. *Robbie enjoys destroying peers' belongings. For example, one day a student brought a new music tape to school. The student obviously was proud of his tape, a newly released heavy metal track. Robbie feigned interest in the tape, saying he wanted to read the words on the jacket. After a quick, cursory look at the jacket Robbie took a pen and pulled the tape out of the cassette, damaging it beyond repair. Also, Robbie has taken large boards from the industrial arts classroom to break windows around the school. He seems to take pleasure in destroying property.*

The CD student (9) has deliberately engaged in setting fires to cause serious damage.

FIRE-SETTING EXAMPLES. *Robbie was near the fire extinguisher when there were several false alarms. He claimed innocence even though he was the only student out of class at those times. Once, after the fire trucks and firemen arrived Robbie was heard saying, "Those suckers."*

Brian, another student with CD, has a history of fire-setting. He especially likes to set fires in the middle of roadways, watching as cars swerve to avoid them. Like Robbie, Brian has been present at enough fires to merit a court judgment on the basis of circumstantial evidence. Brian repeatedly pleads innocent. (See Chapter 26 for more about Brian.)

The CD student (10) has broken into someone else's house, building, or car.

BREAK-IN EXAMPLE. *Evidence has been building concerning Robbie's activities in his neighborhood. Various houses have been burglarized, and there have been numerous incidents of car theft and joy-riding. Robbie's grandmother has been unable to account for him during those times. The police have questioned him and other boys in the neighborhood, and they are zeroing in on Robbie as a major suspect.*

The CD student (11) often lies to obtain goods or favors or to avoid obligations.

LYING EXAMPLE. *Robbie is a con artist. For example, he told another student that the points earned in the school's behavior management system may be given away. Robbie told one student that if he gave Robbie his points, Robbie would not hit him anymore. When it came time for the teacher to add up the weekly points and take the class to the school store to exchange for treats, Robbie claimed that he had a right to the other student's points. He became belligerent when the teacher tried to explain that the system did not work that way. Robbie told the teacher he would do "real damage to your fuckin' system" if he did not get all the points for which he had already bargained. He had no point count of his own, for Robbie did not buy into the system when it involved his own behavior.*

The CD student (12) has stolen items without confronting a victim.

STEALING WITHOUT CONFRONTATION EXAMPLE. *Many items around the school have been missing. Coincidentally, Robbie has usually been in the areas where the missing items had been. These items, singly, are unimportant, but, collectively, they add up in monetary value and school security. They include pencils, pens, and keys.*

The CD student (13) often stays out at night despite parental prohibitions, beginning before age 13.

STAYING OUT AT NIGHT EXAMPLE 1. *Often Robbie stays out late at night, a habit that began when he was about 11 years old. His grandmother cannot manage him. She has tried to stay awake in order to reprimand him, but typically she falls asleep around midnight. His grandmother has no real record of when Robbie comes home.*

The CD student (14) has run away from home overnight at least twice.

STAYING OUT ALL NIGHT EXAMPLE 2. *On several occasions Robbie has not slept in his bed, and his grandmother reported that she did not see him before she left for work. She has no idea where he goes or with whom he stays.*

The CD student (15) often is truant from school, beginning before age 13.

TRUANCY EXAMPLE. *Starting when he was 11 years old, Robbie has missed a lot of school. At first, he told his grandmother that he did not feel well, and she would allow him to stay home. Later, Robbie would leave the house but not catch the school bus, which resulted in unexcused absences.   Given his behaviors at school, teachers and students feel relieved when he is absent. So far, Robbie's absences have not exceeded the legal limit, but a truant officer has been assigned to the case.*

Despite the criteria that are listed for CD, adolescents with a conduct disorder are a varied group. And despite the established criteria, CD is still a controversial and unsettled classification. Its complex etiology involves biological, psychological, and social factors (Hendren 1991). The overlap with ODD makes CD that much more difficult to identify.

OVERLAP BETWEEN ODD AND CD

Based on the previous discussion of ODD and CD, it may readily be concluded that these two extreme disruptive behavior disorders have much in common despite some qualitative dissimilarities. Both show an unremitting display of annoying, destructive, dangerous, and even illegal behavior (Earls 1994).

The overlap between ODD and CD has been referred to as a "transitional state" as if they were dimensions of the same condition. Earls (1994) mentions the inclination to view ODD as a milder, developmentally related form of conduct disorder. Malmquist (1991), who concurs, suggests it is possible that ODD becomes CD when the challenging, angry, and provocative behavior spills over into antisocial acts.

Routh and Daugherty (1992) also view this as a continuum of disruptive behavior disorders. They cite one study where no significant differences were found between CD and ODD youngsters and note that maintaining ODD in the taxonomy is likely to create "diagnostic noise" whenever conduct disorder is studied. They propose a continuous dimensional approach to the definition of conduct disorder, rather than the discrete, categorical approach advocated in the APA's *DSMs*.

What seems to have emerged, then, is a picture of one broad diagnostic category that encompasses a spectrum from mild to severe forms. McMahon and Wells (1989) have suggested that given a CD's persistent pattern of conduct in which the basic rights of others and major age-appropriate societal norms or rules are violated, and given the ODD's pattern of negativistic, hostile, and defiant behavior without the more serious violations of others' rights that are seen in CD, the severity of either should be judged by the number of different behaviors in which the youngster engages. Egan (1991) adds that the violation of others' rights is less severe with ODD than CD; ODDs are more passive in their aggression. Malmquist (1991) offers an analogy that oppositional behavior is to passive-aggressive personality disorder as antisocial behavior is to antisocial personality disorder. Indeed, *DSM-IV* (1994) has changed the emphasis to severity level, specifying mild, moderate, and severe levels of conduct disorder, if not a continuum of ODD and CD together.

Loeber and Schmaling (1985) offer two subtypes of one disruptive behavior disorder. Their model, summarized in Table 9.1, divides the ODD and CD characteristics into two types, overt and covert aspects.

It has also been suggested that ODD may be the covert aspect, CD the overt aspect of a broad disruptive behavior disorder (McMahon and Wells 1989). Ooppositional-defiant youngsters tend to demonstrate their aggression by covert means in contrast to youngsters with conduct disorder (Egan 1991).

The empirically derived subtypes of conduct disorders may also have divergent developmental progressions, differing individual and familial correlates, and differing prognoses (McMahon and Wells 1989).

There are seven specific points of overlap between ODD and CD that are worth mentioning.

First, extremely disruptive behavior disorders are widely prevalent. They are the most frequently occurring child behavior disorders, with prevalence in the general population estimated at 3 to 4 percent (McMahon and Wells 1989).

Second, these disorders are serious and long-standing. It has been said that these disturbances remain stable once they appear in middle childhood, although the actual behaviors composing the diagnostic picture become increasingly diverse and serious as children move into the adolescent years (Earls

Table   9.1
Disruptive Behavior Disorders: Overt and Covert Characteristics

---

Overt Characteristics

Disobedient
Sassy
Blames others
Shows off
Irritable, cruel, fights
Loud, threatens
Temper tantrums
Attacks people, jealous, sulks
Impulsive
Argues, poor peer relations, teases
Demanding
Stubborn, moody
Screams
Hyperactive

Covert Characteristics

Disobedient
Negative
Lies
Steals
Sets fires
Bad companions, runs away, truant, in a gang
Alcohol/drug abuse

1994). Again, this point relates to an ODD-CD continuum.

Third, as mentioned in Chapter 7, insensitivity to others is at the core of these disorders.

Fourth, common to both CD and ODD is a diminished capacity to learn from experience.

Fifth, both ODD and CD show noncompliance (i.e., excessive disobedience to adults) as the keystone behavior.

Sixth, both ODD and CD are at-risk disorders; students who engage in either type of behavior are at risk for later difficulties (McMahon and Wells 1989).

Seventh, the very existence of both CD and ODD is sometimes questioned. For example, Earls (1994) notes that it is unclear if CD and ODD are disorders or temperamental problems. Much still eludes us even though the problems subsumed under the psychiatric definitions of ODD and CD have been a major preoccupation of the child mental health, educational, and juvenile justice systems for many decades.

DISRUPTIVE BEHAVIOR DISORDERS AND THE FEDERAL DEFINITION OF ED

Among the Individuals with Disabilities Education Act (IDEA) criteria for ED there is no specific reference to disruptive behavior disorder, or to conduct disorder and oppositional-defiant disorder. To qualify for special education a student must show an emotional disorder in addition to any social maladjustment or abnormal behavior pattern.

Rob's bad temper, argumentative nature, noncompliance, deliberate annoyance, blaming of others, touchiness, anger, and spitefulness constitute an abnormal behavior pattern. Probably no one would deny that he manifests a disruptive behavior disorder. However, Rob was found eligible for special education services in the ED area because there appeared to be issues of *depression, an inability to learn that cannot be explained by intellectual, sensory, or health factors,* and *an inability to build or maintain satisfactory interpersonal relationships with peers or teachers.* Additionally, reference was made to *inappropriate types of behavior or feelings under normal circumstances.* His affect, as teachers reported, is sad. He is bright and has no vision or hearing problems. He is a healthy, athletic boy. He has difficulty with relationships because he is argumentative and presents a know-it-all attitude; he does not follow adult directions readily; he does not accept responsibility for his own behavior; he is easily annoyed by petty issues and does not understand others' points of view; and he is vindictive. Rob certainly shows signs of impaired social and emotional functioning, all of which interfere with his school functioning.

Rob appears to have an oppositional-defiant disorder associated with disruptive behavior. Some educators have expressed surprise that he was found eligible for special education services in the ED area; they believe that Rob is simply a mean kid. His behavior certainly has not evoked sympathetic responses from teachers.

This brings up an important consideration. As Earls (1994) notes, the impact of a child's behavior on others, rather than personal distress of the individual child, is what gets the most attention and influences decision making. Egan (1991) noted that the inner experience of the ODD child is one of helplessness, neediness, and frustration, but any emotional problems such a student may have receive secondary, if any, consideration.

After an exasperating ninth-grade year, with numerous disciplinary referrals for noncompliant behaviors, Rob clearly needed a more restrictive placement. Following conferences between school staff and Rob's parents, as well as the parents' exploration of other programs, including a private school for troubled adolescents, the parents had Rob evaluated by a psychiatrist, who concluded that Rob might benefit from medication for depression.

Rob's resource teacher and parents agreed not to tell Rob's classroom teachers that he was taking the medication, Paxil. Feedback, it was agreed, would be more objective if teachers were unaware of the biochemical intervention. During the first week of the two-week medication trial, teacher reports were dramatically different, shedding more light on the contribution of emotional disturbance to Rob's behavior.

MEDICATION EFFECT EXAMPLE. *From Rob's LD basic skills teacher the comment was simply, "Rob has been fine."*

From Ms. S, with whom there had been ongoing problems, came a satisfactory rating for the week and comments such as "much better," "very polite," "improved, not argumentative; still asks a lot of questions, but arguing isn't a factor."

From Mrs. C, one of Rob's humanities teachers, came the word "wonderful." She reported on a situation that brought a totally unexpected response: When faced with taking a harder version of a test, the one that was expected of the nonLD students, Rob initially showed displeasure but shortly settled down. Mrs. C was able to explain to him that he was capable of the harder version and should trust her judgment. Rob was able to negotiate reasonably, he took the harder version of the test, and he earned a high score.

From Rob's geometry teacher came the comments, "He's taken a sudden interest in making things up" and "Behavior is no problem."

The efficacy of a biochemical intervention suggests, in Rob's case, that his oppositionality may be related at least partially to depression. Indeed, Rob's behavior typically had been accompanied by nonverbal indicators of unhappiness (a sad face, dull eyes, sagging posture, and a sluggish gait) and lack of pleasure in misbehavior. While Robbie also has been diagnosed with depression, he enjoys his misbehavior.

The need to consider the possibility of emotional disorder in noncompliant youngsters is also addressed in Chapter 25, which focuses on the pros and cons of including social maladjustment in the definition of ED. Relevant issues are also discussed in Chapter 26 concerning interrelated disorders.

SUGGESTED EDUCATIONAL STRATEGIES

A student with a disruptive behavior disorder needs to learn to be less argumentative, to temper his or her feelings, to cooperate with others, and to comply with rules. Strategies that would be effective include those that prevent and respond to problems. Suggested educational strategies also relate to needs for external control and appropriate engagement.

Some suggested educational strategies are the following.

1.   Even though many noncompliant students may not readily buy into behavior management systems, try to reward them when they are compliant.

2.   Establish consequences for misbehavior and follow through consistently. This cannot be overemphasized because these students typically push the envelope and are quick to point out inconsistencies and unfairness. As the principal of a public day school for ED adolescents said, "Start out like we can hold out."

3.   Structure cooperative activities where students monitor one another. Peer pressure is highly effective with students who defy and constantly test adult authority.

4.   Conduct all disciplinary feedback in private so that the student can save face with peers.

5.   Involve the student in identifying solutions to problems so that the student is empowered and cannot claim that a solution was imposed on him or her arbitrarily.

6.   Provide logical consequences to teach the reality of the social order and to show that the rules do not stem only from the authority figure.

7.   Do not back the student into a corner. Provide choices that are realistic, logical, and clear. When students can choose instead of being told what to do, they react less negatively toward adults and academic requirements.

8.   Do not argue. Present instructions, choices, or whatever, with clear expectations for time and conditions, and move away. Hovering over the student will probably foster resentment and resistance. Give the student space to make up his or her mind and appear that he or she is doing so independently and willingly.

9.   Build a personal relationship to enhance your power of persuasion.

10.   Try alternative strategies before seeking outside help. This shows the student that the adult has the authority and power to deal with him or her.

11.   Display classroom rules.

12.   Give a weekly progress report that can be used at home or at school. This is good for behavioral or performance contracts.

13.   Allow the student to do assignments in different ways. Communicate that the issue is not if he or she will do the assignment but how (i.e., choice of method).

14.   Use group pressure to redirect the student. For example, "Everyone except Jennifer has their book out."

15.   The student may curse in anger. Moralizing or lecturing about proper language is usually ineffective. Respond to the inappropriateness of the behavior by responding to the feeling or need that underlies it. One tactic is to defuse the anger with humor or a smile. The student may curse for shock value, and the adult can stop the behavior by not responding in kind. Do not, in effect, give the student what his or her behavior suggests he wants. When a student curses out of frustration, the appropriate response is to acknowledge the difficulty of the task and to offer help. At another time, the teacher might suggest alternative ways to express anger. The immediate need is to reduce tension. Also, take the time to listen to the student without moralizing or making value judgments.

16.   Many students who misbehave say that a calm teacher helps them stay calm.

17.   Focus on specific behaviors when rewarding or disciplining, and catch the student complying. With a framework of positive attention to compliant behavior, the student will have less reason to shift responsibility to others when he or she misbehaves. An adult who tries to find ways in which the student is complying will also be less likely to be targeted for revenge.

18.   Treat the student at his or her age level. Expect the student to make his or her own decisions as much as possible.

19.   Make rules that are not for the adult's convenience or comfort but for the student's welfare. For example, rather than rules about profanity, gum chewing, tardiness, talking, and movement, focus on rules that help the students interact and learn.

20.   Logically relate punishment to misdeeds. For example, a student might be taken before a group of peers to gain understanding of a problem and possible solutions. One logical solution might be to give a failing grade, rather than detention, for incomplete assignments.

21.   Confront the student about misbehavior in a low-key, forthright manner that serves to inform rather than incite.

22.   Therapists, tutors, and counselors should work cooperatively with school staff. If the student is exposed to different approaches, he or she will use the loopholes as further justification for misbehavior. As these students can be very manipulative, a consistent approach, with differences worked out away from the student, is best.

23.   A stimulus-based strategy is interspersal of high probability tasks, which involves embedding stimuli associated with high rates of problem behavior with stimuli associated with low rates. For example, present a direction that the student is likely to follow just before the direction that is likely to be followed by a maladaptive response. The probability is good that the student will comply with the second command.

24. Teach a sense of responsibility so that the student can develop self-discipline.

25. Deemphasize conformity so that the student might freely explore alternative solutions to problems in an atmosphere of constructive disagreement. Such an environment reduces disruptiveness and noncompliance.

26. Handle early difficulties by attempting to find interesting and meaningful activities and by showing friendliness and caring. This approach can defuse potential resistance.

27. Have a conference with the student to explore his or her interests and to suggest better use of time. Suggest alternatives to disruptive behavior or yearly goals. Use a nonjudgmental, nonthreatening tone. The optimal time to hold this conference is when the student is behaving appropriately. Direct the student to evaluate the negative effects of his or her own behavior. If these steps are unsuccessful, hold class discussions in which peers can suggest ways to help the student behave appropriately. (The student should be informed of this step in advance.) If these efforts still are not successful, referral to a trustworthy person outside class could be made to have a cordial but informative conference. At that time the student should be told that tolerance for the behavior is decreasing, and a change plan should be developed. The adult in charge of discipline should also see the student, set and clarify behavioral limits, and draw up a contract outlining the changes to be made. The student then should sign the contract, and copies should be given to the student and teacher. Finally, the student should be told that the parents will possibly be involved.

28. If in-school efforts do not work, suspension is an option. Parents should be asked to ensure that the student remains at home and does assigned academic work. After returning to school, a reentry conference should be held with the student, teacher, and school disciplinarian, and the student should be asked to commit to change. A new behavior contract should be drawn up and signed. Expulsion should be discussed as a possible outcome for chronic disruptiveness, and the student should be reminded that outcome is up to him or her. Continued suspensions may lead to a change of placement through an individualized education plan (IEP).

29. If expulsion becomes necessary, an alternate educational plan must be developed, and all procedural steps must be followed per IDEA discipline regulations, including a manifestation review to determine if the student's disability caused the rule-breaking, if he or she was receiving appropriate programming, and if a behavioral plan had been developed and followed to address his or her needs.

30. The *transactional analysis* (TA) framework can be effective with the defiant and repetitively challenging student. Long in the literature (e.g., Kravas and Kravas 1974), TA offers teachers and other change agents a method of observing and responding to student behaviors. The adult, after closely observing the student, can identify which ego state (Parent, Child, or Adult) the student is using to express himself. If the student too often shows behavior representing one of these

states, he or she can be helped to show behavior from other ego states. For example, when the adult responds to a student's misbehavior with Adult controlling or judgmental messages (e.g., "Don't ever talk to me that way, young man"), the adult may unwittingly reinforce the student's childish behavior. An alternative response is to appeal to a more objective part of the student's personality (i.e., his Adult ego state: "This is obviously important to you. Let's talk about it in private"). Try to hook the student into a rational discussion of issues; appeal to the Adult in him or her, moving away from the Child's emotions and impulses. TA is useful in sensitive situations in which teachers and students view things differently and in which authoritarian directives by teachers appear to have harmful consequences.

31.   When a student has temper outbursts, a first step is to help the student describe the thoughts, feelings, and bodily sensations he or she experienced just before the outburst. Later, role-playing can help the student understand the conflict and try out calm behaviors.

32.   Videotaping students during typical incidents involving noncompliance can be an effective tool. Students often are shocked to see their aggressive body language and provocative attitude. This method also helps cut denial and shifting of blame onto others.

33.   Reinforce the student for working through his or her difficulties with others without resorting to retributional behavior.

34.   Provide positive role models who do not use retributional behavior to problem solve. These models can be peers or adults. If the student's parents tend to use retributional methods, it is helpful for the student to see school staff solving problems in a positive way.

35.   Do not accept excuses for irresponsible behavior.

36.   Emphasize individual success or progress rather than winning or "beating" other students.

37.   Do not leave a lot of unstructured time for the student.

38.   Do not allow the student to be unsupervised anywhere.

39.   Treat the student with respect. Talk in an objective manner at all times. Avoid accusatory or authoritarian language. Instead, use "I" messages (e.g., "I expect") rather than "you" messages (e.g, "You, move now!").

40.   The student may deny any wrongdoing to avoid embarrassment and negative consequences. When the student's version of what occurred differs from what was witnessed, describe both versions to the student for his or her reference without making accusations. (He or she may stop listening during a direct confrontation.) Most important, the student should be helped to calm down in order to think about the behavior and its consequences.

41. Ensure that consequences for improper behavior do not stigmatize the student. Nonpunitive consequences might include restitution, for example, replacement of stolen items or cleaning up spray-tagged lockers.

42. Encourage all students to monitor their belongings. Do not provide temptations.

43. Introduce and maintain positive, consistent class management that incorporates an opportunity to think through consequences before choices are made.

44. Deal with the student's refusal to perform an assignment in such a way that the rest of the group will not be exposed to contagion; for example, refrain from arguing with the student, place the student at a carrel or other quiet place to work, remove him or her from the group or the classroom.

45. Teach the student to recognize when he or she is becoming upset or angry and suggest ways, other than cursing or engaging in behavioral outbursts, to express his or her feelings.

46. Do not allow the student to participate in a situation unless he or she can demonstrate self-control.

47. Provide the student with a place to go when he or she gets upset or angry (e.g., a time-out room).

48. Teach the student to verbalize feelings before losing control (e.g., "The work is too hard" or "Please leave me alone, you're annoying me").

49. Monitor the behavior of other students to ensure they are not teasing or stimulating the student to become upset or angry. Prevent peers from provoking the student into reactive, verbal responses.

50. Teach the student ways to deal with conflictual situations (e.g., reasoning, walking away, asking an adult to intervene).

51. Look for warning signs (e.g., arguing, loud voice) that the student is getting upset or angry and intervene to change the activity.

52. Allow natural consequences to occur as a result of the student's cursing or outbursts (e.g., not being able to participate inspecial activities, being removed from the situation, social rejection by peers who do not behave that way).

53. Offer the student opportunities for creative self-expression: writing, sculpting, drawing, acting, and so on. Do not emphasize grading in these activities.

54. Teach the student to respect others' belongings by respecting his

or her belongings. For example, do not go into the student's desk without his or her permission.

55.   Make certain the student has the necessary school supplies. If the student says he or she cannot afford them, work out a deal whereby he or she can "buy" supplies by points earned for appropriate behavior. Or work with the student's family to establish ways in which the student can earn the items he or she needs for school.

56.   Deal with stolen belongings privately rather than publicly.

10

Overview:
Eating Disorders

Birth, growth, reproduction, death. They are the outlines of life. But what rounds it and gives it resonance is the way it tastes. (Richman 1995, p. C5)

Food is life, and we need it. We take it for granted, and we associate it with special events. When we are old, feel insecure, or are ill, it is to "comfort foods" that we turn. In hard times, food assures us that the world still has color, taste, and smell and always will no matter how bad things get.

     Two typical adolescents share memories about food. First, Stephen's recollection, then Megin's.

When I was very little, my brother and I used to eat hard-boiled eggs. The eggs that we didn't eat, we would throw at each other. I miss those times.

My father and I don't get to do too many things without the rest of the family. But a while ago, he took me to a Mets game. And being with my Dad (even watching a sport I wasn't very fond of) made the whole day special. Everything about it (the ballpark hot dogs, the mustard, an ice cream bar that was like a sundae on a stick) is still sharp in my mind, still special.

     While food is the staff of life for some individuals, for others it is a problem. Some people may want too little or too much of it. They may overindulge in particular food preferences or ingest unnatural substances. Some people eat too little. They may fear food will fatten them beyond a standard of beauty. For others, food is a substitute for parental attention and affection.

SUBSTITUTING FOOD FOR ATTENTION EXAMPLE. *As the mother of this 19-year-old readily admits, food is Lisa's substitute for attention and affection. Consequently, Lisa is overweight. Try as she might to lose weight by taking classes in dance and the martial arts, Lisa thinks about food constantly. One school day Lisa had a choice: to attend a birthday party for one of the teachers or to remain with her social skills group. While Lisa barely knew the celebrating teacher, she opted for the party. Subsequently, Mr. H, her government teacher, criticized her for failing to check in with him at the end of the period for catch-up work. She lied that she had not attended the party. Lisa became very upset and started to cry when confronted with the truth, evident by cake crumbs on her lip. Mr. H reminded her that he had agreed to release her for weekly group meetings, not for parties. Lisa's rational judgment had been overriden by her desire for party food, especially on a day when she had only had a Slim Fast and bottle of mineral water for lunch.*

Food is not only central to biological life; it is essential to psychological life as well. Each person has a self-image that relates closely to eating habits. When an individual has a healthy outlook on life, food usually is taken for granted and is part of an orderly life routine. On the other hand, when an individual has an unhealthy outlook on life, food may become excessively important and the resultant behavior disorderly. For example, many people overeat when they are unhappy.

Eating disorders among adolescents are some of the most pressing health concerns (Feldman and Elliott 1990). Common eating disorders among this group include anorexia nervosa, bulimia nervosa, and obesity. Anorexia is a disorder characterized by extreme weight loss caused by a refusal to eat; bulimia is characterized as a combination of gorging and purging food; and obesity involves chronic overeating and extreme weight gain (assuming there is no organic problem over which the individual has no control).

These eating disorders are serious even though their incidence rates are not high. *Anorexia nervosa*, the focus of Chapter 11, is primarily an adolescent phenomenon. Relatively rare, it has an estimated incidence ranging from 0.5 percent among females aged 12 to 18 years (Herzog and Copeland 1985) to 1 percent among girls between the ages of 16 and 18 (Crisp et al. 1977). Even at the U.S. Naval Academy, anorexia has become an issue, and the Academy has had to face this "quiet problem"; according to Argetsinger (1995), two female midshipmen have been hospitalized for anorexia. Anorexia is probably increasing in frequency, though moderate and severe forms remain uncommon (Graham 1991). Bulimia and obesity are more common than anorexia. *Bulimia* is more common in adults (Russell 1985), but 5 to 18 percent of the 12- to 18-year-old female population are afflicted with it (Herzog and Copeland 1985). An estimated 15 percent of adolescents show *obesity* (Poissonet, La Valle, and Burdi 1988).

All three of these eating disorders are serious. Anorexia and bulimia may, in a relatively short period of time, result in severe health problems and even death. About 5 percent of anorexics who do not recover develop bulimia (Russell 1985). Anorexia, according to some experts, is one of the few psychiatric disorders that can follow an unremitting course resulting in death

(Brooks-Gunn and Reiter 1990); it is debilitating and dangerous, with a mortality rate of 10 to 15 percent (Palla and Litt 1988). Obesity, on the other hand, is not associated with extreme health problems in the short run, but it may result in serious health problems in the long run. As Millstein and Litt (1990) note, with the exception of morbid obesity, early death caused by complications associated with obesity, there are no known adverse medical consequences of adolescent obesity. The likelihood of continuation into adulthood, however, makes obesity a hazard to future health.

Eating disorders are culture bound. Leon and Dinklage (1983) note that severe eating disorders, especially anorexia and bulimia, are related to societal affluence. In countries where food is scarce, most people do not have the luxury of overeating or gaining attention through refusing to eat. In India, for example, there is a scarcity of food and a commensurately low incidence of anorexia. Affluent countries, such as the United States, show high incidence of both obesity and anorexia. Eating disorders are also strongly related to gender. Most individuals with eating disorders are female, although bulimia is distributed somewhat more equally between males and females. Anorexia is uncommon among males; females represent from 90 to 95 percent of all cases (Brooks-Gunn and Reiter 1990; Millstein and Litt 1990; Russell 1985; Steinhausen 1994). Because adolescent depression is also more likely to occur among girls than boys (Brooks-Gunn and Reiter 1990), obesity (often linked to depression) is more likely to be found among female adolescents.

AN INCREASE IN EATING DISORDERS

Eating disorders have increased since the early 1980s. This increase may be related to a growing emphasis on thinness as the ideal body image. Eating disorders also may be precipitated by feelings concerning body changes that occur during adolescence (Millstein and Litt 1990), with the weight change (upward or downward) resulting from a combination of emotional condition and perception of ideal physical image. Obesity, for example, may be considered self-punishment for not meeting the ideal image. The incident at the Naval Academy may have been caused by a military atmosphere that places a strong emphasis on physical fitness and dismisses students if they do not meet weight qualifications, as well as the fact that prestigious colleges attract at-risk students who are driven to perfection and indulge in rigid self-discipline (Argetsinger 1995).

The increase in eating disorders among youths may be caused by modern stressors such as fragmented families, violence, and pressure for high academic grades and achievement scores. The most common form of adolescent obesity may result from chronic overeating among depressed, passive individuals with low self-esteem, further aggravated by stress (Mellin 1983). Also, as Erickson (1978) points out, obesity can result from stressors such as the death of parents or siblings, birth of a sibling, parental separation, personal failures, and illness.

11

Anorexia Nervosa

Are they men eating reflections of themselves?
Wallace Stevens

While "anorexia" means, literally, loss of appetite, anorexics do not report absence of hunger. The problem is that they refuse to eat. It is, thus, a misconception that anorexics lose their appetites.

Anorexia, though, is not simply a refusal to eat. A much more complex problem, it encompasses a refusal to maintain body weight, an intense fear of gaining weight, and a distorted image of one's body weight, size, or shape (*DSM-IV* 1994). In order to reach their desired weight, anorexics may diet, avoid meals, induce vomiting, use laxatives and diuretics, or exercise excessively (Steinhausen 1994).

Among adolescents, anorexia nervosa (AN) is a significant, self-induced weight loss, a body image distortion, and an endocrine disorder involving the hypothalamic-pituitary-gonadal axis resulting in delayed menarche or secondary amenorrhea (World Health Organization, ICD-10, 1990). It is also a specific psychopathology with behavioral symptoms (Russell 1985; Steinhausen 1994).

Refusal to eat and the associated psychopathology that drive the anorexic toward self-injurious behavior render its victim a "pitiable ruin" (Schwartz and Johnson 1981, p. 287). Sara's words during her hospitalization for AN attest to a pitiable condition.

I think about killing myself, but I would not do it. I feel like crying many days. I worry that bad things will happen to me. Things bother me many times. I do not like being with people many times. It is hard to make up my mind about things. I have trouble sleeping many nights. I am tired many days. I feel alone many times.

PITIABLE CONDITION EXAMPLE. *Sara also experienced auditory and visual hallucinations, and when she slept she had nightmares about "being hurt in different ways. " She was severely depressed, had difficulty concentrating, and lost interest in people. She thought about suicide and tried to hurt herself, once burning herself with a curling iron. She said that a voice told her to do so. She fought with peers. She had headaches and stomachaches, and she became a hypochondriac, complaining so frequently of illness that she missed 39 days of school during sixth grade. Altogether, Sara's life, night and day, was hellish. There was no peace of mind, little sleep to heal, and no emotional calm.*

AN is not simply a behavioral disorder; it is a complex disorder that represents behavioral and emotional concerns as well as medical complications. It has been categorized by some professionals as a psychophysiological, or psychosomatic, disorder, a physical condition in which psychological factors are known or presumed to play a causal or at least contributory role. A distinct feature of this psychosomatic disorder isthat there is actual damage to the body.

The disorder is distinguished by four criteria (*DSM-IV* 1994). These follow with illustrative case material.

The first criterion relates to the refusal to maintain body weight at or above a minimally normal weight for one's age and height. Most studies of AN cite a criterion of at least 25 percent loss of original body weight. By this standard, the statistically normal female, who is 5'5" tall at age 16, should weigh 110 pounds and would meet this criterion if her weight fell to 82 pounds or less.

WEIGHT LOSS EXAMPLE. *By the time Sara was 11 years old emotional turmoil led to a diagnosis of AN following a weight loss of 35 pounds.*

The second criterion relates to an intense fear of gaining weight or becoming fat, even though underweight.

FEAR OF GAINING WEIGHT EXAMPLE. *When Sara was hospitalized with AN during sixth grade, she reported seeing "big hairy ugly" images of herself and a dead body in her room.*

The third criterion relates to the disturbance in the way in which one's body weight or shape is experienced, undue influence of body weight or shape on self-evaluation, or denial of the seriousness of the current low body weight.

BODY IMAGE EXAMPLE. *Sara does not want to be treated differently because she lost some weight. Having experienced hospitalization and intense psychotherapy, she wants nothing further to do with special help. Unwilling to be singled out, she does not want to leave her friends even for one period during the school week to meet with her resource teacher. When offered the opportunity to join an all-girl, seventh-grade support group led by the school's social worker and a guidance counselor (both females), Sara refused. Resistance persisted, even when her mother told her that if Sara did not participate in the support group she would have to resume private therapy. Sara believes that she is doing fine. She does not want to talk about anything associated with eating or her weight.*

Further, her self-image is distorted. She struggles with body image issues. Her ideal image has curly, long hair, beautiful features, and a curvaceous body. Actually, Sara is developing into that image despite her perception that she is ugly and fat. Indeed, her perception is everything; she sees a fat body and eats according to what she sees.

The fourth criterion relates to an absence of at least three consecutive menstrual cycles in post-menarcheal females.

MENSTRUAL CYCLE EXAMPLE. *Sara had not begun to menstruate when she evidenced signs of AN.*

Complementing the *DSM-IV* criteria are those of Feighner (1972): a distorted attitude toward eating food or weight that overrides hunger, reassurances, and threats; an absence of medical illness to account for the weight loss; no other known psychiatric disorder; and at least two of the following: amenorrhea, lanugo (downy hair), bradycardia, episodes of bulimia or vomiting (self-induced or otherwise).

AN ISSUE OF CONTROL

One of the key attributes of AN is a feeling that others are responsible for one's emotions and actions. For example, when trauma occurs, one reaction is to feel victimized by someone or something that had control. Sara, for example, was traumatized sexually and feels powerless much of the time. Bruch (1966) notes that the anorexic does not believe that her eating habits are her responsibility; outside forces make her eat this way. Strict dieting, in this view, is one way to control an otherwise uncontrollable life.

The anorexic's control, furthermore, is rigid, fueled by a perceptual disturbance. Not only are physical dimensions distorted; sensations of hunger and satisfaction are misperceived. Essentially, the anorexic substitutes external signals for internal ones. In other words, rather than eating when hunger is felt, the anorexic may sit down with the family but eat strictly controlled amounts. Perception, not bodily sensations of hunger, controls eating behavior.

Consequently, anorexics become defensive. Because they deny their bodily sensations and refuse to eat adequately, they must develop explanations and excuses. They become impervious to others' opinions and influence. Only their own perceptions matter to them.

This attempt to overcontrol a part of one's functioning is what makes AN an internalizing disorder. The anorexic tries to impose order and control by disorderly means, going to great lengths to self-delude and cover up a serious problem. Eventually the disorder causes the anorexic to try to control everything related to food intake. Because food is so basic an issue, eating becomes a major bone of contention.

NOT A MODERN PHENOMENON

Some professionals contend that AN is an outcome of a modern cultural obsession with thinness. Others maintain that AN has been with us for a very long time. In fact, both views are based upon fact.

Eating disorders, particularly AN, have been evident since early times. Various accounts of asceticism, starvation, and emaciation in young women have come to us from the Middle Ages. The first published account of classical AN, with the symptoms that are recognized in the modern era, is a 1694 paper written by Richard Morton. This paper described an 18-year-old girl and a 16-year-old boy who developed a condition Morton referred to as "nervous atrophy."

Before use of the term AN the condition may have been called "phthisis," which refers to the wasting and emaciation characteristic of tuberculoisis. Long before anything was known about the tubercle bacillus, phthisis was attributed to grief, fear, too much thinking, and other "passions of the mind." Gull, lecturing about phthisis in 1868 at Oxford University (Steinberg 1983), was the first to use the term "anorexia nervosa." AN, then, has been described for centuries in different societies and cultures.

Those who believe that AN is a modern phenomenon point to a pervasive obsession with personal appearance, shape, and thinness. Vincent, writing about the ballet world and its obsession with weight, commented, "If obsession with fat is a national pastime, then surely dancers are Olympic contenders" (1979, p. 6). It may be extreme to use one small group to define a cultural phenomenon, but the phenomenon is nonetheless real. "By today's standards, Venus is a tad chunky, and a well-intentioned friend might even advise her to enroll at Weight Watchers" (Vincent 1979, p. 10).

The premodern and modern eras are replete with examples of faddish attitudes about weight. For example, sixteenth-century Frenchwomen swallowed sand in order to ruin their stomachs and acquire a pale complexion (Vincent 1979). At the beginning of the twentieth century, a buxom woman was the ideal. In the 1920s flat chests and lean, angular looks were the ideal. Then, by the 1940s, a well-fed look matched the post-World War II rationing era and became the sign of attractiveness. When Twiggy was the rage of the 1960s, at 5'7" and 92 pounds, she represented yet another body ideal in a chain of twentieth-century ideals.

Co-existing cultures provide a perspective on AN throughout history. Concurrent with Western modern industrialized and technologically advanced societies are agrarian cultures that extol obesity. Overfed women in some cultures represent the indolent, well-to-do class. In some African cultures, brides-to-be reside in special houses for weeks or years to fatten themselves for matrimony (Vincent 1979).

Overall, the pattern has been toward a leaner standard of beauty. The

1990s in the United States have been notable for a fitness movement and a drive to be thin. There is evidence that the prevalence of AN has been increasing (Bemis 1978; Leon and Dinklage 1983).

SOME THEORIES

Subtle emergence. While the incidence of AN is dramatic and seems to be increasing, AN development in individual cases is more subtle. The anorexic's early development has been described as relatively trouble free. Parents often describe their anorexic daughters as having been even-tempered, docile, and affectionate in their early years. There may have been food fads, excessive tidiness, or difficulty in forming friendships, but nothing dramatic or alarming. Against this background AN may appear quite suddenly. One day the girl appears to be thinner. Amenorrhea may be the first symptom to precede weight loss (Russell 1985).

Many causes have been cited for AN. There are four theories about the psychological progression of anorexia. These theories relate to life changes that may contribute to the development of this disorder. Contextual factors are multiple and have received most attention in the evaluation of AN. These theories involve family dynamics, sexual peculiarities, stress, and psychodynamics.

Family dynamics. Waller, Kaufman, and Deutsch (1975) point to family dynamics, particularly open conflict between mother and daughter, in the development of AN. The onset may occur when the psychological significance of relationships must be faced and adjustments are required, as when the daughter is leaving home to attend college. There may be an eating disorder in the family, with individual histories of obesity and overeating, as well as a family history of psychosis or neurosis, especially involving eating issues.

Sexual peculiarities. In the evolution of AN, sexual aberrations have been reported. Lack of sexual desire and impotence are notable.

Stress. Interpersonal stress and trauma have also been associated with AN. As far back as 1954, Kay and Leigh estimated that two-thirds of their patients experienced major changes in interpersonal relationships prior to the onset of AN. Other specific psychological precipitates in a sample of 140 anorexics were a death or a serious illness in the family, personal illness, and failure at work or school (Dally 1969).

The trauma of sexual abuse probably precipitated Sara's AN. However, other factors were contributory.

CAUSES OF ANOREXIA EXAMPLE. *Sara's home life is stressful. Her parents divorced when she was seven years old, and her mother remarried when Sara was nine. Sara's relationship with her stepfather is confrontational. She wants to control their relationship. She likes her stepfather but feels that he is intrusive. Not surprisingly, the stepfather lacks self-confidence in his parenting role. Often, he feels like an outsider. Sara, her mother, and her younger bro-*

ther were an intact family before the stepfather's arrival. Sara also feels rejected by her biological father, who limits his contact with her.

Additionally, Sara was sexually abused at age five and experienced physical trauma when she was in sixth grade. She was threatened by a female student, who followed her home one day, brandishing a knife. The girl entered Sara's home on two occasions.

Finally, Sara attended five different schools between preschool and sixth grade. Even though all schools were in the same county, it meant change and adjustment. No sooner did Sara make friends and begin to feel comfortable when she had to change schools.

Psychodynamic theory. Among the theories of psychogenesis are psychodynamic explanations, which focus on unconscious wishes and fears. Frequently described among AN cases is an unconscious wish to reject the possibility of pregnancy or to reject the idea of growing up. This theory asserts that AN represents an unconscious desire to retreat from adolescent maturing and development of secondary sexual characteristics. There also may be an unconscious desire to avoid threatening sexual conflicts. Dally (1969) found that sexual conflict often precedes the onset of AN.

Other psychodynamicists refer to a morbid fear of fatness (Goldbloom and Garfinkel 1989) or a history of obesity associated with taunting and social failure. Some, too, ascribe a symbolic search for personal mastery along with a fear of failure and need for empowerment.

Another psychological explanation is that AN is a form of hysteria that develops when there is inconsistency between action or desire and word (Proctor 1958). For example, when a youngster is exposed to religious sermons that emphasize damnation for engaging in sexual behavior, there may be conflict with a strong desire to be sexually active. This explanation of hysteria relates to Sara's situation: physical intrusion and hurt perpetrated by a familiar adult.

SEXUAL ABUSE EXAMPLE. *Sara's sexual abuse was by a trusted adult. The molester, a friend's father, told Sara that he was a doctor whom her mother had asked to physically examine her. This happened several times and included touching and penetration. Sara said, "He told me if I told anyone he would hurt me." The perpetrator also criticized Sara's weight.*

Learning and AN. Learning theories focus on the acquisition of behaviors to explain AN. These theories (e.g., Gold et al. 1980) emphasize environmental factors that maintain the anorexic's behavior, specifically events that reinforce the anorexic's dieting and related behavior. For example, an anorexic mother may encourage and be a role model for her daughter's spindly frame and fashionable thinness. There may also be secondary gains from attention and sympathy.

Organic Factors. Despite the persuasiveness of psychogenesis or learning as explanations for the disorder, professionals cannot avoid citing organic issues because of the effect of food refusal on the body and because the body is its venue; organic theories address issues of affect or effect, and both. Biologically oriented theorists (e.g., Gold et al. 1980) emphasize such possibilities as hypothalmic dysfunction. Others such as Waller, Kaufman, and Deutsch (1975) note the common features of weight loss, constipation, weakness, exhaustion, amenorrhea, emaciation, increased hair over the body, and loss of head hair.

Biochemistry may play a role in the genesis of AN. Researchers at the National Institute of Mental Health (NIMH) found that young women suffering from AN had elevated levels of the hormone vasopressin. They concluded that a behavioral problem may change to a biochemical problem when the anorexic's weight drops below a critical level, which triggers a biological reaction. Among 16 anorexics in one study, the vasopressin levels were above normal, which led to an imbalance in fluids (*New York Times* 1983). Vincent adds: "Knowing that such a high percentage of body weight is water, one may easily appreciate that rapid weight fluctuations are always the result of fluid shifts and have nothing to do with the fate of fat" (1979, p. 46).

When women experience a considerable weight loss, levels of hormonal secretions also may be suppressed. The most obvious manifestation of such a fall in hormone level is amenhorrhea and impaired fertility (Warren 1985). Most endocrine and metabolic changes probably are secondary to starvation, but there is evidence for primary neurochemical abnormality (Herzog and Copeland 1985). Hormones, then, may play an important part in the genesis of AN.

HORMONAL LINK EXAMPLE. *Not only did Sara achieve developmental milestones early, but she had more female hormones than usual, which resulted in "plumped out" breasts when she was an infant. She developed into a very attractive young woman. By the time she was 13 years old, following hospitalization and therapy for AN, she was physically well developed and very pretty, with warm brown eyes, high cheekbones, and long, wavy hair the color of chestnut with natural blond streaks. She needed no make-up, but when she used cosmetics she looked glamorous, her appearance belying her young age.*

Despite much research on AN in the past 25 years, uncertainty remains about its fundamental cause. This is apparent in the aforementioned theories. It is probable that diverse psychosocial and biological factors interact. This disorder, then, appears to involve a complexity of psychological and somatic elements, a blend of psychological and organic issues.

SOME FACTS

Demographics. The demographics of AN involve socioeconomics, gender, age, country of origin, affiliation, and racial group. Steinberg (1983) notes that AN appears to be related to higher socioeconomic status.

Racially, there is a curious fact: AN is virtually limited to patients of white racial origin. This has been confirmed by U.S. and British clinicians (Russell 1985).

In terms of country of origin, AN is extremely rare in developing countries. Although AN is known worldwide, it is found primarily in Europe, Australia, and North America. As indicated earlier, it seems to be related to social circumstances where availability of food is not a problem. The incidence is increasing in the United Kingdom, particularly among the private school population (Steinberg 1983).

As for gender, AN is primarily a disorder of females. The ratio of females to males has been found to be about 10:1 (Steinberg 1983).

Finally, affiliation appears to be an important demographic consideration. Within the countries where AN is found, it is common in groups that are selected for thinness. Ballet dancers and models, for example, are ripe for AN.

Onset. AN appears to be largely a disorder of adolescence and young adulthood; most cases occur between the ages of 16 and 20. In Halmi's (1974) research, only 8 percent of the cases showed onset before 10 years, which makes Sara's case relatively rare.

Prevalence. According to the American Anorexia/Bulimia Association, 1 percent of teenage girls suffer from AN, and as many as 20 percent of college women have bulimia symptoms. Herzog and Copeland (1985) reported in the *New England Journal of Medicine* that about 0.5 percent of females between 12 and 18 develop AN.

Progression and prognosis. This self-imposed starvation evolves over time. The worst part of AN typically occurs over a two- to three-year period. AN usually starts with a benign diet and evolves into shifting weight goals and an escalating sense of being overweight even as weight loss occurs. Abstention from high-calorie foods develops into global food aversion. In the beginning of the dieting process there is selective food refusal, and in the critical later stage food refusal is pervasive.

Numerous attempts have been made to collect follow-up data on anorexics. Some individuals completely recover from AN, but it is often a chronic disorder characterized by periodic remissions and relapses (Schwartz and Johnson 1981). Some anorexics die from the disorder or from its complications (Van Buskirk 1977). According to Crisp and colleagues (1977), the overall recovery rate is between 40 and 60 percent. Graham (1991) concluded that one-third of anorexics fully recover after comprehensive treatment; one-third retain reasonable body weight but remain morbidly preoccupied with their appearance and often have personality problems affecting relationships, especially with the opposite sex; and one-third fail to reach or maintain satisfactory weight, are chronically underweight, or develop periodic binging and consequent weight fluctuations. Females in the last group, who began AN prior to puberty, may remain short in stature and never menstruate. Others point to permanent undernourishment and eccentric attitudes toward food, erratic eating patterns, and emotional difficulties. Overall, the prognosis is both variable and unpredictable (Russell 1985). Despite persistence of attitudinal, emotional, and social issues, follow-up studies show that up to 50 percent recover fully. This means restoration of normal weight and cyclical menstruation. However, given that severe medical complications, including death, may result, professionals still tend to associate AN with a relatively poor prognosis.

SOME SCHOOL SIGNS OF AN

As a disorder characterized by subtle early signs and overcontrol, AN is not likely to present itself in glaring, obvious ways. It is more likely to elude quick detection. While it has unique behavioral features, it is a subtle disorder, compared to disorders characterized by undercontrol, with a subtle pattern of behaviors and emotions.

ANOREXIA PATTERN OF BEHAVIOR EXAMPLE. *Sara's teachers were surprised to know that she is a recovering anorexic. However, upon close scrutiny there is a pattern to Sara's behavior and emotions.*

o   *She is inattentive and disinterested at times, and concentration is poor.*

o   *She is frequently absent and when in school often asks to go to the clinic.*

o   *Completion of work is inconsistent.*

o   *Occasionally there are crying spells.*

o   *Quality of work is characterized as careless. She does not check for errors or proofread compositions.*

o   *Self-esteem and self-confidence are poor. Praise is hard for her to accept. She seems to disbelieve positive words from adults.*

o   *She does not accept challenges or take risks.*

o   *She does not ask for help when needed. Sara does not feel that it is all right to have weaknesses.*

o   *Her self-concept and body image are unrealistic. She perceives only her faults and focuses on ways to improve her physical appearance.*

o   *She is unable to discuss alternatives to unsatisfactory behaviors or difficult situations.*

o   *There are frequent complaints that teachers or peers are picking on her.*

o   *Constructive criticism is perceived as a personal attack or insult.*

o   *Sara is extremely sensitive to touch by adult males. Even if a male teacher puts a hand on her shoulder, simply to encourage her or to get her attention, Sara perceives intent to harm.*

o   *Sara also is extremely vigilant about victimization. When some girls pushed her in the hallway one day, she vowed that she would take revenge, even if it meant physical counter-aggression. She believes that she should not have to take abuse from others even if it means she will get in trouble.*

o   *There are periods when Sara becomes "unbelievably social." Teachers complain that at such times Sara talks over them, will not stay in her seat, cannot read during silent periods, talks incessantly, and distracts peers.*

o   *There are also periods of social isolation.*

o   *She does not show positive affect by smiling and laughing.*

o   *The month of May is difficult for Sara. She experiences an "anniversary effect," this being the month in which the sexual abuse first occurred. Sara becomes withdrawn during this month.*

o   *She is moody and sometimes irritable.*

o   *Sara is secretive. She does not want to share her personal life or feelings. When she was in the midst of her worst phase of AN, her clothing was loose and baggy, hiding her body.*

o   *Even small changes in routine are difficult for Sara.*

o   *At the height of her AN Sara wore multiple layers of clothing to keep warm. (Extreme weight loss has been associated with hypothermia.)*

o   *When given corrective feedback for inappropriate behaviors, Sara often tries to blame others.*

AN AND THE FEDERAL DEFINITION OF ED

Within Individuals with Disabilities Education Act (IDEA) there is one criterion for defining ED that applies most obviously to AN. It is *a tendency to develop physical symptoms or fears associated with personal or school problems.* The anorexic's refusal to eat results in an extreme weight loss, which clearly is a physical symptom. Associated with this refusal is an intense fear of gaining weight and of becoming fat.

It has become clear, too, that AN is associated with an *inability to learn that cannot be explained by intellectual, sensory, or health factors.* Typically, students with AN have no cognitive, sensory, or medical problem that would explain poor school performance. Their learning problems are due primarily to a lack of concentration, fatigue, and emotional disturbance, all of which interfere with learning by preventing the student from taking risks, attending classes or school, and engaging in learning activities. This student is too preoccupied with weight and related issues to participate freely and actively in school activities.

While the student with AN manifests perceptual distortion, it is not synonymous with cognitive limitation. Sara, for example, has average intelligence, but her thinking is distorted for emotional reasons. She processes information differently, to the point of occasional hallucinatory perceptions. This student perceives a thin body to be fat and an attractive body to be ugly. The student with AN eats according to what is perceived. As the disorder progresses, the perceptions become more distorted, and eating and weight decrease.

Another significant emotional issue in AN is *depression*, also a federal criterion for ED. Certainly Sara's depressive affect and social isolation exemplify unhappiness.

Sara was found to be eligible for special education services as a student with an emotional disability. By showing that she had an emotional pattern that interfered with her educational progress, she met the above criteria.

SUGGESTED EDUCATIONAL STRATEGIES

For students with AN, teaching strategies must be varied to deal with misperceptions, need for control, rigidity, inattentiveness, inconsistent performance, careless work habits, inability to take risks, tenuous relationships, and social isolation. A comprehensive approach is needed also to deal with low self-esteem, nonassertiveness, absenteeism, distrustfulness, inability to take criticism, difficulty with changes, and inability to accept responsibility for their own behaviors. These problems point to needs for acceptance/approval, internal control, appropriate engagement, encouragement, consistency/routine, and attention.

Some specific suggestions for educating these students are the following.

1.   To encourage the student, ensure that the assigned tasks are appropriate and at the student's ability level.

2.   To promote socialization, pair the student with another student or with a peer tutor. Move later to larger groupings when the AN student is comfortable with one peer.

3.   Provide frequent positive feedback. Provide feedback that indicates the student is successful, competent, important, and valuable.

4.   Provide constructive criticism. In feedback, combine strengths and weaknesses; focus on what was done well as well as what needs improvement.

5.   Do not post work without the student's approval.

6.   Teach the student to relax in a one-to-one format. For example, encourage her to pretend to be in a safe place by visualizing it. Teach other relaxation techniques.

7.   Rehearse new situations prior to the student's experiencing them. Use a one-to-one format. Have the student close her eyes while being guided through each situation, step by step, so she can anticipate it. If closing her eyes is uncomfortable for the student, let her face away, with eyes open.

8.   Have the student list anxiety- or fear-provoking situations in a relaxed, one-to-one format. Discuss past reactions. Give homework to practice relaxing to recalled nervous scenes.

9.   Teach assertiveness. Discuss how assertive responses show in eye contact and facial expression, body posture and gestures, tone of voice, and message content. Have students make a list of situations requiring assertiveness. Role-play common situations, such as returning improperly cooked food in a restaurant. Process feedback, then role-play more appropriate assertive responses.

10.   Rational-emotive therapy (RET) has been effective in cases of social discomfort. RET's premise is that faulty thinking produces negative emotions and that focusing on commonly held irrational beliefs (exaggerating negative consequences, unrealistic demands, and blaming statements) can enhance self-awareness of faulty thinking. Rational thinking can be taught through lectures, discussions, and practice. The emphasis is on developing attitudes of self-acceptance, risk-taking, accepting uncertainty, and tolerating imperfection, all needed by students with AN. For example, the students can be taught that it is irrational to exaggerate negative consequences. A situation involving a new experience, say, talking with the principal about starting a new club, can be explored using the guiding questions, "What's the worst that can happen? What's the best that can happen?" Educators may obtain materials from the Institute for Rational-Emotive Therapy in New York City.

11.   Be explicit about the intention of cues, focus of questions, necessary steps in directions, meaning of references, and reasons for activities, thereby not leaving anything to chance. An itinerary would help the student stay focused.

12.   Activate current knowledge about a new concept so the student can make the bridge from old to new. Semantic mapping is one way. This is a free association of ideas followed by categorizing responses. This readies the student for new information.

13.   Foreshadow things to come or how present work will fit into future work.

14.   Reinforce participation.

15.   Check with the student as soon as lessons begin to ensure that directions are understood.

16.   Use cooperative learning experiences so that (1) the student can work in a social context and (2) the student can learn that each participant can make a meaningful contribution based on individual skills and strengths.

17.   Counteract rigidity by modeling flexibility. For example, use differential grading, say, one grade for writing mechanics and one for content; call for multiple correct responses to questions; or change the order of activities within a block of time with student input.

18.   Establish a private nonverbal cue in relation to a particular behavior that needs changing.

19.   Reinforce students who are exhibiting appropriate behavior, orally labeling what they are doing so the target student can hear. For example, "I like the way you accepted criticism, John" or "Your response indicated you were paying attention, Judy."

20.   Provide class partners with whom the students can share responsibilities and develop trust. During lectures, for example, pause every 10 to 15 minutes so that partners can compare notes and generate questions before proceeding.

21.   Speak with the student privately before class to warn her about upcoming changes or challenges.

22.   Practice active listening. By reflecting back remarks, the student is confirmed.

23.   Empower the student by enabling self-correction of work as often as possible.

24.   Teach the student in a one-to-one format to read her own body and feeling signals so she knows when she is angry, afraid, frustrated, or whatever is associated with withdrawal, outbursts, or other asocial or unproductive behavior.

25.   Teach about stress: what it is, how it is manifest, what situations cause it, and how to cope with it. One coping mechanism is self-instruction. Teach the student to use inner speech to talk herself through difficult situations. Emphasize rational, realistic thinking to appraise situations, to attribute her own behavior, and to structure expectations of her own capacities to handle stressors.

26.   To facilitate attentiveness provide simple directions one step at a time, ask the student to restate directions, break complex tasks down into steps that are achievable, provide additional structure and guidance during transitional periods, help the student estimate time required for tasks, reinforce work completion, and use a multisensory approach, alternating types of work.

27.   Provide a predictable, consistent routine.

28.   Have the student question anything she does not understand while performing assignments.

29.   Demonstrate appropriate ways to respond to constructive criticism. Use peers as models, reinforcing those who respond appropriately to constructive criticism.

30.   Ensure that assistance and support are offered along with constructive criticism and that the student is reinforced for appropriate responses to constructive criticism.

31.   Reduce the emphasis on competition and perfection.

32.   Make the necessary environmental adjustments to prevent stress, frustration, and anger.

33.   Intervene early when there is a problem in order to prevent more serious problems.

34.   Be careful to avoid embarrassing the student by giving her orders or demands in front of others. Provide constructive criticism in a private setting rather than in front of others.

35.   To build relationships with adults, give the student the responsibility of being a teacher's assistant for an activity, responsibility for tutoring another student, responsibility of leading a small-group activity, and responsibility of running errands that require interacting with teachers.

36.   Greet or recognize the student as often as possible in the hallway and at the start of class.

37.   Arrange for one-to-one interactions with the student.

38.   Offer the student assistance throughout the class period or day.

39.   Call on the student often in order to encourage communication.

40.   Encourage the student to communicate needs to other personnel (school counselor, principal, school psychologist).

41.   Attune to the student's attempts to communicate needs (facial expressions, gestures, inactivity, self-depreciating comments).

42.   Teach the student appropriate positive verbal ways to indicate disagreement ("I'm sorry, I don't think that's correct").

43.   Encourage the student to participate in peer mediation when there are conflicts. Coach her in appropriate verbalization for problem resolution as an alternative (e.g., "Let's talk about it").

44.   Maintain trust and confidentiality with the student at all times.

12

Overview:
Mood Disorders

> lightly, grimly, incessantly
> Denise Levertov

In everyday parlance, *mood* is a state of mind or feeling, sometimes called a "spell." Generally, moods are defined as feelings that come and go. Adolescents might define mood as what they feel now. Their parents might describe "moodiness" as adolescent moods that change more often than their underwear.

A *mood disorder*, on the other hand, is not a temporary or passing phenomenon. It is a pervasive and sustained emotional state that, in the extreme, markedly colors one's perception of the world (Kashani and Eppright 1991) and makes a distinct impression on others.

Mood can represent any feeling along the emotional range. However, dictionary definitions typically ascribe a negative tone to mood, for example, adjectives such as "gloomy" and "morose." A teacher who describes a student as moody usually means that the youngster's feelings are sullen or ill-humored.

Inclusion of mood disorders in a book devoted to adolescents with emotional and behavioral disorders is important not only because of the devastating effect of these disorders, but because of the trend. The prevalence of depression, for example, seems to be rising among younger people (Sarason and Sarason 1993). Increasingly, researchers and clinicians are finding that adolescents experience mood disorders, albeit with qualitative differences from adult mood disorders.

The challenge is to identify these disorders within a population subgroup that is developmentally different from the adult subgroup. With appreciation that important changes and crystallization of character occur during adolescence, mood disorders can be identified and understood.

THE AFFECTIVE DISORDERS

Mood disorders are also referred to as *affective disorders*. If the emotion, or affect, is extreme and sustained, it is an acute problem. The affective disorders range from depression to mania, and one may show either or both conditions. The mood disorders may be broken down into two groups, *bipolar disorders* and *depressive disorders*. Either can appear alone as the principal symptom of the disorder, or both can appear cyclically within one individual.

These disorders are among the most prevalent and lethal of the mental disorders. People may die from suicide following a severe depression, and bipolar disorder can create havoc, even self-destruction, in one's life.

Mood disorders occur in about 8 percent of the population at some time. One study found that, within a sample of 20,000 scientifically selected people from five areas in the United States, 7.8 percent met the criteria for a mood disorder one or more times in the past. This prevalence was similar for Hispanics, African Americans, and Caucasians, although African Americans reported a slightly lower rate. Different rates were found for men and women; twice as many women as men reported a mood disorder of some type in either the present or the past, particularly depressive disorders. These results accord with foreign longitudinal studies (Sarason and Sarason 1993).

A mood disorder is distressful; distress is defined as suffering, sorrow, or unhappiness. The derivation, in Old French, is destresse, which means "narrow passage." As will be seen, adolescents who are in distress draw tightly into themselves and seem to be evolving along a narrow pathway; distress disorders adversely affect the personality, causing it to show constricted emotional responses.

Mood disorders usually first appear in late adolescence (Seligman and Moore 1995). An adolescent must adapt to peer pressures, to many teachers simultaneously, and to many new expectations from home, school, and community, in addition to a changing body. Other factors involve the adolescent's family, for example divorce, relocation, dysfunctional parenting, and blended families. It has been found that the strongest predictor of healthy resistance to stress is whether or not a child has had a warm, supportive relationship with his or her mother (Kauffman et al. 1979). Mood disorders, influenced by both genetics and modeling, tend to run in families (Seligman and Moore 1995). This hereditary pattern is particularly strong in men whose mothers were depressed (Gutsch 1988). Other risk factors include loss of or separation from parent, child abuse, parental criminality, perinatal stress, chronic illness, and low level of parental education (Rutter 1979).

The very instability of moods, a common feature of mood disorders (Seligman and Moore 1995), can be a stress factor for an adolescent. Accompanying the current mood may be anxiety about when and if the mood will change. As an asthmatic may experience a severe attack simply in anticipation of blocked breathing, so may an adolescent with a mood disorder experience anxiety in anticipation of an extreme mood state.

DEPRESSIVE DISORDER

One form of distress is depression, which is more than sadness or unhappiness. Depression is an affective disorder that has significant impact on self and others.

Many people experience "down" feelings. These feelings, often called "the blues," may occur in rainy weather, during illness, or after a broken romance. Even events that are expected to be happy may end with sad feelings. Individuals may experience the blues after holidays, describing a letdown following a flurry of activities over days or weeks. While such events may elicit sad feelings and require adjustment, the unhappy moods are normally temporary and usually fade relatively quickly.

The following case exemplifies a short-term response to stress. It illustrates unhappy feelings that are normal and transient.

Jane, age 21, is single and works in a day care center. She sought psychotherapy two weeks after she discovered that the man she had been involved with for six months was married. She reacted with bouts of sadness and crying, felt she was falling apart, took a week's sick leave from her job, and had vague thoughts that the future was so bleak that life might not be worth living. She felt that something must be wrong with her, otherwise she would not have gotten so involved with someone who had no intention of maintaining a long-term relationship. She felt that she had been "really stupid" not to see the signs of her lover's marital status. There were no other symptoms of depression, such as loss of interest or appetite or difficulty concentrating. After 12 therapy sessions Jane was much improved in her outlook and behavior, and so she terminated the therapy. She returned to work, was no longer experiencing crying jags, and was willing to consider the possibility of dating new men. The spell of sadness had ended. (Author personal interview 1995)

In addition to situational, transient depressive moods, there may be depressive moods associated with other disorders. Borderline personality disorder, substance abuse disorder, and disorders where there are physical changes in the brain, for example, often have overtones of depression. While depression, in such cases, is a symptom, it is not a mood disorder per se because the depression is not pervasive and sustained (Sarason and Sarason 1993).

Chapter 13 describes the constricted worlds of adolescents who suffer from chronic unhappiness. It will become clear that this affective disorder is not a short-term reaction to a stressful situation. Some of the signs of depressive disorder include dissatisfaction and anxiety; changes in appetite, sleep, and psychomotor functions; loss of interest and energy; feelings of guilt; thoughts of death; and diminished concentration. This mood, then, affects others, persists, and affects the individual acutely.

BIPOLAR DISORDER

Another form of distress is bipolar disorder, also known as manic-depressive disorder, which is characterized by alternating phases of depression and mania. The manic component is characterized by a flight of ideas, elevated mood, and increased psychomotor activity, and extreme elated behavior. Bipolar disorder, much less common than depression, is experienced by only about 0.8

percent of the general population (Sarason and Sarason 1993).

Although bipolar disorder is infrequently seen in the general population, various studies have found that it occurs in disproportionately high proportions among creative individuals. Leonard Woolf, the husband of Virginia Woolf, a highly creative writer who was affected by bipolar disorder and ultimately killed herself while depressed, described his wife's genius as mental instability. He commented that she followed "the voices that fly ahead" (Sarason and Sarason 1993, p. 310). Other creative people with documented bipolar disorder are Hart Crane, Anne Sexton, and Sylvia Plath. Historically famous figures such as Napoleon Bonaparte, Oliver Cromwell, and Winston Churchill all experienced periods of both severe depression and high energy, elevated mood, and impetuousness, even questionable judgment (Sarason and Sarason 1993).

Like transient depression, mania may occur apart from a bipolar disorder. Certain drugs can cause people with no history of affective disorder to experience manic episodes. Steroids have been implicated in short-term mania. Mania also can result from infections, metabolic disturbances, and growth of tumors. Mania in these cases is a symptom of changed biochemical state and is not classified as a mood disorder.

The peak incidence of bipolar disorder occurs during young adulthood. Many people, however, show evidence of the disorder as adolescents. The discussion of bipolar disorder in Chapter 14 makes it clear that manic-depressive disorder represents pervasive elevative as well as depressive moods, a serious impact on others, cycling moods, and even antisocial behavior. The bipolar adolescent, in short, exists in a constricted world that is illusorily expansive and gloomily depressive.

Both depression and bipolar disorder affect the adolescent's crystallizing personality in ways that differ from adult mood disorders. Extremely depressing or racing moods are associated with cognitive impairment, diminished concentration, cognitive distortion, impaired judgment, indecisiveness, and disorderly behavior. Students with mood disorders are more likely than adults to manifest somatic complaints, irritability, school problems, hyperactivity, and social withdrawal. Adult manifestations, by comparison, primarily involve psychomotor retardation, hypersomnia or insomnia, guilt and delusions (Seligman and Moore 1995). These mood disorders also manifest themselves in crying, neglect of personal hygiene, and needy behavior. All of these factors relate to diminished life functioning and deteriorated academic performance. Teachers who describe disordered adolescent moods as "heavy" are on the right track, for these disorders weigh heavily on the student.

13

Depression

I have been acquainted with the night.
Robert Frost

Some people believe that our society is depressed. One sign of this is the widespread drug culture, described in the book *Prozac Nation: Young and Depressed in America* (Wurtzel 1994), which chronicles crying jags, hospital stays, drinking and drug binges, suicide attempts, unsupportive lovers, ineffective psychotherapists, and widespread use of many prescription drugs, including Prozac. Wurtzel tries to make a case that endemic depression is due to eroded family values. Others have tried to make the same case by pointing to the homelessness problem, voter apathy, crime, and violence. Depression, however, has long been with us. "The lifetime risk of the disabling and more *recurrent* forms of affective illness has probably changed little and remains at no more than 4 to 5 percent" (Whybrow, Akiskal, and McKinney 1984, p. 13).

HISTORY OF DEPRESSION

Depression has been evident throughout history. For centuries, words such as "cold" and "black" have been used to describe depressive dispositions. For example, Shakespeare's description of Hamlet's anguish as weary, stale, and flat suggests depressive affect.

Between the Elizabethan era and the twentieth century, weariness and flat feelings, representing more than sadness, continued to be evident. While sadness is part of the normal range of emotions, depression is different. Harrington (1994) described depression as emotional emptiness or a feeling of flatness rather than sadness or unhappiness.

Despite signs across the centuries, prior to the 1970s it was largely assumed that only adults experience depression. As Kauffman (1985) has noted, traditional psychoanalytic theory holds that depression cannot exist in childhood because psychological self-representation is insufficiently developed. This belief is not shared by all professionals. Friedman and Doyal (1974) noted that the problem has been increasingly acknowledged as a widespread childhood disorder that deserves closer attention. Rutter (1985) commented that since 1975 there has been growing acceptance that depressive disorders can and do occur in childhood, accompanied by an explosion of clinical and research papers.

An interview with a depressed child provides some insight. The following quotation attests to the intense feelings experienced by depressed youngsters.

I am in fourth grade. One day I leave my seat in the classroom and go down the hall to the girls' room. I walk close to the wall, trying not to take up space I feel I have no right to. Inside the restroom, I crouch behind a toilet, my arms wrapped around my knees. I do not cry; I am just wordlessly sad. I have been wordlessly sad for quite a while. People seem to take this for granted. "My hill and dale girl," my mother calls me, and I have no way of knowing that the way I feel is at all unusual. I only know it feels unbearable. And so for relief I sit behind the toilet, where at least it's cool and quiet, away from the boisterous classroom and the noise that seems to hurt my skin. Unable to figure out why I am sad, equipped with only a child's logic, I eventually decide that it is because President Kennedy is still dead. (Thompson 1995, p. 10)

Despite increased attention, there remains a lack of knowledge and understanding about childhood depression. There are various reasons for this gap. One is that many adults, including mental health professionals, equate mood swings with the adolescent phase. Another reason is that adults attribute the external signs in depressed children to other emotional or behavioral disorders. For example, the depression of children with oppositional-defiant disorder may be overlooked. There has been a tendency to define depression by the primarily vegetative signs of the adult syndrome. Lack of knowledge about childhood depression causes it to be widely underidentified and unreported.

Four key points support the existence of clinically significant pre-adult depression.

Depression endures. Research shows that depression endures. One criterion signifying depression is that the symptoms endure from at least three months (Snyder and Huntley 1990) to one year (the American Psychiatric Association's *DSM-IV* 1994). The symptoms of a depressive disorder may change as the child matures, but the disorder itself may be very stable and enduring (Snyder and Huntley 1990). One study found that between 50 and 77 percent of a sample of depressed children were still depressed as young adults and that those who did not show continuity in depression often showed other forms of adult psychopathology (Cytryn et al. 1986). Thus, signs of pre-adult depression are not merely benign, transitory phenomena; they tend to foreshadow important psychiatric maladjustment in adulthood.

Federal law documents childhood depression. The Individuals with Disabilities Education Act (IDEA) defines emotional disturbance (ED) as a general pervasive mood of unhappiness or depression.

It can occur at any age. Depression has been identified as early as infancy (Snyder and Huntley 1990).

Depression is widely prevalent. Depression occurs in one out of six children who are seen in psychiatric settings, and, according to Reynolds (1990b), it is one of the most prevalent forms of pre-adult psychopathology. Petti (1981) reported that, within clinic populations, estimates of the proportion of depressed children range from 12 to 20 percent, and sometimes as high as 68 percent. (The prevalence estimate for mood disorders, 8 percent, reflects a combinatory effect of assorted disorders.)

The difficulty of identifying childhood depression has affected prevalence estimates. It is easier to recognize an externalizing problem such as oppositional-defiant disorder than a disorder that has internalizing features. Many of the cognitive and affective features that are relatively difficult to assess are guilt, self-blame, feelings of rejection, and low self-esteem. "Of all the internalizing disorders, childhood depression may be the most difficult to identify" (Quay and La Greca 1986, p. 77). In light of this difficulty, it is critical that those who work with children recognize the signs of depression.

Even if students cannot articulate their feelings of depression, their behaviors offer important clues. The two essential signs of childhood depression are dysphoria (restlessness, anxiety, or depression) and self-depreciation (Shaffer 1985). Additionally, two of the following symptoms must be present (those qualified by Lewisohn et al. 1994 are bracketed): aggressive behavior; changes in school performance and attitude toward school; somatic complaints; appetite disturbance; sleep disturbance; motor agitation or retardation; loss of interest in usual activities; loss of energy; self-reproach or guilt [pessimistic cognitive style; self-blame]; and impaired ability to concentrate; recurrent thoughts of death or suicide [suicidal].

Lewinsohn and his colleagues (1994) further specify the signs of depression among middle and late adolescence: history of psychopathology, especially substance abuse and anxiety disorders and other problematic behaviors and physical symptoms; emotional dependence; self-consciousness; ineffectual coping resources; feelings of lack of support by friends and family; and heavy smoking.

The foregoing descriptions of childhood and adolescent depression point to a complex mixture of emotional, physical, and social signs. Each individual's cluster of symptoms is unique, but they all are variations on a theme.

DEPRESSION SYMPTOMS EXAMPLE. *Juan Christian, age 16, appears sad, somber, sullen, and withdrawn. His affect is gloomy. He walks with his head bowed. Often he sleeps in class, and occasionally he cuts classes and wanders the hallways aimlessly. He is reticent about sharing feelings and concerns, and when upset isolates himself. He avoids eye contact. It is difficult to engage him in conversation, and when he speaks, he whispers or mumbles. When talking about school issues, he may become tearful. There is a lack of spontaneity. He has had suicidal thoughts, including a plan to jump from a tall building. He feels very anxious and cannot seem to adjust to the world around him. He seems to need affection and interpersonal contact but feels hopeless about having intimate relationships. To defend himself from tormented feelings he pulls into himself "to keep it together." Consequently, Juan Christian withdraws from interactions, responds passively, and remains aloof. Affect at times is inappropriate. For example, he smiled when talking about suicide. Sometimes he is irritable. He is very concerned about his family and does not want to trouble them with his personal needs and pain, so he hides his pain from his parents and denies his own feelings. In the process Juan Christian almost convinces himself that he is all right.*

CLINICAL DEFINITION

DSM-IV (1994) refers to dysthymic, or depressive, disorder with the following pre-adult characteristics. First, the mood can be irritable and duration must be at least one year. Second, two (or more) of the following symptoms are present during the depression: poor appetite or overeating, insomnia or hypersomnia, low energy or fatigue, low self-esteem, poor concentration or difficulty making decisions, and feelings of hopelessness. Third, during the one-year period of the disturbance the first two symptoms have not been absent for more than two months at a time. Fourth, the disturbance is not better accounted for by major depressive disorder that is chronic or in partial remission. Fifth, there is no manic episode at any time.

Although the above clinical signs must be present for a pre-adult diagnosis, the adolescent developmental stage must be considered in relation to these clinical signs. Depression is more likely to occur after puberty than before (Cantwell and Baker 1991) because of hormonal and other neuroendocrine changes. During this phase, there are also major changes in the social environment that contribute to the increased incidence of adolescent depression.

The salient qualitative differences between adult and adolescent depression among adults and pre-adults include the following:

1.   Adolescents may show fatigue, but they also may have intermittent periods of energy.

2.   Adolescents may isolate themselves socially, or they may socialize in inappropriate ways (e.g., with youngsters who match their level of self-esteem, such as "druggies," underachievers, or other at-risk youngsters).

3.   Adolescents may show antisocial behavior, but often it is directed against others, not just to avoid others.

4.   Adolescents may have enhanced sensitivity to social rejection, but rather than go into hiding or lose themselves in their work, they may actively oppose and act out against

perceived threats and rejection.

5.   Adolescents may have sleep problems, but rather than insomnia they may sleep around the clock.

6.   Adolescents may have thoughts of self-destruction, including suicide, but the first signs may be the carving of letters or words on their skin with razor blades.

Seligman and Moore (1995) add that adolescents typically show an irritable, rather than depressed, mood.

These indicators suggest that an individual's developmental status should be considered carefully during diagnosis. Not only are there some subtle, and some not so subtle, differences between adolescent and adult depression, there are also developmental differences between adolescent depression and depression among younger children. There are striking changes with age in both the frequency and form of affective disturbances (Rutter 1985).

Depression has been described across different ages in childhood. Such descriptions can promote recognition of depression's signs and, thereby, identification of this serious disorder in pre-adults. Examples of such descriptions are given in Table 13.1.

Thompson adds to this developmental picture. During her own childhood, specifically between fourth and fifth grades, the following incident happened.

Signs of chronic depression were emerging. I had begun to make frequent trips to the doctor, always complaining of a variety of ailments. Some were real; others had no clear phsyical cause. I seemed to suffer constantly from stomachaches, headaches, a mysterious cough, strange lumps in my lymph gland: a list of ailments baffling to my doctors and worrisome to my mother. The family doctor referred me to an internist, who referred me to a neurologist, who gave me an EEG. It was normal. My urine was tested for diabetes; my blood was tested for leukemia. Those tests were normal, too. Finally, in bafflement, the internist gave up and wrote a prescription for Valium. (1995, p. 24)

Before looking at specific signs in depth, a caveat is in order. We need to consider a cluster of signs, not isolated symptoms. Looking at any one sign may suggest another problem or lack of a problem. For example, a parent might believe that crying spells relate to romantic problems; that impaired school performance relates to poor study habits or application; that sleep problems relate to changing hormones; that decreased ability to deal with classroom demands is due to poor rapport between student and teacher; that lack of friends is due to "nerdiness" that will be outgrown; and that oppositional behavior is due to the adolescent's desire for independence. When all the signs are put together, and when suicidal thoughts or behaviors are thrown into the mix, it becomes more diffi-

Table 13.1
Some Developmental Illustrations of Depression

Age	Description
8	Cody has been going under his desk and crying a lot.
9	Sammy was referred to the school nurse because he always looks tired, occasionally falls asleep in class, and constantly complains of aches and pains.
10	Julia's grades dropped suddenly, she alienates her peers, and she ran away from home.
11	Mary Jane is the star of the volleyball team, a cheerleader, and an honor roll student, but she describes herself as fat, stupid, ugly, and undeserving of friendship.
12	John's English journal entries contain themes of death and lack of self-worth.
13	In art class Sarah sketched a picture of the sidewalk she sees below herself as she peers down between her feet from the ledge of a skyscraper.
14	Laurel hides behind furniture in the classroom. She thinks about suicide and has tried to overdose on pills. A gifted athlete, she has dropped sports. In a gifted/ talented program through eighth grade, she was dropped because of poor effort.
15	Heather feels isolated and self-conscious. She believes that no one wants to be her friend.
18	Jennie felt that the world was on her shoulders. Her guidance counselor tried to get her psychiatric help for signs of depression: insomnia, falling grades, and chronic fatigue, among others. Jennie graduated from high school in June, took a full-time job in order to help support her family and pay tuition for night school. By March she was six months pregnant. About 2:00 one April morning she hanged herself.

cult to write off the pattern as a transient problem. Diagnosis is further complicated when symptoms are intermixed with or masked by others (i.e., expressed indirectly through such problems as hyperactivity, truancy, and oppositional behavior).

EMOTIONAL AND BEHAVIORAL SIGNS

Emotional signs. The emotional signs of depression can be seen in the cases of Heather, Andy, Jesse, Michael, Laurel, Olivia, and Joel. These signs range from sadness to anger, from slow-motion activity and fatigue to restlessness and acting out, from obsessively morbid thinking to indecisiveness. One pattern shown is that of sadness, a feeling of being unloved, negative self-evaluation, poor concentration, irritability, suicidal thinking, social withdrawal, and decreased academic performance. Along with these signs are issues of unresolved dependency conflicts, acting out, a strong need for approval and affection, and self-condemnation. There also is evidence of changed behavior.

EMOTIONAL SIGNS EXAMPLES GROUP 1. *Heather, age 18, shows unresolved dependency. Abandoned by her father when she was a baby, and having had no contact with him except for one phone call in 15 years, Heather feels unloved and rejected. She was sexually abused by an uncle when she was about six years old, and she only began to recall these incidents within the past few years. Her memories are largely olfactory: smells of alcohol and sweat. Heather depended on her mother for many years until her mother remarried, had another child, divorced again, and acquired a boyfriend. It reached a point where Heather was so confrontational and sarcastic in the boyfriend's presence that her mother sent her to live with an aunt; intolerable were Heather's screaming, breaking of objects, and even pounding on the mother's bedroom door when she and the boyfriend were together. Heather took great pleasure in these incidents and sabotaged the boyfriend at every opportunity, including replacing his contact lens solution with tap water. Often, she is irritable; she is constantly on edge and annoyed by other students. Her feelings of rejection and sadness are apparent in this sample of her writing:*

Everyone has to start or do something new. But I never thought it would be me, well it was. Ever since I was in the 1st grade I went to city schools, I knew everyone and was very popular in the schools. But by the end of 9th grade my mom and dad decided they wanted to move, so we did. Here I am at a school where I know hardly anyone and not anyone seems like they want to be my friend. So far I hate my new school, the kids here are a lot different than they were at my old school. I have only about seven friends here, at my old school I had friends in every grade. What I don't understand is why it has been so hard for me to make friends. You feel very different and not wanted and as if people are staring at you.

Joel feels sad because he does not fit in or is not tall enough to fit his image of a basketball player. He also feels sad because he cannot achieve in school and cannot stop himself from moving around in class.

Jesse has become overwhelmed by school work and feels inadequate and devoid of confidence. He sees no reason to live. When things go wrong, Jesse blames himself, as if he can control events beyond himself. Decisions are hard for him, so he tends to avoid having to make them. One solution he has found is to avoid social situations so that he will not risk disappointing others. Jesse remains a loner. It is easier that way.

Laurel, age 14, shows poor concentration, suicidal thinking, social withdrawl, and diminished academic performance. In terms of withdrawal, Laurel often hides behind a file cabinet in the classroom. One teacher commented that she is "totally passive, quiet, spaced out when subject matter is content oriented; can be animated if a topic is related to her interests (for example, drugs)." Several important aspects of her life have changed. Placed in a center for gifted children during the second grade, she remained in that center until eighth grade. During seventh grade her grades went down, and attendance became sporadic. Her friends changed, from those who are academically oriented to those who denigrate school. A gifted athlete who was involved in basketball and baseball, she has lost interest in sports. Laurel wanted to stay in the gifted center, but she could not meet the expectations. She did not work in class, did not do homework, and told her teachers that she was too emotionally upset to work. She is unable to concentrate due to feelings of stress. Laurel's parents believe that she has an attention disorder, but more likely Laurel's inattention is based upon interfering emotions. Altogether, Laurel has changed; the things that gave her pleasure have been dropped, except for music. However, in this area Laurel has become nonconforming and dark. Her music is oriented toward hard rock and lyrics that suggest alienation and grotesque images.

Along with sadness, depressed adolescents often show hopelessness, despair, and pessimism.

EMOTIONAL SIGNS EXAMPLES GROUP 2. *Olivia does not believe that she will ever do well despite good grades, popularity with peers, and strong athletic and dancing abilities. Instead of focusing on her positive achievements, she worries a lot about not doing well.*

Jesse fears for the world and for himself. The weight of the world is on his shoulders, and he is consumed about world events, which in his mind point to futility. He escapes into science fiction movies.

Andy sees no way out of his social dilemma. He believes that he has not made friends for so long that there is no hope. As for girls, they might as well not exist. His pessimism interferes with motivation to change. Also, Andy thinks about death, about leaving everyone and everything he knows.

Michael writes about hopelessness and despair. His compositions are filled with thoughts of death and burial.

Behavioral signs. The notable behavioral signs of adolescent depression include acting out, oppositionality, dissociation, suicidal gestures or acts, and substance abuse. They may attack the external world while seeking an escape from a dark internal world. Acting out may serve as a defense against the feelings of despair and helplessness, a way to escape from painful feelings or cry for help. Acting out, also, can serve to obtain the security that they need, particularly if they feel cheated, abandoned, or rejected. Acts such as promiscuity and physical assault may salve feelings.

Feelings of panic may also threaten an adolescent's ego. Rather than face this unknown disintegration, the adolescent may dissociate, thereby creating something that has comforting familiarity and predictability. Heather claims to have a multiple personality, with alters who provide a world of familiar characters that can meet assorted needs at critical times.

BEHAVIORAL SIGNS EXAMPLES GROUP 1. *Jesse feels such overwhelming sadness that he took an overdose of antidepressant pills. He is so depressed that he appears comatose at times.*

Laurel was hospitalized after overdosing on pain killers. Her oppositionality has taken another, more active form. She has a tendency to associate with students who get in trouble, who use inappropriate language, and who cut classes. Laurel makes an effort to appear different. Her blond hair is tinted green or purple, and ink tracings appear on the veins of one arm. Her parents complain that she does what she wants and has an "oppositional streak."

Krakowski summarizes the overt aspect of depression. This illustration clarifies the interplay between internalizing and externalizing aspects.

The depressed child does poorly in school. He frequently projects his parent-directed hostile feelings onto his teachers and peers. In this manner he is able to release his hostility and at the same time retaliate against his parents. Guilt-ridden, he may provoke in order to fulfill his need for expiation. The provocation may be achieved by insubordination, obstructionism, passive resistance, pouting or insolence. (1962, p. 60)

BEHAVIORAL SIGNS EXAMPLES GROUP 2. *Heather's negative self-esteem is evident in statements about her inability to read and fear of reading aloud to classmates, feelings that she cannot concentrate in class, and feelings that she may never finish high school.*

Andy's typical reaction to criticism is to stonewall. When a teacher provides constructive criticism, Andy shuts down and becomes silent.

Olivia explodes verbally at a teacher when criticized. It is as if someone has assaulted her to the core.

Michael does not react well to criticism. For example, when reminded to put a pair of scissors away, he enacted a bizarre ritual, dramatizing his compliance and going far beyond the necessary motions, as if mocking the teacher. He turned compliance into opposition.

James is angry at his father for abandoning him and at his mother for babying him, on the one hand, and for setting unrealistically high expectations, on the other. For example, his mother is convinced that James is intellectually gifted. She smothers James. James has begun to lash out physically against peers and against his mother.

David O, age 15, has difficulty dealing with his weaknesses and tends to deny them. When his mood is good, he can accept help, but when he is depressed, he rejects it. He works well with adults whom he trusts, but it takes a long time to develop trust. David places such unrealistic expectations on relationships that he cannot deal with criticism and limit-setting, even by those he trusts. He becomes angry and oppositional at those times.

The acting-out behavior of students with depression may also be impulsive, disorganized, and full of verbal aggression. In the face of such noxious behaviors it is hard to remember that this student is unhappy.

ACTING-OUT EXAMPLES. *Her teachers describe Myra, age 14, as a very articulate, outgoing student who does a great deal of calling out, yelling, and talking in the classroom. She is extremely disorganized and cannot seem to stay focused and on task. Despite high-average intellectual ability, Myra fails to complete work, has difficulty getting started on tasks, and forgets to do homework. She has trouble with the transitions between activities and classes because she is easily sidetracked. Generally, she has difficulty following through on commitments. Altogether, Myra is not a calming influence in her classes. She has been diagnosed as depressed.*

Ricky, age 13, shows acting-out behavior that is full of verbal aggression. He has poor impulse control and is disorganized. His kindergarten through fifth-grade years were good ones, but between sixth and eighth his grades began to decline and his behavior began to look aberrant. During that period his mother suffered a long-term illness and died. By eighth grade Ricky's emotional-behavioral status was poor. He had difficulty concentrating; could not complete school work; was easily agitated; was forgetful and disorganized; sought attention and approval; and was frequently absent. He agitated peers, e.g., by bumping into them purposely; ran away from home; and had numerous disci-

plinary referrals resulting in suspensions for such behavior as throwing objects in class and refusing to report to the office; challenging another student in class to fight; punching a student in the face; throwing a student's property out the school bus window; possessing cigarettes, a lighter, and drugs; aiming an armed bow and arrow at the teacher during archery class; and using profanity. Subsequent to referral for special education services, projective testing showed a child who felt trapped in a life that was bleak and full of loss. One story character, e.g., was a girl who "felt that her heart had been torn out of her chest." The school psychologist concluded that Ricky was depressed and anxious. Despite forceful appearances and a desire to be strong, Ricky seemed overwhelmed with feelings of isolation, loneliness, loss, insecurity, and rejection. His self-esteem appeared to be low, and he seemed to crave nurturance. It is no wonder that Ricky became involved in a gang, which offered acceptance and approval.

Depressed students may also act out in antisocial ways, which, it is theorized, is part of a struggle to reestablish equilibrium. In the process of normal development the child experiences some guilt for growing away from the objects of first love (parents). There is some grieving for what must be left behind in order to achieve autonomy. In this grief there is a phase of anger. For a depressed youngster, this phase is serious and protracted; the anger is abnormally strong and may be acted out in antisocial ways.

ANTISOCIAL BEHAVIOR EXAMPLES. *Chris has tried to achieve balance and security, but in abnormal ways. He has cheated in school and has stolen in his neighborhood. He broke his curfew when under probation. Chris is, however, not simply a juvenile delinquent. He has pervasive emotional difficulties stemming from parental discord around custody issues. In order to counteract depression, Chris takes risks that provide the "rush" that helps him re-establish equilibrium. For example, by breaking his curfew Chris took a chance that his probation officer would find out and send him to detention.*

The peers with whom Laurel associates not only endorse cutting classes and using foul language, but also they set fires and abuse drugs. Laurel's depression is associated with a strong inclination toward delinquent behavior.

Depressed adolescents may also have an overwhelming need for approval and affection because of inadequate nurturing. Seeking attention is one way to capture what is missing. Consequently, affiliation with others who are not associated with the cause of the pain provides hope for much-needed intimate relationships. However, efforts to forge these relationships typically are desperate with much disappointment and disillusionment.

NEED FOR APPROVAL EXAMPLES. *Heather has invested enormous emotional energy in her friends and boyfriends. She has trouble saying "no" to sexual advances because she desperately needs approval and affection. With boys, she has been having trouble distinguishing between love and friendship; the lines become blurred, and she often loses these relationships because of misunderstandings. Heather became pregnant before finishing high school. She found affection with a young man and satisfied a craving to have a child that would need her.*

David O was abandoned at birth in his native African country by his father, and at age three by his mother, both of whom immigrated to the U.S. While David was raised by close relatives, he has suffered deep, lasting feelings of rejection. When he came to the U.S. at the age of 10, he reunited with his mother and father, whose stormy marriage had finally settled down to a stable union with several new siblings. David's re-adjustment to his family has been full of conflicts. He has run away several times and lived at an alternative house for a while. He has shown a strong need for approval and affection. He vacillates between feeling very good about himself or feeling depressed and angry.

Another feature of adolescent depression is a mix of symptoms. Adolescents who are depressed often go through transient periods that change within a short time. A typical occurrence is apathy alternating with garrulousness.

MIXED SYMPTOMS EXAMPLES. *David O vacillates between indifference and sociability. When he is feeling good about himself, he relates well with peers and feels like part of the crowd. When he is playing a team sport, particularly one that is coached by someone with whom David has a good relationship, he feels wonderful. When he also has a girlfriend, David feels supported and able to accomplish many things in school. At these times, David is so much on top of the world that his ambitions, such as the goal to achieve straight "A's," are unrealistic. When he is between girlfriends or between sports seasons, without the supportive relationships that he craves, David is closed about discussing any problems, distances himself from others, goes into an academic slump, and is suspicious of and confrontational with peers. On one occasion he started a fight because a classmate "was looking at me funny." David seems to be an all-or-nothing young man; either things go his way or they do not. The good periods are short-lived because he does not have the emotional security to sustain them. Consequently, David's behavior invariably tips the balance, and he enters yet another downward spiral.*

Olivia, too, shows changeability. She tries to mask her sadness by being a social butterfly and by indulging in numerous sports and dance activities. When she does not think anyone is looking, her face is a mask of sadness.

Similarly, Sara looks very sad when she is alone. When she is with peers, however, she assumes a social persona and acts like queen of the hop.

For Adam, efforts to mask his depression are at times outrageous. False bravado has become his trademark. To escape feelings of sadness, Adam has gone so far as to dance on classroom desktops; however, the sad feeling, momentarily kept at bay, never leaves him.

An additional emotional-behavioral pattern shown by depressed adolescents involves identity confusion. In this pattern, adolescents idealize someone or something, as if it is the answer to all their problems. It is, essentially, a quest for a hero. The adolescent also may, out of bitterness and disappointment, identify with counterculture or subculture groups.

IDENTITY CONFUSION EXAMPLE 1. *David O's temple is sports, his gods coaches. He is a good athlete, but his devotion to sports exceeds normal bounds. During football season he carries his ball to all his classes. He says he even sleeps with it. Mr. J, known by his basketball players as Coach Joe, takes an unusually keen interest in the boys, circulating questionnaires weekly about academic progress, supervising an after-school detention for players with low grades, and taking players to dinner when they show academic progress. David thrives on this attention, which is understandable given his background. Having a hero, Coach Joe, has helped to allay feelings of depression and to give David a sense of hope and connection. A turning point came one summer while he participated in a basketball league. That summer he spent a lot of time with Coach Joe, who mentored David and took special interest in him. The two spent intensive time together, Joe often driving David home and having long talks with him. Joe counseled David to have fun, not take sports too seriously, and to balance sports with academics. For David, Coach Joe "was like a dad to me." Later that summer, David began to spend more time with his younger brother. He said he wants to take an interest in his brother while he grows up. Since that summer he has cooperated more with his teachers, has been respectful toward authorities, and is more serious about academics. He has also begun to understand that his emotions have interfered with academic progress and relationships. He told his resource teacher, "I can see, now, that my feelings took over at times and I got out of control." David's attitude is now more open and positive. He has begun to engage in the process of change. One important sign is that he no longer carries the football off the field.*

Identity confusion can become an acute problem. Combined with self-condemnation, it is deeply troubling. Billy shows many signs of depression as well as devaluation of himself and overvaluation of his parent.

IDENTITY CONFUSION EXAMPLES 2 AND 3. *Billy, age 14, rarely smiles; his demeanor is sad. His affect is flat and lacks variety, spontaneity, and humor. He moves slowly, lets his hair fall over his eyes, and walks with his head down. Judging from his polite behavior with adults, one would not guess that he is angry, but he hates his father, who does not encourage Billy to have his own identity. The father expects that Billy will imitate him as a good student and outstanding athlete. Billy repeatedly condemns himself as stupid for failing to get the grades his father expects. If he cannot meet his father's expectations, then he may as well not exist. The father does not understand Billy's love of music; it is contrary to his own interests and what he believes will earn someone a place in society, yet Billy lives for his guitar and the small band he has formed. His father, however, wants Billy to be a hockey player and top academic, but Billy's learning disability makes academic work a struggle, and he has no desire to be an athlete. Billy's father keeps him up late at night working on homework, forcing Billy to recite facts to memorize, and making him write compositions over until they are letter perfect. The father dotes on the younger son, who is an exceptional student and athlete. Consequently, Billy feels rejected, and at every opportunity he aggresses against this brother. Lacking a belief that he is important, and lacking a solid identity, Billy also believes that he has no right to his own feelings, as if feelings are right or wrong. Consequently, Billy is out of touch with his feelings. When asked how he feels, Billy says "fine" with no conviction, as if it is an automatic, socially conventional response. When asked what has gone through his mind to arrive at the conclusion that he is fine, Billy draws a blank.*

Jesse, too, suffers from acute identity confusion. He is caught between reality and fantasy. Unable to fulfill his own ideals and ambitions, particularly his dream of being an actor, Jesse is in constant despair. On the one hand, Jesse has an ideal image of himself on stage, firing up an audience with a sparkling performance. The reality is that Jesse is lethargic, vegetative, sad, and sluggish. Teachers have wondered if Jesse could move fast enough to exit the school building if it caught fire, so acting seems very unrealistic. He is immune to suggestions to read more, experience more, audition for school productions, and, generally, to experience life in the mainstream instead of on the sideline. He will not actively prepare for acting, so his dream eludes him.

PASSIVITY

Some depressed individuals believe their emotional problem is a weakness that they could overcome if they tried harder (Seligman and Moore 1995). The belief in one's inability may be too powerful an emotion, causing inertia. Billy, for example, believes that his father is correct when he says that Billy lacks motivation. Consequently, Billy does not seek help, either in school or elsewhere. His passivity prevents him from being active in school and from engaging actively in psychotherapy. He keeps the therapy appointments because his mother drives him there.

Passivity such as Billy's relates to learned helplessness, a phenomenon that has been identified in many students with learning disabilities. These students often experience feelings of inadequacy that pervade their lives. After many years of repeated failure, they may come to feel that they cannot overcome their problems and that fate and other people are responsible for both their successes and their failures. Their learned helplessness is combined with a feeling that they cannot achieve because they do not try hard enough.

DEPRESSION AND THE FEDERAL CRITERIA FOR ED

This chapter illustrates, in depth, one IDEA criterion for ED: *a general pervasive mood of unhappiness or depression.* This criterion is given additional meaning in this chapter.

Often there is also *an inability to learn that cannot be explained by intellectual, sensory, or health factors.* A student who is depressed is not likely to succeed academically. A student who has not slept is dull and inattentive in school; such a student shows impairment of perception, concentration, and memory. Billy, for example, has difficulty in school. Everything, he said, seems to go by him, and he has difficulty remembering what happens in the classroom. Certainly Laurel's inability to learn cannot be explained by intellectual factors because she is intellectually gifted, but she has only enough energy for music. Laurel cannot achieve academically because of interfering emotions, particularly depression.

Depression also relates to the student's *inability to build or maintain satisfactory interpersonal relationships with peers and teachers.* A student who is angry and oppositional, or who acts out and overreacts to criticism, is difficult to teach.   Likewise, a student who is extremely passive is hard to reach. A student who hides behind a file cabinet is not accessible for instruction. Interpersonal relationships with peers may be equally difficult to build or maintain. Depressive behaviors engender discomfort and rejection from peers. Peers are likely to conclude that depressed peers do not like playing with them (Rudoph, Hammen, and Burge 1994). Students cannot look into the minds of their peers to see the internal conflict and emotional distress; what they see is what they judge. This phenomenon suggests a vicious cycle. First, the depressed student feels unworthy of peer interaction and withdraws. Peers sense that something is wrong, but rather than conclude that the individual is unhappy, they believe that he or she is rejecting them. Hence, peers withdraw, and the depressed student concludes, with even greater intensity, that he or she is unworthy. The cycle is complete.

Finally,   depression often is associated with *a tendency to develop physical symptoms.* Sleep disorder is one sign. Somatic complaints may include headaches, stomachaches, and assorted physical signs. Laurel, for example, has stomach problems and nausea, along with sleeplessness, joint pains, and dizziness. Jesse, too, frequently complains about sickness. Billy complains about frequent sleeplessness and headaches, and Olivia has many physical signs, including asthma and a sleep disorder.

SUGGESTED EDUCATIONAL STRATEGIES

This complex, multifaceted problem demands teaching strategies that are commensurately multidimensional. What makes this disorder especially challenging is the range of behaviors among and within individuals, from sluggishness to hyperactivity, from self-reproach to anger and oppositionality.

Some suggested educational strategies are the following.

1.   Mildly and moderately depressed individuals have found relief through both cognitive and behavior therapies; a combined approach is more effective than either one used alone. Educators can apply these approaches in their settings. For example, a student who has been focusing primarily on negative feelings and who has lost interest in physical activity could be directed to take increasingly longer walks around the building and grounds, with the assignment to concentrate on the surroundings and report back about what was seen. The student might also be directed to keep a log of environmental details observed during walks. Also, a student who has trouble concentrating in class could be directed to take five minutes at the start of class to write concerns on a piece of paper, which would be given to the teacher to hold. The teacher would return the paper to the student after class with the comment, "See, the list is still here even though you were a part of other things." If the student had a productive session, he or she could be praised for getting on with business. Gradually, the teacher should wait for the student to ask for the list back, which the student might forget to do when he or she learns that the worries that felt so important at 9:00 no longer do at 10:00. Hopefully, the student will learn (1) that he or she can let go of the bad feelings and (2) that by doing so nothing terrible happens.

2.   Elicit from the student what activities are enjoyable for him or her. An assessment of mood might also be done by asking the student to rate his or her mood at the end of each day relative to activities in which the has engaged. (This could be done with an entire class to assess moods, particularly following a traumatic schoolwide event.) Conduct the activities and have the student write the satisfactions arising from them.

3.   Graph the student's academic progress with him or her, increasing task difficulty in a safe, step-by-step manner. If the student balks at a task, there is proof of success on a task preceding the feared one.

4.   Increase the reinforcing characteristics of the environment. For example, schedule activities from least enjoyable to most enjoyable, thereby building in hope and a forward orientation. A corner could be redecorated with warm colors and pictures, and a comfortable chair and rug added. A student who has completed work could have downtime time to relax, read a magazine, listen to music with headphones, or talk quietly with a peer.

5.   Set aside time for class meetings in order to discuss or deal with feelings as they spontaneously surface in class.

6.   Encourage or reward the student for interacting with peers. Encour-

age or reward peers for interacting with the target student.

7.   Deal with aggressive, hyperactive, and oppositional behaviors as you would with all students. (See Chapters 8 and 9 for specific suggestions.) Students who are depressed do not need to feel further guilt and self-reproach for their behaviors, thus their behaviors should receive the appropriate corrective response. Hopefully, strategies will convey the message that the student is liked, but some of his behaviors may not be appreciated and need to be changed.

8.   Reinforce and chart/graph small steps of progress. Often, depressed students do not believe they are achieving because goals seem distant and elusive. Rewarding each success enables them to feel good about their performance, and seeing an upward trend line on a chart/graph gives them a concrete verification of progress.

9.   Reinforce task-specific behavior. Depressed individuals tend to be overly sensitive to feedback, either overvaluing it or undervaluing it. In either case, they set themselves up for further disappointment if they cannot consistently merit the accolades or for further misperception if they cannot match the accolate with the performance. Honest, specific feedback communicates precise skill status and accurate self-evaluation. Discriminative feedback is best: Inform the student about both strengths and weaknesses in terms of skills and behaviors. Rather than writing "Good job!" on a composition, write down what was written well and what needs further work. For example, the ideas and content might be insightful and comprehensive but the writing mechanics might be weak. Such feedback encourages the student to move forward, with direction for learning and development.

10.   For the student who is angry or aggressive, even when the underlying problem is depression, crisis management strategies are appropriate. If the student is out of control, do not try to talk with him or her; the student is not going to listen anyway. Time is needed to calm down. Time-out, which works in many cases of aggressive behavior, needs to be applied consistently, each time an aggressive behavior occurs. Time-out typically produces an immediate reduction in disruptive behavior. In an extreme case, it may be necessary to send the student home. At the first opportunity, when the student is calm, talk with him or her about the feelings he or she experienced before the outburst, what might be changed to prevent further outbursts, and how much you want to support learning and growth. However, remind the student that outbursts are unacceptable and will receive a firm response. During this conference, a contingency contract could be developed.

11.   Structure the environment so that the student has many opportunities to interact with peers.

12.   Conduct a sociometric activity with the class in order to determine the peer(s) who would most like to interact with the target student. Use the results to assign students to work groups and to arrange seating.

13.   Structure cooperative activities so that the student will learn that his or her skills and abilities are important in productivity. These activities also will

encourage friendships and break down social isolation.

14.   Take the time to convey your concern and interest.

15.   Provide the student with as many academic and social successes as possible so that peers may view him or her in a more positive light.

16.   Make the necessary environmental adjustments to prevent the student from experiencing stress, frustration, or anger.

17.   Structure the environment so that the student does not have time to dwell on real or imagined problems.

18.   Help the student identify his or her inappropriate behaviors, and teach the student how to change those behaviors.

19.   Ask the student to pick a peer with whom to work on a specific assignment. Encourage the student and peer to interact in nonacademic areas (e.g. break time). Do not force the student to interact with any students with whom he or she is not completely comfortable.

20.   Have the student keep a journal of positive, "up" feelings that are experienced each day. Require the student to write at least one positive entry daily.

21.   Reinforce those students in the classroom who make positive, supportive comments to peers.

14

Bipolar Disorder

Fire is the symbol: the celestial possible.
                              Wallace Stevens

Alone, in silence
Even as the crowd swells
Alone, in confusion
Caged up where your mind dwells
Self-esteem washed away
Left, alone, in silence
There but only part of you
Half you cannot find
Alone but never free to leave
Alone, that always stays
Alone, in silence
On this endless day

                              Carrie

Some believe that Robert Louis Stevenson drew on a deep personal understanding of bipolar mood disorder for *The Strange Case of Dr. Jekyll and Mr. Hyde*. The theme of the story overwhelmed Stevenson's mind; there is evidence of it in almost all of his works (Harman 1992).

Psychiatry professor Kay Jamison has studied the link between artistic creativity and mood disorders, particularly bipolarity. To Jamison, herself afflicted, Stevenson's novel has come to symbolize bipolarity, a condition of long, severe mood swings, from the tortured depths of depression to the thought-racing, hyperactive, deluded heights of mania. Jamison's *Touched with Fire* (1993) addresses the connection she perceives between creative genius and manic-depression.

Whether or not one accepts that certain creative geniuses have had bipolar disorder, Stevenson's story is probably the best available psychological allegory. His character, Henry Jekyll, enacts the disorder, giving voice to the tortured spirit of the manic-depressive, whose dual nature yearns for integration.

The allegory of Jekyll and Hyde has been woven into the common knowledge base. For example, in describing her son's early development, Rick's mother alluded to Stevenson's dual-nature character.

DUAL-NATURE CHARACTER EXAMPLE. *Rick was evaluated at age 10 for special education services. His mother said that he had "Jekyll and Hyde behaviors." When he is good, she said, he is an angel, helping with the household chores and cuddling with his parents; when things are not going well, Rick threatens to jump out the window of his bedroom and says he hates life.*

It is believed that Edgar Allen Poe also suffered from bipolar disorder. Poe's story, "The Pit and the Pendulum," is a metaphor for a condition that swings, like a pendulum, from the depths of depression to the heights of mania. The core psychological problem is that bipolar individuals cannot modulate their feelings and behaviors in order to achieve balance.

BEHAVIOR MODULATION EXAMPLE. *Rick had difficulty modulating his behavior and feelings. He cannot achieve balance and readily dissipate strong feelings. When other students annoy him, he feels that it is all right to aggress against them. Consequently, Rick typically reacts out of proportion to situations. For example, when a classmate took a pencil from his desk, Rick tried to strangle the boy. Hostile feelings last if Rick cannot express himself physically. One sign is hand tremoring, which happens when Rick needs to hit someone to relieve tension.*

Stevenson's Dr. Jekyll, who seeks a solution through laboratory experimentation, creates a drug that will separate the two personalities, thereby relieving his torturous duality. Jekyll's concoction foreshadowed the modern era's psychotropic drugs such as Lithium. Modern psychotropic therapy has helped manic-depressives integrate their emotions.

PSYCHOTROPIC DRUG THERAPY EXAMPLE. *Laura takes Lithium to stabilize her moods and Prozac to counteract depression, but most of the time she refuses to take the medications, which exacerbates the problems. On the other hand, when she takes an antipsychotic medication, she likes the resultant "high." Laura's need for excitement is partly satisfied by watching horror films, the content of which spills into her compositions. For example, she wrote about children killing their parents. In history class, for example, she became bored because the teacher was not covering anything she liked, such as war and atrocities, especially tales of people burning alive. She also experiences a social high when classes change; she darts through the halls to meet with friends, to watch boys, and to stuff notes into friends' lockers. There is much giggling and talking behind hands. Laura becomes so worked up that her face flushes and her hands shake. The ringing of the bell to end classes is like a conditioned stimulus that sets her in motion and prompts emotional salivation in anticipation of each seven-minute social feeding frenzy.*

Despite the fact that many individuals with bipolar disorder have been helped by drugs, they are likely to be controlling (Benjamin and Wonderlich 1994). They seem to try to make others match their moods rather than try to adjust their moods to others. Self-control is a major concern for bipolars; they constantly seek internal equilibrium and a way in which to relate to others.

PSYCHOTROPIC DRUG THERAPY EXAMPLES 2 AND 3. *In Sarah's case, affective instability, anxiety and depression, concentration difficulties, aggressive fantasy, morbid ideas, and tendencies both to withdraw and to act out continue despite intensive treatment. When she withdraws, she tries to renew herself and to figure things out: how to get along with others, what others feel about her, and how to control herself. When she acts out, feeling that she cannot change enough to satisfy others' demands, she believes that others must change to match her mood. If they do not adjust to her, Sarah becomes suspicious and cynical and tense, angry, frustrated and dissatisfied with everyone and everything. She rails at the demands made on her and claims that others do not accept her as she is. In her manic phases, Sarah tries to control the pace and content of conversations. Thus, it is difficult to converse with her. Her manic phases are also fraught with opposition and defiance. She may become violent, throwing chairs and physically fighting.*

Rick also is bipolar. He uses aggression to test limits and to control others. When frustrated, he tries to force others to see and do things his way. For example, if a peer playfully teases Rick, his response may be to physically aggress against the peer, "to keep him in line." If Rick scores poorly on a test, he may refuse to follow directions, become uncooperative, or act out. These responses have forced others to back down and give Rick what he needs: for example, some space, a chance to earn extra credit to improve his grade, or a way to avoid peers. Rick's extreme behavior controls his world.

Bipolar disorder is not just a mixture of normal feelings and mood swings. It is a disorder of extremes and contrasts that affect the individual's developmental, educational, and personal pursuits. Adolescents, particularly, may manifest the disorder in developmentally unique ways, and their educational and personal endeavors are impacted significantly in ways that relate to their age and stage. For adolescents with bipolar disorder, there is not only the normal challenge of independence versus dependence, there is also a serious inner duality that involves extreme mood swings.

INNER DUALITY EXAMPLES. *Laura looks like a Norman Rockwell American girl: blue eyes, round face, red hair in a pony tail, a chunky build just a year away from baby fat, freckles, and a mouthful of braces.   Upon second glance one sees macabre fantasies, precocious sexual interests, a flushed face and shaking hand when excited, and a child spinning in place in order to get a "rush."   Who is this child, a contrast between innocence and darkness, evident in Laura's poem?*

> *Forests of green*
> *Get awakened by the sound of a shot*
> *Lilies wake from their beauty sleep*
> *To catch the dew that falls*

During depressive phases Rick is cooperative and compliant, although socially withdrawn. At these times, too, he stares into space, puts his head on his desk, and sometimes sleeps. Altogether, he lacks energy and is unmotivated. During manic phases Rick has rushes of motivation and makes promises to make up weeks of past-due school work in short order. With increasing frequency he has requested passes to the office, where he sits and watches office staff work and people come and go. Rick is content doing this, avoiding the drag of demands that he cannot consistently meet in the classroom, and avoiding his own anger when thwarted during energy rushes when his mood elevates.

SOME FACTS

Family history. Statistics show that many bipolars are related to individuals with affective disorders. Hirshfield and colleagues (1986) found that from 60 to 65 percent of bipolars had family members with some history of major depression or bipolar illness.

Prevalence. Mood disorders in children have long been underdiagnosed in the United States because of the belief that a child's emotional and personality immaturity mitigates against such a disorder (Weller and Weller 1991). Only in the past decade has the existence of bipolar disorder been recognized in childhood and adolescence. Bipolar disorder is believed to afflict 2.5 million Americans (Fried 1995). Precise estimates among the pre-adult population are unclear owing to the disorder's rarity in this age group. While less common than depressive disorder (Keller and Baker 1991), it is a condition that merits study, for it is destructive, often psychotic, and frequently lethal (Jamison 1993).

Gender. Bipolarity occurs equally in males and females. Although depressive episodes are more prevalent among women, manic episodes occur with equal frequency in both genders.

Age of onset. As clinicians may not be prepared to recognize children with bipolar disorder, and as parents have little information available to them (Spivack 1994), understanding of the prevalence and the time of onset is unclear. The belief that bipolar disorders usually begin in late adolescence or early adulthood, rarely in childhood or early adolescence, is still held by many mental health professionals. More research and practical information are needed to clarify the onset issue.

AGE OF ONSET EXAMPLES. *Sarah was diagnosed as bipolar at age 14. Her elementary school years were described as "a golden time" by her parents. She had good academic skills, was a gifted athlete, and related well to classmates. During middle school, she took a downward plunge, and emotional problems surfaced. She began taking illegal drugs. By ninth grade Sarah was associating with "fringy" kids, those who take drugs and denigrate school. By the middle of ninth-grade Sarah was referred for special education evaluation. Her grades had declined, she had begun to cut classes, she did not complete assignments, and, generally, she appeared unmotivated.*

Rick was 14 when he was diagnosed as bipolar. Since early school years teachers had reported moodiness, a "short fuse," and problems relating to peers. He was referred to a school psychologist in kindergarten because of oppositional, manipulative, and aggressive tendencies and subsequently was placed in a self-contained program for ED students.

Laura was diagnosed as bipolar when in third grade. Her psychiatrist was reluctant to diagnose her as bipolar at such a young age, but the symptoms merited it.

Cause. Bipolar disorder, a biological, inherited disorder (Spivack 1994), is not usually diagnosed until adolescence. Early signs may suggest another condition, or it may be interpreted without the benefit of a bigger picture, such as family history.

CAUSE EXAMPLES. *Rick's maternal grandfather had had a manic condition for most of his life. Binge shopping, hyperactivity, and grand, unfulfilled promises were characteristic. His family always thought of him as eccentric. Rick's mother began to rethink the nature of her father's actual condition when Rick was diagnosed as bipolar.*

Sarah's mother had struggled for years with clinical depression, for which she had taken numerous medications. Sarah's father experienced severe mood swings.

Course. Many adolescents admitted to hospitals with severe depression later show a clinical course compatible with bipolar disorder. When bipolar disorder occurs in childhood or adolescence, it is associated with suicide and rapid cycling between depressive and manic phases. Episodes of bipolarity last from two to four months. The average time between symptoms is 33 months. Left untreated, a person with bipolar disorder can expect to have at least 10 manic or major depressive episodes in a lifetime, and cycling between episodes may increase in frequency. Treatment can help shorten the episodes and lessen the severity of symptoms.

It is critical to bipolar disorder to identify appropriate levels of services for this complex condition. Medication, intensive personal and family therapy, environmental interventions, special education, and hospitalization may all be required at one time or another or concurrently. Psychotherapy helps a youngster understand herself or herself adapt to stresses, rebuild self-esteem, and improve relationships.

Swinging from the pits to the heights is a serious problem, and bipolarity is a serious psychiatric disorder (see Table 14.1). Such signs represent the duality with which the individual struggles, including dramatic motoric, cognitive, and emotional shifts. It is, thus, understandable that adolescents with bipolar disorder may experience *dissociativeness*, a feeling that they are outside of their own bodies, watching themselves. Frequently they report feelings of fragmentation, which may be a response to the intensity of manic emotions.

The seriousness of bipolar disorder is also reflected in suicide statistics. "The thing that doesn't get emphasized enough is the fact that manic-depressive illness kills people. There's an extremely high suicide rate attached to it. It's the most important thing about the illness" (Jamison quoted in Fried 1995, p. 13).

Sarah has had two psychiatric hospitalizations, one during seventh grade and one during ninth grade, because of extreme violence and rage and lack of response to outpatient treatment and medication, as well as prolonged substance abuse involving marijuana and LSD. Themes of death and dying run throughout Sarah's poetry, excerpted here.

> *He was going to be caught and he knew it*
> *He just didn't care*
> *And he knew it even more when he heard the wail of the*
> *Sirens coming after him*
>
> *But he didn't run, instead he lit another cigarette*
> *He sat by a tree and leaned his head back*
> *Closing his eyes he let out a deep sigh*
> *And he could hear the barking dogs getting closer*
>
> *Now he had been found, and he felt relieved*
> *The police ran for him, but he was too quick*
> *He grabbed the knife (It had claimed one life already)*
> *And he plunged it deep inside his chest*

To summarize, Sarason and Sarason offer a comparison of the emotional, cognitive and motor characteristics of bipolar disorder, contrasting manic and depressive patterns (1993, p. 308). This comparison, excerpted for Table 14.1, clarifies the ups and downs of this mood disorder by defining patterns of manic and depressive characteristics in bipolar disorder.

Psychotic features. As indicated previously, psychotic features may occur in bipolarity when the mood disturbance is at its worst. Five out of 11 hospitalized manics in one study had hallucinations and delusions, and paranoid

Table 14.1
Emotional, Cognitive, and Motor Characteristics of Manic and Depressive Patterns

Characteristics	Manic Pattern	Depressive Pattern
Emotional	Very sociable	Socially withdrawn; loss of enjoyment in favorite activities
	Impatient at any hindrance; very irritable distractible; attention moves constantly	Irritable; poor concentration; complains of boredom
	Elated; euphoric; usually happy or silly; "wired"	Gloomy, hopeless; persistent sadness; frequent crying
Cognitive	Racing thoughts	Slow thinking
	Desire for action	Obsessive worrying
	Positive self-image	Negative self-image
	Delusions of grandeur; unrealistic highs in self-esteem	Delusions of guilt
Motor	Hyperactive; increased talking: too fast, too much, changes topics too quickly; and cannot be interrupted	Slow motor activity
	Does not become tired	Tired; frequent complaints of physical illness such as headaches or stomachaches; low energy level
	Needs less sleep than usual	Difficulty sleeping (major change in pattern)
	Fluctuating appetite	Decreased appetite

grandiosity and delusions may also be present (Weiner 1983). Disordered thinking may be a secondary symptom of depression and mania (Fried 1995).

Manic-depressive, or bipolar, illness encompasses a wide range of mood disorders and temperaments. These vary in severity from cyclothymia (characterized by pronounced but not totally debilitating changes in mood, behavior, thinking, sleep, and energy levels) to extremely severe, life-threatening, and psychotic forms of the disease. (Jamison 1993, p. 13)

Seligman and Moore (1995) note that bipolar disorders include distinct periods of diverse moods, including depressive, manic, hypomanic, and normal mood episodes. The depressive episodes usually resemble episodes of major depressive disorder.

Bipolar mood swings may appear in the classroom as erratic behavior. Teachers may report ups and downs of a chronic nature.

BIPOLAR MOOD SWING EXAMPLE. *Sarah's work habits have been described as erratic. Her creative writing teacher described brief "spurts" of activity and longer "lulls." Sarah says her work habits depend on her mood.*

MANIC FEATURES

Mania is associated with acceleration and energy, with the body racing to keep up with thoughts and feelings. Mania typically lasts at least one week. The individual experiences an elevated, expansive, or irritable mood. Besides racing thoughts, also called "flights of ideas," and elevated mood, typical signs include disorganization, hyperactivity, inflated self-esteem, combativeness, insomnia, overtalkativeness, grandiose delusions of intelligence or power, delusions of persecution, impaired concentration, agitation, excessive spending, and pleasure-seeking. Costello and Costello (1992) add that during the manic state energy is expended uselessly and seemingly endlessly and that there is unrealistic optimism. There may even be violence because strong, unleashed emotions can lead to uninhibited behavior. The individual, too, typically disregards the consequences of pleasure-seeking behavior (Seligman and Moore 1995). Indeed, if the individual in a manic state is blocked or criticized, irritability or belligerency is likely to occur, as well as abusive and profane language.

MANIA FEATURES EXAMPLES. *Sarah's mania is characterized by easy annoyance at other students. Trivial issues "tick me off," she said. On one occasion, Sarah tried to be helpful to another student, picking up something the other girl dropped. When the other student failed to thank her, Sarah said that it was everything she could do to control herself and not "punch the bitch out." Many times, Sarah feels so frustrated and angry that she wants to "throw people across the room." The only reason she controls herself is that she does not want to be hospitalized again. During mania she is overly talkative and tries to dominate conversations, flowing from one topic to another without pause.*

Rick, also, has shown some violence. On one occasion, when his brother, tired of Rick's sloppiness, threw away all of Rick's clothes and toys that littered his side of the bedroom, Rick retaliated by slashing the brother's mattress with a knife and cutting his favorite clothes with scissors.

Types of Mania. There are three types of mania: hypomania, acute mania, and delirious mania. Of these three, hypomania is the least disturbed and most common. It features supercharged mood, overactive behavior, poor judgment, unwillingness to listen to reason, grandiosity, and desire to control. Called "mild mania," the hypomanic phase is considered to be the one silver lining among the disorder's many thunderous clouds. During hypomania there is increased energy, expansiveness, risk taking, and fluency of thought, which can lead to periods of superhuman productivity (Fried 1995). It is focused frenzy.

Also evident in bipolar disorder is enjoyment of the "rushes" of mania and the desire to avoid the down times. In a pursuit of highs and avoidance of lows, these students may have repeated legal troubles and show academic underachievement.

HYPOMANIA EXAMPLE. *Laura has engaged in recurrent illegal activities, along with violence and lying. She calls her illegal actions "risk taking." For example, during fifth grade she stole food at school; during sixth grade her parents found empty beer and wine bottles in her bedroom, she cut the Christmas lights in neighboring houses, and she stole and destroyed a neighbor's mail; and during seventh grade she cut classes and left school grounds. In terms of violence, Laura threatened her brother with a knife when he tried to make her clean up cereal on the kitchen counter. She also pushed her mother several times when her mother tried to discipline her. As for lying, Laura told her parents that the wine and beer bottles were part of a collection; she claimed that she was keeping cigarettes for a friend when her parents found a pack in her room; she conned her younger brother out of his allowance by telling him that she would donate the money to a baseball fund; she told her third-grade teacher that she had had a baby sister who died; she told her mother that she stayed after school to work when actually she had gone to a mall with a friend; and she forged her mother's signature on a permission note so that a friend could take Laura's bus.*

These students also typically seek to enjoy the heights of their mood swings. They may do so in frenetic fashion, as if to ward off the depressive feelings. Some bipolars neglect to take their mood stabilizing medications because they prefer the elevated moods.

In acute mania, which may grow out of hypomania, the individual's speech is incoherent, and there are extreme symptoms such as a frightening level of irritability. Acute mania may arise without warning.

The third type, delirious mania, is the most extreme form. The individual is completely out of control, a "wild maniac." Hallucinations and delusions appear, and behavior becomes dangerous. Sedation and physical restraint are needed; the individual's sleeplessness will probably lead to exhaustion.

Manic Grandiosity. Manic grandiosity deserves further explanation. Grandiosity involves exaggerating reality, with many tall tales of fantastic, unbelievable exploits. It is beyond lying. As these students regard themselves as adults, they want to take charge (Spivack 1994).

MANIC GRANDIOSITY EXAMPLES. *During a grandiose moment, Rick proclaimed that he was going to propose a computer homework bulletin board system to his middle school principal, as if she is his colleague. The plan is for teachers to post homework assignments so that students might access them through their home computers. Rick has worked out a conceptually big scheme; however, he has no idea how to deal with the details of implementation. He fails to see the discrepancy between the grandiose idea and his own daily functioning (he almost never does homework) or the practical obstacles to implemention.*

Laura has fantasies about becoming a famous writer. During the same week that she declared this career interest she also announced that she wanted to convert to Judaism, become a vegetarian, earn a million dollars by the time she was twenty-one, and marry a rich, handsome man and bear three children. The order of these accomplishments is unclear. She does not want to be bothered with details. The only thing that Laura accomplished during this particular week was to write two pages of a creative writing assignment.

Manic Sexuality. The adolescent with a bipolar disorder is unusually adult-like in sexual interest and behavior. These students may pursue sexual activity as if they are emancipated adults. Provocative postures, gestures, verbalizations, and actions are typical for them (Spivack 1994).

MANIC SEXUALITY EXAMPLES. *Sarah is proud of her sexuality. She feels that she is a mature person now that she has a steady boyfriend with whom she is sexually active. She describes their sex life as great fun.*

Laura has been vulgar and precocious in sexual matters. During fourth-grade she put her Ken and Barbie dolls in sexual positions. During sixth grade she showed recurrent fascination with "dirty sexual words."

Carrie's provocative movements at school dances make faculty extremely uncomfortable.

Manic Aggression. When adults try to reaffirm boundaries and limits, the student with a bipolar disorder typically rages. However, if adults do not set realistic limits, symptoms may worsen (Spivack 1994). One serious symptom is aggression, shown against self or others. In a manic state, the individual's functioning is markedly impaired due to underlying depression, consequently hospitalization may be needed to prevent self-injury.

DEPRESSIVE FEATURES

During depressive episodes, which tend to last longer than manic ones (Seligman and Moore 1995), thoughts of suicide are likely. Jamison describes one of her own depressive episodes:

All I wanted to do was die. I couldn't function, but I did function. There's an interacting shell you present to the world. But I had no fun, which for me was inconceivable. Life, to me, was fun. Then, all of a sudden I had no pleasure in doing anything. I had no name for it, no notion of what it was. Several of my teachers called me aside and said I looked terrible. But they didn't say "depressed." Back then, nobody thought people in high school were capable of feeling like that. (quoted in Fried 1995, p. 27)

Jamison's depression broke after several months. Even untreated, the mood eventually swings back, with quick recovery. Fried describes the aftereffects of Jamison's depressive episode.

When you recover, you're so normal. It's one of the things that can be deceptive. It's like having a very bad flu, during which you promise that you'll do this, that and the other thing, and you're going to appreciate life more when you feel better. I'm amazed at how rapidly one feels normal and takes it for granted. (1995, p. 27)

The depressive features that are evident in a student with bipolar disorder are similar to those of depression in general. The reader is referred to Chapter 13 for a detailed coverage of depression in adolescents. The essential difference is that in bipolar disorder the depressive features are cyclical.

DEPRESSIVE EPISODE EXAMPLES. *Rick's evaluation by a school psychologist at age 10 revealed numerous depressive features. There were feelings of helplessness and hopelessness. Negative feelings about himself often surfaced, at times intense. When comparing himself to peers, he tended to view himself as less capable and less effective, which presented as sadness. At one point, Rick completed the sentence stem, "My biggest mistake was" with "being born." This sadness alternated with overvaluing of the importance of his personal worth.*

Sarah experiences recurrent depression. Because her self-esteem sags from time to time, she demands a lot of attention in order to sustain a viable level of self-worth. There are times when she acts out, too, to get attention. When she feels sad, Sarah believes that her parents do not love her.

Laura's depressive episodes tend to occur during the winter months; her manic flowering typically is during the springtime. When depressed, she is prone to physical illness along with sad feelings. During one winter Laura asked her mother to pick her up at school numerous times because of a sprained ankle, lost eyeglasses, fever, sick stomach, and a jammed finger.

BIPOLAR DISORDER AND THE FEDERAL DEFINITION OF ED

One ED criterion under the Individuals with Disabilities Education Act (IDEA) is *a tendency to develop physical symptoms*. Sarah and Laura meet this criterion. Sarah has developed numerous physical symptoms: chronic back pain, headaches, and sleep problems. At times, both Sarah and Carrie have panic attacks when their hearts race and they feel chest pains. Sarah has also reported "sharp and stabbing" stomach pains. Sarah said, "When I think of school I feel stressed." She would like a reduced school schedule so that she can go home at midday and relax. Laura shows numerous physical symptoms during depressive phases.

Fears associated with personal or school problems are also defining for ED, generally, and bipolarity particularly. For example, Sarah said, "My worst fear is losing my friends." New to her high school, she feels like an outsider and hangs on to her few friends for dear life.

Also, a student with a bipolar disorder shows signs of a *general pervasive mood of unhappiness or depression*. The bipolar condition involves depression alternating with mania, but even the manic phase involves an undercurrent of depression.

Students with bipolar disorder have an *inability to build or maintain satisfactory interpersonal relationships with peers and teachers*. It is difficult to relate to a student whose moods change radically. The unpredictability may be unnerving and even frightening. For example, Rick's English teacher observed two separate incidents when a classmate took a pencil from Rick's desk. On one occasion Rick reacted by staring sleepily at the boy; on another, he tried to strangle him. Altogether, Rick's teachers are constantly kept off balance by him, and their fear about potential aggression is worsened by his unpredictability.

As for peers, many of Laura's classmates avoid her because she is wild at times and glum at other times. Classmates describe her as "spooky" and "weird."

The federal criterion of *inappropriate types of behavior or feelings under normal circumstances*, may be applied as well. Certainly, Rick's attempt to strangle a peer for taking a pencil is an inappropriate response. Also, Sarah's desire to strike a peer for failing to show gratitude for a simple gesture is inappropriate.

Finally, students with bipolar disorder show *an inability to learn that cannot be explained by intellectual, sensory, or health factors*. As seen in actual cases, these students are unable to focus on school work. When they are depressed, their thinking and energy are profoundly compromised. They cannot get out of the emotional pit. When they are manic, their ideas and emotions fly so fast that they miss the essentials. What does a mundane grammar assignment mean when they can be planning a way to revamp the entire ninth-grade English curriculum?

Their inability to learn has nothing to do with cognitive ability, abnormal senses, or physical health; their learning problems have everything to do with the pendulum that causes their moods to swing from depression to mania and back again. These students expend emotional energy struggling with a duality that interferes with their learning.

SUGGESTED EDUCATIONAL STRATEGIES

The types of teaching strategies needed for students with bipolar disorder encompass, first, many of those that are appropriate for depressed students. Second, appropriate strategies relate to a need for consistency and stability, a need to improve peer and adult relationships, and approaches that will dispel fears about the future by structuring activities and ensuring predictability.

Some appropriate strategies are the following.

1.   Maintain a predictable routine. When changes occur, give the student advance warning.

2.   Have the student keep a daily journal, highlighting the best and worst events of the day and how he or she felt during the day. Review the journal once each week, noting mood patterns. This strategy can promote the student's self-awareness and help the adult understand and plan activities.

3.   Maintain close communication with parents as moods can change rapidly. School and home must work together to prevent escalation of behaviors to a severe level and to respond to problems. Communication should also be fostered among school, parents, and therapists; the effects of medication should be monitored closely.

4.   Encourage the student to get involved in extracurricular activities that provide tension relief and opportunities for creativity. Drama, for example, is a good outlet.

5.   Because the bipolar student is unable to adapt to change quickly, provide accommodations. For example, Carrie was unaware that her twelfth-grade English teacher expected that the students would have read certain books during the summer between eleventh and twelfth grades, as well as complete a written journal about those readings. When Carrie arrived for the first English class of twelfth grade and learned about the assignment, she was thrown into an emotional upheaval. Before the teacher had an opportunity to reassure Carrie that she could have extra time to catch up, she jumped to conclusions about her ultimate grade and future. It took about a week to calm her and to plot an accommodative course. The teacher maintained a flexible, understanding position, and Carrie eventually rallied and caught up after the parent, the teacher, Carrie, and the ED resource teacher met to design a realistic, extended time frame. Carrie, once calmer, could see that she would be able to catch up.

6.   Ensure that the student knows the course requirements.

7.   Closely monitor the student using progress checks. Ask all classroom teachers to provide feedback about completion of work, any outstanding assignments, and social-emotional status. Give copies of progress reports to the parents and therapist.

8.   Pair students during lectures and presentations. Every 10 to 15 minutes stop the activity so that they can check their understanding, compare notes, and ask questions of each other and the teacher before proceeding. This helps the student follow the activities.

9.   Establish a private, nonverbal cue with the student to remind him or her to refocus, pay attention, and participate.

10.   Stand near the student during activities in which there is more chance that he or she will drift mentally or distract other students.

11.   Build self-esteem by reinforcing appropriate behavior, by corrective feedback that balances error spotting and positive comments, and by integrating the student's interests into activities. Another way is to give the student responsibility for helping a peer who is less skilled.

12.   Build self-awareness through structured interpersonal activities. Begin by pairing the student with a peer of his or her choice for projects. Help the pair divide the labor, set goals, and proceed to work. Supervise interaction closely in order that the peer with whom the student interacts does not stimulate the student's inappropriate behavior. Group projects will probably be difficult for this student for a number of reasons. For example, the student may be intolerant of other students' ability differences, and he or she may be unable to focus on work division because he or she is focused on the final product or unrealistic ideas of a final product. Pairings would be more effective than larger groupings, and even pairings should be closely monitored and helped to structure the work and to process ideas. Cooperative working will help the student become more aware of her own strengths and weaknesses as well as of others' in relation to himself or herself.

13.   Modify situations that cause the student to be reluctant to participate (e.g., degree of difficulty, competition, fear of failure, threat of embarrassment).

14.   Make sure that classroom activities and the social atmosphere do not provoke difficulties with desired classroom interactions (e.g., a noisy classroom may overstimulate the student).

15.   Encourage the student to share things of special interestor unique accomplishments.

16.   Hold class meetings in which issues and concerns common to all members are discussed. Start with relatively impersonal, neutral, and group-oriented topics, for example, the value of rules. As students and teacher get to know one another

better, more experiences can be shared and feelings explored. One important goal, which is highly relevant to the ED student, is that the students gain understanding that their difficulties are shared by others and are not due strictly to their own inadequacies. For example, exploring students' reactions to changes, pop quizzes, and many other stressful events casts such experiences in an impersonal light that sets the stage for dealing with such events.

17.   Teach the student problem-solving skills so he or she is better equipped to manage potential problems (e.g., talking, walking away [timing himself out, cooling off], calling on the teacher to arbitrate, and compromising).

18.   Ask the student to self-evaluate his or her mood prior to the start of class. Use a scale of 1 to 3, with 1 representing "down," 2 "O.K.," and 3 "hyper" or "psyched up." This self-rating can be done quickly and routinely using words or finger signals. (These self-ratings could be recorded for ongoing assessment purposes.)

19.   Accommodate the student's unique, perhaps even unconventional, style by allowing options to complete assignments and projects. Structure the choices and be firm about sticking to the chosen methods. A written contract can provide concrete verification of the agreed upon terms.

20.   Be there for the student. Despite the ups and downs, a predictably reassuring relationship is important.   This student needs to know that despite his or her changeable behaviors and moods, there is at least one adult who constantly accepts him or her.

21.   When there are peer conflicts, use mediation techniques. The bipolar student needs to get realistic feedback about others' feelings and the behaviors that evoke such feelings. Resolution helps the student get closure and move on without unresolved tension and guilt.

15

Overview:
Anxiety Disorders

For fear of him the keepers did shake, and
became as dead men.
　　　　The Bible, The Gospel according to Matthew

FEAR AND ANXIETY

Fear. In order to understand anxiety it is necessary to understand fear. There are
five important attributes of fear.

1.　　It is an emotion that is focused on a specific person,
　　　object, or situation, such as fear of dark places or snakes.

2.　　Fear is an emotion of apprehension, or uneasiness,
　　　about the future. Some synonyms are dread, fore-
　　　boding, and misgiving. In short, fear is an emotion
　　　about what may occur.

3.　　Fear may be rational or irrational. A fear that is realistic is
　　　rational. For example, it is rational to fear a snake's bite
　　　when face-to-face with a poised snake. On the other
　　　hand, it is irrational to have a reaction to an unreal or
　　　nonexistent danger. It is irrational to dread snakes while
　　　in a city elevator, far removed from any snakes.

4.　　Fear is anxiety's parent emotion.

5.　　Fear signals fight or flight.

　　　Anxiety. Anxiety is an emotion that can be helpful; it provides necessary
information about the quality and adaptive efficiency of our transactions with the

environment (Krauss and Krauss 1994). For example, a little anxiety in a test situation can give us a performance "edge." On the other hand, anxiety can be dysfunctional, adversely impacting a person's life. It may pervade a person's life. It has been called "angst," or fear of fear.

Unlike anxiety, fear ceases when help comes, the situation changes, or danger passes. Anxiety is not situational; it is a lasting feeling of unavoidable doom, a pervading expectancy of disaster. The anxious person is extremely vigilant. Thus, while fear is a reaction to impending danger, real or imagined, anxiety is difficult to relate to tangible sources of stimulation. Anxiety is a nonspecific, diffuse, and anticipatory emotion.

Generalized to more diverse situations, anxiety involves more of the cognitive component. For example, people who fear mice may cry and experience rapid heart rate when they see a mouse, but they are not likely to develop thoughts about their own incompetence when there is no mouse in sight; out of sight, out of mind. By comparison, students who are anxious about school think a lot about that situation; they may be anxious about separating from their mothers; they may cry at the sight of the school bus; they may become nauseous at the sight of the school building; and they may have ongoing thoughts about academic failure. Eventually, the anxious student's thoughts become complex in terms of rationalizing why he or she should not go to school and devising avoidance tactics. Their responses evolve into a complicated cluster of symptoms that do not clearly relate to the school situation.

During a child's development, fears and anxieties are intertwined. In early development, fear of animals, darkness, and separation from parents are common. Young children are diffusely anxious about a lot of things because the world is relatively new to them. Hence, they may scream, urinate, and think about monsters whether or not a scary situation is at hand; the issue of fear versus anxiety is not a very meaningful distinction in early childhood.

In later childhood and into adolescence, on the other hand, fear and anxiety begin to separate qualitatively. While fear and anxiety share some features by this stage, they are increasingly different, and a divergence between them can be discerned. By adolescence, the individual is able to experience anxiety covertly and through behaviors and actions that cannot obviously be traced to a particular situation or circumstance. At this point, anxiety can be differentiated from the parent emotion, fear, by the disguise of its cause.

Nearly everyone feels fearful from time to time; given certain circumstances, it is normal to be fearful. An individual who has never ridden a horse may feel fear when faced with a saddled rental pony. A student facing a final examination, an expectant mother, and a man going into a job interview may all experience fear, and even a bit of anxiety. These are normal fears, but they pass when the circumstances change. Fears are a part of life, and it would be abnormal not to have them when faced with situations that require us to perform differently, especially well, or courageously.

Anxiety, on the other hand, is a sustained emotion that can render cognitive functioning dysfunctional and can lead to generalized dysfunction. It can be a crippling emotion, less a challenge to learn and more a loss of freedom.

Some people experience feelings of anxiety that come to dominate their lives. In extreme cases, individuals may wash their hands 50 or more times a day to remove unexplained germs. Others, who are considered to be victims of agoraphobia, may refuse to leave the safety of their homes for many years. Still others, suffering from undiagnosed anxiety disorders, may suffer intractable insomnia that disturbs their sleep and affects the quality of their lives. (Pasnau 1984, p. 3)

People who suffer from anxiety may also experience sudden panic attacks with accompanying feelings of impending doom and intense fear. Still others may suffer anxiety following a traumatic event, such as rape or other violence. Thus, fear can be bothersome, but anxiety can be disabling. Chronic anxiety is as painful as physical pain (Peck 1978).

DISABLING EFFECTS
There are four notable disabling effects of anxiety:

1. Emotional paralysis: Fear propells us to act. Anxiety, on the other hand, immobilizes us. Anxious people do not believe that anyone, or they themselves, can save them. Often, they feel doomed.

2. Low self-esteem: Anxiety reduces our ability to act and increases our doubt that we can be effective. Inability to act and self-doubt lead to low self-esteem and feelings of weakness, inferiority, and helplessness.

3. Social effect: Anxiety often causes us to withdraw from others and may result in feelings of anger, irritability, and hatred of others.

4. Cognitive breakdown: Anxiety affects intellectual functioning, especially memory and expressive ability. It can lead to cognitive breakdown. Eysenck (1991) believes that anxiety plays a major role in cognitive dysfunction. As the individual tries to disguise the cause of anxiety and rationalize behavior, thinking becomes distorted and dysfunctional.

ANXIETY EXAMPLE. *Feeling helpless to change her father's perception of her as irresponsible, and feeling powerless in the face of her domineering parent, Myra attributes feelings of stress to school demands. Anxiety does not diminish despite increased academic effort. Myra has bouts of tears, has difficulty sleeping, and feels woefully inept to deal with the stress. She feels overwhelmed. Her thinking has become dysfunctional. She rationalizes that she has too much work to do and too little time to do it. Myra is stuck; she cannot accept that there are ways to cope with school demands because her anxiety has caused her otherwise superior intellect to break down.*

Childhood anxiety was largely ignored prior to the twentieth century. The emphasis was on fears, with the understanding that they would pass as the child matured.

The literature on anxiety disorders has increased dramatically since the 1980s. The most frequently researched conditions are panic disorders, obsessive-compulsive disorder, and post-traumatic stress disorder. Many articles about anxiety disorders have appeared in psychology and psychiatry journals (Norton et al. 1995).

The reasons for this dramatic increase relate partly to funded research. The National Institute of Mental (NIMH) became very interested in anxiety disorders and began the first wave of funded research. By the mid-1980s, the NIMH was spending $3 million a year on anxiety research. While this was a modest investment, compared with $19 million on schizophrenia and $15 million on depression, research into treatment strategies, diagnosis, and genetic susceptibility to anxiety was progressing rapidly. This was followed by drug company research predicated on a need to establish which drugs are effective for particular anxiety disorders.

Another reason for increased attention to anxiety disorders in childhood and adolescence is evidence about the relation between childhood and adult anxiety disorders. Gittelman (1986) suggested that adult anxiety states are first likely to become manifest in childhood.

Also, increased attention to anxiety disorders relates to the stress of modern living. For example, one mental health problem that has been gaining attention is ataque de nervious, a response to acute stress found primarily in Hispanic women (Oquendo 1994). This intriguing disorder involves seizure- and panic-like responses, dissociation, suicidal threats, acting out, impulsivity, agitation, and screaming. While apparently prevalent in middle-age women, further research and attention may illuminate the early signs of this disorder, particularly during adolescence and young adulthood.

SOME FACTS

Prevalence. Anxiety disorders have been estimated to affect a sizable part of the general population and to be widely prevalent. Anxiety is one of the three major mental disturbances; the others are depression and stress (Wolman and Stricker 1994). According to a household survey conducted in the mid-1980s by the NIMH, 8 percent of the U.S. adult population had symptoms that could be diagnosed as anxiety disorder. Another 11 percent suffered from serious anxiety symptoms that were related to physical illness (Pasnau 1984). Another study concluded that about 15 percent of the population will suffer anxiety sometime during their lives (Robins et al. 1984). Despite such published figures, some experts question the reliability of data about these disorders in adults, and even more in children and adolescents. Many mental health professionals believe that the prevalence of anxiety disorders is seriously underestimated.

Conceptualization of children's anxieties is in a prescientific state because of methodogical and measurement problems. The construct is poorly defined, with unclear and variable behavioral referents that change over the course of development in unknown ways. Too many children are allowed to fail in school before consultation is sought, and then referral is sought not because of anxiety reaction but because of scholastic failure.

Onset. During the pre-adult phase, the most frequently affected are those of peripubertal adolescent ages.

Gender. It is more likely that females will be diagnosed with all types of anxiety disorders (Holmes 1994).

Cause. The current understanding is that biological, cognitive, and behavioral factors all play important roles, operating at differentlevels and influencing one another in the etiology and maintenance of these disorders (Emmelkamp and Scholing 1994).

Signs. There are four signs of anxiety disorders. The first is a pervasive mood characterized by tenseness, panic, and apprehension. Second, there is a cognitive component characterized as worry and inattention as a result of focus on potential disaster. This cognitive component adversely impacts routine functioning in such activities as school work. Third, there is a somatic component, which is either immediate or delayed. Immediate body signs include sweating, dry mouth, shallow breathing, rapid pulse, increased blood pressure, a throbbing sensation in the head, or feelings of muscular tension. Delayed body signs occur if anxiety is prolonged, including chronically elevated blood pressure, muscular weakness, and stomach cramps. Fourth, there are motor signs of anxiety disorder, including restlessness, fidgeting, pointless motor activity such as toe tapping, and an exaggereated startle response to sudden noise. The motor component can interfere with functioning (Holmes 1994).

Impact. Anxiety disorders are the most costly of all mental disorders in terms of indirect and direct costs. Indirect costs include lowered work productivity. Direct costs are reflected in time and expense needed to treat these disorders, which are crippling and severe. The costs to individuals and the society reflect a need for more and better research. There is a need for more understanding of anxiety disorders among adolescents as well as the diverse ethnic and cultural groups that melt into U.S. clinics, hospitals, and schools.

Types. Anxiety disorders have been generally divided into two categories: phobic disorders and anxiety states. In phobias, anxiety is focused on one object or situation. In anxiety states, the anxiety is more diffuse and not related to any one thing; it is experienced as omnipresent or free-floating. An individual who is experiencing an anxiety state may feel that his entire life is enveloped in an electrified cloud or that every move bodes doom from which there is no escape.

Separation anxiety, defined as abnormal difficulty separating from key attachment figures, a specific phobia according to the American Psychiatric Association's *DSM-IV*, is discussed in Chapter 16 as one issue in the complex phenomenon of school phobia. Overanxious disorder (classified by *DSM-IV* as generalized anxiety disorder), involving worry about everything or difficulty controlling worry, is considered in Chapters 17 and 18 (obsessive-compulsive disorder and post-traumatic stress disorder, respectively). While there are other types of anxiety disorders, those featured in the next three chapters are the most frequently found among schoolchildren.

Those things that hurt should instruct. However, no mentally healthy person would welcome such extreme anxiety as characterizes post-traumatic disorder, school phobia, or obsessive-compulsive disorder. Indeed, the pain shown by adolescents with these disorders interferes with their being and becoming, which includes their learning. They try to avoid the pain that set them on an anxious course. In the ongoing, evolving psychological process of avoidance they build layer upon layer of emotional defenses. Their pain is disguised in a knot of motor, behavioral, and psychological symptoms. They avoid dealing directly with the anxiety, as if to dance around their problems. School phobics set up school as the straw man; obsessive-compulsives create assorted ideas to think about and things to do to avoid dealing with their real problem; and post-traumatic adolescents avoid, selectively perceive, and numb their emotions to steer clear of painful thoughts and memories.

Freud, in his time, would unite these disorders as "neuroses." He viewed them all as the ego's attempt to defend itself against anxiety, which he defined as a feeling that is evoked when an unacceptable idea becomes conscious (Nevid, Rathus, and Greene 1994). Thus, a school phobic youngster cannot accept that his mother is dependent on him and he on her to a point of codependency, so the student scapegoats the school. If he stays home with his mother, according to this theory, it is to stave off the pain of separation. By Freud's theory, an obsessive-compulsive student cannot accept the idea that she cannot achieve her parent's desire for perfection. Hence, obsessive ideas of perfectionism and compulsive acts evolve. Finally, Freud likely would say that a student with post-traumatic stress disorder cannot accept the pain of remembering a catastrophic experience. Consequently, assorted motor responses (e.g., crying and physical avoidance), physiological responses (e.g., headache and stomachache), and cognitive responses (e.g., images of monsters, thoughts of danger and bodily injury, and avoidance of certain thoughts) develop.

Further, if, as the Freudian school of psychiatry maintains, "neurotic" behavior stems from the threatened emergence of unacceptable anxiety-evoking ideas into conscious awareness, it is those individuals who are most consciously aware who will suffer most from an anxiety disorder. By this reasoning, ignorance may be bliss; unawareness may spare one from an unrelenting, protracted anxiety disorder that establishes itself in the psyche and relents only with intensive, prolonged therapy requiring, in turn, strong awareness and a good memory. Thus, the stronger the learned connection that establishes the anxiety disorder, the harder it may be to unlearn. To untangle the web that has been spun by the youngster with an anxiety disorder, more is involved than desensitizing him or her to a fearsome stimulus.

The students who illustrate the three anxiety disorders featured in Chapters 16, 17, and 18 are strong learners. Their IQs are all in the above-average range. Consequently, the cognitions and behaviors that they have learned for dealing with emotional pain are strong and entrenched. For example, one of the school phobics, John, could not be helped in the school setting. He was placed on homebound instruction, and eventually his parents enrolled him in a private home study program. It is doubtful that John will ever return to a normal school situation.

16

School Phobia

Upon the mountains of my fear I climb.
W. H. Auden

Anxiety disorder is the most prevalent of all major groups of mental disorders in our era. Phobia, a subtype of anxiety disorder, is the most common anxiety disorder. It is estimated that phobias occur in about 13 percent of the general U.S. population at any given time (Holmes 1994; Lindemann 1994).

Phobias are so common that they may be trivialized and become a source of humor, but their commonness does not negate their seriousness. A phobia is a significant disability that is associated with a decrease in the quality of life, depression, suicide, financial difficulties, emergency room visits, and the risk of drug abuse in adolescents and young adults (Lindemann 1994).

The word "phobia" comes from the Greek word phobos, which means "flight." In Greek mythology, Phobos provoked fear in his enemies, causing them to flee.

A phobia is a persistent and irrational fear of a specific object, activity, or situation. For example, a phobia of flying covers all airplanes under all circumstances even though 100 percent of aircraft obviously do not crash during their trips.

A phobic individual is aware of the irrationality of the fear but cannot stop the emotion. It is this feeling of dread that makes a phobia an anxiety disorder. For the individual with a phobia the core fear becomes an angst that impairs functioning. Fear of fear takes over.

Fear typically incites the phobic to flee the fearsome object or situation. Even to the individual is unable to shake the fear. Instead, the risk and potential harm become exaggerated, and the phobic's anxiety takes over. The response is pervasive, internalized, and out of control. The phobic person has no control over this chronic, excessive fear (Hyde 1977).

While the fear becomes further removed from the original situation or object, the feeling is more crippling. The anxiety does not escape phobic individuals, even though, in fact, they may have no direct experience with the source of the original pain. Indeed, to the phobic the emotion, typically accompanied by tremor, faintness, nausea, perspiration, and feelings of panic, is and disabling.

Three things distinguish fear from phobia. These are: (1) inappropriateness of the reaction, (2) excessive preoccupation with the feared situation or object, and (3) the intensity of the feeling (Hyde 1977).

Phobias are categorized in terms of what triggers the fear, how the person reacts, and the thing feared. Separating the phobias into these categories has been controversial, but it is one way of making sense of the array of these anxiety disorders. The categories are *agoraphobia*, *social phobia*, and *simple* (or *specific*) *phobia*. The American Psychiatric Association's *DSM-IV* (1994) classifies specific phobias into animal, environmental, or situational types. All three phobias share anxiety in a phobic situation, avoidance of the situation, and an inability to control the reaction.

Phobias become debilitating lifestyles fraught with avoidance behavior. This multifaceted phenomenon occurs despite the person's awareness that the fear is excessive, unreasonable, and irrational. For example, someone who is phobic about airplanes will avoid this mode of travel, even though it affects choice of occupation and an array of lifestyle decisions. Intense emotion is evoked when one tries to change a phobic's behavior pattern, which has been carefully organized around avoidance.

The childhood phobia of greatest concern is school phobia, yet it is not clearly classified among psychiatric disorders. *DSM-IV* (1994), for example, refers to it only in cases in which the anxiety is not better accounted for by another mental disorder, such as separation anxiety disorder. A school phobic lifestyle causes a child to miss important learning and socialization experiences. It is an isolative lifestyle. One of the serious implications is that the child's behavior pattern will merit eligibility for special education services in the emotional disturbance category. Absence from school also presents legal problems and serious implications for the child's education. School phobia (SP) can rule the child's life and deny him normal experiences.

Historically, the term school phobia is a late addition to the terminology used to describe youngsters who are chronically absent from school. Around 1932, *persistent nonattendance* was the term used to label youngsters who chronically missed school. The term *school phobia* came into use between 1941 and 1958. Until about 1965, all forms of persistent absence from school were labeled *truant*.

Along the way, it became clear that school phobia and truancy diverge in important ways. Hersov (1985) studied truancy and school phobia and found that school phobics were more overprotected by their mothers, had eating disturbances, nausea and abdominal pains, sleep disturbances, anxieties, and histories of family psychological problems. Truants, on the other hand, were found to have absent parents and externalizing problems, such as poor conduct, and they were found to be heavily court involved.

SOME FACTS

Prevalence. In its severe form (which is uncommon), school phobia may be seen in from 1 to 2 percent of psychiatric clinic and school populations (Graham 1991; Millman, Schaefer, and Cohen 1980). Among school populations, the estimate is 8 percent (Erickson 1978). Prout and Harvey (1978) noted that each year 17 out of every 1,000 schoolchildren refuse to attend school. By late adolescence, school phobics are likely to become dropout statistics. This issue confounds prevalence rates.

Gender. Like phobias in general, school phobia in the past tended to be seen more often in girls than boys. However, in recent years, this trend has been changing. In 1991 Graham noted that SP is seen equally in boys and girls.

Onset. Krakowski wrote about factors that may precipitate school phobia:

Rarely is the school, itself, responsible for formation of school phobia, although it should be stressed that a threatening teacher or a difficult school assignment may precipitate the phobia if the conflicting stresses happen to coincide with other difficulties of a scholastic or social nature in a child who is simultaneously in conflict with himself or with his home environment. (1962, p. 51)

Onset also has been associated with recovery from organic illness. If the child has actual somatic symptoms, the problem becomes more complicated when the mother displays excessive concern about the child's physical welfare. It is not school officials to whom a student with school phobia first becomes known. Typically, this youngster is taken first for medical consultation, not only because of the acute panic-like states related to the school situation, but also because of the frequently co-existent physical complaints (Krakowski 1962).

In the past, SP was thought to peak in the middle of the elementary school years, making it seem less common at the secondary level. Currently, it seems to be more common among adolescents than among young children. Lindemann (1994), for example, reported a median age of onset at 13 years. Costello and Costello (1992) refer to three peaks: at transition to school (about age five), at age 11, and between ages 14 and 15. Millman, Schaefer, and Cohen (1980) refer to a peak between ages six and 10.

These three peaks represent different phenomena. Onset that occurs during the first one to two years after a child has begun school probably represent separation anxiety. Onset during age 11 (fifth or sixth grade) coincides with an increasing emphasis on achievement. Finally, onset may occur soon after a child transfers to the upper school level, and at this age, about 13, the student may be emotionally insecure and unsure about fitting into new social groups or may be fearful of higher academic demands (Costello and Costello 1992).

Interestingly, the school phobic's earlier development has been described as typically uneventful prior to signs of SP. Krakoswki (1962) commented that SP affects youngsters who have not usually dreaded attending school and who have, until the sudden onset of the disorder, shown good scholastic progress and normal attitudes toward both teachers and peers. Graham (1991) concludes that prior to the development of school phobia most of these children have been good, quiet, conforming children who were having no trouble at school or with keeping up with work.

Socioeconomic status. The role of socioeconomic status is debatable. Graham (1991) concluded that SP is not peculiar to any socioeconomic stratum; however, Last and colleagues (1987) found the disorder to be associated with high socioeconomic status, particularly among adolescent boys. In homes where children are relatively unsupervised school attendance may be a problem, but this is more an issue of truancy than school phobia. Clearly, more research is needed.

CAUSES OF SCHOOL PHOBIA

The causes of school phobia are diverse, probably a mixture of contextual (school, family, and community), developmental, biological, and psychological factors.

Psychological causation. Separation anxiety is often cited as a significant factor. The parent-child relationship in some SP youngsters is characterized by an unresolved codependence; the child depends upon his mother, and the mother depends upon the child (Krakowski 1962). Dread of something in school is often combined with separation anxiety about leaving home (Millman, Schaefer, and Cohen 1980). Going to school may be equivalent to losing mother, while staying home is reinforced by mother. In some cases, the disorder is associated with anxious and depressed mothers who have maintained overly close relationships with their children. These children may be special to their mothers as the last born or be special for some other reason, such as premature birth. Also, the mother may depend upon the child for companionship if the father is absent due to death, separation, or passivity (Graham 1991). The mother, often the primary caretaker, may teach her child to fear school by strongly sympathizing with, thereby reinforcing, complaints. "The mother herself views school negatively as an impersonal place, and communicates the message that she wishes the child to remain at home" (Erickson 1978, p. 279). In effect, the separation anxiety of the school phobic's mother starts at the moment of the child's birth.

Biological causation. Biological causation was cited nearly 25 years ago. For example, Schechter, Toussieng, and Sternlof (1972) suggested that SP relates to precocious physical development based upon observations of bony pelvis growth and budding breast nipples of nine-year-old females.

Contextual causation. The emergence of SP relates to school, which may actually be a source of difficulties for the youngster. For example, he or she may have a learning disability. One school phobic boy found the physical education course particularly problematic because he had not developed pubic hair and dreaded the lockerroom shower situation. Also, the family may have an illness or disability requiring care that the youngster feels guilty about not providing while attending school.

TYPES OF SCHOOL PHOBICS

Kennedy (1965) proposed two types of SP: neurotic and characterological. An example of the characterological type is an older child whose school refusal episodes are continuous. Erickson (1978) adds that this type likely is the product of a disturbed personality and maladaptive family dynamics. Similar to that identified by Waldron et al. (1975), this type is also characterized by psychological defenses such as displacement, projection, and externalizing. Cretekos (1977) described this type as extremely anxious in school and other situations. The characterological type blames the school for the phobia.

CHARACTEROLOGICAL SP EXAMPLE. *Billy H, age 13, is very enmeshed with his mother, who is a high school drop-out, unemployed, and spends a lot of time caring for a physically disabled younger son. Billy complains a lot to his mother about school: that the work is unstimulating, the rules are stupid, and so on. Because Billy's IQ is in the gifted range his mother believes the school is not challenging him. However, Billy also has a learning disability and needs special education support. When Billy attends school, he sleeps or behaves so badly that teachers refer him for discipline. He dances atop desks, walks out of classes, and talks incessantly. His pot smoking and late hours do not help. If he stays out late at night, his mother lets him sleep the next day, and they sit around listening to music and watching TV like old friends on a holiday. When Billy's father finds out how his son has spent his day, the parents argue. However, the overall pattern does not change, except that Billy and his mother may conspire more carefully.*

The neurotic type of SP is exemplified by a younger child whose SP begins suddenly. The family of this type of SP child is adjusted, generally, but there may be separation anxiety in the context of a mutually hostile-dependent relationship between mother and child (Waldron et al. 1975). Further, the school phobic's mother may strongly identify with the dependent child and try to gratify the child's every wish, which may mean sacrificing her own needs, and protect the child from physical discomfort or unpleasantness (Erickson 1978).

Waldron and colleagues (1975) have proposed a third type of SP in which the student is consciously concerned about the parent, who has an actual medical illness or serious, clinical depression. Along with the parent's problem are maladaptive family dynamics and long-standing psychological defenses, particularly displaced and projected emotions (from home to school) and externalizing (blaming school for the phobia). This school phobic is a combination of Kennedy's neurotic and characterological types.

SCHOOL PHOBIA EXAMPLE 1. *John, age 13, was on homebound instruction during the last part of sixth grade due to SP. He has just begun middle school and is enrolled in seventh grade. The school staff has had a conference with John's mother to agree on a plan to ease John into school. His mother says that she wants John to attend school. It was agreed that John would have core academics in the morning, with relatively small classes and a team of teachers known for sensitivity and flexibility. Also, John is scheduled to have electives and a study period in the afternoon. Physical education has been scheduled with an adaptive physical education teacher during the time she works with students having physical disabilities, for John is overweight. Despite the school's planning for John, which would alliow him to see his guidance counselor on an as needed basis, and to see an itinerant ED resource teacher twice each week, John calls his mother every day, asking to be taken home. He has a lengthy list of complaints about the school, which he articulates well due to excellent verbal skills. While school staff have considered every complaint, most are unreasonable. Most complaints are unreasonable. For example, John complained about the English teacher's instructional methods despite the fact that he has not attended her class. Altogether, John does not try to make things work; he is intent on finding reasons why he should not be required to attend classes. John's father works long hours, leaving his wife to deal with their three children. His mother is in psychotherapy for severe depression; John's sister is in psychotherapy for chronic anxiety attacks; and his younger brother needs ongoing medical treatment for ADD as well as special education for a learning disability. Like John, his sister has been chronically absent from school. The mother does not work outside the home and is, thus, able to take phone calls from her children throughout the day. While she says that she wants all of her children to be successful in school, her behavior belies that goal. For instance, she told the school staff at her youngest son's school that she wants him to be independent but fears that the school may make unrealistic demands on him. She prefers to drive this child to and from school so he can avoid the "hassle" of the school bus. The staff at his school have worked hard to support his independence. For example, they encourage him to carry his book bag by himself, reasoning that his disability is in the mental, not physical, area. Each afternoon the boy, carrying his book bag, leaves the building with his mother. Once away from the building, staff have observed, she takes the bag and carries it to the car. After two months in seventh grade John's attendance and complaint pattern has not changed, despite numerous attempts to modify his schedule and make accommodations. School efforts were finally sabotaged completely by the mother when John's resource teacher tried to convene a parent meeting with the staffs of all three schools in which the family's children are enrolled in order to devise a consistent plan for dealing with the these students. Initially agreeable to meeting, John's mother shortly thereafter withdrew him from school and enrolled him in a private home correspondence program.*

This type of SP may involve not only an ill mother but, again, a "neurotic" codependency that is ingrained in the mother-child relationship. The mother may sacrifice her own needs and invest herself in protecting her child from any unpleasant and uncomfortable experience. In the process, she satisfies her own need to be needed.

SCHOOL PHOBIA EXAMPLE 2. *BB, age 13, is rarely in school more than three days each week. On the days he attends, he is tardy. When in the building, he may go to the clinic, visit his counselor, or avoid classes in other ways. BB's father has a job that requires extensive travel. At one point, he moved to an East Coast city to take a job while his wife and three sons were in Texas. The mother, therefore, was the boys' primary caretaker until the family reunited on the East Coast. She had a tragic childhood, losing both parents and growing up with elderly relatives. She admits having strong unresolved feelings about her loss and strict, joyless upbringing. She has been working part time to keep busy, but has made it clear to her employer that she needs to be available for her children at all times. BB, the oldest child, complains constantly about school: about loud and unruly peers, about unfair teachers who "pick on" him, about unfair rules, and so on. His mother has done everything she can to make life easy for BB. For example, she has not required him to take the school bus because it arrives "much too early." Further, when she drives BB to school, she drops him off wherever he wants, despite the designated drop-off area, so that he will not have to walk far. She writes notes to excuse BB from dressing for physical education, and from making oral presentations if he is having an allergy attack. She does his homework, and she picks him up during the school day no matter how minor the physical complaint, whether it be skin rash, sneezing bout, headache, or cough. When BB's poor grades, work avoidance, and insubordination with teachers indicated the need for a more intensive, structured special education program, BB's decision not to change from total mainstreaming was decisive. His mother refused to sign the IEP, which documented the need for a more intensive program. The school staff finally contacted BB's father. The mother complained about this move, but things changed for the better. However, as soon as the father left town again, the situation reverted to school avoidance as usual, with BB in control. By the end of the school year, when it was clear that BB would fail seventh grade, his mother agreed to put him in a day treatment program while she sought counseling. By that point, she could see that BB's school refusal and her enabling behaviors were impacting the rest of the family. The younger brothers were starting to avoid school. The process of reversing years of enabling and school refusal was difficult. The mother is unable to control BB, who is large and strong. Any change on her part is met by fierce resistance. For example, when she threatened to call his father to report that he would not go to school, BB grabbed the phone from her. When she said that she would use a neighbor's phone, BB took her keys and blocked the door. After these incidents the parents agreed to place BB in a hospital program for the summer while they sought family counseling.*

Waldron and colleagues (1975) proposed yet another type of school phobia involving fear of a real situation. For example, there may be fear of failure and loss of self-esteem or fear of bodily harm. Students with poor self-esteem are vulnerable to such crises. Specific examples include students who have been bullied and hurt repeatedly and fear further injury, or students who have learning disabilities and fear further proof of their inability to achieve and perform in the classroom. Anxiety and ambivalence become displaced onto the school (Millman, Schaefer, and Cohen 1980).

SCHOOL PHOBIA EXAMPLE 3. *Sharon, age 14, cuts English class on days that oral reading is scheduled. She has a learning disability in reading, and she has built up an intense need to avoid a situation that makes her look "retarded" in front of other students.*

SP AND THE FEDERAL DEFINITION OF ED

The Individuals with Disabilities Education Act (IDEA) defines ED partly as *a tendency to develop physical symptoms or fears associated with personal or school problems*. Clearly, SP exemplifies this criterion. The school phobic may fear school situations where academic failure, loss of self-esteem, and even bodily harm are possibilities. Or the personal problems of the school phobic may relate to the mother's unresolved needs or parent-child codependency. School phobics are fearful of school for assorted reasons related to personal or school problems, which often are associated with symptoms of nausea, stomachaches, and dizziness.

School phobics also cannot *build or maintain satisfactory interpersonal relationships with peers and teachers* if they do not attend school. While a youngster like John may acquire an education by correspondence course, he cannot benefit from the socialization experiences that are available in school, nor can he develop skill in adapting to varying instructional styles and personalities. He has no same-age peers at home, and family dynamics do not offer healthy socialization. After all, the social experience of school is the important "hidden curriculum" that prepares students for life as adults who can live both independently and cooperatively.

The youngster with school phobia also shows signs of *inappropriate types of behavior or feelings under normal circumstances.* Indeed, this youngster's behavior is predicated upon pervasive anxiety, so that much of his behavior is abnormal. For example, when teachers treat BB like all the other students, he feels unfairly treated. His experience of normalcy is a situation devoid of the real work of growth and learning.

Finally, a school phobic experiences *a general pervasive mood of unhappiness or depression.* As school phobia is an anxiety disorder, depression probably accompanies it (Wolman and Stricker 1994). John and BB both look at other students with longing; they seem to want to belong to their peer group. However, they are emotionally invested in being separate from their peers. Enmeshed in a pattern of refusal that denies them a normal life, they seldom smile or appear happy.

SUGGESTED EDUCATIONAL STRATEGIES

Numerous strategies are appropriate for a student who is school phobic. Before presenting specific strategies, it is necessary to point out that SP requires two general approaches depending on the intensity of the phobia. Acute SP calls for immediate return of the youngster to school, along with parent counseling; chronic SP requires an intense intervention such as family psychotherapy. Combinations of methods are needed (Prout and Harvey 1978).

This student needs to learn without undue fear and anxiety, to improve relationships with others, to gain self-control, to overcome fear of failure, and to overcome depression. Above all, this student needs strategies that overcome avoidance of the school situation. The adult's attitude should exemplify optimistic expectation that the youngster will spend as much time in school as possible, even if feeling ill. Early return to school is agreed by all as necessary (McDonald and Sheperd 1976).

The following specific suggestions combine clinical and educational approaches because the youngster is not in school fully.

1.   Develop an attendance contract with specific rewards and punishments.

2.   Desensitize the youngster, returning him or her gradually to the school grounds, the building, the classrooms, and the schedule one step at a time. Systematic desensitization should involve learning to relax while hearing about threatening situations. From least to most threatening, the youngster (while relaxing) becomes less anxious to imagined or real situations.

3.   An approach for characterological school refusal is a combination of an attendance contract and daily tutoring by the regular teacher. Short-term homebound instruction might also be considered along with other strategies.

4.   A shortened day is effective (i.e., from 15 minutes to three hours). Do not increase the amount of in-school time in large amounts. For example, although a student may declare that he or she is ready to jump from 15 minutes to three hours, it might be more realistic to increase the time at the rate of one hour every two weeks.

5.   The student might spend time in the principal's office, counselor's office, or clinic.

6.   Instruct the student to express his or her feelings, to face them head on.

7.   Strengthen the student's negotiating skills regarding tasks. Self-advocacy must be built. Increase, too, opportunities for task negotiation.

8.   Increase praise for effort.

9.   Reinforce the student's seeking peer help (networking).

10.   Do not show any hostility or negative feelings about the student's poor attendance. Instead, praise attendance, no matter how minimal.

11.   Ensure that the student obtains academic work missed (guidance counselors typically collect assignments).

12.   The teacher and one or two peers might make home visits and encourage the SP youngster to return to school. Visits are most effective if they occur soon after the youngster refuses to attend school.

13.   The youngster might take the family pet to school for emotional support.

14.   The youngster's progression might be from homebound instruction to a special class to a resource room and finally to a regular class with resource and/or itinerant special education support.

15.   Ensure that all academic expectations are realistic, with a high probability of success.

16.   If the youngster has a computer at home, he or she might E-mail the teacher and peers while on homebound instruction. The student could play games via computer and participate in content area discussions and projects.

17.   Enlist a paraprofessional (volunteer, companionship therapist, big brother or sister, aide, or the like) to pick the student up and drive him or her to school, thereby removing the parents from the conflict. The volunteer could be given permission to bring the student to school late after driving him or her on scenic tours. After school the pair could drive to an ice cream parlor, or other reinforcing site, and discuss the day's events at school.

18.   Role-playing could be used in therapy, and the school situation should be monitored and supported.

19.   Group therapy or a school support group could focus on social assertiveness and peer relationships.

20.   Psychoanalytically oriented approaches focus upon improving the insight and ego strength of these youngsters as well as restoring family equilibrium, particularly to reduce power struggles.

21.   Individual therapy for the mother is indicated to reduce hostility, inner conflicts, and dependency. The mother typically needs to change her attitude.

22.   The SP youngster typically needs therapy to alter his or her self-image.

23.   Learning theory effectively reduces fear and school avoidance and lessens separation anxiety. Adaptive responses are induced by contingent reinforcement. Positive reinforcement follows the adaptive response (operant conditioning). Also, the youngster is reinforced for each small step toward returning to school (shaping). An alternative to systematic desensitization is to pair an enjoyable activity with the feared situation (counterconditioning), so that pleasurable reactions gradually overcome fearful responses.

24.   In implosive therapy, another method based on learning theory, anxiety is diminished by presenting vivid, scary scenes so that the youngster experiences intense anxiety with no dire consequences.

25.   Anxiety about tests, reading, public speaking, math, or any other school situation can be reduced through relaxation training in a group. After the training, the student should practice the feared behavior.

26.   Parents need to be taught to use behavioral methods, particularly principles of reinforcement. Behavioral methods lead to less parental guilt and more control and effective involvement.

27.   When he or she is in school, provide the student with time and encouragement to establish rapport.

28.   Do not force the student to socialize in school. It is more important to offer opportunities for positive reinforcement from socialization than to demand a display of socialization skills.

29.   The student who withdraws from socializing needs careful attention to what constitutes positive reinforcement (e.g., a student who receives social praise from a teacher or an authority figure may decrease socializing behavior because of embarrassment). Use a reinforcer survey, observe, or interview the student and parents to develop a list of positive reinforcers specific to the student.

30.   Assign a peer to sit or work directly with the student. Gradually increase group size when he or she has become comfortable working with one person.

31.   Call on the student when he or she is more likely to respond successfully.

32.   Allow passive participation as a social choice across learning activities.

33.   Reduce the emphasis on competition; increase the emphasis on cooperative activities so that the student will learn that his or her abilities and skills make an important contribution.

34.   Show respect for the student's opinions, responses, and suggestions, even if they do not effect changes. The student simply needs to be heard

and to be encouraged to play a role in class proceedings.

35.   Provide the student with many social and academic successes, and provide positive feedback to herald his or her successes.

36.   Modify situations that cause the student to be reluctant to participate (e.g., degree of difficulty, competition, fear of failure, threat of embarrassment).

37.   Confer with the student privately as often as possible, daily at first, to get feedback on how things are going. For example, ask the student to rate his or her comfort level on a scale of 1 to 5: 5 meaning "very comfortable," and 1 meaning "very uncomfortable." Encourage the student to reveal what it would take to move the rating up to the next higher rating. Then discuss how you could do that together.

38.   Make certain the student has a schedule of all activities in order that he or she knows what to expect at all times.

39.   Simulate or practice any new or different activity or social situation with the student before the actual activity takes place.

40.   Have the student choose peers with whom he or she will participate in any new or different activity or situation.

41.   Make sure the student is familiar and compatible with the peers with whom he or she will participate in the activity or social situation.

42.   Ensure that the student feels as comfortable as possible about his or her physical appearance. Compliment the student on his or her appearance.

43.   Maintain a positive attitude about the student's participating in new or different social situations or activities. Do not force the student to attend new or different social situations or activities, but reinforce him or her for participating in new or different situations and activities.

44.   Give the student permission to leave any social situation or activity if he or she becomes uncomfortable.

17

Obsessive-Compulsive Disorder

> The rule is, jam tomorrow and jam yesterday
> but never jam today.
>> Lewis Carroll (*Alice in Wonderland*)

Some professionals question the existence of obsessive-compulsive disorder (OCD) in children. During normal development, they note, children often show ritualistic behavior. March, Leonard, and Swedo (1995) refer to normative age-dependent obsessive-compulsive behavior; for example, the common desire among young children for things to be done "just so" or insistence on elaborate bedtime rituals. Mild compulsions such as stepping over cracks in the sidewalks are common, and milder forms of OCD look like simple fears or habit disturbance. There are normal variants of compulsive behavior, with three peaks at around two years, seven to eight years, and early adolescence (Kessler 1972).

In evaluating students who show compulsive behavior the defining characteristics must be addressed in order to determine if the behavior reflects an underlying psychological problem. Do the symptoms interfere with daily living, including school performance? Do they consume a lot of daily time? Is the student of an age that normally is associated with such behaviors? Is this a chronic problem?

Another developmental consideration is separation of child and adult OCD manifestations. For example, recognition that obsessional thoughts, impulses, or images are a product of one's own mind is characteristic of older adolescents and adults with OCD, not of children. The adult with an obsession knows that it is his own imagination that is giving him trouble, but children rarely complain about their own pathology, their moods, feelings, unwanted thoughts, or undesired impulses. For this reason, their diagnoses are usually made on the basis of overt manifestations alone.

Megan, 17, is a high school senior and honor student who is involved in extracurricular activities and college applications. However, between kindergarten and seventh grade, Megan developed OCD. She experienced intrusive, frightening thoughts and ideas, and she designed rituals that she repeated until they were exactly right. When her mother found her in the bathroom one night, she tried to steer Megan back to bed. "I can't," Megan said as she shook off her mother and proceeded carefully, repetitively, in sets of three, to tap her foot over the door's threshold. Her mother tried again to force her out of the bathroom, but Megan cried, "I have to do this!"

Other adolescents show perfectionistic behavior, also a sign of OCD. A perfectionist regards anything short of perfect as unacceptable. Products must be completely accurate and flawless. Taken to the extreme, as OCD represents, things must be done in a certain manner or the youngster becomes very upset. In school, compulsive students are excessively careful, do work over and over, and must have perfect desks and work papers.

OCD is made manifest in thoughts and behaviors that become ritualistic in the process of avoiding the source of anxiety. Its purpose is to relieve discomfort that is intensified by stress. The youngster's attention is diverted from the source of emotional pain by performing rituals. Obsessive thoughts and compulsive behaviors appear as the must-think and must-do results of anxiety. Essentially, the disorder is an inability to be reassured by the senses, to know that certain things are as the rest of us take for granted.

This connection between OCD thoughts and behaviors is sequential and integral. Sequentially, obsessions are typically preceded by anxiety, and compulsive behaviors nearly always are preceded by obsessional thoughts, like a chain reaction. The behaviors come about because the individual can no longer control anxiety by selected thoughts; the compulsive rituals serve to allay anxiety. This sequential phenomenon, with anxiety at its core, gathers momentum as it progresses. The obsessive and compulsive components of OCD work off each other in tandem fashion. Thus, OCD thoughts and behaviors integrally relate. Obsessions and compulsions are reinforced as they reduce the individual's anxiety. Thus, the thoughts and behaviors continue because they are reinforced.

By learning theory, the OCD pattern is perpetuated by negative reinforcement. In a learning paradigm, this means that the individual avoids an aversive stimulus by performing the behavior. In this case, obsessive thoughts or compulsive actions are reinforced because they stave off anxiety. Just as an individual may continually fasten a car seat belt to avoid the nagging buzzer, one may practice a behavior compulsively, or think a thought obsessively, in order to avoid an unpleasant feeling.

Although obsessions and compulsions help individuals with OCD reduce anxiety, they interfere with the OCD individual's functioning. The word "obsession" is appropriate; in Latin, the word *obsidere* means to besiege. This is a serious, disabling disorder. It causes marked distress, is time consuming, and significantly interferes with normal routine, school functioning, social activities, and relationships.

This interference has been described by Rapoport as "ritual and doubts run wild" (1959, p. 177); in other words, crippling obsessions that create absurd, embarrassing, or frightening thoughts that repeat in the mind in an endless loop and result in compulsive behavior. The thoughts or rituals, whether meaningless or loaded with meaning, cannot be put out of the mind or stopped. The student who is stuck in the doorway to the classroom may say, "I have to do it over again to get it right."

Rapoport (1959) noted that the parent of an obsessive-compulsive child must understand the pain of the anxiety and also its control over one's behavior. The child has absolutely no control over what he or she is doing. OCD symptoms take over. In Megan's case, the parents reasoned that there was a logical explanation for the behavior: the death of a pet, trouble with a friend, or the family's relocation. However, there is no logical explanation for the thoughts or behaviors. This lack of control is a tyranny of nonsense. Obsessively, the individual ruminates; compulsively, he ritualizes. To the observer, the individual's rituals are totally aimless and make no sense. Normal human reasoning and logic have little or no role in this disorder.

OCD EXAMPLES 1 AND 2. *Sara shows OCD, in addition to anorexic symptoms. Her anxiety, stemming from early sexual abuse, became manifest in OCD, specifically repeated counting of objects, lines on the road, and people's words. Her rituals take up so much time that she avoids people. She has difficulty concentrating in school because of preoccupation with the rituals.*

Another student, Sarah, has a bipolar disorder, but she also shows signs of OCD. For example, her magical number is 18. In the classroom she will count the wall tiles until she reaches the number 18. Sometimes she counts in sets, say three groups of six, to reach 18. When she reaches her "favorite number," she says, there is a feeling of satisfaction. This ritual consumes a lot of Sarah's time, but she cannot stop.

OCD is not a new phenomenon. Shakespearian audiences were acquainted with the disorder, in reality if not in name, in the form of Lady Macbeth's handwashing ritual. "Out, out damned spot!" has been a popular quotation for generations to describe intrusive thoughts and repetitive behaviors resulting from pervasive anxiety. Lady Macbeth, the reader may recall, had murder on her mind and hands.

A basic function may be out of control, but the individual with OCD is not psychotic. However, this has not always been the understanding. Until the mid-nineteenth century, OCD phenomena were considered to be a sign of insanity. Over the years, OCD came to be considered one of the "neuroses" (Rapoport, Swedo, and Leonard 1994).

Although it is not a new phenomenon, OCD has a short history in terms of recognition among pre-adults. As of the early 1970s, there were few published reports on OCD in childhood. Rapoport, Swedo, and Leonard (1994) noted that, until recently, OCD was unfamiliar to most child psychiatrists.

As often happens in the mental health field, study of childhood OCD resulted from the study of adult cases. Retrospective reports that as many as one-half to one-third of adults with OCD first showed the symptoms in childhood or adolescence led to focused attention by the child psychiatric community on this chronic and often disabling disorder (Rapoport, Swedo, and Leonard 1994).

SOME FACTS

Prevalence. Holmes (1994) found that, among adults, the prevalence rate is about 2 percent of the population. Another estimate is from 1 to 3 percent of clinic populations (Erickson 1978). The rarity of occurrence among children and adolescents is documented by Quay and La Greca (1986), who found from 1 to 2 percent in clinical samples. March, Leonard, and Swedo (1995) found 1 percent in a community sample of 5,000 New Jersey adolescents.

Referrals may not reflect actual prevalence. Compulsive behavior is more readily observed; by the time compulsive behavior has been observed, the obsessions have long existed. Also, often, compulsions are practiced in private or may be unobservable, such as mental counting rituals. OCD is much more common than we ever thought. Because most OCD sufferers keep their afflictions hidden, the disorder has not been well documented. However, the best estimate is that more than four million people have OCD. (Rapoport 1959)

Onset. The typical age of onset in children is between the ages of 10 and 14; most individuals with OCD develop their symptoms before the age of 25. The statistical mode onset age has been found to be seven, and the statistical mean about 10 years.

There appears to be an early onset group and an adolescent onset group. The early onset group seems to be twice as likely to be male and to have a family member with OCD or a tic disorder. Among children under the age of seven or eight, rituals such as hand washing commonly flag the disorder (Swedo et al. 1989).

In Megan's case, signs of disturbance appeared during kindergarten. She did not want to be away from her mother, she was cautious, and she was fearful of new situations. During third grade, she worried that she would commit suicide and did not want to be left alone with such objects as plastic bags. By seventh grade, Megan showed well-developed rituals, including counting to herself, blinking, touching objects, and touching certain squares in a specific sequence on the patterned living-room carpet.

Course and prognosis. About half the time, OCD begins in childhood (Rapoport 1959), and children suffer from OCD with the same symptoms as adults. OCD has a poor prognosis. Because the obsessional and compulsive symptoms may go unnoticed for years (often the gap between onset and treatment is from 10 to 20 years), the condition may become serious before any intervention is tried. There are obsessional states that are subtle and diffuse, thus difficult to diagnose. For example, an OCD boy who broods, constantly checks himself, and cannot make up his mind may look like an irresponsible dawdler to impatient parents. Compulsive behavior (e.g., counting) is typically secretive. Megan hid her rituals while she was at school in order to look normal. In OCD's early stages, the behavior may seem commendable to the parents. It may take parents a long while to realize that the child has lost control and is compelled to repeat the hand washing, the bed making, or whatever it may be (Kessler 1972). Thus, by the time OCD has reached the observable stage, the individual may be crippled by rituals. Obsessions can be dormant for weeks or months and then something not associated with anything in the environment, something internal, sets them off.

Several criteria are used to diagnose OCD. The youngster may have either obsessions or compulsions. The majority of those diagnosed have experienced both. Too, the symptoms must cause marked distress, be time-consuming (more than an hour each day), and significantly interfere with normal routine, occupation (such as school), and relationships (March, Leonard, and Swedo 1995). OCD symptoms change over time. For example, a compulsive washer will turn into a checker after years of washing. With Tourette's syndrome, the individual can temporarily inhibit jerks, tics, and vocal outbursts; this temporary inhibition is possible with OCD as well.

OCD EXAMPLE 3. *Mark, age 13, is so disabled by OCD that he cannot change classes within the allotted time. He engages in many ritualistic behaviors. Going through doorways, which is especially difficult for him, involves numerous sets of behaviors that have to be performed in a certain order.*

Overall, this disorder is chronic and intractable. One study of patients with OCD, who were reevaluated from two to seven years after receiving both cognitive-behavior therapy and pharmacotherapy, revealed that only 11 percent were totally asymptomatic. Many youngsters with OCD can expect substantial improvement but not complete remission of symptoms (March, Leonard, and Swedo 1995). The movements are under the individual's control and can be stopped for minutes, even hours, but they always return. The intractability of OCD is reflected in a popular 1997 film in which the lead character, played by Jack Nicholson, asks, "Is this as good as it gets?"

Cause. There are three major theories about what causes OCD. One relates to the anxiety paradigm, another relates to neurological impairment, and the third views OCD as a thought disorder. The anxiety paradigm posits that the core anxiety can start either insidiously or acutely; trauma may precipitate OCD, or it may develop gradually. Because the behaviors may occur in private, the onset may not be observed. Anxiety may drive OCD, but what created the anxiety becomes blurred over time.

OCD may be the result of a neurological impairment. Some professionals theorize that OCD and Tourette's syndrome (TS) are flip sides of the same coin. As early as 1885, Gilles de la Tourette made a connection between obsessions and motor tics. In the current era, it has been observed that compulsions occur in about one-third of cases with Tourette's syndrome. Rapoport (1959) proposed that obsessions are "tics of the mind." Rapoport also refers to OCD as a "cinder of thought" that irritates mental processes, allowing the individual no rest. According to this theory, the rituals and thoughts of OCD have a tic-like quality, out of context and uncontrollable. Rapoport's book, *The Boy Who Couldn't Stop Washing* (1991), gave the disorder a name. Rapoport's rationale includes the following six points.

1.   Pharmacological evidence indicates that at least one drug, Anafranil, blunts or removes the obsessions or compulsions. Reactions to other drugs suggest a connection between OCD and TS.

DRUG THERAPY EXAMPLE. *Jed was given a prescription for a stimulant medication in order to help him concentrate on academics. Immediately, an undesirable reaction was seen. He alternated between catatonia, appearing zombie-like, and increased hyperlexia, compulsive reading of anything in sight. The stimulant likely increased the tics, which led to an increase in Jed's effort to control external signs of his internal eruptions.*

2.   Obsessions and compulsions are strongly associated with specific neurological diseases, such as movement disorders and epilepsy. A high proportion of patients have had minor tics or twitches of the face or hands.

3.   Many of the families of OCD patients are psychologically normal.

FAMILY HISTORY EXAMPLE. *Psychologically, Jed's family is basically sound, although the mother is somewhat obsessive. She has hounded the school system for years to institute massive accommodations for Jed's multiple needs: learning, social-emotional, and attentional. She has not made many friends among teachers and administrators in Jed's schools, mostly because she obsesses about minor issues and expects school staff to match her commitment hour for hour. By disposition a highly anxious person, she tries to control a problem that is eminently uncontrollable and elusive. The father, who seems to be more realistic in his attitude toward his son's difficulties, recognizes the bigger mental health picture; however, he is very supportive of his wife's efforts and attends all school meetings with her. Together, these parents have taken their son to every imaginable specialist for diagnosis and treatment. They have paid for several private services. Presently in tenth grade, Jed has had the same tutor since he was in third grade, the same clinical psychologist for about as long. The family, including Jed's older sister, has no other problem except for the enormous pain and grief they all suffer trying to understand and cope with Jed's disorder in all of its compelling complexity.*

4.   The universality of symptoms that override cultural norms suggests

a biological, hereditary component.

5.   As Tourette's syndrome is considered to be a disease of the basal ganglia (Rapoport 1959), OCD and TS appear to be two sides of the same neurological coin.

The individual expends mental energy trying to inhibit his thoughts but loses, over and over again, as made evident by the repetitive behaviors.

The urges that erupt may be angry ones. The adolescent with OCD who experiences intense anger has difficulty controlling it. These individuals spend enormous energy trying to control their hostile impulses.

ATTEMPT TO CONTROL OCD EXAMPLE. *Jed, who has Tourette's syndrome with OCD, has had many negative experiences among his peers over the years because of tics. He has launched a crusade of self-control. He tries hard to control facial expressions so that he will not show a "weird smile" to his peers. He has devoted so much time to controlling his tics that his emotional life has been stunted. He believes that he can go through life without friends, completely self-sufficient. His hostility ranges from ignoring people to arrogant disdain to verbal attacks. Jed reads compulsively to release tension that builds up at school. Indeed, morning teachers who have observed Jed during afternoon classes have seen a different student, one who is more testy and irritable.*

6.   A new biology of this disorder has been influenced by studies of brain abnormalities.

The American Psychiatric Association's *DSM-IV* (1994) points out that OCD is not due to the direct physiological effects of a substance or a general medical condition. It has been important to rule out these issues in diagnosing OCD, and these eliminations have helped pave the way toward other theories of causation, such as neurological impairment.

OCD is also conceptualized as a thought disorder. It follows from a theory of neurological disorder that OCD may involve disordered thinking; a neurobiological theory points to brain dysfunction as the brain is the locus of thought processes.

A student who believes that it is immoral to participate in team sports, who believes that a teacher will go to hell for caring about others, who is obsessed about religion, whose primary goal is to be less nice to others lest his personality change if he is nice, and who speaks of putting a teacher under his "jurisdiction" so that he may control her shows signs of a thought disorder. Jed shows just such disordered thinking.

OCD individuals have doubts and suspicions that run wild. At times, these individuals may seem to be paranoid in their thinking.

PARANOID THINKING EXAMPLE. *Jed distrusts others. It takes him a long time to interact with others in nonhostile ways. His doubts about others' intentions are rife, his suspicions about others' motives pervasive. For example, Jed frequently shows up late for his library study time without a hall pass. It has become obvious to the school staff that there are blocks of unaccountable time. They decided to tell Jed that he needs a pass to use the library, and that he needs to check in with a particular teacher. The matter seemed straightforward; however, Jed's reaction was accusatory. First, he accused the staff of babying him. Then he accused them of blaming him for not following rules. Finally, he accused staff of singling him out for punishment. In response, the staff tried to explain liability and safety issues, as well as the fact that all students are expected to be accountable for their whereabouts, but Jed has not accepted this reasoning.*

Finally, a thought disorder cannot persist in a vacuum. While the individual may try to create an inner world, and to align external stimuli and messages with that internal world, a clash between reality and idiosyncratic thinking is inevitable. In the maturing process, adolescents with OCD are bound to reach recognition that their obsessional thoughts, impulses, or images are a product of their own minds.

IDIOSYNCRATIC THINKING EXAMPLE. *Jed's internal world is becoming more and more idiosyncratic. His perceptions are unique, and he is unyielding in his beliefs, impervious to attempts to match his expectations with realistic feedback, and unrealistic in his goals. His thinking has become brittle and inflexible, unaccepting of alternative ideas. His psychololgist has commented that a breakdown is imminent and that this is typical in such cases (Tourette's syndrome-OCD) between the ages of 16 and 18.*

Altogether, the best judgment at this time is that OCD results from a combination of vulnerabilities. This disorder appears to be an outcome of physical and psychological problems (Caldwell 1996).

Gender. Among children, OCD occurs primarily in boys. However, during adulthood, it occurs equally in men and women.

THE OBSESSIVE COMPONENT

Definition. Obsessions, which are persistent, intrusive and unwantedthoughts, urges, images, or impulses, may be single words, ideas, or combinations of words and ideas. Additionally, the individual cannot get the obsession out of mind even though it may be repugnant. The individual tries to resist the obsession, but it is uncontrollable.

DSM-IV (1994) defines obsessions as follows:

o   recurrent and persistent thoughts, impulses, or images that are experienced, at some time during the disturbance, as intrusive and inappropriate and that cause marked anxiety or distress o   not simply excessive worries about real-life problems

o   attempts to ignore or suppress such thoughts, impulses, or images, or to neutralize them with some other thought or action

o   recognition that the obsessional thoughts, impulses, or images are a product of his or her own mind (not imposed from without) (p. 207)

OBSESSIVE COMPONENT EXAMPLE. *Jed's avowed plan to be neutral in regard to feelings and interpersonal relationships is classic in terms of the above criterion. He wants to be robot-like in his demeanor, i.e., to show no crack in the armor and no chinks in the thought pattern. It is as if the toxicity of his anxious thoughts and urges can be neutralized by controlling thoughts or by compulsive behaviors such as hyperlexia.*

    Types and manifestations. Obsessions are of two types: (1) precautionary ideas about safeguarding (e.g., health and cleanliness) and (2) repugnant ideas (e.g., fantasies about hurting someone, sexual perversions, or doing something "dirty" and shocking). Common obsessions are repetitive thoughts of violence, contamination, and doubt (e.g., thoughts that one has done something to hurt another). Further, obsessions often revolve around a unique topic. Thus, an obsession is not like a worry, which usually relates to everyday experiences.
    Rapoport, Swedo, and Leonard (1994) found the following obsessions in a sample of children and adolescents with primary OCD. The list begins with the most frequently found obsessions: dirt, germs, environmental toxins; something terrible happening; symmetry, order, exactness; scrupulosity (religious obsession); bodily wastes or secretions; numbers (lucky, unlucky); sexual thoughts; fear of harm to self or others; household items; and intrusive nonsense sounds, words, or music.

THE COMPULSIVE COMPONENT

    Definition. Compulsions, behaviors that are repeated excessively in a stereotyped manner, may be simple or elaborate actions. Compulsions are defined by *DSM-IV* (1994, pp. 207-8) as follows:

o   repetitive behaviors (e.g., ordering, checking) or mental acts (e.g., praying, repeating words silently) that the person feels driven to perform in response to an obsession, or according to rules that must be applied rigidly

COMPULSIVE COMPONENT EXAMPLE 1. *Sarah at age 14 complains about her counting ritual. After describing this compulsion, which involves her favorite number, 18, as well as a paper folding compulsion, she said, "It's the most obnoxious thing!" Her mother has a long history of mental illness, and one of her brothers has been diagnosed as both emotionally disturbed and learning disabled. Sarah has experienced multiple hospitalizations since she was 11 years old and currently is receiving psychiatric and psychological treatments. Numerous medications have been tried: Lithium, Depacote, Zoloft, Disipramine, and Tegretol. Sarah readily talks about her emotional problems, diagnosis, and experiences with medications. Her talkativeness may be one way to ward off intrusive thoughts that precede the "obnoxious" compulsion to count and fold.*

o   goal of preventing or reducing distress or preventing some dreaded event or
        situation

COMPULSIVE COMPONENT EXAMPLE 2. *Jed's intense desire to not be nice and to not care about others may be his way of preventing a collision with reality and of delaying awareness that his obsessional thinking, impulses, and images are a product exclusively of his own mind. To interact regularly and intimately with others likely would upset the balance that he has tried to achieve.*

o   no connection of behaviors or mental acts in a realistic way with what they
        are designed to neutralize or prevent

COMPULSIVE COMPONENT EXAMPLE 3. *Sarah's counting ritual, using her magic number, has no connection with any known situation in her life. Her anxiety may be traced to early experiences within her family, but the source of her favorite number is obscure.*

Thus, the behavior's purpose is not obviously linked to the symptom. While the individual seems to achieve a goal, say hand washing to avoid germs, it usually is senseless and ineffective. (For example, the hands were not dirty before they were washed.) What the individual is doing, essentially, is trying to ignore, suppress, or neutralize obsessive thoughts and associated feelings by enacting compulsions. In that sense, the repetitive behaviors are purposeful only so far as they are responses to obsessions and serve to alleviate anxiety.

o   clearly excessive

COMPULSIVE COMPONENT EXAMPLE 4. *Mark's compulsive behaviors are clearly excessive. As he tries to go through a doorway, he does not simply make one ritualistic movement. Unlike the superstitious ritual of a young child who steps over the crack in the sidewalk so as to avoid "breaking grandma's back," Mark's compulsions seem endless. He turns around, touches the door frame, takes a step forward, then one back, and then recycles through each behavior in order, again and again.*

Finally, there is little, if any, self-control. Like an obsession, a compulsion cannot be controlled. The individual realizes it is an irrational behavior and takes no pleasure in it. He or she will become tense and anxious if the behavior is not performed or is interrupted. The inability to stop the compulsion addes to the anxiety felt.

COMPULSIVE COMPONENT EXAMPLE 5. *If anyone interrupts his private reading, Jed becomes irritable and even hostile. His resource teacher had thought that this time would be ideal for meetings. She soon learned, through Jed's sullen or hostile responses, that he had no intention of foregoing even five minutes of this time. When prompted, he will use the time to study, especially if a test is looming, but even that activity is delayed until the very end of these periods.*

   Types and manifestations. The compulsive acts of OCD fall into two categories: (1) restrictions, prohibitions, or precautions and (2) penalties or punishments. A precautionary compulsion is exemplified by wiping doorknobs free of germs. Everyday activities such as eating, dressing, and washing may be elaborated into highly complicated rituals, sometimes caricaturing parental demands for care and cleanliness (Kessler 1972). Penalty compulsions are exemplified by hand washing, counting, checking, and touching, which are self-imposed punishments for having certain thoughts.
   Rapoport, Swedo, and Leonard (1994) identified the following compulsions in a sample of children and adolescents with primary OCD. These manifestations are presented in descending order of frequency: hand washing, showering, bathing, toothbrushing, and grooming; repeated rituals (e.g., going in or out of doors); checking (e.g., locks, stove); miscellaneous rituals (e.g., writing, speaking, reciting the alphabet or number sequences); removal of contact with contaminants; touching; preventing harm to self or others; ordering and arranging; counting (e.g., buttons on other people's clothing, tiles on the ceiling); hoarding and collecting rituals; and cleaning rituals (e.g., household or inanimate objects).
   March, Leonard, and Swedo (1995) note that the most common compulsions in children are washing and cleaning (self) and that most children experience washing rituals at some time during the disorder's course. According to Rapoport (1959), OCD is a world-wide phenomenon, and no matter where it is found washing is the most frequently observed compulsion.
   Treatment. Until recently, OCD was one of the most untreatable disorders. Today, treatment typically combines drugs and behavior therapy aimed at the symptoms. It remains one of the great ironies in psychiatry that OCD, the illness most cited to illustrate the fundamental principles of psychoanalysis, should be the disorder that benefits the least from this treatment (Rapoport 1959). There is no known cure, and the disorder may be lifelong. However, promising behavioral treatment involves confrontation of the obsessive ideas and compulsive behaviors.

OCD AND THE FEDERAL CRITERIA FOR ED

The definition of ED contained in the Individuals with Disabilities Education Act (IDEA) refers to characteristics that adversely affect educational performance and to inappropriate types of behavior or feelings under normal circumstances. Certainly, OCD *adversely affects educational performance.* This disorder interferes with all aspects of daily living, including school performance. It is a persistent disorder that involves intrusive thoughts and excessively repeated behaviors, which preoccupy the student. A student who is preoccupied with mental or overt rituals cannot concentrate on instruction.

Also, students with OCD show *inappropriate types of behavior or feelings under normal circumstances.* A student who cannot walk through a doorway between classes without performing time-consuming, elaborate rituals shows abnormal behavior.

With so much time consumed with obsessions and compulsions, the student shows *an inability to build or maintain satisfactory interpersonal relationships with peers and teachers.* For example, Jed's unique perceptions and unyielding beliefs and opinions have put off both peers and teachers, and his belief that he can function completely alone translates to social isolation.

The student with OCD has *a tendency to develop fears.* This tendency is excessive. The anxiety that drives OCD is overwhelming and impedes the daily routine and educational progress. The fear of fear takes over these students' lives, compelling them into an endless loop of obsessive thinking and compulsive behavior.

Finally, *depression* has been associated with OCD (Rapoport 1959).

SUGGESTED EDUCATIONAL STRATEGIES

Teaching strategies for students with OCD should address their anxiety, problematic relationships, and their need for a predictable routine to obviate some of the student's need to impose an inner-directed routine on the external one. Strategies are recommended specifically to address needs for acceptance/approval, external control, internal control, appropriate engagement, and encouragement. Altogether, students with OCD need a multifaceted approach, of which behavioral strategies should be a small part inasmuch as they have not been very effective in diminishing compulsive behavior (Rincover et al. 1979).

Some suggested strategies for educating students with OCD are the following.

1.   Because overly high expectations can lead to compulsive behavior, ensure that assigned tasks are reasonably designed to promote challenge without frustration.

2.   As students become compulsive in order to feel safe or to avoid anxiety, anxiety can be gradually desensitized by positive responses to appropriate

behaviors and extinguishing (e.g., ignoring) compulsive behaviors. Compulsive behavior can be made less gratifying by reinforcing noncompulsive behavior.

3.   Label feelings verbally to help the student's awareness.

4.   Encourage flexible thinking. For example, structure activities that require two or more responses to questions or alternative ways to express ideas.

5.   Develop a close relationship with the student. Work with the student on assignments to help him or her to focus, and seek him or her out to do special activities together.

6.   Do not require the student to address groups. Public speaking can be very anxiety-provoking for the student with OCD, as for the student with Tourette's syndrome.

7.   Redirect attention to appropriate activities in order to stop inappropriate behaviors.

8.   Suggest alternative behaviors through coaching. For example, suggest that, instead of verbally lashing out at a peer when angry, the student should walk away. Later, he or she might try saying what is on his or her mind in an appropriate manner (tone, choice of words, voice volume). Role-playing might be used to rehearse appropriate verbalizations.

9.   Counselors and psychologists can help the student with OCD develop the cognitive capacity to understand his or her difficulties. In this process, it is recommended that age-appropriate defenses against anxiety be strengthened rather than abruptly removed. Similarly, any direct confrontation of OCD symptoms will be counterproductive, as will any approach that attempts sudden change.

10.   Acceptance and a nonpunitive approach provide security and comfort, a hedge against anxiety.

11.   Relaxation exercises can relieve tension and anxiety.

12.   Role-playing and drama activities can provide the student with opportunities to explore the thoughts and feelings of characters and other people.

13.   Internal control can be developed by giving open-book and take-home tests. This relieves the anxiety of memorization and time pressure.

14.   Self-awareness can be promoted by having the student record both the number of times he or she feels the need to perform a ritual and the number of times he or she does not perform the ritual. Maintaining a chart will help the student see progress.

15.   Teach internal control through self-instruction. For example, teach

the student to talk himself or herself through difficult situations. This impacts what the student attends to, how he or she appraises various events, to what he or she attributes behavior, and his or her expectations about his or her own capacities to handle stress. This strategy also enhances self-awareness.

16.   Provide simple directions one step at a time so that anxiousness will not interfere with learning.

17.   Break complex tasks down into steps that can be achieved.

18.   Provide additional structure and guidance during transitional periods.

19.   Accept all responses as worthwhile at some level.

20.   Identify the student's learning style and incorporate it into activities.

21.   Consistency and routine provide security.

22.   Continuously monitor understanding. For example, pause every 10 to 15 minutes during a presentation to ask students, in pairs, to share their notes and clarify any misunderstandings or to generate questions before moving on.

23.   Ensure that the student knows what the activity's goal is so that there is a clear, overriding objective; redirect any "stuck" behavior toward that objective.

24.   Record or chart the number of times the student expresses concerns or worries about school or home to make the student aware of the frequency of this behavior.

25.   Take the time to listen so that the student realizes that your concern is genuine.

26.   Explain that certain concerns or worries are legitimate and normal for students (e.g., tests and grades).

27.   Have the student keep a daily journal of thoughts. Initially, review the items daily, with discussion of each item in terms of the following questions: "Did things go O.K., even though you were worried about them?" "Did it help to 'park' your concern in the book so you could concentrate on your work?" "Did you need to write the item down more than once?" The journal can be used also as an assessment tool.

28.   Identify persons the student may contact with worries or concerns (e.g., guidance counselor, school nurse, social worker, school psychologist).

29.   Make the necessary adjustments in the environment to prevent the

student from experiencing stress, frustration, or anxiety. Structure the environment in such a way that time does not permit opportunities for the student to dwell on concerns or worries.

30.   Provide the student with alternative approaches to testing (e.g., oral administration, shorter tests, oral responding, separate nondistracting room).

31.   Assign a peer to work with the student in order to keep the student focused.

32.   Call attention to the student's accomplishments, publicly or privately, depending on which is more comfortable for him or her.

33.   Teach the student alternative ways to deal with demands, challenges, and school pressures (e.g., dealing with problems when they arise, exerting self-control at all times, sharing concerns with others).

34.   Teach the student appropriate ways to react to personal or school experiences (e.g., calling attention to the problem, practicing problem solving, moving away from the situation if it is threatening).

35.   Do not force the student to make decisions or choose courses of action. It is more important to offer opportunities for reinforcement through making positive decisions and choosing positive courses of action.

36.   Help the student identify a short-term academic goal (e.g., within three to five days). Then help the student develop a few objectives to attain the short-term goal. Provide assistance to follow through with the plans. Positively reinforce attempts. Finally, use his or her success in this situation to build toward other successes to replace indecisive behavior.

37.   When the student expresses indecisive, stuck behavior, establish with him or her positive steps that he or she may choose now. Provide positive comments and reinforcement for positive action.

38.   Teach the student to identify antecedents to anxious behavior. The journal described earlier could help in this activity. Once the student learns to recognize triggering situations, work to develop coping strategies to use at those times. For example, if the stress is experienced during test situations, coach the student to set aside time to prepare for tests and to develop strategies for true-false, multiple-choice, and essay formats.

39.   Teach the student to ask questions and actively engage in other information-gathering activities before he or she is expected to make decisions.

40.   Help the student develop a list of likes and dislikes to reference when making choices.

41.   Provide the student with a variety of activity choices. Reinforce him or her for making choices.

42.   Give the student ample time to think and process feelings at a specific time each day. The end of the day, when all work is completed, and during study period, are both good times. Have the student review his or her journal if he or she has been keeping one, giving attention to positive and negative thoughts and feelings and identifying accomplishments. Use success to build toward goal-directed behavior for ensuing days.

43.   Help the student chart progress toward developed goals.

44.   When the student does not choose to participate in an activity, make sure that he or she is involved in an alternative one. Later, review with the student the academic and social pros and cons of his or her choice.

45.   Give the student responsibility for helping a peer make choices in the course of group activities.

46.   Provide the student with many social and academic opportunities to experience success.

47.   Allow the student to pick a special event or activity for the class. If the student is very anxious about making a decision or is easily embarrassed, minimize the amount of group attention the student could receive from making such a choice. Thank the student for his or her input following the activity if such attention would not be too embarrassing for the student.

48.   When the student experiences dissatisfaction, frustration, or anger concerning a choice he or she has made, reassure the student and remind him or her that best effort is more important than perfection. After the student has calmed down, review the situation with him or her to determine a modified approach for future reference.

49.   Emphasize individual success and progress over winning or "beating" others; deemphasize competition.

50.   Do not expect the student to confront his or her "worst nightmare." Help the student build toward a desired goal in small, nonthreatening steps.

51.   Supervise classroom activities closely so that peers do not stimulate inappropriate behavior or ridicule the student; an individual with OCD may be easily intimidated or influenced.

52.   Provide the student with a variety of ways to develop rapport with teacher (e.g., writing notes, e-mailing concerns, talking privately about concerns).

53.   Through observation and interaction with the student, identify

when he or she will most likely experience an inability to make decisions. Develop with the student coping mechanisms and other choices he or she may opt to use in these situations (e.g., going to the restroom if she needs to cry). Reinforce the student for using developed strategies.

54.   For the student who is afraid of making mistakes, provide examples of how people can learn from mistakes (e.g., trial-and-error learning).

55.   Teach the student to use a self-reinforcement system for making choices. For example, as a consequence for participating in a required activity, the student is able to engage in a well-liked hobby activity.

56.   To prepare the student for making choices, ask him or her to rehearse choice-making in a role-play situation or simulation.

57.   Encourage the student to think through potential choices in terms of benefits and consequences. Have the student list benefits and consequences before making   decisions.

18

Post-Traumatic Stress Disorder

Pain is human.

Wallace Stevens

Although the concept of post-traumatic stress disorder (PTSD) emerged from studies of adult reactions to major stress, after WWII soldiers returned home, it is not a modern phenomenon. Wars, catastrophes, and disasters have occurred throughout history. The concept PTSD did not gain widespread attention until it was observed in veterans of the Vietnam conflict, many of whom came home with PTSD symptoms.

An even greater understanding of post-traumatic stress came after various U.S. disasters in the 1970s: the Buffalo Creek flood (1972), the Grand Teton flood (1976), the Kentucky Supper Club fire (1977), the San Diego airline crash (1978), the Massachusetts blizzard (1978), and the Three Mile Island nuclear accident (1979). Ensuing research conducted by mental health professionals led to the realization that significant psychological disturbance may be found in a large proportion of disaster victims, and that these victims need crisis intervention or even prolonged psychotherapy. Subsequently, the problem was recognized by Congress in the Disaster Relief Act, PL 93-288.

A "shock" reaction, which appears to unfold in stages, was observed. First, there appears to be stunned, dazed, apathetic, stuporous, disoriented, amnesic behavior. Other stages following the initial shock are characterized by cooperation or passivity. Finally, "recovery" is evident. However, it is during this recovery phase that clinical signs of anxiety, apprehension, and tension appear. During this state, nightmares are common, and victims typically feel a need to retell experiences repeatedly, often doing so with identical emphasis and detail each time (West and Coburn 1984). Feelings of guilt and depression are also seen during the recovery stage.

Generally, the event precipitating PTSD is an extraordinarily stressful one, so extraordinary that its repercussions are severe. The severity of the reaction attests to the severity of the trauma. The psychosocial repercussions are normal reactions to extraordinary circumstances (Figley 1986).

If the individual's psychological reaction to an extraordinary circumstance is normal, why should post-traumatic stress disorder be a psychiatric category? Indeed, some have argued that it should not be considered a psychiatric disorder (Yule 1994). However, PTSD is a severe, chronic emotional impairment, and its classification as a psychiatric disorder seems appropriate. It is not a passing phenomenon, and it meets the criteria of an anxiety disorder. There is discernible impact on the individual suffering from PTSD.

PTSD can strike at any age, for extraordinary circumstances can occur at any time. Children and adolescents, as well as adults, may develop PTSD in the face of unexpected, overwhelming stress. A growing body of literature has delineated PTSD symptoms in children and adolescents. Most of these data concern youngsters who have experienced the death of a parent or sexual abuse (Cantwell and Baker 1989).

Adult studies have contributed to the understanding of PTSD because it is through the studies of adults that we have come to understand PTSD in children and adolescents. The findings of these studies indicate that (1) many adults who experienced sexual abuse as children have identifiable degrees of impairment (Miller-Perrin and Wurtele 1990) and that (2) the trauma-related symptoms shown by sexually abused children and adolescents are similar to the symptoms evidenced by adults.

This understanding is new. Historically, professionals have found it difficult to accept the existence of psychological and psychiatric sequelae in child disaster victims (Benedek 1985). This reluctance is, perhaps, most notable concerning sexual abuse victims, an attitude that was probably provoked by Sigmund Freud, who believed that children's accounts of sexual events were fantasies (Masson 1984). This position created resistance among both therapists and victims to address the reality and severity of child sexual abuse (Miller-Perrin and Wurtele 1990).

Since Freud's time there have been divergent attitudes. At one extreme have been those who maintain that childhood sexual experiences with adults can be beneficial (e.g., Yates 1978). Even those who argue about the existence of PTSD-type emotional difficulties in children contend that their symptoms subside relatively quickly (e.g., Yorukoglu and Kemph 1966), or they attribute the symptoms to long-standing psychiatric problems (e.g., Bender and Grugett 1952). At the other extreme are those who believe that child victims are harmed only later as adults (e.g., MacFarlane 1978).

Understandably, if the attention is concentrated on adults, it will be difficult to comprehend children's reactions to extraordinary stress. The development of assessment protocols for pre-adults generally has lagged behind such work with adults.

One rare study of pre-adults is noteworthy. Burgess and colleagues (1984) studied 66 children and adolescents who had been exploited through sex rings and pornography shows. The researchers found assorted post-traumatic stress responses: 68 percent of the youngsters reported intrusive thoughts and flashbacks, nervousness when reminded of the events, and vivid memories, dreams, and night terrors; 62 percent showed reduced involvement in daily activities, withdrawal from friends and school activities, and refusal to attend school; and 74 percent showed symptoms of abnormal arousal responses, specifically hyperalertness, easy loss of temper, dislike of "being startled," sleep disturbance, irritability, and difficulty concentrating.

THE OFFICIAL DEBUT OF PTSD

PTSD was introduced as a category, with operational definition, in the third revision of the American Psychiatric Association's *Diagnostic and Statistical Manual of Mental Disorders (DSM-III)* in 1980. It was in 1980, then, that PTSD made its debut as an official psychiatric disorder.

The disorder is defined by its internal response, not by the external event(s); it is the internal, subjective experience that marks PTSD from other disorders (Yule 1994). PTSD is an emotional response subsequent to the event, with feelings that make the event continue to feel real, with assorted signs of emotional fallout after the extraordinary event; hence, the name post-traumatic stress syndrome.

Moreover, because PTSD is an internal response that plagues the individual long after the stressful event is over, it may be distinguished as an anxiety disorder. As some professionals have not wanted to classify PTSD as an anxiety disorder, this issue is still under debate. *DSM-IV* classifies PTSD as an anxiety disorder, and it meets many of the criteria outlined in Chapter 15.

Typologies of stress disorders, in general, are arbitrary distinctions owing to the lack of research. In regard to children and adolescents, this paucity is due largely to the relatively recent recognition of PTSD among pre-adults.

Two types of disorders are related to stress (Nevid, Rathus, and Greene 1994; *DSM-IV* 1994): *acute stress disorder* and *post-traumatic stress disorder*. Both disorders share three features: (1) They are caused by exposure to traumatic events, (2) they produce stress-related reactions, and (3) they involve feelings of intense fear, helplessness, or a sense of horror emanating from the trauma.

Acute stress disorder and PTSD separate in terms of specific post-traumatic reactions. For example, while students with PTSD may show disorganized or agitated behavior, they can function; those experiencing acute stress disorder cannot perform necessary tasks to function, they show extreme anxiety, and, typically, they dissociate, or detach, from their surroundings; they seem to be present in body but not in mind. An acute stress disorder immobilizes the individual, whereas PTSD allows the individual at least marginal functioning.

An acute stress disorder is temporary, limited to the days and weeks immediately following a traumatic experience. *DSM-IV* (1994) describes a specific time frame of from two days to four weeks, with occurrence within four weeks of the traumatic event. On the other hand, PTSD persists for months or even years or decades, and it may not develop until many months after exposure to the stressful event. As a result of its chronicity and intensity, PTSD can interfere with a student's educational progress and make it likely that special education services will be needed.

SOME FACTS

Onset. Because trauma can occur at any time, PTSD may occur at any time during childhood or adolescence.

Prevalence. It has been estimated that between 1 and 2 percent of the general population may be diagnosed as having PTSD at any given time. Solid prevalence data are unavailable, partly because previous work on PTSD focused on combat veterans, particularly Vietnam conflict veterans. Yule (1994) noted that, given the individual differences in reaction to objectively similar stressors, it will never be possible to predict precisely how many children will react adversely to a particular event.

Gender and family factors. Reliable data about gender and family factors are unavailable.

Predisposition to PTSD. Despite the understanding that PTSD occurs as a reaction to events that most people would regard as stressful, not all individuals react to extraordinary stress by developing PTSD. Among children, the most likely to be affected are those predisposed to psychiatric disorder (Graham 1991). Some highly resilient youngsters can maintain emotional equilibrium despite extraordinary stress.

SPECIFIC CLINICAL SIGNS

PTSD was well defined, with eleven clinical criteria, for both children and adults, in *DSM-IV* (1994, pp. 209-11). These criteria are listed below with illustrations from actual cases.

o   exposure to a traumatic event in which the individual experienced, witnessed, or was confronted with an event or events that involved actual or threatened death or serious injury, or a threat to the physical integrity of self or others

TRAUMATIC EVENT EXAMPLE. *Sara, whose anorexia is detailed in Chapter 11, has had extraordinarily stressful experiences: repeated sexual abuse by an adult male when she was five years old, subsequent sexual abuse by a nine-year-old, and repeated physical threats by a knife-wielding sixth-grade classmate.*

o   response that involved fear, helplessness, or horror

FEAR RESPONSE EXAMPLE. *Subsequent to her experiences of sexual abuse, Sara developed fear of being in groups and, generally, lost interest in people. She has avoided groups inside or outside of school. She plays alone at home and agrees to one peer visitor at a time. Moreover, that playmate must be someone she has known for a long time. Sara has reduced the threat of further harm. By seventh grade she said, "I do not like being with people many times."*

o   re-experience of the traumatic event, for example, recurrent, intrusive, and
           distressing recollections of the event, including images, thoughts, or
           perceptions

RE-EXPERIENCING TRAUMA EXAMPLE. *Sara continues to experience her
trauma; recurrent thoughts plague her, and she thinks she hears voices talking to
her, one telling her to hurt herself. Her abuse perpetrators seem to superimpose
themselves on her thinking; they "speak" to Sara and threaten her. In that sense,
they maintain power over her.*

o   recurrent dreams of the event, which may be frightening dreams for children

NIGHTMARE EXAMPLE. *Sara's sleep is restless, and she has periodic
nightmares about being hurt. She has trouble sleeping many nights.*

o   acting or feeling as if the traumatic event were recurring, including a sense of
           reliving the experience, illusions, hallucinations, and dissociative flashback
           episodes

RELIVING EXPERIENCE EXAMPLE. *During her waking hours Sara has
occasional visual and auditory hallucinations. When she was hospitalized at age
11 for anorexia, she reported seeing a "big hairy ugly" person, as well as a dead
body, in her room. While she avoids talking about the abuse, Sara experiences
intrusive thoughts. She re-experiences the trauma, and at these times loses her
ability to concentrate on what she has been doing, at home or at school.*

o   intense psychological distress at exposure to internal or external cues that
           symbolize or resemble an aspect of the traumatic event (frequently referred
           to as an "anniversary" effect)

ANNIVERSARY EFFECT EXAMPLE. *The pleasures normally abundant during
the onset of spring are lost on Sara. May is the anniversary month of the first
time she was sexually abused. She becomes especially distractible, fails to follow
through on school assignments, and, generally, seems listless and worried during
the spring.*

o   physiological reactivity on exposure to internal or external cues that
           symbolize or resemble an aspect of the traumatic event

PHYSIOLOGICAL REACTIVITY EXAMPLE. *Sara has difficulty relating to
men. When a male teacher talks to her, even for routine purposes, Sara shows
physiological reactions such as blanching or blushing. For example, when her*

male guidance counselor tried to help her understand that tight-fitting, low-cut clothing is inappropriate in school, Sara reacted by alternately blushing and blanching. After the initial physiological reaction Sara was unable to put the situation in perspective. Rather, the counselor, in her view, was a threatening figure who targeted her for insult and verbal abuse.

o   persistent avoidance of stimuli associated with the trauma and numbing of general responsiveness (not present prior to the trauma), e.g., efforts to avoid thoughts, feelings, or conversations associated with the trauma; efforts to avoid activities, places, or people that arouse recollections of the trauma; inability to recall an important aspect of the trauma; markedly diminished interest or participation in significant activities; feeling of detachment or estrangement from others; restricted range of affect (such as inability to feel love); and sense of a foreshortened future (does not expect to have a career, marriage, children or a normal life span)

AVOIDANCE OF STIMULI EXAMPLE. *While Sara had been a joyful child prior to the sexual abuse, subsequent to the abuse she not only avoided group activities and showed shyness around people, but she avoided reminders of the abusive events. She does not want to participate in psychotherapy, and she rejects her resource teacher's efforts, all to avoid the possibility of recalling the original trauma. While Sara plays the role of a normal adolescent, she masks her feelings. She pretends that she is fine, hiding behind a persona of sociability. Rather than becoming close with anyone, she is everyone's best friend.*

o   persistent symptoms of increased arousal (which were not present prior to trauma), e.g., difficulty falling asleep or staying asleep; irritability or outbursts of anger; difficulty concentrating; hypervigilance; exaggerated startle response

SYMPTOMS OF INCREASED AROUSAL EXAMPLE. *Sara has difficulty concentrating, and her memory is often faulty as she struggles to select what is safe to recall. She constantly filters her experiences. She has trouble falling asleep and stays up late at night reading. "It is hard to make up my mind about things," she said. Occasionally, Sara also has explosions of anger, usually around issues of participating in therapy or counseling. She fights with peers. She is hyperalert, easily startled, especially by men; a male teacher who touches her shoulder gently will evoke a flinch.*

o   Duration of disturbance longer than one month

LENGTH OF DISTURBANCE EXAMPLE. *Sara's distress has lasted far longer than one month. The original abuse occurred when she was five years old, and her PTSD symptoms have been evident for about eight years.*

o   clinically significant distress or impairment in social, occupational, or
         other important areas of functioning, such as school

SOCIAL IMPAIRMENT EXAMPLE. *Sara has been unable to function in
school at the level her intelligence would suggest. Socially, her functioning is
impaired to the extent that she is unwilling to participate in groups, and when she
does participate, she tries to control the situation. Her controlling behavior is a
turnoff to peers.*

As well as specific clinical indicators, PTSD has been associated with
certain long-term negative effects. Aside from protracted anxiety, which is central
to PTSD, with such signs as headaches, stomachaches, flashbacks, recurring
nightmares, phobic behavior, social withdrawal, and school refusal, there are six
important long-term effects of PTSD.
      Low self-esteem. One long-term effect of PTSD is diminished self-
esteem. These students may have a nagging sense that they caused or deserved
the trauma.
      Guilt. Guilt is strong in individuals with PTSD. A youngster may feel
guilty to have survived. Guilt is especially acute when others suffer more or die.
Guilt is one of the many symptoms shown by youngsters in the aftermath of
exploitation by sex rings and pornography shows (Burgess et al. 1984).

LOW SELF-ESTEEM AND GUILT EXAMPLE. *Sara shows numerous long-
term signs of PTSD. Her low self-esteem is reflected in an eating disorder. She
developed anorexia nervosa subsequent to sexual abuse, and as is typical in
anorexia, Sara has feelings of ugliness and worthlessness. Also, she feels guilty
about what she might have done to incur abuse.*

      Depression. Depression is the most commonly reported symptom among
adults who were sexually abused as children (Browne and Finkelhor 1986).
Another study showed that adults who were sexually abused as children tended
toward self-destructive behavior such as suicide and suicidal ideation (Briere 1984).
Adult and child post-traumatic symptoms are similar, and research has documented
long-term depressive features in PTSD children and adolescents (e.g., Burgess et
al. 1984).
      Physical effects. Documented long-term physical effects in PTSD cases
include sleep disturbances (Briere 1984), obesity (Meiselman 1978), and eating
disorders (Oppenheimer, Palmer, and Brandon 1984). (Recall that Sara has
anorexia.) Sleep disturbances were seen among the post-trauma youngsters who
participated in sex rings and pornography (Burgess et al. 1984).
      Cognitive dysfunction. This includes an inability to concentrate
(Courtois and Watts 1982) as well as dissociation and "spaciness" (Briere and
Runtz 1985). Burgess and colleagues (1984) documented concentration difficulty
among youngsters who had participated in sex rings and pornography. (Recall

Sara's concentration difficulty, evident long after the traumatic events.)

Sexual maladjustment. Almost all clinical studies document problems related to sexual adjustment among victimized women (Briere 1984). As often happens, the female sexual abuse victim may dress seductively and flirt openly. This sexual behavior contradicts the logic of the situation; it would seem that an abuse victim would desire sexual camouflage in order to decrease the chance of abuse recurring. However, this is not the case with youngsters who have been sexually abused. Many develop dysfunctional sex lives, exemplified by prostitutes and pornography film actors, many of whom have histories of early sexual abuse.

SEXUAL MALADJUSTMENT EXAMPLE. *Sara exhibits confused sexual identity. While she has suffered emotional trauma due to sexual abuse, it brings her attention, and on one level that means a lot to a child, especially one whose father has left the home. Furthermore, Sara's distorted self-image may help her compensate for feeling dirty or ugly because of the sexual abuse. She wears curve-enhancing clothing and styles her long hair in a wavy, sensual manner, all of which makes her look older and seductive, belying her emotional condition as a scarred, scared child. She is, emotionally, a child in a woman's body, sending mixed messages and experiencing mixed feelings about how to deal with the sexual part of life.*

Further insight into this phenomenon comes from research on child sex rings. Children develop strong attachments to the offender, who occupies a position of authority and familiarity (Burgess et al. 1984). Hence, the child has strong ambivalent feelings: both devotion to and fear of the adult offender. Developmentally immature youngsters have difficulty making sense out of these conflicting feelings. In these rings, too, some children are threatened to ensure the secrecy of the ring and its activities. Finally, through the grooming process these children are systematically "brainwashed" into believing that the activity is acceptable.

PTSD IN THE SCHOOL SETTING

School personnel should be alert for signs of PTSD, not only the aforementioned clinical signs and long-term negative effects, but also signs that are likely to be apparent in the school setting. A caveat, however, is in order: It will probably be the pattern of these signs, rather than any one sign, that will be revealing. Nine points are worth mentioning.

The student has had a severe experience that would be distressing for nearly anyone. For example, students nationwide are experiencing loss of schoolmates through AIDS, drunk driving, homicide, and violence. Grief has come to this generation that previous generations did not face. At one high school, for example, a student was killed when the vehicle she was driving turned over on a Friday night following a beer party. Despite the fact that school was not in session the next day, and assuming that word would travel fast, the guidance counselors and administrators opened the school for all students who needed to talk. The offices were filled that Saturday. Understanding that trauma has a predictable aftermath can help educators provide appropriate follow-through.

Subsequent to trauma the student avoids talking about it, acting as if it did not happen. Students who avail themselves of the opportunity to talk with a high school administrator or counselor following a tragedy are not the problem. The student who does not want to talk is the one to watch. This may be a sign of incipient PTSD. To a student who says, following a stressful event, "I don't want to talk about it," the wise clinician should respond, "Now is when you need to talk."

The student shows reduced interest in the usual activities. This is a sign of assorted problems besides PTSD, among which are drug activity and depression. A student who drops all interests and wants to be alone certainly should be watched.

The student is detached. The student who seems unaffected by something that would be normally stressful is at high risk for PTSD. One of the clear signs of PTSD, as discussed earlier, is a desire to avoid recollection of the trauma.

The student shows a restricted emotional range. The student who seems to be in an emotional rut is at risk for PTSD. This is a youngster who has crawled into a narrow affective world in an attempt to be safe. It is an avoidance response.

The student has lost interest in the future. A student who seems unconcerned about what will happen next month, next year, or anytime in the future may be at risk for PTSD. It is especially telling if the student had been interested in planning ahead but now focuses on the present. One might say he or she is stuck in the present, tense.

Regressive behavior is observed. A student who regresses to thumb sucking, hair twiddling, or baby talk is at risk for problems, particularly PTSD. Regressive behavior is a common sign that an individual has experienced something traumatic and is too overwhelmed to cope, reverting to the comforting behavior of an earlier period.

There is increased arousal. Irritability, anger, distractibility, hyperalertness, and jumpiness are symptomatic of PTSD. The hyperstartle reaction, discussed earlier, may point to a student who has suffered severe trauma.

There is academic deterioration. As with other disorders and problems, including drug abuse, academic deterioration is a sign of PTSD. Students who have shown a downward spiral in grades and in effort may have experienced something severe enough to derail them.

PTSD AND THE FEDERAL CRITERIA FOR ED

PTSD includes many features that qualify it as an emotional disturbance under the Individuals with Disabilities Education Act (IDEA) guidelines. Let us look at these specific features.

First, PTSD is a condition that exists *over a period of time and to a marked degree.* As discussed earlier, PTSD, by definition, is a disorder that persists for at least one month but more typically for years and even decades. As seen in Sara's case, the effects of the events that traumatized her during early childhood have persisted into her adolescent years.

Second, there is *an inability to learn that cannot be explained by intellectual, sensory, or health factors.* Academic deterioration and inability to work up to potential are characteristic. As seen in Sara's case, inability to concentrate, distractibility, and avoidance of group activities impact on her school progress. Certainly, a student who hears voices telling her to hurt herself, and who experiences intrusive thoughts, is unavailable for instruction. "Being there in body but not in mind" appears to be an apt description of such a student. This may be especially pertinent considering that a student with PTSD will probably have sleep deprivation, which will also impact adversely on school performance. This student's inability to learn cannot, overall, be attributed to intellectual, sensory, or health factors but, rather, to an interfering emotional disorder.

Third, PTSD affects the *ability to build or maintain satisfactory interpersonal relationships with peers and teachers.* A student who is fearful of adults as potential abusers, for example, are not open to relationships needed for learning. Students who fight with peers, withdraw socially, and who seem aloof and detached are not going to appeal to other students.

Inappropriate types of behavior or feelings under normal circumstances are also characteristic of PTSD. Students who do not have an emotional disturbance will not flinch when a teacher gently touches their shoulder to get their attention (drug abuse aside). What may seem normal to others will evoke a reminder of earlier trauma in the student with PTSD. Recall Sara's annual reaction to spring: Rather than hope springing eternal, she manifests signs of anxiety.

A tendency to develop physical symptoms or fears associated with personal or school problems also may be evident. Recall that Sara developed both PTSD and anorexia nervosa subsequent to sexual abuse. As part of this pattern, Sara has recurrent headaches and stomachaches, which result in frequent school absences or visits to the school clinic.

Finally, the student with PTSD is likely to exhibit *a general pervasive mood of unhappiness or depression.* Catastrophe, grief, or any event that would be experienced by the normal person as stressful will affect some students so adversely that it could put them in a chronic state of depression. For example, for years after Sara's sexual abuse she had crying spells. As will be discussed in Chapter 26, there is often overlap between depression and PTSD in children and adolescents.

SUGGESTED EDUCATIONAL STRATEGIES

A variety of teaching strategies is indicated for the student with PTSD because this student's academic performance has deteriorated, low self-esteem is evident, depression is likely, there is an inability to focus on schoolwork, and interest in activities and the future is low, showing poor engagement. Certainly in developing strategies the student's need for empowerment should be considered, as well as needs for acceptance/approval, internal control, appropriate engagement, encouragement, and consistency/routine.

The following educational strategies are suggested for a student with PTSD. These strategies represent this student's needs for acceptance, sensitivity, focusing, structure, consistency and predictability, safety and privacy, strategies that build from the individualized to group ones, relationship building, and a positive approach.

1.   Communicate acceptance through nonverbal cues (e.g., smiling).

2.   Draw the student into group activities. Begin by pairing the student with one other student. When the relationship is successful, introduce other students to the group. Do not force the student to interact with others, particularly students with whom he or she is not completely comfortable.

3.   Provide alternative modes of expression. Art and drama offer good outlets for expressing repressed feelings and exploring an emotional range.

4.   Allow the student to record lectures by tape.

5.   Encourage the student to "talk back" at characters by writing in book margins. This helps the student maintain interest, prepare for discussions, and practice assertiveness.

6.   Use nonverbal signals worked out privately to prompt attention.

7.   Build a bridge to the future. Start day by day. For example, plan desirable activities that may interest him or her in the immediate future: first later the same day, then the next day, the next week, and so on.

8.   Provide a safe, private place where the student may indulge in regressive behavior (e.g., hair twiddling). This might be an earned period of time for participating in group activities.

9.   Refocus and alert the student in the here-and-now by infusing his or her name into discussions at random points.

10.   Sit or stand beside the student to keep him or her focused on work.

11.   Build a close relationship gradually by structuring a consistent, predictable routine, assuring successful experiences, and setting reasonable expectations, then establishing interpersonal connections to build trust, empathy, and a personal relationship. Provide the student with a variety of ways to develop rapport (e.g., writing notes to you and talking about concerns privately). In the process, actively listen, reflecting back what the student says to confirm his or her statements and to affirm him or her as a person.

12.   Teach the student to stop reading periodically to self-question, checking comprehension, and to summarize what has been read.

13.   Allow the student to correct his or her own work first before you check it. This conveys trust and builds ownership of and pride in what the student accomplishes.

14.   Encourage the student to read his or her own signals so that he or she knows when he or she is angry, irritated, afraid, stressed, or frustrated. The student could be given a private journal to keep track of feelings and associated events. Gradually, the student could be encouraged to share journal entries.

15.   Structure several short work periods rather than one long one.

16.   Seat the student away from distracting noises.

17.   Provide a consistent, predictable, safe environment, schedule, and routine.

18.   Facilitate attentiveness by alternating types of work and by using a multisensory approach.

19.   Check the accuracy of homework assignment recordings.

20.   Shorten or modify assignments.

21.   Provide written directions and homework assignments whenever possible.

22.   Provide the student with alternative activities to perform in case some activities prove upsetting.

23.   Provide the student with as many positive interactions as possible (e.g., recognize, greet, and compliment the student's attire).

24.   Discourage the student from engaging in those activities that cause him or her unhappiness.

25.   Teach the student alternative ways to deal with unpleasant social interactions (e.g., deal with problems when they arise, practice self-control at all times, share problems or concerns with others).

26.   Maintain maximum supervision of the student's interactions and gradually decrease the amount of supervision over time. Do not assume that the student is being treated nicely by other students.

27.   Temper criticism. When correcting the student, be honest yet supportive. Never cause the student to feel bad about himself or herself.

28.   Allow the student to try something new in private before doing it in front of others.

29.   Structure the environment so that the student does not have time to dwell on real or imagined problems.

30.   Take the time to listen in order for the student to realize your concern and interest.

31.   Modify situations that cause the student to be reluctant to participate (e.g., degree of difficulty, competition, fear of failure, threat of embarrassment). Ensure that the student is familiar with the peers with whom he or she will participate in an activity. As much as possible, ensure that the student is compatible with those peers.

32.   Provide the student with opportunities for small-group participation as opposed to large-group participation.

33.   Have the student question any directions, explanations, and instructions not understood.

34.   Be careful to avoid embarrassing the student by giving him or her orders or demands in front of others.

35.   Go with the student or have someone else accompany the student to those activities in which he or she may not want to participate. Gradually decrease the length of time the adult stays with the student.

36.   Carefully assess the activities in which the student does not want to participate. If something unpleasant is causing the student to not participate, do all you can to change the situation.

37.   Have the student engage in activities that require minimal participation. Gradually increase the student's participation as he or she becomes more comfortable.

38.   When the student expresses concerns or fears, make certain he or she knows you value sincere thoughts and feelings. Acknowledge the thoughts and feelings and do not minimize them.

39.   Encourage the student to evaluate his or her progress, academically and socially.

40.   Help the student develop ways to self-reinforce following social successes.

41.   Obtain background information on the student that will help you to avoid discussion of sensitive topics. Knowledge of a previous "anniversary effect"

will also help raise sensitivity to the time of year when the student may be hyperreactive and acutely sensitive.

19

Overview: Abnormal
Adolescent Development

Adolescence is a phase fraught with numerous developmental struggles and
expectations. Adolescents must modify their unconscious concepts of parental
figures, assume appropriate standards of morality, identify with a sex role, and
make decisions and choices about their educational and vocational future.

Anna Freud (1958) believed that adolescence, as a stage, is an
interruption of peaceful growth and that it is abnormal for the adolescent to
maintain equilibrium. In her view, disharmony is to be expected, and fluctuations
between love and hate of parents, vacillation between asceticism and sensual
sprees, excessive independence or dependence, intense suffering and ecstatic
happiness, and other fluctuations are healthy. Currently, the understanding is that
such fluctuations are normal but are predominantly moderate among most
adolescents. However, it is also understood that maintaining even moderate
psychological balance is particularly difficult if the previous stages of
development have not been peaceful or smooth. The course can be especially
rocky if development is abnormal. For adolescents who are vulnerable, these
struggles can be overwhelming and can adversely impact development.

There are pervasive themes of dysfunction in adolescents with
developmental disorders in the following critical areas of functioning:
psychological, sexual, social, educational/occupational, and cognitive.

Indeed, for some adolescents, prepubertal development was not smooth.
When development has been complicated by disabilities, additional struggles are
carried into adolescence, and the challenges of this new stage will be more difficult
for these youngsters than for their nondisabled peers.

SPECIAL CHALLENGES EXAMPLE. *Fred's parents immigrated to the U.S.
from Afghanistan when his mother was pregnant with him and when both parents
were very young. It was a political emigration and an unsettling time for the
couple. They first settled in California, where Fred was born, and then moved to*

the East Coast. They had few skills and no mastery of English. Fred's father got a job, and his mother stayed home with the baby. She was fearful of her new community and did not know the neighbors. With no friends or family in the area, the family was isolated. Whatever they did socially was as a family. The mother did not take Fred outside to play, she did not read to him or stimulate language acquisition, and the parents could afford few toys. By the time a second child was born, Fred was showing signs of extreme hyperactivity, and his mother had difficulty managing him. A Public Health visiting nurse tried to teach Fred's mother parenting skills, but there was a language barrier, and the mother did not want a stranger in her home. The nurse's report reflected the mother's feelings of being overwhelmed by Fred's troublesome behavior and her inability to learn the skills needed to discipline him and stimulate language development, either in Farsi or English. Rather, his mother indulged Fred, waiting on him, giving him whatever he wanted, tolerating negative reactions to discipline, and setting no limits. Too poor to access appropriate professional services, and too proud to seek public services, the parents unwittingly exacerbated Fred's communication problem.

Adolescents with special developmental challenges include those with communication disorders (Chapter 20), learning disabilities (Chapter 21), and Tourette's syndrome (Chapter 22). These three developmental disorders were selected because they are seen relatively often in our schools, compared with other developmental disorders. Students with these disorders, who are likely to be found in the mainstream of education or close to it, need special education support.

20

Communication Disorders

A sentence uttered makes a world appear.

Wallace Stevens

Communication, central to human existence, has been pivotal in our very evolution as a species. The individual's acquisition of the language of the culture is perhaps the single most dramatic and exciting event in the entire panorama of human ontogeny (Looft 1972). Despite its importance, however, communication skill is a relatively new topic in child and adolescent development.

The focus of this chapter is on face-to-face communication, which occurs by means of speech sounds accompanied by intonation, stresses and pauses, gestures, facial expression, eye contact, posture, and physical distance between interacting parties. Altogether, it is a complex behavioral repertoire of verbal and nonverbal elements: sound, grammar, meaning, and function (Dodd 1980).

As a behavioral repertoire, language is best conceived holistically: as a capacity for using speech and language to learn how the world operates; to receive, analyze, organize, and store information; to share that information with others filtered through a cultural value system; and to adjust the manner of communication in accord with prior knowledge of the age, social status, and other characteristics of listeners. Competent communication, then, is the ability to integrate those various language skills into a seamless whole in an orderly process (Meyen 1990).

Integration implies that communication requires a functional coordination of many aspects of language. Thus, in describing language acquisition we must also describe how the components of language are coordinated. We must account for function, or how to get things done with words. "The only way language use can be learned is by using it communicatively" (Bruner 1983, p. 119).

COMMUNICATION AS A SOCIAL SKILL

Communication, as a function to get things done in the human-cultural context, is a social skill. As such, communication involves interaction and pragmatic subfunctions.

Communication is interaction. Communication is not only a cognitive process but also a social process because it occurs in an interactive context, involving a message that is conveyed from one person to another. Language provides a systematic way of communicating to others, of affecting their and our own behavior, of sharing attention.

The interactive nature of communication is reflected in the evolution of transactional models to explain the relation between language and socio-emotional development. Specifically, such models propose that developmental outcomes are the result of dynamic interrelationships between child behavior, a caregiver's responses to that behavior, and environmental factors that influence both child and caregiver (Bishop 1994). Personality development is affected from birth on by the infant's capacity to engage and become oriented to the caregiver and by the caregiver's ability to engage the infant's attention and orient the child to those aspects of speech, perception, and thinking that will be important in his or her life.

Implicit in communication, then, is a social exchange. "Clearly, [communication] involves social interaction as well as cognition" (Worell and Stilwell 1981, p. 180). For true communication, there must be an exchange. Implicit, too, is an essential contingency; if you say something, then someone will respond. In this social exchange, there are three parts: sender, receiver, and message (Heward and Orlansky 1984).

Communication is pragmatic. As a social skill, communication is pragmatic. That is, speech has a function, or purpose, to influence others and to interpret others' speech; pragmatic skill involves the ability to take into account what someone else could see, know, or understand (Dodd 1980). Thus, pragmatics requires combining the other basic language skills in a social context. Pragmatic skill, then, is linked to the development of social skills; it is critical for interacting appropriately and effectively with others. "Pragmatics cuts across both speech and language because it overlaps with social customs; it is the system that makes language form (syntax and morphology) and content (semantics) applicable to life situations" (Meyen 1990, p. 262).

Unfortunately, the importance of pragmatic skills is not widely recognized. Typically, teachers are advised to refer students for speech-language evaluation if the way the child talks is more noticeable than the content of what the child is saying, i.e., if mispronunciations, dysfluencies, unusual pitch, rate, hoarseness, omitted words or word endings, words used in unusual ways, or atypical word sequences call attention to the manner of expression more than to the message (Meyen 1990). Students with pragmatic problems may not receive adequate attention for their communication difficulties.

PRAGMATIC PROBLEM EXAMPLE. *Jeff, age 14, has been in special education programs since third grade when he was placed in a self-contained program for ED students. At that time, he was socially immature and showed inappropriate behaviors. In middle school, he continues to show social immaturity, but he has learned to behave appropriately. However, Jeff does not engage well in social conversation, tending to focus on his own interests and not taking turns speaking. Very noticeable is his inability to make transitions between topics, which typically confuses listeners. Jeff's parents have been trying for years to get speech-language services for their son, to no avail. Repeatedly, they have been told that Jeff manifests none of the standard signs of a communication disorder. The school's speech clinician offers a social skills group, focusing on pragmatics, and Jeff's parents think that this would help Jeff. However, the school system denied the parents' appeal for additional services in the speech-language area. While his resource teacher added pragmatics goals to Jeff's IEP (individualized education plan), and uses exercises to build his pragmatics skills, Jeff could have benefitted even more from peer group pragmatics learning activities.*

SOME FACTS

Prevalence. Many preschool children labeled with "developmental disorder" as a primary handicap have speech and language problems. Later, after they enter school and begin to show reading and writing problems, they are more likely to be classified under the category specific learning disability. This practice masks the prevalence of communication disorders and causes underestimates of the numbers of school-age children needing speech-language services. Prevalence rates are even higher when problems such as elective mutism caused by emotional trauma are factored into statistics.

Types. There are many types of communication disorders. Some are organic, for example, cleft palate and paralysis of speech muscles. Others are functional, with unknown origin and possible environmental causation.

Functional communication disorder involves receptive and expressive language. Some factors involved in functional communication disorders are developmental delays, cognitive limitations, environmental deprivation, hearing impairments, emotional deprivation, and behavior disorders. Some profesionals believe that autism is an extreme form of functional communication disorder that is caused by a combination of cognitive limitation and developmental delay. The autistic pattern is sometimes referred to as functional retardation. An example of an environmental deprivation is the child who has little stimulation in the home and has few opportunities to speak, listen, explore, and interact with others. Such a child will likely have little motivation for communicating and limited communication skill.

Speech problems may involve articulation (the way sounds are produced); fluency (speech rate and rhythm); and voice (pitch, volume, and quality of speech). Language problems may involve syntactic structure (organization of phrases and clauses); morphology (use of prefixes and suffixes to build words); semantic content (concepts and vocabulary); or pragmatics (the application of semantics, syntactics, and morphology to interactive communication with differing listeners in varied settings). Pragmatics cuts across both speech and language because it overlaps with social customs. This chapter emphasizes functional communication and pragmatics.

Course. Many parents of children who have communication disorders report early signs of problems. These problems often involve behavior, language acquisition, and learning of self-care skills, an interrelatedness that attests to the holistic nature of communication skills. Communication disorder also is evident in older youngsters. In fact, there is much room for further pragmatics research among adolescents. Later language development (age five through adolescence) has not been as extensively studied as earlier development. Because communication disorders are often reported during the formative years, these problems are considered developmental.

COMMUNICATION DISORDER EXAMPLE. *Although Fred was in good health, developmental milestones were reached somewhat late. For example, he walked at 13 months, drank from a cup at 30 months, and was not toilet trained until age three. Enrolled in a county adult education department parent-toddler program when he was two years old, he was removed for disruptive behavior. About this time, he was monitored by a Public Health Service nurse, who reported severe speech delay and "an out of control youngster with little parental guidance." One report described a large child running about the house, climbing into and playing in the sink, pounding furniture, and flipping the TV on and off. It was also noted that Fred's mother did not respond to his efforts to verbalize; she did not take him outside to play, fearing that he would hurt himself. Further, Fred did not make eye contact, showed no interest in toys, and did not sleep well. At age four, Fred was given Ritalin for hyperactivity and uncontrollability. Around this time he insisted on sleeping with his mother and would cry and scream if she put him in his own bed. When Fred was 11 years old, his behavior was similar to that of a five-year-old. He acted responsibly at times, at other times he would ask nonsensical questions; he reacted strangely to people and did not seek friends.*

People who cannot communicate effectively have problems and experience frustration. Children who cannot express their thoughts and feelings in words, or who cannot absorb information through listening, are certain to encounter difficulties in school and the community (Heward and Orlansky 1984). Furthermore, the child who lacks a framework for thinking about himself in relation to past and future events, and to regulate arousal and emotional states, may find it difficult to show self-control and to defer gratification. The child's communicative difficulties are likely to lead to social rejection, educational failure, and emotional-behavioral problems.

In fact, students with communication disorders constitute the second largest group of students receiving special education services in our schools, after students with learning disabilities (Freiberg 1992). Communication problems are found also in conjunction with other disabilities, such as behavior problems Bishop (1994).

There is a particular need for further pragmatics research among special populations. Some attention has been given to the functional language of youngsters with learning disorders. For example, Levine (1990) outlined the following pragmatic skills for this special population:

o   knowing the "right" words: using the right words in the right way in a
         special language peculiar to peer group and locale

o   communicating feelings: putting true feelings into language in order to be
         understood fully

o   making language fit the situation: "code switching," changing the way
         one talks depending upon the context; saying things that sound right for the
         situation

o   choosing a topic: picking topics that do not seem "weird" or disconnected to
         the moment

o   knowing when to stop talking: knowing how long to talk about something;
         not being boring (pp. 210-211)

Research to date and practical evidence attest to increasing interest in pragmatics among special populations. Let us look at both research and practical evidence.

Research. Research has focused on the pragmatic functions of adults with mental retardation (Bedrosian and Prutting 1978), of children with severe language impairments (Miller 1978; Snyder 1975), and language problems related to interpersonal difficulties among students with learning disabilities (Bryan 1974; Smith 1983). Richman, Stevenson, and Graham (1982) concluded that severely language-delayed children, those speaking only a few single words by age three, are at high risk for later behavioral and educational difficulties. Boucher (1984) found that in social situations boys with learning disabilities (LD) used less complex verbal language and were less verbally informative than nonLD peers but showed a pragmatic style that was more encouraging of cooperation and joint problem solving, and sought more information than nonLDs. Contrary to previous findings, the boys with LD were able to adapt their verbal language to listener age. In short, this study showed that LDs could play functional, complementary social roles through language. Further study (Boucher 1986) showed that LD and nonLD boys were similar in terms of semantics usage and ability to accommodate to listener age (i.e., to play social roles).

One particular study deserves mention. In their research on pragmatics, Carr and Durand (1992) noted that in some children bizarre behavior is a way of communicating, and understanding their message is important for getting through to these children. At the Suffolk, Long Island Child Development Center, research has shown that severe behavior problems, such as those manifested by autistics, are not senseless acts but primitive attempts to communicate. Aggression, self-injury, and tantrums are often the only effective ways some children have of making their needs known (Carr and Durand 1992). The communicative nature of their bizarre behavior was demonstrated in data showing that autistics are more aggressive and self-injurious when seeking adult attention or attempting to escape from unpleasant situations. These children's behaviors, essentially, are saying, "Please pay attention to me" or "Please don't ask me to do this."

The idea that bizarre behavior may be a form of communication has a long history. Over 2,300 years ago, Plato suggested that newborns communicated with their caregivers by crying and screaming. French philosopher Jean-Jacques Rousseau wrote that when children begin to speak they cry less, a natural progression when one language is substituted for another. Researchers have found that the more skillful one-year-old infants are at communicating by facial expression, gesture, and speech, the less they cry.

Practical evidence. Practical evidence suggests that people working with students who have emotional disturbances need to devote attention to communication disorders, including pragmatics. For example, at the School for Contemporary Education (SCE) in Annandale, Virginia, a school for students between the ages of seven and 22 who have emotional and behavioral disorders, there were 135 students enrolled as of March 1995. Of these 135 students, 110 were receiving speech and language services. The guiding premise at SCE is that most students with emotional and behavioral disorders have communication problems related to social and problem-solving skills and self-advocacy strategies.

In their working with children who have emotional disorders, Carr and Durand showed that teaching these children how to communicate their needs reduces their odd behaviors. By manipulating situations and tasks, they found that increases in abnormal behaviors signify needs for attention or reduced task difficulty. "Once we understand the message in the behavior, we attempt to teach the child better ways of communicating" (Carr and Durand 1992, p. 166). When a child demonstrates that a task is too difficult for him, he is taught appropriate ways to ask for help (e.g., by saying, "I don't understand"). Children who are unable to speak are taught to use sign language to convey their messages.

NONVERBAL COMMUNICATION

Most attention to language development, and specifically social communication, has focused on verbal skills. Even pragmatics acquisition has focused primarily on the development of verbal language skills that will foster social relationships. In a holistic paradigm, inattention to nonverbal communication is a serious gap. Mehrabian (1968) found that, in face-to-face interactions, 55 percent of the emotional meaning of a message is expressed nonverbally, i.e., facially, posturally, and gesturally, and that 38 percent of a message is expressed through tone of voice.

Thus, wordless communication is a must for fitting into the social world (Nowicki and Duke 1992). Serious misunderstandings can occur if nonverbal messages are misinterpreted, or if we send nonverbal messages that inaccurately reflect our emotions. Because this type of communication is continuous, a nonverbal deficit will generally be more pervasive and have a greater impact than a verbal difficulty (Nowicki and Duke 1992).

A communication disorder in the nonverbal area, *dyssemia*, thus, is critical for social functioning (Nowicki and Duke 1992). If youngsters are dyssemic, they have difficulty (dys) in using nonverbal signs or signals (semes). As is true with a verbal communication disorder, a student with dyssemia may be unable to understand or "read" nonverbal messages. One specific example is "receptive facial dyssemia," the misreading of facial expressions.

While verbal language is represented in both written and unwritten modes, nonverbal language is unwritten. It is a code that must be learned during social interactions. The rules, while subtle and informal, are critical for establishing ourselves as social beings.

Six essential channels of nonverbal communication have been identified (Nowicki and Duke 1992): (1) rhythm and use of time, (2) interpersonal distance and touch, (3) gestures and postures, (4) facial expressions, (5) paralinguistics, and (6) objectics. These six areas involve both receptive and expressive aspects, as do verbal language skills.

Rhythm and use of time. Rhythm and use of time relate to the very pace of life. People who show skill in rhythm and use of time can adjust to others' tempos. A related ability is emotional rhythm. Individuals who typically react strongly to situations may adapt poorly to individuals who characteristically react mildly. A strong reactor may interpret a mild reactor as an uncaring person. Tension and misunderstanding result from mismatched rhythms and senses of timing.

RHYTHM EXAMPLE. *Myra's teachers are frustrated, for Myra is typically two to three minutes late to every class. When she arrives, she has difficulty finding a desk and settling down. Despite conferences with teachers to explain that Myra marches to a different beat, patience is wearing thin. Teachers attribute Myra's tardiness to an uncaring attitude rather than to Myra's disorganization, poor sense of time, and distractibility.*

Interpersonal distance and touch. Interpersonal distance and touch relate to personal space. A deficit in this area involves trouble in defining one's own spatial boundaries. Four proximity zones have been identified: (1) Intimate space, permitted for communication among family members and intimates, is estimated to occur within 18 inches of one's body; (2) personal space, within 18 inches to four feet of one's body, is reserved for conversations with friends and acquaintances; (3) social space (four feet to 12 feet) is reserved for loud talking without a privacy constraint; and (4) public space (12 feet or farther) is reserved for communication through postures and gestures that draw others into the social zone.

The social boundaries vary from culture to culture. The proximity zones, however, may be violated within cultures.

Often, students fight when boundaries have been violated. For example, a student may claim that another student pushed him first, starting the fight. What the claimant may fail to understand is that it was he who violated the space that led the other child to push him away, into a zone that was more acceptable.

INTERPERSONAL DISTANCE EXAMPLE. *When Alan wants to communicate with others, he is literally "in their face," usually within the intimate zone, despite his resource teacher's constant reminders that it is inappropriate to converse with acquaintances this closely. Alan also begins conversations with her about personal issues in the hallway (i.e., within the public space).*

Understanding appropriate touching is a nonverbal skill that is related to interpersonal distancing. Because touching entails zero interpersonal distance, it occurs in the intimate zone. Of all cultures, Americans like touching nearly least, and touching sexual areas, especially by someone over the age of eight, is a significant breach of social etiquette. There are rules about where we may touch. For example, in nonintimate contacts it is acceptable to touch others along the outside of the body line, say the outside of the arms.

Some students with emotional disorders do not want to be touched and withdraw from attempted hugs or touches. On the other hand, other students with emotional disorders cross into the intimate zone in ways that peers and teachers find offensive.

INAPPROPRIATE TOUCHING EXAMPLES. *Mary, age 18, touched her teacher's pregnant belly. The teacher felt it necessary to tell Mary how uncomfortable she felt when touched in that way by someone who is not her husband, relative, or close friend.*

During ninth grade, Rob did not care for his science teacher. She was young and pretty but inexperienced with oppositional adolescents. Ms. S tried various approaches for dealing with Rob, which he interpreted as uncertainty on her part. Ms. S's efforts to manage his behaviors were met with determination on Rob's part to take revenge and make Ms. S look bad in front of the other students. One day, when Ms. S tried to explain a quarterly interim grade to Rob, he asked if he could use her highlighter to mark the missing assignments on his list. Before Ms. S could find the highlighter Rob put his hand into the side poc-

ket of her slacks and extracted the marker. Understandably, Ms. S found this behavior to be an invasion of her intimate space and immediately wrote a discipline referral. Rob, on the other hand, felt that he had a perfect right to go into her pocket because he needed the highlighter and he knew where Ms. S had put it.

Gestures and postures. Gestures and postures also are important in nonverbal communication. Children who understand and send a broad repertoire of clear-meaning gestures may hold a distinct interpersonal advantage over those who cannot (Nowicki and Duke 1992). On the other hand, poor use of gestures, which usually involve one part of the body, results in stilted communication.

Postures, too, are used for "reading" others' messages. Whether up close or from a distance, postures, which involve all or most of the body, communicate attitudes and feelings. For example, slouching suggests disinterest. Teachers often look at how students sit at their desks to gauge engagement and interest in instruction.

Walking, a moving posture, also creates impressions. One can convey confidence (e.g., by walking with the head up and a firm, even stride). Former pickpockets have helped the public understand that this appearance of self-confidence can help prevent muggings.

The emotion of depression is conveyed by assorted postural signs combined with movement, vocal, and facial indicators. Stooped posture and bowed head, slow actions, glum facial expression, flat voice, and plodding movements all suggest depression. A mismatch between verbal and nonverbal indicators also may suggest an affective disorder.

GESTURE AND POSTURE EXAMPLES. *The mismatch between Jed's gestures and vocal tone creates confusion as to his true meaning. He can use his hands in a smooth, slow manner to signal "stop" or "slow down," but accompanying vocal tone is hostile and loud. It is unclear if Jed means that he simply wants the receiver to slow down or stop or if he wants the receiver to slow down or stop as well as understand that Jed is impatient and annoyed.*

The mismatch between Rob's posture and verbal content creates confusion. His posture sags in the classroom, yet he typically says that he is willing to work. Consequently, his teachers hesitate to demand much of him. Typically, they report that his body language overrides his verbal message; they assume that he is unwilling to work.

Joel's teachers find it difficult to believe that he is paying attention when his body is slumped in his chair and his head is swiveled 90 degrees away from the center of instruction. Joel claims that he is listening at these times, and most of the time he is able to respond to questions with accurate answers, but teachers rely nevertheless on Joel's body language.

Billy's posture communicates his affect. He sits and walks with his head down and body stooped. His gait is slow and halting. Everything about his posture suggests depression.

Facial expressions. Facial expressions are nonverbals that give us away most of the time; people take us at "face value." Not only do faces always catch our attention, but social difficulties are often related to problems with matching facial expressions to feelings and with making eye contact. Effective eye contact and appropriate smiling are the two most frequently noted characteristics of socially successful children (Nowicki and Duke 1992). We read facial expressions and produce them to reveal true feelings. Interpersonal problems can develop when we use the wrong facial expression or the correct expression with the wrong intensity (i.e., fail to modulate).

FACIAL EXPRESSION EXAMPLES. *Rob rarely smiles. He may verbalize that he is feeling O.K., but fleeting eye contact and lack of smiling belie this assertion.*

Alan rarely makes eye contact when someone else is speaking. On the other hand, he makes inappropriately intense eye contact, locking onto the other's eyes, when he speaks. Alan, consequently, communicates that he demands to be heard and is relatively disinterested in listening.

Paralinguistics. Paralinguistics, or "paralanguage," involves nonverbal language that is heard (i.e., the sounds we use to show how we feel). Specifically, paralanguage involves tone, loudness, intensity of voice, humming, whistling, sound patterns, and speed of talking. We respond to voice tone long before we react to the actual meanings of words (Nowicki and Duke 1992).

PARALINGUISTICS EXAMPLES. *Jed's voice is poorly modulated. As he speaks often with a loud, abrasive tone, listeners are turned off by what appears to be hostile behavior. Jed complains that others do not understand him, but what he does not seem to understand is that others cannot hear his intent because of the vocal noise that scrambles the messages.*

Alan talks too loudly in the social zone about matters that are private, and he talks too quickly so that many of his words are not heard. He complains that others do not listen to him, but listening to him is difficult due to the rush of words and the volume, which often reaches ear-piercing level.

Objectics: how we look and smell. Finally, an area of nonverbal communication, highly relevant to adolescents because of their intense interest in peer group membership, is objectics. This area involves fashion sense and the signals communicated through dress, cosmetics, jewelry, hairstyle, and perfume.

Objectics reflect the particular culture. In U.S. society, for example, hygiene is basic for social interactions, and body odor is a problem in objectic communication.

OBJECTICS EXAMPLES. *Billy wears his emotions on his sleeve, literally. His hair is unkempt and falling into his eyes; his t-shirts are dirty and worn; his jeans are dirty, torn, and frayed beyond what is fashionable; his shoes have gaping holes; and he emits an acrid odor. Altogether, Billy's personal hygiene and appearance suggest that he does not care about himself or about social blending.*

Charysse changes her hairstyle almost weekly in a desperate attempt to fit in and garner approval from her peer group.

James wears the same clothes for days on end, and he is careless about hygiene. His body odor is offensive, his hair is unkempt, and his clothing is spotted. His peers avoid him, and James seems oblivious as to why.

Fred has poor personal hygiene. His eyeglasses are clouded by dirt; his hair is uncombed; his shoelaces are untied; and his body odor is unpleasant.

Joel wants to fit in. He wears the latest fashions and hounds his parents to buy what his peers wear. If they wear baseball caps in school, Joel insists that he should be allowed to do so; if his peers cut holes in the knees of their jeans, he insists that he should be able to do so; and if his classmates wear beaded necklaces, Joel follows suit, even if he has to make them himself.

Vigilant about appearance, Laura misses a lot of instruction. She continuously surveys the social landscape to see what is in style, and she is critical of peers who are not in fashion. While she cannot blend into the crowd behaviorally or emotionally, she can do so by wearing the latest jewelry, perfume, and clothing.

VERBAL COMMUNICATION

As mentioned earlier, verbal language has received far more attention than nonverbal language. For that reason, this chapter devotes more space to nonverbal communication.

Verbal miscommunication can also affect relationships adversely. For example, if a student asks odd questions in the classroom, others will be disinclined to interact with him. A student who is in his own world cannot establish the mutuality with peers needed for relationship. Peculiar verbal behavior relates to communication disorder. Altogether, both receptive and expressive verbal language problems may lead to an adaptive behavior problem.

VERBAL COMMUNICATION EXAMPLES. *When Fred was 12 years old it was determined that, in addition to a learning disability and speech-language difficulties, he had an emotional disability. Fred needed behavioral controls to reduce inattention and fantasy activity. He did not relate well to peers or to adults. Frequently, he mimicked others' behavior at inappropriate times. For example, he began to laugh at something when all others were finished laughing. Sometimes Fred laughed "out of the blue," as one teacher commented. This behavior often provoked comments or glances from peers. Fred frequently rocked and talked or mumbled to himself. When asked what he said he would usually reply, "Nothing." Even though Fred was polite, friendly, and cooperative, it was difficult to interact with him.*

During seventh grade, Fred's teachers made the following comments, which attest to the connection between his communication disorder and social-emotional functioning.

o   *Sometimes Fred raises his hand and asks an irrelevant question such as, "Have you had a vaccination for hepatitis?" or "Have you eaten at Jack-in-the-Box? You could die from eating their food."*

o   *In teen living class Fred follows me around and asks odd questions.*

o   *Fred said that he feels trapped. Several times he described a passageway with "rocks closing it."*

SUMMARY: ADOLESCENT CHALLENGES

The adolescent with a communication disorder has numerous challenges aside from those characteristic of this developmental stage. These students have special social challenges resulting from verbal and nonverbal miscommunication. Social isolation is likely when communication is one-sided and misunderstandings are pervasive. If the student does not blend in due to lack of nonverbal skills, rejection is likely.

Sexually, an adolescent must learn how and when to say "yes" to the appropriate peer. An adolescent who says "yes" with the voice while standing outside the intimate zone and frowning is sending a mixed message. At this important time of life orderly communication is essential. Sexual confusion is likely for an adolescent with a communication disorder.

Psychologically, problems are likely for adolescents with communication disorders. For example, if a youngster cannot receive accurate information or express himself, then feelings of loneliness and self-doubt are likely.

Educationally and occupationally, receiving and sending accurate messages are critical. For example, if a student conveys the message that he is present only in body, then a teacher will likely pay less attention to him, thereby offering less help. Learning, consequently, will suffer. Further, a student must be able to receive accurate information about the world around him in order to guide himself toward appropriate postsecondary choices, including higher education and employment.

Cognitive limitations, frequently associated with expressive or receptive language problems, often are evident in academic achievement, social relationships, and information processing difficulties.

COGNITIVE LIMITATION EXAMPLE. *Fred was three years old when he was found eligible for special education due to a developmental delay in cognitive skills. He needed a highly structured, self-contained environment in order to meet his needs for continuous and intensive remediation and compensation in deficit areas. Fred was placed in programs designed specifically for children with autism and language delays. By the time he was seven years old, Fred needed speech-language therapy, and when he was nine years old, Fred showed cognitive deficits in auditory processing, particularly auditory memory and auditory discrimination. By this time, his achievement was below expected in reading comprehension, mathematics computation, written and oral expression, and listening comprehension.*

Cognitive deficits may be associated with communication incompetence in other ways. Such deficits may be manifest in thought disorder, fantasy activity, or unusual perceptions.

MANIFESTATION OF COGNITIVE DEFICIT EXAMPLE. *Fred has a rich fantasy life. One teacher commented: "It's not that Fred can or cannot ignore the inappropriate behavior of others; he does not appear aware of inappropriate or appropriate behavior of others. He is in his own world." Not only is Fred in his own world; his fantasy life helps him cope with social rejection. For example, during sixth grade he fantasized that there would be a war in which all sixth graders were captured by the Bombay army. In this fantasy, Fred defeated the army and saved his classmates, which, he further fantasized, brought him much adulation and gratitude. Rather than bringing him adulation and gratitude, his fantasy led to peer rejection.*

So, Fred goes somewhere else to escape the stress of a confusing world. He studies road maps, which provide a comforting concreteness and constancy compared with the ever-changing social landscape, which, after all, contains changing expectations and confusing verbal messages (especially verbal and nonverbal cues that do not always match). Above all, Fred feels that everyone wants him to change. His response to change is, "I like things just like they are."

Fred knows no rational strategies to make and keep friends. He often is involved in fights, and frequently he feels misunderstood. He cannot read the social cues needed for mutual understanding, the foundation of friendship.

In terms of thought processes, Fred is "out to lunch." He cannot separate reality from unreality, and he often makes bizarre remarks. It is difficult to communicate effectively if one's thinking does not match others' reality. Similarly, there can be no meaningful communication if one is preoccupied with one's own thinking.

INABILITY TO SEPARATE REALITY FROM UNREALITY EXAMPLE. *Fred's communication problems include limited insight into his own or others' behaviors, manifest by oversensitivity to situational variables, a tendency to engage in perseverative actions, and poor interpersonal functioning. Fred's understanding of situations is literal. Consequently, his social perceptiveness is poorly developed. He has few means to validate beliefs or impressions. Interpersonal relationships are defined in terms of observable, concrete activities rather than intent or role-taking. Without an emotional bond with others, Fred is confined to understanding others in terms of his own literal reading of social messages. For Fred, there are no shared meanings.*

An adolescent whose cognitions are discordant because of language impairment cannot manipulate the symbols of our language in order to think and learn. The very questions framed will lead this student in a direction far afield of where he needs to be. Logic will be idiosyncratic. As mentioned earlier, cognitive deficits may be manifest in thought disorder, fantasy activity, or unusual perceptions, and cognitive limitations often are associated with expressive or receptive language problems. Communication is limited if there are cognitive problems, which may be evident in academic achievement, social relationships, and information processing difficulties. Altogether, use and understanding of language influence cognitions, and cognitions influence language development. The two interrelate.

THE FEDERAL DEFINITION OF ED
Although the Individuals with Disabilities Education Act (IDEA) definition of ED does not refer explicitly to a communication disorder, there are clear indicators that ED and communication disorder interrelate in important ways. For example, Nowicki and Duke (1992) noted that nonverbal behaviors reflect our very emotional stability. Most students with emotional and behavioral disorders have communication difficulties relating to social skills, problem-solving skills, and self-advocacy. At the intersection of ED and communication disorder there is often an interrelated condition that adversely affects educational performance.

In Fred's case, for example, the interaction among his learning disability, emotional disability, behavioral disorder, and cognitive deficiencies became clear in the IEP statement about the current level of school functioning. The IEP team decided that Fred needed to be considered for placement in a program that could assist him with greater intensity and that a regular education program, with self-contained classes in the learning disabilities program and pullout service in the program for students with emotional disabilities in addition to speech-language services, was insufficient. What follows is part of the IEP statement about Fred's functioning during his seventh grade school year.

IEP EXAMPLE. *Between September and March Fred showed significant downward progression on IEP social-emotional objectives. Specifically, Fred increasingly has had difficulty controlling impulses; ignoring others' inappropriate behaviors; reflecting on and discussing feelings behind actions; interacting appropriately with peers; and accepting adult redirection toward appropriate behavior. Further, Fred has begun to aggress physically toward peers and has become more dependent on adults, with extreme nervousness and frustration when he is expected to perform independently. Also, Fred functions as a social isolate. Peers tease him, and he has no friends at school. One teacher commented, "Fred is in his own world." Odd nonverbal behaviors sometimes occur, e.g., facial grimacing.*

Fred needs intensive, continuous support and structure in both academics and electives. Even minor changes are difficult for him. He needs the security of sameness, concreteness, consistency, and predictability.

Currently, Fred is taking stimulant medication for hyperactivity and is participating in both individual and group psychotherapy.

The IEP team during this meeting agreed to refer Fred to local screening [child study]. A multipurpose referral will be completed to request a case review and to determine if additional evaluation is needed.

Subsequently, the school's screening committee reviewed previous documentation of Fred's functioning, together with the IEP statement. The committee recommended that an IEP conference be convened following approval from the coordinator of special education services for a significant change in placement. Following administrative approval for a more restrictive placement, Fred's parents visited two programs and decided on one. Fred was placed in a middle school co-facility program for ED students where he could also receive LD and speech-language services.

Fred's present middle school is a boisterous, booming, and buzzing world. Fred is bewildered by it; it adds to his anxiety. Fred experiences new fears and creates fantasies in order to cope with the stimuli that bombard him. He needs a smaller, quieter, more structured program where he can receive both academic and clinical support. Specifically, Fred needs continuous feedback regarding language and social perceptions. He needs an interrelated program that provides a social skills group, counseling, and behavioral contracts to focus on appropriate behavior and the communication skills needed to achieve academically and socially.

In terms of specific federal criteria, a student with a communication disorder cannot *build or maintain satisfactory interpersonal relationships with peers and teachers.* A student who communicates in peculiar, idiosyncratic ways, or who shows pragmatic dysfuntion, likely will be rejected by others. Such a student cannot establish mutuality and will be socially isolated.

If students have communication disorders, they may show *inappropriate types of behavior or feelings under normal circumstances.* Students who cannot read the social landscape cannot align their behavior with situational realities. Even the emotions of such students will be predicated on misunderstandings. Inappropriate behaviors or feelings will ensue when reception and expression of information are askew.

A student with a communication disorder may also suffer from *a general pervasive mood of unhappiness or depression.* While Fred does not experience major depression, he is not happy. He is unsure that things will work out for him, and most of the time he is certain that bad things will happen. He is uncertain about how to make decisions, he is unsure if he is loved or even liked by others, and he is anxious. Further, he is easily overwhelmed as a result of his inability to respond to a verbally demanding environment and his inability to use and understand language. Unhappiness is a logical outcome when a student is confused, fearful, and apprehensive because of a pervasive inability to engage in meaningful communication. Pervasive miscommunication, understandably, may lead to pervasive unhappiness.

Finally, a student with a communication disorder may develop *fears associated with personal or school problems.* If this student is unable to receive messages in an orderly manner, any demands to adapt and to change will be met with fear. A student who cannot make sense of the world around him likely will retreat into a world of his own, complete with his own fantasies and fears. As seen in Fred's case, the inability to process information from the world around him led to many fantasies and fears; he created his own world to replace the one that made demands on him that he could not meet.

SUGGESTED EDUCATIONAL STRATEGIES

Teaching strategies for students with communication disorders should be clear and unambiguous (i.e., model good communication). They need clear verbal and nonverbal messages to structure their expressiveness and receptiveness. Also, they need to learn and practice communication skills in a naturalistic setting (Rice 1986).

The following are some suggested educational strategies.

1. Students with communication problems can be helped to perform socially and academically by modeling communicative interactions. For example, treating with patience and courtesy students who are unintelligible, dysfluent, and impaired verbally and nonverbally provides a model for other students in their own interactions with classmates who have disordered communication skills.

2. Reduce the heavy verbal comprehension load by limiting directions to one or two steps, giving essential information in short utterances and keeping

sentence subjects close to verbs. Also, avoid indirect commands and either/or statements.

3.   Show the student what to do rather than tell him or her.

4.   To help with expression, allow the student extra time to respond, ask him or her to act out or gesture what cannot be expressed verbally, and gently encourage the student to continue when he or she initiates communication.

5.   Provide two or three one-word answers from which the student may pick the correct one.

6.   Ask the student to raise his or her hand when a true statement is made as opposed to a false one.

7.   Use open-ended questions to encourage divergent language.

8.   Combine oral and written language activities, which is an holistic approach. Provide the student with written directions and instructions to supplement verbal directions and instructions. Use a multisensory approach.

9.   Do not rush the learning process; make sure the student enjoys the process.

10.   Role-playing activities are good for identifying others' verbal and nonverbal styles. Many situations can be enacted, e.g:

o   Two friends have not seen each other for years,
        and they see each other walking down a street.
        What would their facial expressions show?

o   A teacher is reprimanding a student. How would
        they both look?

o   Two students are standing in the cafeteria line. A
        third student cuts in. One student's facial expression
        shows anger, the other amusement. What has
        happened?

Role-playing gives the student opportunities to rehearse communication skills.

11.   Directly teach units on nonverbal behavior. Use activities in which students observe others' nonverbal communication. Identify and discuss the meanings of various postures, facial expressions, clothing, interaction distances, vocal volume, and so on. Make videotapes of classroom activities and watch them without sound. Focus on particular nonverbal behaviors and discuss their meanings. Contrast them with verbal behaviors; for example, how meanings were better communicated. Have students make a "dictionary" of postures using magazine photos. Label the pos-

tures according to meaning, for example, "tired," "bored," "angry." Have the students keep track of the use of time and punctuality of others. Discuss the meaning of punctuality: What does being late mean to a friend who is waiting for you? How is this different from keeping a teacher waiting? The principal? A doctor? A grandparent? How do the students feel when they are kept waiting? Taped television sitcoms also can provide good content to evaluate verbal and nonverbal behaviors.

12.   Use cooperative activities. In the division of labor, designate an observer to record effective and ineffective verbal and nonverbal behaviors. Discuss observations in a constructive manner and rotate roles so that all group members have an opportunity to observe.

13.   Play charades to develop content vocabulary and to practice nonverbal skills.

14.   Develop cross-cultural understanding of nonverbal behavior. Tape television programs from other countries or cultures and have students identify differences in various nonverbal behaviors. Discuss misunderstandings that can arise between people from different cultures, even within the school.

15.   Make certain the student's hearing was checked recently.

16.   Have the student repeat or paraphrase what is said in order to determine what was heard.

17.   Give the student short directions, explanations, and instructions to follow. Gradually increase the length of these statements as the student shows success.

18.   Make certain the student is attending to the source of information (e.g., making eye contact, hands free of writing materials, looking at book). Also, place him or her near the source.

19.   Emphasize key words in lectures.

20.   Speak clearly and concisely when delivering directions, explanations, and instructions, and use an appropriate pace and loudness.

21.   Reduce distracting stimuli (e.g., noise and motion in the classroom) in order to enhance the student's ability to listen successfully.

22.   Pause at key points when presenting information or when delivering directions, explanations, and instructions in order to determine student comprehension. Some refer to this as "dip-sticking."

23.   Teach specific listening skills (e.g., stop working, look at the person presenting information, and have note-taking materials ready).

24.   Give the student information to listen for in advance of a presentation.

25.   Teach the student to repeat information just heard silently to help him or her remember important facts.

26.   Ensure that information communicated is on the student's ability level.

27.   Have a peer provide information the student did not hear. The language and vocabulary of peers may be more comprehensible.

28.   Present one concept at a time. Ensure that the student understands each concept before presenting the next.

29.   Directions may need to be given to the student individually to ensure successful follow-through.

30.   Give directions in a variety of ways in order to enhance the student's ability to attend.

31.   Reinforce the student for communicating thoughts and feelings in a way that appropriately engages the listener's attention.

32.   Do not force the student to talk. It is more important to offer opportunities for positive reinforcement for voluntary speech.

33.   Let the student know you value his or her thoughts and opinions, regardless of how well or poorly ideas are communicated.

34.   When the student has difficulty with verbal communication during particular situations or activities, adjust behavioral expectations to match her or his strengths and needs. Gradually increase expectations based on performance.

35.   Encourage students to give one another positive feedback for positive verbal exchanges.

36.   Help the student develop more interesting, positive verbal and nonverbal communication skills by recording him or her with audio-visual equipment. Review the tapes with the student using specific communication criteria.

37.   Provide experiences in communication through the arts, including writing, acting, singing, and painting.

21

Learning Disabilities

Failing a social test can be much more painful
than failing a spelling test!
Levine (1990, p. 201)

BACKGROUND

Some background about learning disabilities (LD) is in order before discussing emotional-behavioral issues. It is necessary to provide a perspective on terminology, prevalence, and the importance of studying LD adolescents.

Terminology. "The term *learning disabilities* emerged from a need to identify and serve students who experience continuous school failure yet elude the traditional categories of exceptionality" (Mercer 1979, p. 37). In the process of identifying and serving these students, numerous definitions have emerged.

Early definitions typically stressed neurological factors. Later definitions, which placed greater emphasis on academic factors, typically referred to (1) a discrepancy between ability and achievement, (2) a learning problem that excludes or is not due to mental retardation, sensory impairment, emotional disturbance, or lack of opportunity to learn, and (3) a requirement for special education. Although, by the 1990s, the emphasis on academic factors was apparent, neurological factors had not disappeared. Despite a number of differences, most of the current definitions of learning disability have six points in common: (1) a significant discrepancy between expected and actual academic achievement, (2) difficulty with academic learning, (3) a disorder in one or more of the psychological processes, (4) an uneven growth pattern, (5) a central nervous system dysfunction (evidenced, for example, by auditory and/or visual information processing problems), and (6) exclusion of learning problems primarily due to mental retardation, emotional disturbance, environmental disadvantage, sensory handicaps, or physical disabilities (Graham, Harris, and Reid 1990).

The American Psychiatric Association's *DSM-IV* (1994) integrates academic and psychological processing concerns in its classification of learning disorders, referring to academic skills that are substantially below the skills expected given the individual's chronological age, measured intelligence, and age-appropriate educational level. *DSM-IV* also refers to a disturbance that significantly interferes with academic achievement or activities of daily living that require reading, mathematics, or written expression.

No universal definition has been embraced by those working in the LD field, and identification of these students remains troubled by disparate practices. Lester and Kelman (1997), for example, found that variation in LD diagnostic levels across states is significantly related to distinctions in diagnostic practice as well as, or instead of, actual disorder prevalence. Thus, one must keep in mind when reading research reports and theoretical perspectives that it cannot be assumed that results or premises are generalizable beyond the particular samples referenced. A student who is found to be LD in one school district may not be identified as LD in another district.

Although federal guidelines in the form of laws and regulations (notably the Individuals with Disabilities Education Act, or IDEA) exist, each state must demonstrate compliance or suffer certain consequences, one being the withholding of federal funding. In turn, school districts must file compliance plans with their state departments of education or suffer consequences. The principal variation of definition is in the regulations and criteria at the state level. Implementation methods, not criteria, occur at the local district level.

Currently, the operational definition used in most school systems involves a quantifiable discrepancy between ability (determined by IQ) and achievement in one or more of the basic academic areas (reading, mathematics, written language), along with a definable processing deficit, or neurological disturbance. For example, if a student's full-scale IQ is 120 and his reading standard score is 100, he may be determined to have a learning disability. This depends, however, on the discrepancy criterion, which varies between 15 and 20 or more points. If that ability-achievement discrepancy is accompanied by a processing deficit (e.g., memory, processing speed, auditory perception, visual perception, or visual-motor integration), a case is usually made for classification as LD.

Another factor frequently considered is the comparison between verbal and nonverbal IQ scores. If there is at least a 15-point difference between the two scores, serious consideration may be given to classification as LD.

LD CLASSIFICATION EXAMPLE. *According to his school system's criteria, Billy has a learning disability, specifically in written language. His full-scale IQ is 104, which is average, but his verbal and nonverbal abilities diverge widely. At last evaluation, his verbal IQ score was 113, nonverbal 93, a 20-point difference. Poor psychomotor speed and difficulty bridging information from auditory memory to paper attests to an information processing problem. That information, combined with a written language standard score of 80, which is 30 points discrepant from his verbal IQ and 24 points discrepant from his full-scale IQ score, led the eligibility committee to determine that Billy qualified for LD services.*

Along with a trend from primarily neurological identification criteria to a blend of neurological and academic criteria has come a trend toward identifying only those students who are failing to achieve at expected grade level. This trend has emerged at a time when numbers of identified LDs are ballooning. School districts have responded to the enormity of these numbers by putting a brake on identification. Many school systems have taken the position that if a student is achieving at grade level, no matter what the apparent discrepancy between ability and achievement or between subparts of the IQ test, and despite evidence of processing problem(s), eligibility for LD services is unlikely.

Prevalence. As a result of the variations in definition, it stands to reason that LD prevalence estimates will vary. Estimation of the LD population is confounded with states' practices of classifying as LD or educable mentally retarded (Lester and Kelman 1997). Estimates have ranged from 1 percent to 30 percent of the school population (Lerner 1976). Despite lack of uniformity in the definition of LD, it is the most frequently labeled of all handicapping conditions (Freiberg 1992), and prevalence figures continue to rise. In the 1976-1977 school year, 1.79 percent of the school-age population were identified as LD; by the 1983-1984 school year, 4.57 percent were so classified (Graham, Harris, and Reid 1990). According to a 1984 U.S. Department of Education report, the number of LDs receiving special services rose over a seven-year period to over 1.7 million, a 119 percent increase (Kelly 1992).

The LD adolescent. Historically, the focus in the LD field has been on the pre-adolescent years. A basic assumption in the LD field, as well as in education as a whole, has been that educational efforts are most productive if they are focused on the young child (Alley and Deshler 1979). Five factors have led to this focus: (1) pressures from parents and organizations concerning young children who cannot master basic academic skills, (2) materials and methods designed for young children, (3) teacher preparation oriented toward young children, (4) research focused on pre-adolescents, and (5) resistance within the high school establishment to provide LD services (Mercer 1979).

Also, many believe that finding exceptional students during the early years (e.g., in Head Start) will prevent further learning problems. However, experience has shown that the early identification process has not significantly decreased or eliminated the number of LD adolescents.

As prevalence numbers have grown, so has interest in learning disabilities among adolescents. Since about 1975, there has been a dramatic growth of interest in programming for learning disabilities at the secondary level. Unfortunately, many of these programs have been extensions of service models used for elementary-level students. This age group has been denied services for years (Alley and Deshler 1979).

EMOTIONAL AND BEHAVIORAL ISSUES
Secondary programming has not met the students' needs, particularly in emotional-behavioral areas. Programs for LD adolescents have tended to focus on

academic skills. During adolescence, however, "failing a social test can be much more painful than failing a spelling test" (Levine 1990, p. 201).

There is ample evidence of social failure among LD adolescents. Students with LD commonly experience significant problems in social adjustment, social perception, and motivation. Among LD students frustration is pervasive; disruptive behavior is typical; negative self-concept is frequent; emotional well-being often is absent; social judgment is often poor; and attitude typically is not positive. Emotional lability has been noted in LDs by Bryan and Bryan (1975).

Children with learning disabilities have also been shown to have lower social status (La Greca and Stone 1990; Taylor, Asher, and Williams 1987) and to be perceived negatively by their nondisabled peers as well as their teachers (Cardell and Parmar 1988; Siperstein and Goding 1985). In one study (Wenz-Gross and Siperstein 1997), students with learning problems were interviewed to assess their social networks in order to gain a better understanding of their social world. In accord with a previous study (Hoyle and Serifica 1988), Wenz-Gross and Siperstein found that students with learning problems were less likely to view their peers as a source of support than students without learning problems, and they reported less intimacy, loyalty, self-esteem, and contact in their friendships than students without learning problems.

As adolescent peers play an increasingly important role in shaping identity; in providing social comparisons for performance, in developing a sense of belonging outside of the family, and in buffering stress (Aseltine, Gore, and Colten 1994), lack of peer support may place students with learning problems at greater risk as they move through adolescence and into young adulthood (Wenz-Gross and Siperstein 1997). Social-emotional difficulties, then, warrant nonacademic teaching approaches or inclusion in programs that focus on reeducation of social skills and emotions. Excluding LDs from the emotional disturbance category is problematic because emotional overlays may accompany a learning disability and because many students with LD do not develop in a normal emotional-behavioral pattern (Mercer 1979).

Prior to the emergence of the LD field, in fact, many LDs were found in programs for students with emotional disturbance (ED). When the LD subfield emerged, however, many parents opted for LD programs. The LD label appeals to parents, who can get help for their youngsters and avoid such stigmatizing labels as ED. LD, as a label, may be used more for cosmetic than rational purpose (Kelly 1992), which is a logical outcome when a field is long on theory and short on fact. In the process of choosing the LD label, attention to emotional-behavioral issues have been typically neglected. The social and emotional problems do not go away, but specialized attention for academic problems is often preferred by parents.

Among all the emotional-behavioral concerns raised, the most relevant for school purposes are negative self-concept, poor social adjustment, anxiety, low frustration tolerance, withdrawal, and disruptive behavior. Altogether, LDs may show either internalizing or externalizing problems, and typically they show both types of problems.

Students who have trouble adjusting tend to impose either too much or too little structure on their behavior. Those who over-structure their performance tend to devote so much time to the unimportant details that they have no time left to perform the assigned learning tasks. Those who are unable to structure their behavior often fail to attend to tasks long enough to complete them. (Faas 1980, p. 5)

Negative self-concept. Self-concept, an impression of one's own abilities in varied settings, is important for the adolescent, whose identity is in a critical stage of development. Adolescents with good self-concept will be able to engage in the active process of becoming aware of their own attributes. On the other hand, feelings of poor self-concept can cause problems if they interfere with productive responses (Mercer 1979). A student with poor self-concept is likely to say, "I can't do that."

Research has found significant differences between LD and nonLD students on two measures of self-concept: (1) intellectual and school status and (2) popularity (Pickar and Tori 1986).

NEGATIVE SELF-CONCEPT EXAMPLES. *Donnie's father wanted to introduce him to a nice girl who attends their church. Finally, an introduction was made. Later, when the father asked Donnie, age 17, how it went, Donnie shrugged, said "O.K.," and tried to wiggle out of answering the question in detail. The father, however, persevered, commenting that the girl was beautiful, smart, and a good student. Pushed, Donnie blushed and admitted that he was not interested in the girl because she had asked him up front how he was doing in school. At the time, Donnie was failing French and barely passing algebra.*

Jesse, age 15, has average intellectual abilities but struggles with reading and writing as well as with retention of information. Testing indicated underachievement in both areas in addition to weak visual-motor coordination, and Jesse was identified as LD. Often he feels overwhelmed by work and inadequate; he lacks confidence. He tries to achieve because he wants to succeed and please his parents, but his self-esteem is poor.

There are several consequences for LD adolescents whose self-awareness skills are inadequate. For one, a person with an unclear self-image will receive less confirming feedback from others (Kronick 1976). These individuals will not understand how feedback applies to them.

INADEQUATE SELF-AWARENESS EXAMPLE 1. *Billy's self-image is unclear because he has not been successful in creating his own identity; his self-image is enmeshed with his father's expectations for him. Consequently, Billy is unable to believe that he has a learning disability because his father does not believe that he has one, and he is unable to believe that he is doing his best in school because his father does not. In short, Billy fails to see how feedback about his true learning style applies to him because feedback does not match his self-identity.*

Second, the student with a learning disability may have difficulty perceiving and assessing affect (Wiig and Harris 1974). Self-awareness may become stuck on information that is no longer valid, consequently others' behavior toward the student may be misinterpreted.

INADEQUATE SELF-AWARENESS EXAMPLE 2. *Andy, age 15, distorts his father's intentions. To Andy, the idea of physical closeness and proximity means something negative. For many years, his father had difficulty accepting Andy's learning disability; it was a disappointment that his only son had a disability. After some counseling, his father was able to change his attitude, and he began to try to get close to his son. One way was to help Andy with his homework. However, Andy could not reconcile his father's changed behavior with his own entrenched idea that his father did not accept him, so the attention confused him, and Andy misinterpreted his father's changed behavior. His father would beckon Andy to sit with him on the family room couch so that he could work with him. When Andy became discouraged, his father would put his arm around him. Andy concluded that his father intended to sexually abuse him.*

Third, the student with a learning disability may have trouble perceiving the situational gestalt. Consequently, he may receive an ambiguous message regarding the social situation (Kronick 1976).

INADEQUATE SELF-AWARENESS EXAMPLE 3. *Donnie has a verbal IQ of 100 and nonverbal IQ of 77, which means that he has difficulty integrating verbal and nonverbal information. A discrepancy of this magnitude occurs in only 5 to 10 percent of the general population. Despite a good fund of general information and good abstract verbal reasoning, Donnie's ability to perform tasks that require visualization of spatial relations and nonverbal reasoning is relatively weak. Not only does Donnie have problems in mathematical computation, geometry, and chart or map reading; he has difficulty spelling by visualizing words. Rather, his approach to spelling is phonetic, which is a laborious process of sounding out to himself while trying to encode words. Similarly, Donnie's approach to dealing with emotionally charged situations is to simplify them. His awareness is constricted so that he does not perceive the big picture. Characteristically, he has little understanding of what drives his own or others' behaviors. Consequently, he typically behaves inappropriately, often impulsively and with action (either avoidant or confrontational) rather than reflectively and with words. The end result is a pattern of inconsistent strategies to manage stress.*

Finally, when a student perceives messages as ambiguous, the resulting communication will be commensurately unclear, shallow, and lack appropriate affect (Kronick 1976).

INADEQUATE SELF-AWARENESS EXAMPLE 4. *When Donnie's father discovered that his camera, needed for his work, was missing from the family car immediately after Donnie had used the car, he confronted his son. Donnie appeared to hear his father's words of concern, and his eyes teared as he asserted that he did not know anything about the camera and did not remember its being in the car. His father stormed out of the house, and Donnie withdrew to a corner of the living room to watch TV. Upon prompting from another family member, Donnie left to help his father search for the camera. When it was not found in the home area, his father became very angry. He yelled at Donnie about carelessness, and he threw the car keys at his son, telling him not to come home until he found the camera. That message seemed to impress Donnie; the matter now seemed clear and serious. He drove to a friend's house and in short order found the camera. His story was that one of the girls who had been in the car had inadvertently taken the camera when she left the car the previous night. Donnie had been unable to deal with the situation in a direct manner; his method of coping with the ambiguity was to withdraw.*

Poor social adjustment. Students with learning disabilities typically have difficulty establishing relationships with peers. Research has been consistent in showing that students with learning disabilities are not as well liked by their classmates as other students (Gresham and Reschley 1986; La Greca and Stone 1990).

Social relationships with adults, too, are difficult for LD adolescents. Evidence shows that mainstream teachers' initiations and responses to LD students are more negative and corrective than they are with students without disabilities (Siperstein and Goding 1985). Dorval, McKinney, and Feagans (1982), for example, found that general education classroom teachers initiated conversations more frequently with mainstreamed LD students than with average-achieving students, but that these initiations were primarily directed to inattentiveness and rule infractions. Similarly, Slate and Saudargas (1986) found that LDs received more individual contacts with their teachers but that these contacts related to their being engaged in an activity other than schoolwork.

Across all relationships, LD adolescents need to develop three skills in order to promote social adjustmente. With both peers and adults, LDs need to develop these skills: (1) providing supportive verbal communication, (2) engaging in active and empathic listening, and (3) judging and using nonverbal communication in ways that will instill trust (Alley and Deshler 1979) and promote communication.

First, supportive verbal communication implies self-disclosure. Mutual trust within a group is promoted when members share information about one another. LD students typically lack the ability to self-disclose. They do not seem to know how to balance the essential elements of self-disclosure, specifically timing and movement, toward trust in small increments (Alley and Deshler 1979).

POOR SELF-DISCLOSURE EXAMPLE. *Andy had just begun to work with his new resource teacher when he claimed that his father was sexually abusing him. Andy had been meeting with his previous resource teacher for half the school year and had never mentioned such a matter to her. In fact, the "abuse" that Andy reported had occurred quite some time ago.*

Also, in communication, it is important to engage in active and empathic listening and to show support. Adolescents with LD often show an inability to converse in a functional manner. Their contributions to conversations may be irrelevant, off-track, or even odd, as if they have not been attuned to the conversational flow or situation.

NONEMPATHIC LISTENING EXAMPLE. *Donnie's conversational skills do not promote relationships with adults. The offbeat nature of his questions and comments more often promotes laughter and a quizzical reaction. If he has not seen a relative in a while, Donnie will ask a question that catches the adult off guard. For example, Donnie asked an uncle, whom he had not seen for some time, if he, a policeman, had ever shot anyone and how he felt. This may not have been unusual save for the fact that Donnie asked the question during a family gathering when everyone had just sat down to dinner. Donnie's questions often come out of the blue, do not fit the situation or flow of conversation, and make big leaps to topics that have not been part of any recent discussion. Another example is his asking, "Do you believe in psychic stuff?" in the midst of a conversation about an elderly relative's health and well-being. He entirely missed the facial cues showing concern and sadness about this relative's status and the fact that she was sorely missed at the family table.*

Anxiety. Among LDs, often there is anxiety about competence, particularly the ability to handle new tasks and situations. In the face of unfamiliar demands, LD adolescents may become excessively talkative, show irrational fear, or exhibit physical symptoms (Mercer 1979). Faas (1980) noted that LD students waste time trying to avoid or delay facing the material they should be studying.

LDs also may become passive in the face of anxiety. One problem that has been observed among LDs is that of *inactive learning*. Often, they remain on the periphery of academic and social involvement in the classroom (Torgeson 1982). McIntosh and colleagues (1994), too, found that secondary LDs participated very little in activities, were not engaged in the learning process, and exhibited particular signs of inactive learning: They infrequently asked for teacher assistance, did not volunteer to answer questions, participated infrequently in teacher-directed activities, and interacted infrequently with both teacher and classmates. The researchers also concluded that the response styles of LDs features little self-monitoring of what is being learned or what parts of information are being missed. Limited interaction may be their strategy for getting through the school day with a minimum of difficulty (Brozo 1990).

Low frustration tolerance. Frustration is a common emotional reaction when an individual's desires are thwarted. A pattern of frustration intolerance may develop in response to repeated obstacles to goal achievement, resulting in reduced effort or decreased performance (Mercer 1979). Often we see LD adolescents avoid challenging tasks or stop shortly after starting new tasks. Consequently, learning is inhibited. This student may say the work is too hard, or he or she may write the same answers to all of the mathematics problems.

Also, LD students often have low frustration tolerance in the social arena. Unreasonable feelings and overreactions are typical.

LOW FRUSTRATION TOLERANCE EXAMPLE. *Andy not only has little tolerance for teacher feedback, preferring to work his own way, but he is intolerant of criticism or teasing by peers. Even when peers try to engage Andy in playful joking or teasing, he perceives their behavior as hostile and them as sources of rejection. Consequently, Andy frequently overreacts to playful situations. For example, while he enjoys basketball, Andy cannot control his temper. Often he yells obscenities at other players for perceived insults to himself.*

Manipulation often occurs among LD students when they are frustrated. Some students try to manipulate their teachers into forgetting to have them read or complete their assignments by causing disturbances or trying to become teachers' pets (Faas 1980). Such disturbances usually take the form of aggressive behavior toward the teacher, other class members, or the school's equipment and property. Aggression, thus, is a frequent response of frustrated LD students. They spend time getting into and out of trouble, leaving little time to concentrate on schoolwork. That is the point.

MANIPULATION EXAMPLES. *Andy has tried to get on his teachers' good sides. Instead of working on dreaded tasks, Andy frequently offers to do errands such as run attendance sheets to the office.*

When David O has trouble with an assignment, he typically diverts attention from what he should be doing by starting trouble with a peer. Once, for example, he accused a boy of looking at him funny. The ensuing aggressive sideshow consumed the rest of the class period.

Withdrawal. A common emotional response to social incompetence is withdrawal. Withdrawal, in turn, leads to less interaction and even more rejection (Mercer 1979). LDs frequently experience this self-defeating cycle.

WITHDRAWAL EXAMPLE. *Jesse is socially withdrawn. Most of the time he is too preoccupied and introspective to reach out to others. Jesse is comfortable interacting with teachers, but even in those situations interactions are superficial; he prefers to discuss current events or "Star Trek" plots, rather than personal matters. He avoids emotionally charged situations. He is open with his resource teacher about world affairs, but he is not open about intimate topics. As Jesse is unavailable to peers he is not a part of their interactions. Feeling rejected, he withdraws further. The cycle continues.*

Disruptive and disorderly behavior. Besides emotional difficulties, LDs often have behavioral disorders. One study (Fink 1990) found that LD students were referred to the school office more often than nonspecial education students for disciplinary infractions.

One problem seen in many LD adolescents is impulsivity, or the inability to think before acting. It is an externalizing problem of undercontrol.

IMPULSIVE BEHAVIOR EXAMPLE. *Andy's behavior often is impulsive. He is reactive rather than thoughtful in his approach to situations. Despite coaching in strategies to cope with social situations, Andy forgets in the heat of the moment, consequently anger and frustration override. Andy does not think about the effect of his behavior on others.*

Delinquency, another problem of undercontrol, also is seen frequently among adolescent LDs. LD has been found to be associated with illegal activities (Fink 1990).

DELINQUENCY EXAMPLE. *Chris, age 15, has a learning disability and shows impulsivity, lack of self-control, and poor judgment, all of which increase the likelihood of delinquent and oppositional behaviors. He has been involved in the juvenile court system because of mailbox vandalism, shoplifting, and driving without a license, and he has abused alcohol and marijuana. Chris has been assigned a probation officer and community service for his illegal behaviors. Chris feels "stuck" and would like to get rid of his record, but he cannot seem to break out of the pattern. He does not recognize that it is his responsibility to think about the consequences of his behavior, exert self-control, and make good choices.*

On the other hand, overcontrol, or internalizing, also may be seen in LD adolescents. This problem may be evident in their focusing on irrelevant or unimportant information, causing them to perseverate on tasks so long that instruction passes them by. Overcontrol can be disruptive of their own learning.

OVERCONTROL EXAMPLE. *Billy spends so much time thinking about all the details of one task that he is unavailable for other information. When a teacher presents an idea, Billy tries to think about everything he knows. He also becomes anxious about assignments. The teacher may begin by saying that the students will need to complete the check-up questions at the end of a chapter. While the teacher is specifying the exact question numbers, Billy is thinking about whether or not he has paper, where his pen is, and an assortment of details that could wait until he has all the necessary information. Usually he misses the most important details, such as what the assignment is and when it is due.*

SUMMARY: DEVELOPMENTAL   CHALLENGES

Adolescents with learning disabilities have special developmental challenges: social, psychological, cognitive, sexual, and educational and occupational challenges. Socially, a big challenge is to fit in with the peer group. For an adolescent who is socially immature, and whose perceptions of social situations is imprecise, blending is a problem. Many LD students have friends who are two or three years younger. One 13-year-old LD girl is most comfortable with a 10-year-old friend playing with Barbie dolls. Because of their social flaws, relative to age-mates, LD adolescents frequently are unpopular.

Poor social judgment, also often seen in LD adolescents, can lead to bad choices of friends. They may put trust in peers who manipulate and use them. An LD adolescent may literally be left holding the bag: a bag of cocaine that a peer did not want to be caught holding. One LD student confided that he abetted a peer's cover-up of a school theft because he needed friends.

Psychologically, LD adolescents often are insecure. Because they have experienced academic failure they may feel incompetent. As adolescents spend a lot of time comparing themselves to peers, the self-evaluations of LDs are often negative. Billy, for example, wishing that he had debating skills so that he could influence others, said, "I'm sick of having to back down." In other words, he wishes that he had the verbal skills to argue for himself effectively. It is an ongoing struggle for LD adolescents to identify their strengths and take pride in them. If their strengths do not match their peers' values, the dissonance can be painful.

If parents do not help their LD adolescents understand their own strengths and weaknesses, emotional problems are likely. For example, because Billy's father does not want to recognize his son's learning disability and compels Billy to take courses that are too difficult for him, Billy is depressed, feeling trapped in a failure pattern.

Learning disabilities are largely language based, and school curricula are largely verbally oriented. Cognitively, the inability to manipulate verbal or numeric symbols is a disadvantage for an LD adolescent. Aside from the academic challenge, there is the related social challenge. Students who do not process information as quickly as their peers may be rejected or ridiculed. Peers may call them "retards." Students with learning disabilities must overcome a popular belief that LD is synonymous with being "dumb" or "slow."

Sexually, an adolescent who misperceives social cues may be unable to develop satisfactory relationships with the opposite sex. Due to immaturity, LDs typically are "late bloomers." Romantic relationships often elude LD adolescents until later adolescence. There are many subtleties to be learned in order to relate to the opposite sex, particularly communication, which is a challenge for LDs.

Educationally and occupationally, one of the biggest problems for LD adolescents is making realistic choices. They may be unrealistic about the courses they should take in high school, as well as the occupations to which they aspire. For example, the LD student who has a math disability may wish to become an engineer, or an LD student with a visual-motor coordination deficit may dream of becoming an artist. One LD student needed to be steered in the direction of graphic art because her computer skills and eye for composition far outweighed her free-hand art ability.

LD AND THE FEDERAL DEFINITION OF ED

As pointed out, the federal definition of specific learning disability excludes ED as a primary component. The exact guideline is as follows: The term does not apply to children who have learning problems that are primarily the result of visual, hearing, or motor disabilities, of mental retardation, of emotional disturbance, or of environmental, cultural, or economic disadvantage.

While it is assumed that an LD student is not primarily a student with an emotional disturbance, it is understood that students who experience learning problems often have emotional-behavioral disorders. For example, one study (McBride and Siegel 1997) found that adolescents who committed suicide were relatively more impaired in terms of learning problems, and another study (Dalley et al. 1992) found that successful LD students reported fewer depressive symptoms than LDs identified as unsuccessful, but more than their nondisabled peers. Efforts to deny the co-occurrence of ED and LD are not based on evidence. Much of what is presented in this chapter shows that there are significant emotional-behavioral concerns in LD. Frequently, the argument revolves around the erroneous assumption that learning disabilities cannot occur in conjunction with other handicapping conditions, despite evidence to the contrary (Graham, Harris, and Reid 1990).

The case of Ricky, a student with severe depression who was introduced in Chapter 13 because of his acting-out behaviors, illustrates how one school-based eligibility committee made a "false negative" judgment when they concluded that Ricky no longer had a learning disability. This school's staff were vigilant about overidentifying LDs, in light of the school system's widely publicized goal of reducing the number of LDs. Consequently, they were drifting toward failure to identify true LDs.

FAILURE TO IDENTIFY LD EXAMPLE. *When Ricky was in eighth grade, he was evaluated for continuing special education eligibility. Three years before, he had been found eligible for LD services. Due to multiple disciplinary referrals, and due to the psychologist's finding that Ricky's emotions were overwhelming him, the committee ignored strong evidence of a learning disability. Specifically, there was a 22-point discrepancy between verbal and performance IQ scores, which the psychologist noted was "highly significant" for verbal processing deficits; below average auditory processing, with significantly weak auditory memory; a visual-motor integration deficit; and a 17-point discrepancy between written language and ability. Moreover, Ricky's academic achievement in written language was at the fifth-grade level.*

In the face of the evidence of co-occurring emotional and behavioral disorders, it is probably wise to keep the door open to an interrelationship between ED and LD. (See Chapter 26 for more discussion of interrelatedness.) Excluding these difficulties from the official definition of LD, or ignoring them in the decision-making process, will not make them go away.

Some professionals have attempted to address the issue of interrelated disabilities by proposing a generic definition that stresses the similarities among all mildly disabled children and adolescents. Hallahan and Kauffman (1976), for example, suggested that *mildly handicapped* be used to delineate students who have traditionally been classified as ED, EMR, or LD.

Since that proposal was made, the federal guidelines have changed. They now allow for the possibility that a student may be both LD and ED. IDEA provides for *multiple disabilities*, a provision that has been undisturbed by IDEA 1997. Implicit here is the idea that a student may qualify for this category by showing concomitant impairments, the combination of which causes such severe educational problems that they cannot be accommodated in special education programs solely for one of the impairments. While this guideline may be used by school systems more frequently with students who have hard handicaps, such as deafness and blindness, the door appears to have been opened for officially combining LD and ED.

Indeed, in this chapter, it has been shown that some students with learning disabilities may have equally pervasive and impairing emotional and behavioral difficulties. For one, *an inability to build or maintain satisfactory interpersonal relationships with peers and teachers* is evident. A student who has poor listening skills and who has impaired ability to communicate will have difficulty making friends and keeping them. Further, a child who is anxious and passive in social situations will have trouble connecting with others.

Second, LDs may show *inappropriate types of behavior or feelings under normal circumstances.* Students who aggress against others (even if it is for the purpose of bypassing their own frustration) create conflict and problems in the classroom. Conversely, students who withdraw from others in the face of rejection and incompetence present problems to teachers and peers. Students who are impulsive and reactionary create nagging problems in the classroom.

Finally, students with learning disabilities may show *depression,* another ED criterion. As discussed in this chapter and in Chapter 13, a number of the primary sample cases show both LD and depressive features.

In the secondary sample, as well, depression is evident. Donnie, for example, has a long history of depression, which probably began when he was a preschooler. At that time, his parents separated and a period of animosity and dispute over custody ensued, including parental kidnapping and dramatic rescuing. It was, altogether, a chaotic and frightening time for a little boy.

In the face of a constantly shifting home situation, which was the pattern for the next 14 years, Donnie became detached. This was an adaptive response in the face of emotional arousal. His experience with unpredictability, and with painful events out of his control, explain his detachment. This emotional style, however, interfered with his ability to negotiate life's tasks, both at home and at school. He became uncomfortable with his own feelings and with emotionally charged situations. As a result, Donnie lost access to the kind of spontaneous responsiveness that fuels one's vitality. Lacking spontaneity, motivation, and zest for life, Donnie developed chronic depression. At 17, he attempted suicide by overdosing on barbituates.

Altogether, there is a growing body of evidence that LD students with learning disabilities have significant internalizing problems, such as depression. For example, Thompson (1986) reported that internalizing problems occur more often than externalizing ones in children with LD. Further, Stein and Hoover (1989) concluded that students with LD experience more anxiety than peers without disabilities.

SUGGESTED EDUCATIONAL STRATEGIES

Teaching strategies for LD students should address a range of internalizing and externalizing emotional-behavioral problems as well as academic problems. Additionally, interventions should focus on teaching LD students how to utilize support within their network and how to provide support to others (Wenz-Gross and Siperstein 1997). Strategies could also focus on the development of comforting skills and affective and social perspective-taking abilities to increase peer support (Burleson and Keenkel 1994).

Alley and Deshler (1979) proposed a *learning strategies model* for LD adolescents to facilitate acquisition, organization, storage, and retrieval of information for the academic curriculum and for the demands of social interaction. The present focus is on the need to cope with social demands, specifically needs related to peer support, low self-esteem, self-awareness, perception of social situations, competence anxiety, passivity, frustration tolerance, impulsivity and disruptiveness, and making realistic choices.

The following are some suggested strategies for helping the LD secondary student.

1.   Direct instruction (DI), a stimulus-based method, has been effective in reducing disruptive behavior (Nelson, Johnson, and Marchand-Martella 1996). DI is a comprehensive system that involves all aspects of instruction from organization

to curriculum presentation, with clear and unambiguous demonstration. It could involve modeling of new material, guided practice to ensure understanding, and independent practice. One recommended DI sequence is as follows: (1) Frame the lesson (goal, evocation of attention, reviewing), (2) present new content area information (facts, principles, and concepts told or shown), (3) conduct guided practice (assisted application), and (4) use independent practice (with monitoring and immediate response to questions). Indirect instruction, on the other hand, has questionable value for students with mild learning disabilities. Collaborative instruction, as frequently practiced in team-taught, or inclusive, classrooms, has not been found to be very effective for secondary LD students. Boudah, Schumacher, and Deshler (1997) found that student engagement was low, only some strategic skills increased, and test and quiz results decreased slightly among mildly disabled students under that model.

2.   Help the student make realistic choices and set realistic goals. Often, LD students overestimate their abilities and select texts, materials, courses, and activities that are too difficult for them. In an effort to attain their goals, LD students may resort to cheating or devote all their energies to striving for one unattainable goal to the detriment of all other activities. Conversely, LD students may underestimate their goals and select those that require minimal energy and work.

3.   Inaccurate self-awareness of their own abilities, an identity problem, may affect the LD student's study skills. This student, consequently, may diminish his or her effort by studying too little or block his or her energy by either studying too late (cramming) or "freezing" during a test. With low self-esteem, an LD student is less accepting of failure and threatening experiences, and probably will not apply himself or herself and face the situation head-on.

4.   Identify sources of failure and threats to success with the student in order to promote accurate perception of social situations and taking responsibility for the consequences of his or her own behavior. One strategy is to hold regular class meetings in which students' problems are discussed. Peers can resolve issues by confirming or denying the target student's view of a situation. A school counselor might be involved to help students cooperatively identify the source of their problems. Another strategy is role-playing, which can effectively increase students' awareness of situations and possible solutions that do not negatively affect the self-esteem of LD students.

5.   Explore the student's strengths and weaknesses with him or her to promote a more realistic evaluation of competencies and to enhance self-esteem through competent performance on specific tasks.

6.   Use a daily activities journal to develop the student's awareness of his or her strengths and weaknesses. Direct the student to write about at least one daily instance of positive feeling or action and one instance of negative feeling or action. If the student cannot think of one positive feeling or action, have him or her describe a positive means to overcome or circumvent the negative feeling or action. From this structured journal, the teacher can learn about the student's criteria for strengths and

weaknesses. No grade should be given for this activity, but it is recommended that supportive statements be written in the journal, which is returned to the student. The student could be given weekly grades, checks, or points for meeting the criteria of (1) daily writing and (2) inclusion of both positive and negative feelings or actions.

7.   "Rap" sessions or class meetings can help students gain a clearer perception of their behavior and the consequences of it. Some rules should be followed: (1) At the start, distinguish between what may and may not be discussed, (2) determine what discussion methods are appropriate or inappropriate, and (3) determine your (the adult's) leadership style (authoritarian, which is best suited to teaching factual information, or facilitative, which promotes group problem solving) and stress your leadership strengths. One guideline is that topics should be open-ended, not limited to those for which there are factual answers (e.g., "When does third period start?"). The idea is to stimulate thinking, with the possibility of providing factual information that the LD student may have missed. Factual background may be needed by all the students to facilitate discussion. The following specific guidelines are suggested for rap sessions:

o   Pose specific problems that challenge the students
       and that relate to their experiences.

o   When there is disagreement, direct the confrontation
       to a noncomittal option without offering a judgmental
       opinion to the group. Clarify similarities and differences
       among options.

o   Summarize a student's statement if some students do not
       understand his or her intent or reasoning, and ask
       the student if your summary reflects his or her thoughts.
       The teacher could also synthesize several students'
       discussion points.

o   Be alert to subtle signs of interest and disinterest.
       Do not let some students monopolize the session.

o   Supplement with resources: films, experts, field
       trips, and so on.

o   Be sensitive to differences between silences
       that indicate topic exhaustion and attempts to
       develop new options. One tactic is to say,
       "Have we covered all the options for this problem?"

o   Tie in unrelated discussion to the topic at hand.
       "Do you agree with Tom or Jane? Why?" This
       procedure helps the LD student's awareness of
       the direction of the discussion and confirms that
       he is providing irrelevant information or feelings.

8.   In counseling, transactional analysis and reality therapy can help LD students develop self-awareness and self-esteem.

9.   Provide a climate of warmth and concern to enhance trust.

10.   Actively listen to the student. Provide both verbal clues, such as paraphrasing and summarizing, and nonverbal clues, such as eye contact and head-nodding.

11.   Give the student feedback that is in plain language and supported by facts (e.g., "I don't think you feel you are important to other students," not "You have low ego functioning").

12.   Give the student feedback that is specific (e.g., "Jovan's rejection is important to you, but now we should talk about other boys you could play ball with," not "You'll grow out of it").

13.   Give feedback that does not alienate the student (e.g., "Sherelle probably does not know you well enough to go out with you," not "Sherelle probably thinks you are weird because she does not know you").

14.   When giving feedback, avoid the words "right," "wrong," and "you should."

15.   Give your opinion only when asked for it. Similarly, offer a solution only if it is requested. Some students want to vent or complain but do not want or are not ready for solutions.

16.   End each class session with a positive remark, even if it is not more than "I look forward to seeing you tomorrow."

17.   Use cooperative group structures to build trust and self-awareness of social and academic skills. Use activities and games that demonstrate that individuals gain more from cooperating than from working alone or competing. This format also is effective for students who are self-centered and unable or unwilling to perceive and act to meet the needs of others. The student is encouraged to contribute to the group's success and to feel needed. Finally, cooperative structures promote interdependence, a realistic blend of independence and dependence, or an ability to determine when to be independent from others and when to be collaborative. These activities encourage self-assessment of abilities relative to types of activities.

18.   Directly teach nonverbal communication, specifically how to judge and evaluate nonverbal messages. (See Chapter 20 for possible topics.)

19.   Teach the components of acceptance: liking other people, tolerance, flexibility, and sympathy. Employ role-playing and discussions of situations in which examples are made using contrasting approaches.

20.   Promote self-confidence and social comfort by group activities in

which individual interests are brought out, thereby promoting knowledge among peers. This strategy combats withdrawal and timidity.

21.   Rearrange natural conditions so that the student is not rewarded for inappropriate behavior.

22.   For the student who is impulsive, reinforce an appropriate behavior that cannot co-occur with an inappropriate one. For example, call on the student when he or she appears ready to interrupt, thereby blocking his or her calling out without raising a hand.

23.   Be a good model. Demonstrate a positive attitude, approach problems with confidence, and apply sound approaches and reasoning in handling problems. Students learn more from what adults do than what they say.

24.   Encourage the student to make value judgments about what he or she is doing or has done that contributes to his or her problem. LD students need to recognize that they are a part of their own problems and that they must make a commitment to change their behaviors, with solutions in which they are invested.

25.   For students who impulsively guess or who place little value on reasoning, teach problem solving by having them solve problems aloud, followed by a correct explanation, and then a comparison of their different approaches with the ideal.

26.   An organized classroom reduces student uncertainty and stimulates a sense of control.

27.   Strike a balance between fostering a strong, supportive relationship and independent functioning.

28.   Recognize that change is not easy for these students, particularly affective styles and ingrained habits. Be satisfied with small increments of change. One recommendation is to maintain charts of behaviors to provide evidence that change is in the desired direction.

29.   Grading may be modified to provide nonthreatening feedback to the student who is anxious about competence or about having sufficient time to meet course requirements. One method is student self-comparison: Student and teacher meet and determine appropriate instructional goals, and the student's progress toward these goals is tracked. Another method is a grading contract: Teacher and student determine the amount and quality of work the student must complete to receive a specific grade. In framing the contract, the parties should agree on what the student hopes to learn; the activities, strategies, and resources that will help him or her acquire the skills; the products the student will complete to show mastery; evaluation strategies; and assignment time lines including lateness penalties and grading procedures. The student might also be given a pass/fail option; put on a mastery level/criterion system involving pretest to determine specific learning activities and posttest to show mas-

tery and credit given so that he or she may move on to the next skill; differentiated grading, with grades given in different areas of achievement, for example,   grading for ability (improvement), effort (time and energy spent), and achievement (mastery of content); shared grading (e.g., teachers collaborating in an inclusive classroom to assign grades based on observations and established guidelines); and descriptive grading in which the teacher writes comments and gives examples regarding student performance that address the student's skills, learning style, effort, and attitude.

30.   Provide classroom accommodations, particularly in an inclusive setting: extra time, reformatted tests to shorten segments, a calculator for functional math when higher concepts are the objective, oral testing, use of peer questions on tests, preferential seating, summaries and reviews, multisensory instruction, highlighting of important information, giving one direction at a time, shortened assignments, outlines/synopses, small-group instruction, alternatives to compositions, and test retakes.

31.   Acknowledge privately and publicly the student's unique contributions.

32.   Ask the student to restate directions.

33.   Break complex tasks down into achievable steps.

34.   Teach the student to divide tasks into small, manageable parts and to decide on the order in which to do them.

35.   Provide access to computers to carry out assignments.

36.   Use aides or peers from upper grades or courses as tutors during independent work periods.

37.   Give open-book or take-home tests when possible.

38.   Teach the student to read his or her own signals so he or she knows when he or she is angry, afraid, frustrated, or whatever else leads to outbursts, shutdown, or other unproductive behaviors.

39.   Have the student maintain his or her own progress chart to become more self-aware. Focus on one social behavior at a time. For academic behavior, self-recording, self-evaluation, and self-graphing have been found to improve completion of homework assignments (Trammel, Schloss, and Alper 1994) and can work well in all academic areas.

40.   Teach self-advocacy and assertiveness.

41.   Use self-correcting materials for immediate feedback and independence. Students with a history of academic failure benefit from private feedback. Also, this method prevents practicing of errors before the teacher can get to

the student to provide corrective feedback. Self-correcting materials also help the student maintain attention. Computer learning activities can provide this type of experience.

42.   Use a *Q-sort* approach to targeting social skills needing development. First developed by Stephenson (1953), this method identifies the degree of discrepancy between the "real" and "ideal" selves. The teacher can make up index cards with one attribute written on each (e.g., get work done on time, poke or hit classmates, play with objects while working, work slowly, work until job is finished, interrupt teacher, pay attention, disturb class with noises). The student sorts through the cards twice, first for real self (how he or she really is) then for ideal self (how he or she would like to be). The student puts the cards in rank order, from "most like me" to "most unlike me." He or she may put more than one card at one rank in the ordering. By number coding the ranks, the teacher can compare the real and ideal rankings by scores. Those attributes that differ by three or more points between real and ideal rankings could be targeted for discussion and intervention.

43.   *Sociometric* data can help to group students for activities, to identify social isolates, and to identify leaders. An easy approach is to list all class members and have each student rate the others in terms of yes, no, or maybe. Separate ratings can be done of concerns (e.g., "Who would you be willing to work with for a group project?"). Sociometric scores can readily be derived by assigning points: 0 to no, 1 to maybe, and 2 to yes. The students must be assured of privacy in order for this method to be effective.

44.   Use *life space interviewing* following peer conflicts. This method, which develops self-advocacy, models active listening, and encourages realistic perception of events, involves four steps (Morse 1971):

1.   Each student involved in the incident gives his version of it without interruption.

2.   The teacher listens and, without judging, asks questions to determine the accuracy of each student's perception.

3.   If the students cannot agreeably resolve the problem, the teacher may have to suggest an acceptable plan to deal with the problem.

4.   The students and the teacher work together to develop a plan for solving similar problems in the future.

The technique can reduce the student's frustration while supporting him or her during an emotionally charged situation; it reinforces the behavioral and social rules; and it helps the student solve his own problems in a supportive context.

45.   For the student who shows some perceptual confusion, provide a map of the school for his or her notebook and post the map in the classroom as well. Highlight locations of restrooms and water fountains.

22

Tourette's Syndrome

There is a child in your class who is very perplexing. She is bright, friendly, anxious to please, generally well-behaved and polite. However, for no apparent reason, she disrupts the class with snorting noises. She also blinks her eyes constantly, even though the eye doctor says she doesn't need glasses. She also persists in jumping around in her seat. You have spoken to her and her parents about her behavior, but she has persisted. You wonder: Is she looking for attention because her parents have recently separated? Is she unusually anxious about something? Does she have some emotional problem that is not obvious? Finally, someone suggests to you that the child may have Tourette Syndrome. (Bronheim 1991, p. 17)

The symptoms of Tourette's syndrome (TS) have been reported since antiquity (Leckman and Cohen 1994). The syndrome was first documented in the 1400s (Lemons and Barber 1991); however, the diagnosis at that time was possession by the devil (Garelik 1986). One of the earliest accounts, written by two Dominican monks in 1489, concerned a priest who suffered from multiple complex motor and vocal tics.

[I]n all his behaviour he remained a sober priest without eccentricity, except during the process of any exorcisms; and Tourette's Syndrome when these were finished, and the stole was taken from his neck, he showed no sign of madness or any immoderate action. But when he passed any church, and genuflected in honour of the Glorious Virgin, the devil made him thrust his tongue far out of his mouth; and when he was asked whether he could not restrain himself from doing this, he answered: "I cannot help myself at all, for so he uses all my limbs and organs, my neck, my tongue, and my lungs, whenever he pleases, causing me to speak or to cry out; and I hear the words as if they were spoken by myself, but I am altogether unable to restrain them; and when I try to engage in prayer he attacks me more violently, thrusting out my tongue." (Lohr and Wisniewski 1987, p. 191)

Many theories of causation were proposed between 1886 and the 1950s. Some pointed to psychological dysfunction or inflammatory disease (Lohr and Wisniewski 1987). Currently, theories and treatments tend to fall into the psychiatric, neuropsychological, biochemical and educational realms, far removed from religious theories and treatments.

Treatments for TS have varied as much as and in accordance with the theories about its causation. The first reported treatment was exorcism; subsequent treatments have included blood letting, prolonged sipping of water, rhythmic traction of the tongue, drug and medicinal treatments (from cocaine to mustard plasters), psychotherapy, hypnotherapy, and behavior modification.

Since 1885, when Gilles de la Tourette described this disorder (Jagger et al. 1982), made up of multiple tics, phonic and verbal productions, and behavioral changes, there has been a cascade of research studies. The result has been a clearer appreciation of the phenomenology, natural history, etiology, physiology, and treatment of TS (Towbin et al. 1992).

"Tic," the central word in TS, derives from the word ticque, which originally was used in veterinary medicine to describe the movements made by horses when restrained. The term did not enter the medical literature until the middle of the nineteenth century. By the start of the twentieth century, the term was used to refer to convulsive, inopportune, and excessive movements.

Currently, the word "tic" is used to describe a variety of involuntary movements extending from simple muscle contractions to complex spoken phrases. The major features distinguishing tics from other conditions are the rapid and transient nature of the movements, the lack of evidence of underlying neurological disorder, the disappearance of tics during sleep, and the ease with which they may be voluntarily reproduced or suppressed. Their rapidity and lack of rhythmicity differentiates tics from the stereotyped or manneristic behavior seen in some autistic and mentally retarded children (Corbett and Turpin 1985) The tics of TS seem to increase as a result of tension or stress and decrease with relaxation or concentration on an absorbing task. Individuals with TS describe relief when a tic occurs. Categories of tics are presented in Table 22.1, along with examples.

While TS involves, primarily, abnormal movements, the intensity of these tics varies greatly from person to person and also in the same person at different times. The movements can be very severe and manifest as violent spasmodic jerking that may even catapult the person from his chair, repeated head shaking and shouting that can provoke blindness following retinal detachment, or violent blows to one's eyes that can induce hemorrhage and loss of sight. They can also be intensified by emotional factors, such as fear, embarrassment, and fatigue; diminished by fever; relieved by alcohol; and modified or completely suppressed by voluntary control (Enoch and Trethowan 1991).

SOME FACTS

Prevalence. While the incidence of TS is low (estimates range from 0.0003 to 0.5 percent among schoolchildren), transient tic behaviors are common

Table   22.1
Simple   and   Complex   Tics

Types of Simple Tics	Descriptors
Motor	eye blinking; eye darting; pursing lips or pouting; facial grimacing; jerking motions of the head, arm, leg, hands, feet, or stomach; snaps of the jaw; neck or shoulder shrugging; kicks; and movements of the trunk
Vocal	throat clearing; coughing; grunting; barking; yelping; squealing; lip smacking and tongue clicking; short exhalations ("puh puh puh"); lip "pops"; sniffing; squeaking; spitting; and verbalization of initial consonants

Types of Complex Tics	
Motor	jumping; biting; repeated touching (other people or things); copropraxia (obscene gestures); smelling; twirling; running; making peculiar "faces"; wincing; throwing; grabbing; pinching; bending; posturing; bouncing; banging; skipping; dancing; kicking; eye and lip rubbing; imitating movements or gestures (echokinesia, echopraxia); and self-injurious actions including hitting or biting oneself
Vocal	uttering parts of words or phrases out of context and and coprolalia (socially unacceptable words); ecolalia; palilalia (echoing others or self); odd prosody and inappropriate accentuation of syllables; and repetitious sounds or words, e.g., "I have to go now, now, now, now, now," "all right, all right," "shiiiiiit, shitttttt, shshshshshshit."

among children, especially between the ages of 7 and 11 years. An estimated 25 percent of children between 6 and 12 exhibit transient tics (Kessler 1972), and 5 percent has been estimated for tic occurrence between the ages of 7 and 11 (Leckman et al. 1994). Graham (1991) concluded that mild tics occur in about 10 percent of children at some stage of development. Thus, while tic behaviors are fairly common among children, tics that meet the defining criteria for TS are not.

   Demographics. The incidence of TS appears to be unrelated to race or socioeconomic status (Leckman et al. 1994), although individuals of Jewish or East European heritage may be more commonly affected. People with these origins may have a greater genetic predisposition toward TS, but it seems more likely that referral bias and other cultural factors affect the expression and tolerance of the symptoms.

Gender. Incidence is greater in boys than girls. There appears to be a male to female ratio of about two to one.

Onset. If the disorder is going to appear, it almost always does so before age 21, and sometimes as early as two years of age. The norm is from six to seven years of age (Lemons and Barber 1991). The most common first symptom is a facial tic, such as rapidly blinking eyes or mouth twitches. For some individuals, the disorder begins abruptly with multiple symptoms of movements and sounds; throat clearing and sniffing or tics of the limbs may be the initial signs (TSA 1994).

Course. TS is chronic and usually present for the duration of a person's life. Symptoms typically change (Bronheim 1991), and there are periodic changes in the number, frequency, type and location of the tics and in the waxing and waning of their severity. Symptoms can sometimes disappear for weeks or months at a time (Tourette Syndrome Association 1994). Tics change slowly but may be stable for years, then suddenly change in strength or pattern. New tics may emerge to replace or add to older ones. Noises or inarticulate words may develop, and assorted repetitive vocalizations or motor or mental rituals may develop (Lemons and Barber 1991). Altogether, the course is unpredictable (Leckman et al. 1994).

Because of the variability there is no typical case. Leckman and Cohen (1994) note that individuals with tic disorders may present a broad array of behavioral difficulties, including disinhibited speech or conduct, impulsivity, distractibility, motor hyperactivity, and signs of obsessive-compulsive disorder.

The factors that influence the continuity of tic disorders from childhood to adolescence to adulthood are not well understood. There is probably an interaction between maturation of the central nervous system and emotional distress along the maturational course (Leckman et al. 1994).

Severity. Typically, TS is not severely disabling. While the expression of symptoms covers a spectrum from very mild to quite severe, the majority of cases seem to be in the mild category. The factors that determine the degree of disability probably include the presence of additional developmental, mental and behavioral disorders. The level of resilience may depend upon support and understanding from parents, peers, and educators and the presence of special abilities or personal attributes (Leckman et al. 1994).

Prognosis. When TS was first identified, the prognosis was thought to be poor, and the majority of cases were assigned to long-term hospitalization (Tourette 1885, 1899). Today, the outlook for TS generally is considered to be good; most individuals experience their worst tic symptoms between nine and 15 years of age. More recent studies suggest a more favorable outcome (Shapiro et al. 1978). Improvement appears to be related to age of onset and initial severity (Corbett and Turpin 1985). Towbin and his colleagues conclude, "From the perception that TS was a rare eccentricity of nature at the turn of the century, we have moved to appreciate a now common, frequently mild disorder compatible with a full, rewarding life" (1992, p. 372).

Other variables. There is no apparent relation of TS to birth weight, birth order, parental age, medical history of individuals or families, or psychiatric history.

In summary, TS is understood generically to be a complex tic disorder with a lifelong course. A triad of components is necessary to make the diagnosis; the presence of generalized tics and involuntary utterances that may be obscene or suggestive, onset in childhood, and a course that involves a fluctuation of signs throughout the life span but typically is not severely disabling.

TIC DISORDER EXAMPLE. *Melissa, age 17, exhibits behavioral difficulties: impulsivity, distractibility, and motoric hyperactivity. She alternates between very loud, disruptive behavior and quiet times when she scribbles on paper or stares into space. At times, Melissa seems unaware of her immediate environment. When the internal stress reaches a boiling point, she simply leaves school and goes home. Melissa has low frustration tolerance. She also experiences racing thoughts and engages in a counting ritual.*

Diagnosis. Despite understanding that TS is, essentially, a neurological condition, diagnosis is made by observing symptoms and evaluating the history of their onset. No blood analysis or neurological testing exists to diagnose this disorder. Some physicians order an EEG, MRI, CAT scan, or certain blood tests to rule out other ailments that might be confused with TS. Rating scales are available to assess tic severity (Tourette Syndrome Association 1994).

Because, as a syndrome, TS involves various signs, both obvious and subtle, it needs to be understood in its entirety. Any sign considered in isolation may lead clinicians and educators to treatment or education plans that address only part of the problem.

Definition. TS is a disorder characterized by tics, which are involuntary, rapid, sudden movements or vocalizations that occur repeatedly in the same way. The tics occur many times a day (usually in bouts) nearly every day or intermittently throughout a span of more than one year.

While the generic definition of TS provides general guidelines about the disorder, the psychiatric definition provides specific markers. The American Psychiatric Association's *DSM-IV* (1994) defines tics as sudden, rapid, recurrent, nonrhythmic, stereotyped motor movements or vocalizations. Leckman and Cohen (1994) add that tics mimic some aspect or fragment of normal behavior, rarely last more than a second, and can occur singly or together in an orchestrated pattern.

The psychiatric definition of TS includes the following five components. Illustrations are from actual diagnosed cases that meet the five criteria.

First, both multiple motor and one or more vocal tics have been present at some time during the illness, although not necessarily concurrently.

MULTIPLE MOTOR TICS EXAMPLES. *Chris B, age 17, shows multiple motor tics. He blinks his eyes constantly and taps his fingers.*

Jed, age 16, shows motor and vocal tics. He jerks his head from side to side, shows facial grimaces, pursing mouth movements, shoulder shrugs, and occasional finger tapping. Vocally, he blurts out rude comments. Occasionally Jed makes throat-clearing sounds. Most motor and vocal tics occur in sets of two or three.

Second, the tics occur many times each day (usually in bouts) nearly every day or intermittently throughout a period of more than one year, and during this period there has not been a tic-free period of more than three consecutive months. Tics can occur at various times. The frequency ranges from a few tics per week to over 90 tics per minute (Lohr and Wisniewski 1987; Leckman et al. 1994). The forcefulness of motor tics and the volume of phonic tics vary from behaviors that are not noticeable (a slight shrug or a hushed guttural noise) to strenuous displays (arm thrusts or loud barking) and exhausting (Leckman et al. 1994).

TIC OCCURRENCE EXAMPLES. *Melissa may suddenly start yelling.*

Chris B's eye blinking is nearly constant, occurring in sets of three and estimated to occur at the rate of 45 blinks per minute.

Third, the disturbance causes marked distress or significant impairment in social, occupational, or other important areas.

IMPAIRMENT EXAMPLE. *By the time Chris B was in high school he manifested difficulty paying attention, poor work habits, and obsessive-compulsive behaviors in addition to motor tics. It was then that his parents decided to send him to a private school. Subsequently, Chris turned a corner. Once the appropriate medication, a combination of Paxil and Ritalin, was found for his TS symptoms, he began to enjoy school and learning. Despite almost constant eye blinking and finger tapping, Chris is optimistic. He likes people, has come to terms with his condition, and even jokes about how he was obsessive-compulsive before it became a well-known disorder. Chris has difficulty making friends. When he encounters someone with whom he would like to start a relationship, it is as if a stone holds his tongue in place. Also, Chris needs to move. He wants to travel the world and have many adventures, e.g., motorcycling and hang gliding. His ideal vocation is in law enforcement because he is fascinated with guns. "This may sound weird," he said, "but I don't want to shoot guns, just hold them." Chris is fascinated with gun designs and their intricate mechanisms, as well as with other objects that have moving parts. The idea of reading, even listening to taped books, repells him. After all, those activities involve little, if any, movement.*

Fourth, the onset of the disorder occurs before the age of 18 years.

ONSET EXAMPLES. *Jed first manifested a tic disorder when he was seven years old. At school he blinked and rubbed his eyes and lips frequently. At home he would spit for minutes at a time.*

David, age 15, first manifested his tic disorder when he was six years old. He would jerk his head from side to side. This occurred both at home and at school.

Michael, age 13, had a bout with facial tics that lasted for several months when he was 10 years old.

Melissa was diagnosed with TS at age six, and Chris B was diagnosed with TS at age seven.

Fifth, TS is not due to direct physiological effects of a substance (e.g., stimulants) or to a general medical condition (for example, Huntington's disease or post-viral encephalitis).

TS CASE EXAMPLES. *Jed, David, and Michael are all healthy boys with no history of significant physical illnesses except, in Michael's case, a mild case of asthma. Jed and David have been active in sports. All three boys have excellent school attendance records.*

Melissa and Chris B, too, are healthy. Melissa's school attendance has been impacted adversely by her inability to tolerate normal school demands, and Chris was sent to a private school because his parents felt that that situation could best deal with his unique learning needs, including a sophisticated medication regimen. Otherwise, both Melissa and Chris have experienced no physical illnesses.

PUZZLING ASPECTS OF TS

Of all TS symptoms, verbal tics are the most baffling. Coprolalia, which is the uncontrollable uttering of obscenities or anything considered by the person to be vulgar, blasphemous, or socially unacceptable, is the most well-known verbal tic, despite the fact that only about 30 to 50 percent of TS cases develop this symptom.

VERBAL TIC EXAMPLE. *Jed has been in psychotherapy for about six years with the same psychologist. As he enters and exits his therapist's office, Jed typically unleashes a stream of obscenities and vulgarities. As the psychologist described it, Jed "dumps." Also, one day after his resource teacher helped him complete an examination in algebra in a quiet, separate room, and while, as she thought, they were engaged in pleasant conversation en route back to the classroom, suddenly Jed lashed out, "Well, that's the first intelligent thing you've said." Jed's remark was stunning and puzzling.*

A second puzzling aspect of TS is the diminution of tics during certain activities. For example, tics diminish greatly during sleep but do not disappear completely (Leckman et al. 1994). Others have reported that symptoms diminish during sexual orgasm.

Third, the involuntary nature of this disorder has been baffling. Most tics can be suppressed for brief periods. One adult with TS reported that he could control his tics 100 percent of the time. Actually, what may occur is that the individual feels a signal symptom, or warning sensation, and then suppresses the overt tic (Leckman et al. 1994), thereby showing a learned component to the disorder.

Youngsters with TS not only can suppress their tics for brief periods, but they may camouflage them. Often, tics are given a purposive appearance (e.g., brushing hair away from the face with an arm). These can then be distinguished as tics only upon close observation, by their repetitive character (Leckman et al. 1994).

TIC SUPPRESSION EXAMPLE. *Jed appears to blend into the social landscape. Only after observing him for some time does the tic pattern become clear. While he reads newspapers and books compulsively, usually facing into a quiet corner of the library, Jed's mouth moves; he may stretch every minute or so; or he may shrug his shoulders every couple of minutes. During a final examination in the library, too, continuous observation revealed that he twisted his head and shrugged his shoulders, on the average, once every five minutes, and these movements lasted about two seconds. Also, his movements occurred in sets of two or three.*

CAUSES

Numerous factors have been considered in the genesis of TS. Eight of these are described here.

First, temperamental factors have been mentioned together with a history of related behavioral symptoms, such as hyperactivity, impulsiveness, and increased muscle tension and reactivity (Rapoport 1959; Walsh 1962). These symptoms may indicate an underlying temperamental vulnerability to TS (Corbett and Turpin 1985).

Second, precipitating factors also have been noted. Varied stressors, such as seeing a pet dog run over, sexual assault, serious home conflicts, serious frights, and acute physical conditions, have been mentioned. In most cases, no acute factors have been evident, but chronic stress is seen in a large proportion of cases (Creak and Guttmann 1935; Eisenberg, Asher, and Kanner 1959; Faux

1966). Acute factors seem more justified in cases of simple tics (Corbett and Turpin 1985).

Third, familial and genetic factors have been cited. Studies suggest a dominant gene; a high proportion of first-degree male relatives show chronic tics (Graham 1991). Cases of TS have been found in mothers and sons, uncles and nephews, identical twins, and among sisters. About 30 percent of persons with TS have a family history of the disorder (Lohr and Wisniewski 1987). One study (1994) found (through longitudinal study) increased rates of tic disorders among children having first-degree relatives with TS (Carter et al. 1994).

Another family factor that has been implicated is psychopathology. It was found, for example, that about one-third of parents of ticqueurs had had psychiatric consultations and half of these were mothers with affective illness (Corbett et al. 1969). It is unclear if parental psychopathology is causally related or merely the result of having a child with severe tics, but it seems likely that parental anxiety may be an important factor in maintaining tics (Zausmer 1954). In mild cases of TS, parents are sometimes overpressuring, and in severe cases primary family factors (such as overpunitiveness) arise because of the child's extremely disturbing behavior pattern (Graham 1991).

Fourth, neurological factors have been implicated. Golden (1977) and Shapiro and colleagues (1978) both found that about half of TS patients showed soft neurological signs, and Golden (1977) reported that eight out of 15 children with TS showed soft neurological signs. Rapoport (1991) and Graham (1991) believe that TS is a neurological disorder, specifically a defect in the basal ganglia.

On the other hand, clinical examination of the nervous system is often negative. Although there has been an increasing number of reported neurological abnormalities, these are usually of a minor nature and difficult to evaluate clearly. Examples are mild motor asymmetrics, ranging from decreased muscle tone or impaired arm swing to a positive Babinski sign. In one study conducted at the Cornell Medical Institute, a careful clinical examination of 22 patients with TS found only 11 with such neurological abnormalities, and those were minor signs of doubtful significance.

Most studies have found a normal IQ distribution among TS patients, but about 50 percent of children with TS show discrepancies between verbal and nonverbal intelligence, with verbal being higher (Shapiro et al. 1978). Researchers have found processing deficits involving visuomotor, spatial memory, and auditory discrimination (Corbett and Turpin 1985), which suggests concomitant learning disabilities.

Fifth, brain chemistry has been implicated. Current research presents considerable evidence that TS stems from the abnormal metabolism of at least one brain chemical, the neurotransmitter dopamine. Graham (1991) pointed to the effectiveness of certain drugs and to similarity with syndromes produced by L-dopa, which suggests an abnormality of dopamine metabolism. Other neurotransmitters, such as serotonin, may be involved (Tourette Syndrome Association 1994). Towbin (1995) suggests that physical structures in the brain may change during behaviors associated with TS.

Sixth, speech and language difficulties have also been implicated. Recent research has focused on linguistic aspects of vocal tics, suggesting that such tics do not occur randomly but are located according to the clausal boundaries or at points of low information within sentences (Martindale 1976; Frank 1978). Other research indicates word finding and speech volume regulation difficulties (O'Quinn and Thompson 1980; Ludlow et al. 1982).

Seventh, psychopathology, or emotional disturbance, has been associated with TS. Two specific psychological disorders associated with TS are obsessionality (Eldridge et al. 1977; Cohen et al. 1980; Nee et al. 1980; Yaryura-Tobias 1982) and sleep disorder (Zarcone, Thorpe, and Dement 1972).

Several psychological models have been proposed to explain both the genesis and the maintenance of tics (Corbett and Turpin 1985). Tics have been described in terms of learning theory, specifically classical conditioning of defensive reflexes that were originally elicited by aversive events. According to this theory, tics are maintained by external events such as parental reactions. Operant models propose that tics are maintained by reinforcement. Psychological models point to critical environmental events that exacerbate TS, such as fatigue, excitement, or anxiety; or events that diminish tics, such as relaxation, concentration, reading aloud, acting on a stage, sleep, or alcohol consumption (Bockner 1959; Challas, Chapel, and Jenkins 1967; Fernando 1976; Goforth 1974; Woodrow 1974; Benditsky 1978).

Eighth, the relationship between epilepsy and TS has been examined by several authors. Some believe that epileptic seizures or other epileptic phenomena do not occur in this condition. Enoch and Trethowan (1991), for example, cited one study of 500 TS cases in which no relation to epilepsy or to any other convulsive disorder was found. However, other studies have indicated that electroencephalograms were abnormal in as many as 75 percent of the cases.

TS AND EPILEPSY EXAMPLE. *Chris B graduated from high school and entered a major university where he was experiencing success and feeling good about himself. In November of his freshman year, at age 18, Chris experienced a grand mal seizure and suffered a severe short-term memory loss. His condition was diagnosed for the first time as epilepsy.*

Many different causative factors may be implicated in the genesis of this disorder. The most appropriate conclusion at this point is that psychological and environmental factors probably modulate the expression of symptoms that derive from an underlying organic dysfunction (Corbett and Turpin 1985).

INTERVENTIONS

Currently, there are broad-spectrum interventions for TS encompassing biochemical, psychological, psychiatric, and educational types. The majority of people with TS do not require medication; however, there are medications available to help control the symptoms when they interfere with functioning. Some effective drugs are haloperidol (Haldol), clonidine (Catapres), pimozide (Orap), fluphenazine (Prolixin, Permitil), and clonazepam (Klonopin). For obsessive-compulsive symptoms that interfere with daily functioning fluoxetine (Prozac), clomipramine (Anafranil), sertraline (Zoloft), and paroxetine (Paxil) have been effective. Stimulants such as Ritalin, Cylert, and Dexedrine are used to help with attentional difficulty, but these drugs are controversial because they may increase tics.

MEDICATION REGIMEN EXAMPLES. *Chris B, on a medication regimen of Paxil and Ritalin during high school, attributed his renewed enjoyment in school and life to medication. However, he said that his tics had increased.*

When Jed was given Ritalin to help him concentrate on instruction, his need for quiet, alone time increased. It was during these midday periods that Jed can relieve his tension and indulge in compulsive, ritualistic behaviors, such as hyperlexia and motor tics.

Melissa's psychiatrist prescribed Zoloft and Prozac for her symptoms. She also has been on Mellaril for depression.

Other interventions for TS focus on families and on education. While the efficacy of education and supportive interventions has not been rigorously assessed, there have been positive results when family expectations and relationships have been reshaped, and when teachers have been prepared to provide a positive, supportive environment in the classroom. (See detailed suggested educational strategies in the last section of this chapter.)

SUMMARY: DEVELOPMENTAL CHALLENGES

Socially, the student with TS frequently experiences rejection. Odd and sometimes aggressive behaviors do not help in making friends or getting along with teachers. A verbally hostile student, particularly one whose outbursts are unpredictable, is not readily accepted by peers or adults. Several authors have noted general difficulties in social adaptation at school (Golden 1977; O'Quinn and Thompson 1980), and the problem of maintaining age-appropriate social skills has been recognized among adolescents with TS (Leckman et al. 1994).

MAKING FRIENDS EXAMPLES. *As mentioned earlier, Chris B has difficulty initiating friendships. This bothers him a lot, but he does not know how to begin making friends.*

Melissa wants to make friends, but she has poor interpersonal relationships because her behavior is unpredictable, which is off-putting to peers.

Jed's arrogance and condescending remarks do not attract peers. His manner of speaking not only confuses but alienates peers.

Psychologically, some of the behaviors shown by a student with TS may be alternative expressions of an obsessive-compulsive disorder or of affective and anxiety syndromes. TS has been associated with panic attacks, phobias, stuttering, and rapid talking. Defining the limits of tic disorders in regard to other forms of psychopathology remains one of the most controversial and difficult areas (Leckman et al. 1994).

The psychological difficulties of students with TS add to specific developmental challenges related to identity, independence, and self-esteem. Verbal outbursts and motor tics may give the student a negative reputation and be incorporated into identity. Students with TS have difficulty becoming independent if they become anxious in new situations. Phobias place limitations on one's ability to function autonomously. Self-esteem is likely to be poor as much of one's self-evaluation depends upon feedback from others; when others express repugnance at compulsive swearing, snorting sounds, or other odd behaviors, the TS student incorporates these data into his self-assessment, with resultant low self-esteem.

Students with TS typically have cognitive difficulties, notably cognitive inflexibility. While the general mental ability of most students with TS can be expected to be in the normal range, there is evidence that these students can "get stuck" cognitively. For example, students with TS may be unable to complete work because they reread or rewrite one word over and over. The analogy is made with a computer program loop, something that cycles back on itself repeatedly (Bronheim 1991). For the student with TS, this "looping" may have special meaning. Cognitive sticking may mean an inability to switch smoothly from one activity to another, to relinquish a negative thought, or to recognize persons or events if out of context.

COGNITIVE INFLEXIBILITY EXAMPLE. *Jed shows cognitive inflexibility. For example, if he cannot do a task, he believes that he will never be able to do it rather than asking for help or trying other problem-solving strategies. Also, Jed does not readily switch activities. For example, for years he typically met his therapist at the clinic, which is on an upper floor. One day the therapist went to the ground floor of the building to get a soda. At the ground floor elevator the therapist and Jed came face to face. Jed turned away, not recognizing his therapist, who was out of context. Another example is that whenever there is a change in the school schedule, Jed is lost. This happens frequently as the school has numerous schedule changes to accommodate pep rallies, fire drills, parent-teacher conferences, and special events, and there are other unscheduled changes due to*

*inclement weather. Typically, Jed is the last student to make the change because
he has difficulty processing what is expected. Jed is very much a creature of strict
routine and habit, and any change in routine is a big problem for him.*

Hence, cognitive inflexibility can adversely impact independence. A
student who becomes disoriented in new places is not a good candidate, say, for a
driver's license, and would be expected to have difficulty even using public
transportation.

There may be significant educational/occupational impairment. For
example, many students with TS have learning disabilities (Burd et al. 1992).
Bronheim (1991) found that a disproportionately high number of youngsters
treated for TS have some form of learning disability, particularly a visual-motor
integration deficit, which makes completion of work and productivity difficult.
Comings and Comings (1987) found that severe reading problems, especially poor
retention of what was read, were extremely common among TS patients. Also,
obsessional thoughts can impede the educational or occupational progress of an
individual with TS as a result of his or her inability to focus on tasks.

LEARNING DISABILITY EXAMPLES. *Jed's learning problem is manifest
primarily in written language. He has difficulty taking notes and writing by hand
due to fine motor incoordination. Despite average intellectual abilities, there is a
discrepancy between his cognitive capacity and his written production. He does
not write quickly enough to keep up with classroom activities. Consequently, he
expends a great deal of effort expressing ideas in writing and handwriting easily
tires him. Jed learns best when written assignments are short and he can think
about the ideas and concepts in advance. He has been using a computer to
complete written assignments. His home computer is compatible with the school
computers so that he can carry disks back and forth.*

*Jed also has difficulty attending and maintaining focus on assignments.
He works so hard to control his tics that he cannot listen or concentrate on
anything else. Jed has particular difficulty with tasks that involve multiple steps.
Because he has trouble attending, by the time he is able to think about one step,
the class is on to another. Consequently, Jed becomes lost.*

*David's learning disability is more global, involving mathematics,
reading, and written language. Like Jed, his written expression is slow due to
difficulty with visual-motor coordination. David has needed a self-contained LD
program since elementary school.*

*David also has difficulty concentrating in class. He misses a lot of what
his teachers say. When the class is engaged in quiet seat work, David shows tic
behaviors such as pen tapping and head jerking. Often, he misses what his
teachers write on the chalkboard or project onto a screen. He often fails to write
down homework assignments, and may not know what to do for homework
unless it has been written on a hand-out or a worksheet.*

Melissa has been diagnosed with a developmental arithmetic disorder. Severe visual-motor and fine coordination inabilities, along with difficulty in visual discrimination, make it hard for her to deal with applied mathematics, particularly calculation.

Despite superior intelligence and outstanding reading and mathematics achievement, Chris B has a learning disability in written language.

Students with TS also find it difficult to cope with demands to target an occupation. These students have unrealistic ideas, or do not process feedback from teachers and guidance counselors. It is difficult for a student with TS to select appropriate courses. For example, a developmental challenge for adolescents is self-advocacy. These youngsters must not only come to grips with their identity, but they must assert themselves to get what they want. For a TS student, who may have poor self-evaluation ability and unrealistic goals, the progression from school to work is uneven, perhaps even arrested. The student with TS faces special challenges in working toward gainful employment.

FUTURE OUTLOOK EXAMPLE. *Jed's poor fine motor skills, irrational ideas, poor interpersonal skills, and poor self-evaluation ability do not augur well for the future. He wants to become an architect, and he believes that he can do this type of work completely alone. He rejects the idea that architects must work with other people. Also, Jed's drawing skills are poor.*

The student with TS also has special challenges in regard to dating and romance. Implicit are the social problems, as articulated above, that often result in isolation. While the individual with TS may experience an abatement of tics during orgasm, this is a relatively brief part of an intimate relationship. If these youngsters cannot get into relationships, they will remain sexually inactive.

Of the students featured in this chapter only Melissa has been sexually active, although her partners have been inappropriate. Jed has never gone out with a girl or expressed any interest in socializing at parties, dances, sports events, or other activities. David has not gone out, either. Chris wants to have friends but does not know where to begin.

TS AND THE FEDERAL DEFINITION OF ED

According to the guidelines of the Individuals with Disabilities Education Act (IDEA) TS is not a category of special education. However, this does not mean that a student may not be included within its parameters. There are, in fact, numerous characteristics of TS that meet the federal ED criteria.

One criterion, *an inability to learn that cannot be explained by intellectual, sensory, or health factors*, relates to TS in various ways. All student examples in this chapter show normal intelligence, sensory, and health factors.

Their inability to learn is not a result of intellectual, sensory, or health limitations.

Rather, learning is impeded by a collection of factors that relate to their *inability to build or maintain satisfactory interpersonal relationships with peers and teachers* and *inappropriate types of behavior or feelings under normal circumstances.* Students with TS have difficulty building or maintaining satisfactory interpersonal relationships because of their odd behaviors. Peers do not want to interact with a student who snorts, grunts, barks, or uses profanity, particularly when profanity is used out of context. Youngsters tend to be frightened by unpredictable behavior. A student whose voice rises and falls for no apparent reason, who isolates himself, or who jerks his head, grimaces, and touches another inappropriately does not endear himself to peers. Furthermore, self-destructive, aggressive, antisocial, and oppositional behaviors make relationship building difficult. Even if students with TS can find compatriots with similar behavior problems, bonding with groups will be difficult because their behavior is unpredictable and sometimes repugnant.

Teachers, too, find themselves put off by these students. A student who tells them they will "go to hell" for caring about others does not gain interpersonal ground. A student who has attention and impulse control problems, or low frustration tolerance, will be difficult for the teacher to manage and, consequently, will tax the teacher's patience. Certainly, the TS penchant for perfectionism will not charm the teacher who tries to move a classful of students forward.

The TS student who shows *inappropriate types of behavior or feelings under normal circumstances* also meets a federal criterion for ED. Within the normal routine of the classroom, a student who suddenly jerks his body or shouts out an obscenity shows inappropriate behavior. A short temper and a tendency to be confrontational are also abnormal behaviors; they indicate a lower than normal emotional threshold. Also, a student who is phobic about being in groups exemplifies inappropriate feelings under normal circumstances.

A student with TS may exhibit *a pervasive general mood of unhappiness or depression*. Melissa, for example, experiences depression. Low self-esteem is evident in her statement, "I've always been stupid." At one point, she was diagnosed with major depression. Chris B showed unhappiness and discouragement about his poor progress in school. He has felt suicidal, and low self-esteem is chronic.

Finally, students with TS may be found eligible for special education services under IDEA's *multiple disabilities* category: a combination of conditions causes such severe educational problems that these students may be eligible for special education even though they cannot be accommodated in special education programs for just one of the impairments. Jed, for example, was determined to be eligible for special services as a student with multihandicaps, and he was placed through the individualized education plan (IEP) process in ED, learning disabilities, and speech-language programs.

According to the Tourette Association of America (1994), identification as *other health impaired* (OHI) may occur under federal law. Such identification entitles the student with TS to services that address specific educational problems in school. Chris B, for example, was determined to be eligible for special education services in the OHI category, and he was placed in ED and LD programs.

SUGGESTED EDUCATIONAL STRATEGIES

A student with TS requires a multifaceted teaching approach that addresses needs for acceptance/approval, external control, internal control, appropriate engagement, consistency/routine, and encouragement. Stress and tension should be prevented as much as possible. As there are differences of opinion about whether or not a tic is a simple learned response that is self-perpetuating or an outward expression of inner conflict, both processes must be addressed because there probably is a causal interaction.

Some suggested educational strategies are the following.

1.   Teach the student with TS to be self-aware regarding mental and physical signal symptoms, for example, a violent image prior to a tic. Heightened self-awareness can promote development of coping strategies, say the use of socially acceptable movements to replace unacceptable ones.

2.   Provide additional guidance during transition periods and warnings of changes. Cognitive flexibility can be promoted with sufficient time to adjust and plan.

3.   Maintain a consistent, predictable routine as much as possible.

4.   Strategies that are appropriate for students with learning disabilities are also appropriate for students with TS (see Chapter 21).

5.   Strategies for enhancing appropriate engagement are also appropriate for students with TS (see Chapter 8). Concentration on absorbing tasks can ameliorate tics.

6.   As this student typically feels anxious regarding self-control, do not put him or her in anxiety-provoking situations. For example, the stress of public speaking may evoke tics. Allow the student to present information in an alternative format. Flexibly schedule oral presentations when the tics are less severe or waning.

7.   As testing is a stressful situation, provide a separate, private room where the student's tics will not distract other students or cause him or her additional stress by such display. This will allow the student to focus on the test.

8.   Use relaxation exercises to relieve tension. Include instruction on the difference between tension and relaxation.

9.   Strategies that have been effective with stutterers may apply. For example, the gestalt approach is recommended (Kaplan and Kaplan 1978). This

approach views stuttering not as an isolated symptom but as an organized self-system arising within the whole person. Like tics, stuttering may be maintained by the individual's experience as an inadequate, deviant stutterer (or ticquer) and by his or her inability to contact those aspects of the self that feel competent, speak (or behave) fluently, and interact in comfort. Consequently, the self system is locked in by the individual's negative experiences. In gestalt therapy, the individual is encouraged to become aware of the here-and-now experiences that maintain stuttering/tics. Tension, breathing, eye contact, and all other moment-to-moment behavior is focused upon so that those parts of the self that maintain the stuttering/tic system may be explored. For example, the student with TS may discover that his or her tics relate to fear of criticism from a particular teacher. Self-awareness promotes understanding of the individual's role in creating his or her own fear and, thus, tics.

10.   Schedule downtime for the student. It is effective to provide a block of time in the middle of the day for the student to transition and relax. Schedule short breaks outside the classroom to discharge tics in privacy.

11.   Provide a support group in which the student can practice fluent behavior and an increased sense of personal power and self-control. Speaking in a small social situation is good practice for speaking in larger groups. In a support group, the student could also role-play stressful events and gain insights into the reasons for tics.

12.   Use a time-out for tics when the student's anxiety level is low. The student could be taught to stop speaking when a tic starts and to turn around for one minute. When ready, he or she could turn back and resume speaking.

13.   Use positive reinforcement (conditioning) and self-monitoring. Establish the length of time that the student is tic free as a baseline. Set a goal with the student for length of fluent behavior and a reward for meeting the goal. Chart on a graph the daily average periods of fluency. Have the student maintain the chart. When the goal is reached, reward the student. Reset the goal for maintainance over a period of days, then weeks. (Behavior therapy may be ineffective with TS if the behavior is maintained by operant reinforcement.)

14.   Use strategies for obsessive-compulsive disorder (see Chapter 17). Systematic desensitization is particularly effective for TS. (Recall its use with school phobics.)

15.   Promote the teacher-student relationship. Anxiety and tics can be reduced through the relationship. Specifically, feelings should be labeled verbally; the adult should be accepting and nonpunitive; and specific suggestions should be made for better alternative behavior. Students will respond positively when they are able to relate to a caring person.

16.   Teach the student acceptable ways to communicate displeasure, anger, and other counterproductive emotions.

17.   Assess situational variables to determine environmental aspects associated with tics. Change those variables that relate to an increase in tics.   Along with this, modify or eliminate situations that cause stress or frustration.

18.   Provide the student with a quiet place to work (e.g., a study carrel) to reduce distracting stimuli. Do not use this as a form of punishment.

19.   Prevent lag time during which the student would be free to engage in inappropriate behavior; do not leave a lot of unstructured time.

20.   Reduce the emphasis on competition that might result in tics owing to anxiety and stress.

21.   Remove the student from the classroom if he or she is unable to show self-control.

22.   Teach the student to self-monitor. For example, if the student is aware of mental and physical signal symptoms, he or she can initiate self-talk, thinking before acting: "What is happening?" "What am I doing?" "What should I do?"

23.   Reinforce the student for communicating in an appropriate manner based on the length of time he or she can be successful. Gradually increase the length of time required for reinforcement as the student shows success.

23

Federal and Practical Definitional Characteristics

We have looked at numerous emotional and behavioral disorders. To gain a meaningful overview of students in discord, let us synthesize what has been presented in the previous chapters. This chapter, which focuses on the federal definition of emotional disturbance (ED) as a set of general guidelines, also includes a list of characteristics (practical defining characteristics) frequently seen among adolescents with emotional and behavioral disorders. This list serves as an applied, operational definition that can be used not only to understand the formal, more abstract definition of ED but also to reflect on the case studies presented. In the federal definition, it is clear that an ED student must show more than transient difficulties; the student must show intense and chronic difficulties that impair educational progress. In the primary cases presented here, as it will become clear, ED students show significant disability in terms of both federal criteria and the practical characteristics delineated in this book.

The federal guidelines for ED classification are as follows, included in the Individuals with Disabilities Education Act (IDEA), PL 101-476, and carried forward into the IDEA amendments of 1997 (PL 105-17), which strengthens academic expectations and accountability for the nation's 5.8 million youngsters with disabilities.

A. A condition exhibiting one or more of the following characteristics over a long period of time and to a marked degree, which adversely affects educational performance:

1. An inability to learn which cannot be explained by intellectual, sensory, or health factors;

2. An inability to build or maintain satisfactory interpersonal relationships with peers and teachers;

3.   Inappropriate types of behavior or feelings under normal circumstances;

4.   A general pervasive mood of unhappiness or depression; or

5.   A tendency to develop physical symptoms or fears associated with personal or school problems.

B.   The term includes children who are schizophrenic. The term does not include children who are socially maladjusted, unless it is determined that they have an emotional disturbance.

The reader is referred to Chapter 26 for a discussion of the current debate about inclusion of socially maladjusted students in the ED category.

All of the primary sample cases, and most of the secondary sample cases, featured in this book have met the federal ED criteria, and those students have been found eligible for ED services by their school systems under state guidelines that replicate the federal eligibility criteria. (Other states and districts provide guidelines that vary from close to loose replication of the federal ones.)

Additional federal law, notably Section 504 of the Rehabilitation Act of 1973 (PL 93-112), which is the first federal civil rights law that protects the rights of individuals with handicaps, may provide protection to students with emotional and behavioral disorders who are not eligible under IDEA. Specifically, Section 504 prohibits discrimination in programs or activities that receive federal financial assistance. Section 504 applies to preschool, elementary, secondary, postsecondary, vocational, and other programs and activities that receive or benefit from federal financial assistance, notably public educational institutions.

To be eligible for 504 protection, an individual must meet the definition of a person with a handicap, which is threefold: (1) There is a physical or mental impairment that substantially limits or restricts one or more major life activity. Physical or mental impairment includes, but is not limited to, speech, hearing, visual and orthopedic impairments, cerebral palsy, epilepsy, muscular dystrophy, multiple sclerosis, cancer, diabetes, heart disease, mental retardation, emotional illness, and specific learning disabilities. A major life activity is caring for one's self, performing manual tasks, walking, seeing, hearing, speaking, breathing, learning, and working. "Substantial" means the inability to access programs and activities because of the handicap. (2) There is a history of, or misclassification as having, a mental or physical impairment. (3) The individual has a physical or mental impairment that does not substantially limit major life activities but that is treated as such a limitation; the impairment substantially limits major life activities only as a result of the attitudes of others toward such impairment; or the individual has none of the relevant impairments but is treated as having such.

Students with attention-deficit disorder (ADD), with or without hyperactivity, may qualify for 504 plans or for IDEA services. Eligibility under both laws is determined on a case-by-case basis. For IDEA, a student must be found to require special education under one or more of the handicap categories; for 504, the impairment must substantially impact on a major life activity, or the student must be perceived or treated as handicapped. Many students with ADD or attention-deficit disorder with hyperactivity (ADHD) qualify for IDEA under ED, behavioral disorder (BD), or learning disability (LD) categories because their emotions and/or behaviors impede their educational progress. Some states provide special education services to these students under IDEA's other health impaired (OHI) category without consideration of criteria other than attentional difficulties and the cluster of related signs.

If parents believe their child is handicapped by ADD or ADHD, the school district must evaluate the child to determine whether or not the child has a handicap as defined by Section 504. Parents may want to refer the child for special education evaluation in case the child may qualify for IDEA under one or more of the handicap categories.

THE EBD MOVEMENT

There has been a movement toward terminology that encompasses emotional and behavioral disorders, or externalizing and internalizing disorders. After decades of disagreement, the terminology "children and youth with emotional or behavioral disorders" (EBD) has been widely accepted. It was adopted by the National Mental Health and Special Education Coalition, formed in 1987, which is coordinated by the National Mental Health Association (NMHA) and the Council for Exceptional Children (CEC) to foster collaboration among various professional and advocacy organizations. The coalition had concluded that EBD more accurately reflects the terminology used throughout the United States.

On February 10, 1993, Congress approved legislation that directed the Department of Education to issue a notice of inquiry concerning the appropriate definition of the term "serious emotional disturbance" (SED) under IDEA. (With IDEA's reauthorization in 1997 the word "serious" was dropped.) Congress further directed the agency, as part of its notice, to publish for public comment the new definition proposed by the National Mental Health and Special Education Coalition. Specifically, the public was asked to comment on both the proposed change in definition and on the term EBD as a replacement for SED.

On January 20, 1998, the CEC sent a letter to the Office of Special Education and Rehabilitation Services (OSERS), U.S. Department of Education, concerning the ED definition, unchanged when IDEA was reauthorized in 1997. The CEC expressed concern that (1) there had been no report to Congress regarding the response to the 1993 inquiry notice, with publication of changes made based upon public input, (2) there had been no published summary of the public comments, (3) the secretary of education had not announced the results, and (4) the proposed definition revision was even more relevant given the improvements of IDEA 1997.

The CEC added in the 1998 letter that the current federal ED definition is neither clear and up to date nor comprehensive in the determination of eligibility for services in this category. For this reason, the CEC noted, the Work Group on Definition of the National Mental Health and Special Education Coalition, composed of about 30 key professional mental health and education associations, developed a substitute, research-based definition for IDEA regulations. This definition, which was widely reviewed and validated, is currently found in the Head Start regulations and is used by other agencies serving this population. That recommended definition is as follows:

Emotional disturbance refers to a condition in which the behavioral or emotional responses of an individual in school are so different from his/her generally accepted, age-appropriate ethnic, or cultural norms that they adversely affect educational performance in such areas as self-care, social relationships, personal adjustment, academic progress, classroom behavior, or work adjustment.

Emotional disturbance is more than a transient, expected response to stressors in the child's or youth's environment, and would persist even with individualized interventions, such as feedback to the individual, consultation with parents or families, and/or modification of the educational environment.

The eligibility decision must be based on multiple sources of data concerning   the individual's behavioral or emotional functioning. Emotional disturbance must be exhibited in at least two different settings, at least one of which is school-related.

Emotional disturbance can co-exist with other handicapping conditions, as defined elsewhere in this law (i.e., IDEA).

This category may include children or youth with schizophrenia, affective disorders, anxiety disorders, or with other sustained disturbances of conduct, attention, or adjustment. (CEC personal communication 1998)

The federal definition, as it exists or as it is proposed, reveals little about individual students; particular emotions and behaviors are not described. Individual characteristics constitute another layer of defining information that cannot be known by reference to a broad definition. Inasmuch as the federal definition abstractly describes a great number of students, with many individual, unique cases under its umbrella wording, it offers no guidelines for designing programs or instructing and managing these students. The proposed definition, too, puts the onus on states and local school systems to compare individual cases to a set of general criteria to determine whether particular behaviorally or emotionally disordered students are unresponsive to direct interventions applied in general education, or whether general education interventions would be insufficient.

By its nature as an all-encompassing, national definition, the federal definition must be broad. Categorical labels, for example, may not lead directly to interventions, but they enable head counts, funding, and other pragmatic activities. For example, the federal definition plays an important part in the identification of children and adolescents with exceptionalities. As Kauffman (1983) noted, the definition that is embedded in the law and federal regulations is the single most important factor in determining which children receive special education services.

TEN PRACTICAL DEFINING CHARACTERISTICS

With the understanding that federal guidelines are broad, practical characteristics that arise from the local districts can be used to inform policy makers and stimulate a broader understanding. Ultimately, understanding emotional and behavioral disorders involves bridging the gap between local and national perspectives.

For this purpose, the author generated 10 key characteristics of secondary students who show emotional and behavioral disorders (see Table 23.1). These characteristics arose out of working in public school districts in Minnesota, New York City, Massachusetts, and Virginia. The characteristics were consistently exhibited by students who had been determined to have emotional and/or behavioral problems.

Table 23.1
**Key Characteristics of Students with Emotional and
Behavioral Disorders**

Characteristics

Low self-esteem
Narcissism
Misperception
Poor body awareness and hygiene
Untrustworthiness
Physical symptoms
Keen sensitivity to others
Depression
Mood swings
Lack of tolerance for untroubled kids

THE TEN CHARACTERISTICS: QUANTITATIVE ANALYSIS

Table 23.2 is a summary of the 13 primary sample cases in terms of practical characteristics shown by each student from the pool of 10 characteristics. These characteristics are coded, and the key is presented at the bottom of the table. Using that summary makes it possible to quantify for further analysis. We can count the characteristics shown by individual cases, or count the characteristics represented in the sample. By ranking the cases in terms of num-

Table   23.2
Quantitative Summary of Primary Sample Using Practical Characteristics

Cases	Practical Characteristics Evident
Adam	1, 2, 3, 5, 8, 9
Andy	1, 3, 7, 8
Billy	1, 4, 6, 8
Chris	1, 3, 8, 9
Fred	3, 4
James	1, 3, 4, 6, 8, 10
Jesse	1, 2, 3, 6, 8
Joel	1, 3, 7, 8
Laura	1, 2, 3, 5, 7, 9, 10
Michael	1, 4, 6, 8
Olivia	1, 3, 6, 8
Rick	1, 3, 4, 6, 9
Sara	1, 3, 6, 8

Key

1	Low self-esteem
2	Narcissism
3	Misperception
4	Poor body awareness/hygiene
5	Untrustworthiness
6	Physical symptoms
7	Keen sensitivity to others
8	Depression
9	Mood swings
10	Lack of tolerance for untroubled kids

bers of characteristics shown, we may also make more conclusions about the overall severity of the disturbance. A student who exhibits all 10 characteristics, for example, could be said to be more in discord than a student who shows only one characteristic. (See Table 23.3.)

At least five other conclusions may be drawn from Table 23.2, all of which raise worthy questions for further research. One conclusion is that all of the primary sample manifest at least two characteristics. In fact, 12 out of 13 cases meet four or more criteria for emotional or behavioral disorders by this operational standard. This perspective adds meaning to the federal definition's phrase "to a marked degree."

Second, it may be concluded that the seriousness of the emotional or behavioral disorder may be discerned by counting the characteristics exhibited by each case. By this approach, it appears that Laura, with seven characteristics evident, is in most discord. James and Adam might be ranked next with six characteristics, and Jesse and Rick follow closely with five characteristics each. Also, this sample suggests that emotional-behavioral impairment may be most pronounced in mixed symptom groups: students with both internalizing and externalizing problems. Indeed, when we examine our primary sample, Laura emerges as the most impaired, with a complexity of emotional and behavioral problems. In light of the federal guidelines, Laura shows pervasive disturbance to a marked degree.

A third conclusion is that the primary sample validates the practical characteristics. All 10 characteristics have been seen in this sample (see Table 23.3).

Table 23.3
Ranking of Characteristics Evident in the Primary Sample

Characteristics	Number of Cases
Low self-esteem	12
Misperception	11
Depression	10
Physical symptoms	7
Poor body awareness and hygiene	5
Mood swings	4
Narcissism	3
Keen sensitivity to others	3
Lack of tolerance for untroubled kids	2
Untrustworthiness	2

A fourth way of looking at the primary sample involves types of characteristics. (See, again, Table 23.3.) Three characteristics stand out: low self-esteem, misperception, and depression. Students in this sample, it may be concluded, show most difficulty in these three areas. On the other hand, students in this sample show least difficulty with tolerance for untroubled peers and with being trustworthy.

Finally, quantitative analysis of the primary sample shows cross-validation with the federal definition, notably, depression (evident in 10 of the 13 cases) and physical symptoms (evident in seven cases). This cross-validation may help us better understand the existing federal definition of emotional disturbance.

Should the proposed EBD definition become policy, all 10 of the present characteristics would validate it as they are "behavioral or emotional responses." Further research could help determine which, if any, particular emotional or behavioral responses might merit reference in a reconstituted federal definition. The present quantitative analysis indicates that four characteristics should receive serious consideration for inclusion in a federal definition: low self-esteem, misperception, depression, and physical symptoms.

THE TEN CHARACTERISTICS: QUALITATIVE ANALYSIS

Qualitative analysis involves linking case content with the 10 practical characteristics. Let us look at each of the 10 characteristics.

LOW SELF-ESTEEM

Low self-esteem is evident in all but one case in the primary sample, which is not surprising. Beck (1995) noted that self-concept is central to emotional disorder. Also, Kauffman (1985) noted that aversive social experiences may produce anxious children who have little self-confidence and evaluate themselves negatively. Certainly, students with emotional and behavioral disorders have more than their share of negative social experiences about which to feel anxious. Primary sample students repeatedly show difficulty with relationships.

Defined as diminished self-evaluation of social ability, of academic accomplishments or competence, or of any area of value, self-evaluation is the impression individuals have of their own abilities in a variety of activities and settings. Self-esteem, as such, is a psychological construct, a mental image that has been built by the individual to sum up self-perceived status.

As a psychological construct, self-esteem is best described as a schema because no coherent conceptualization is currently available (Fennell 1997). In other words, self-esteem is a generic cognitive representation of the self based on experience; it influences how incoming information is processed. Therefore, self-esteem is a product of learning and shapes perceptions. Because self-esteem, as a psychological construct, is not directly observable, understanding of it must be ascertained through inference, which is, in turn, gleaned from the individual's statements and actions. In effect, one's self-evaluation, subjectively determined, is evaluated by others through a perceptual prism.

More specifically, low self-esteem is associated with numerous parameters: It is global (the self-image is of the whole person, undifferentiated and inflexible; the individual cannot appreciate his own various qualities); it is negative and derogatory; it is often persistent and enduring; it underestimates strengths, assets, and qualities; it overestimates weaknesses, deficits, and flaws; and it ranges cognitively from abstract belief to minute-by-minute thoughts.

One way to evaluate low self-esteem is to look for its opposite condition: positive self-esteem. Positive, or high, self-esteem serves as a buffer against stress and typically is associated with a wide range of productive coping strategies (Rutter 1987). Additionally, high self-esteem is clearly linked to enhanced motivation and positive emotional states. Logically, if a student has a positive emotional state, motivation will be enhanced and productive coping strategies unlimited.

On the other hand, students who have low self-esteem typically interact less in groups, tend to be self-conscious and preoccupied with inner problems, avoid disagreements, are more constricted, and are less creative than students with higher levels of self-esteem. Low self-esteem may lead an individual to turn against himself or others (Feldman and Elliott 1990).

Adolescents who have emotional and behavioral problems appear to experience low self-esteem more often than peers who are emotionally healthy. One study of inpatients, ranging from 12 to 16 years of age, in a Boston teaching hospital found that the hospitalized group reported more negative self-perceptions in friendships, job, scholastic, and global domains than nonhospitalized peers. Furthermore, the inpatient adolescents showed more globally low self-esteem; their self-evaluations were less differentiated in terms of domains of concern, so they were more likely to perceive themselves in an all-or-nothing manner (Evans et al. 1994).

While self-esteem is complicated in terms of manifestation as a global phenomenon or as a manifestation of particular domains of competence, for present purposes the student's functional, behavioral signs of self-evaluation are the focus. Self-esteem may be manifest in many areas of functioning: scholastic competence, social acceptance, behavioral conduct, appearance, and parental perceptions and opinions. Let us look at specific functional signs of low self-esteem in our primary sample.

Twelve students in the primary sample show functional signs of low self-esteem. **Laura** is reticent about participating in classroom discussions. She wants to fade into the background. She does not cope well as a group member, whether in the classroom or in a social skills group. She is obsessed about her appearance and peer acceptance beyond what is considered normal for adolescents. Laura does not believe that she has the ability to succeed at academics.

Andy, too, is preoccupied with feelings about peer rejection. His social coping strategies are limited, as evidenced in frequent fights with peers over minor incidents. Andy compares himself with classmates who finish their work faster and with better quality, and his self-evaluation comes up short.

Billy wears his low self-esteem on his sleeve, which typically is disheveled, dirty, and tattered. He believes he is dumb because he has difficulty learning, and he has accepted his father's opinion that he is incompetent because he earns low grades. Billy has invested adults, particularly his father, with overwhelming power over his self-concept; consequently, Billy does not feel that he has the right to evaluate himself by his own criteria. Billy has said repeatedly that if he left home his family would be better off.

Chris's self-esteem is so low that he does not question the validity of his mother's statement that water is not for drinking because it does not contain vitamins. While this notion seems peculiar to him, Chris does not believe he has the right to question her authority. His delinquency illustrates the connection between low self-esteem and the process of turning against others as an outgrowth of turning against one's self.

Sara, also, shows low self-esteem. She believes that she is ugly, fat, and different, and she thinks that she is a problem for her family. Sara's self-esteem is so low that, unlike most adolescents, who aim for a rough imitation of models, her physical self-image has to exactly match some external ideal. She stopped eating so that she could attain that ideal. Her low self-esteem translates into a process of turning against herself to the point of emaciation.

James's negative self-esteem is evident in chronic pessimism. Also, his disheveled, unkempt appearance attests to low self-esteem. He lacks the motivation to care about his appearance.

Jesse feels altogether inadequate. He lacks confidence, blames himself for many problems, shows low initiative, and, generally, is passive and nonassertive. He is not accepted well by peers, who regard him as an oddity as he moves sluggishly with head down and eyes averted.

Low self-esteem is also seen in **Adam's** case. His teachers report that he shows poor self-confidence and insecurity. Adam cannot accept criticism and lashes out when feedback does not match his ideal self-image. Angry at himself for failure, he lashes out at others.

In **Rick's** case, lack of self-confidence is evident in peer interactions. He has been teased, like many children, but Rick believes that he deserves such treatment. He responds to teasing by externalizing and by internalizing. When the stress builds up, he internalizes by developing psoriasis in the form of big, ugly sores all over his face and body, and he externalizes by using physical aggression. For example, he tried to strangle one boy who teased him. Rick cannot tell the difference between playful bantering and teasing. Because he has been unable to cope socially he has lost motivation for anything related to school.

Joel shows dimished self-esteem. He is dissatisfied with himself, especially his height. He has dreams of becoming a professional basketball player, but he is short. Joel is not accepted by many peers because his restlessness and hyperactivity frequently bother them. His choice of friends, the students who do not do well academically and who cause trouble, matches Joel's self-image.

Olivia feels insecure, anxious, and hopeless. Her low self-esteem is apparent in her inconsistent effort. She caves in when criticized and does not make an effort until sufficient positive feedback shores her up to risk again. Low self-esteem also is evident in her inability to assert herself appropriately. Thus, both her motivation and coping resources are limited.

Finally, **Michael's** low self-esteem is evident in his belief that he does not deserve satisfying interpersonal relationships. Michael has said that he is the kind of kid no one wants. He has lost the motivation to try to change, has avoided "shrinks" like the plague, and dwells on fantasies of power mixed with death and dying.

MISPERCEPTION

Mental structures evolve progressively. For example, prejudice rarely appears until adolescence, and depression is rarely seen in pre-adolescence (Elkind 1970). An adolescent's thinking, further, is characterized by three emergent abilities. First, the adolescent can reason by combining factors; he can problem solve and juggle alternative solutions. Parents may bemoan their adolescent's ability to perceive alternatives to their directives and their adolescent's resistance to accepting suggested options without question, but the youngster is developmentally primed to do this.

Second, an adolescent can use a second symbol system. For example, the solution of algebraic problems is now possible. Words, too, may have double meanings, and the adolescent can generate concepts and use introspection to reflect on their own traits. Now that they can see themselves from the outside, they become concerned about how others view them.

Third, adolescents show ability to construct ideals. They can deal with the possible, and the future becomes a reality with which to deal. Along with introspection, the adolescent can think about the discrepancy between real self and ideal self.

Cognitive processes, then, appear to gain importance during adolescence, entering into the individual's interpretations of environmental events, plans, selection of goals, and self-evaluations. In this view it is not so much the actual events and physical stimuli as the individual's interpretation of them that influences actions (Gelfand and Hartmann 1980).

Altogether, an adolescent's thinking is no longer worn on his or her sleeve. Reasoning, concept generation and introspection, and idealization are accomplished largely in secret. There is a lot of mental activity during this stage.

Parents often complain that their adolescent son or daughter is long on argument and short on action. Indeed, this is typical at this stage. Adolescents often say one thing and think another. There is a great deal of intellectual activity, which often manifests itself as criticism of others, particularly adults. Adolescents, in effect, have begun the work of constructing a value system and goals. They just have not begun to understand the work needed to achieve the goals.

Given that a normally developing adolescent is able to reason, generate concepts and introspect, and construct ideals, what can be said about the abnormally developing adolescent, particularly the adolescent with an emotional or behavioral disorder? This youngster shows an inability to reason by using interrelated factors, an inability to introspect and generate concepts, and an inability to construct situations that are possible and not necessarily related to present facts. As cognition and emotion are interrelated, the adolescent with emotional or behavioral problems probably has cognitive problems. Disordered emotions lead to disordered thinking and, ultimately, to disordered behaviors.

Kendall (1993) further explains cognitive difficulties that students with emotional and behavioral disorders tend to have. This explanation involves *cogni-*

tive distortion and *cognitive deficiency.* An adolescent who is fully aware of what is going on around him but still misinterprets it, usually in a harmful manner, shows cognitive distortion. On the other hand, an adolescent who is apparently unaware of actual events shows a cognitive deficiency.

For example, aggressive adolescents show both cognitive deficiency and distortion. They do not use appropriate environmental cues to program their behavior, and they focus on malevolent cues. Furthermore, aggressive youngsters often anticipate that they will have fewer feelings of fear or anxiety than they actually experience. When feelings of fear or anxiety arise, they become angry, as if betrayed by internal and external factors. Such students need to be taught to recognize environmental cues and to control their behavior by altering their distorted thought patterns (Kendall 1993).

Beck (1976) offers a perspective on cognitive errors and the assumptions from which they are derived, blending cognitive distortion and deficiency. The youngster who overgeneralizes believes that if something is true in one case it applies to any case that is even slightly similar. Another example is selective abstraction, the belief that one should be measured exclusively by one set of traits, positive or negative. Finally, a youngster with a thought disorder, by Beck's model, predicts without sufficient evidence, believing that if something was true in the past it will always be true. Beck's model, thus, accounts for emotional disorders in terms of both cognitive deficiencies and distortions.

Such models have stimulated intervention design. Cognitive-behavioral treatment (CBT), for example, has been applied to various disorders: anxiety, depression, ADHD, and learning disabilities, among others. Cognitive structuring is used to modify distorted thinking, assumptions, and perceptions (Kendall and Panichelli 1995), providing the opportunity to broaden perspectives and to modify detrimental cognitive, behavioral, and affective styles.

Let us reexamine some of the specific emotional and behavioral disorders presented earlier in terms of misperception. Among the present cases are numerous examples of thought disorder, which exemplify this important, growing area of concern and study.

ADHD. This disorder has been the target of CBT efforts. Impulsivity, specifically, has been treated successfully with this approach. This is an important intervention because medication does not always address deficits in cognitive processing, and many of the problems shown by these youngsters arelinked to cognitive dysfunction (Kendall and Panichelli 1995).

Anorexia nervosa. Anorexics typically show cognitive distortion, misperceiving bodily appearance and quantities of food. An anorexic girl may overestimate the size of her thighs, stomach, and other body parts, perceiving herself to be bigger than she really is. Commonly, anorexics misperceive amounts of food, believing that their parents are giving them excessive amounts in order to make them fat.

Bipolar disorder. Holmes (1994) noted that cognitive distortion is associated with manic episodes, specifically inflated self-esteem and grandiosity.

Distractibility and fragmented attention have also been observed; bipolar individuals continually shift attention and get distracted. In some cases, the flight of ideas is so rapid and the shifts between topics so fast that it is difficult to follow the manic person's train of thought (Holmes 1994).

Borderline personality disorder. Cognitive distortion has been found to be a key characteristic of individuals with borderline personality disorder. The "splitting" that is often cited in these cases may be a failure to integrate thoughts. For example, rather than perceive the mother as a loving person who sometimes hugs and sometimes disciplines, the borderline individual shifts back and forth between these contradictory images (Sarason and Sarason 1993), concentrating on one to the exclusion of the other, splitting the whole picture into separate pieces, each prevailing at a time.

Antisocial personality tendency. In reference to cognitive activity and antisocial personality disorder (APD), Chapter 5, research shows that APDs manifest the somatic forms of anxiety but not the cognitive. Thus, APDs may not show remorse, worry, or guilt about their misdeeds, but they may exhibit such bodily signs as tense muscles and rapid heart rate.

Depression. Depressed adolescents also often show cognitive distortion. Their self-evaluations and perceptions of past and present events frequently involve twisted facts. Also, they show external "locus of control" (i.e., they attribute their achievements, for better or for worse, to outside factors); they believe that they cannot obtain what they want through their own efforts (Kendall 1993). There have been encouraging results with the use of CBT to treat depression (Kendall and Panichelli 1995).

Currently, the most influential psychological theories of depression are derived from the cognitive perspective (Sarason and Sarason 1993). The core idea of these theories is that the same experiences affect people differently because each person thinks about events differently. One student who does not receive an expected high mark might think: "I am a worthless person. The teacher does not like me. If he did, I would have gotten a better grade." Another student in the same situation might think: "I know I could have done a better job. I am capable of a higher grade. Next time I will try harder." Beck's (1976) cognitive-distortion model of depression, the most original and influential of the cognitive approaches to this disorder, posits that depression is primarily disordered thinking rather than mood and that the depressed person blames any misfortune on his or her personal defects.

Anxiety disorders. Emmelkamp and Scholing (1994) have suggested that recent developments have stressed cognitive representations and cognitive schemata as important determinants of anxiety disorders. In addition, Holmes (1994) identified four specific cognitive components of anxiety disorders. (1) There appears to be *selective attention*, where the individual focuses excessive attention on threats. (2) *Selective recall* relates to retrieval of information. As anxious people tend to store more threat content, they have more such memories on which to draw. Furthermore, because they are more anxious, they are more likely to have an active associative network involving threats, so threat-related memories are more likely to be activated. (3) Among anxious individuals there is a great deal of *misinterpretation* because they are more likely than nonanxious individuals to misinterpret neutral or ambiguous situations as threatening. Such misinterpretation may contribute to anxiety. (4) Finally, Holmes identified *erroneous expectations* among anxious persons. This means that they incorrectly expect situations to be threatening.

Freeman and DiTomasso used anecdotal information to illustrate anxiety qua cognitive distortion and misinterpretation:

P. exhibited a variety of cognitive distortions, most especially catastrophizing. She tended to misinterpret her symptoms as cause for threat to her mental status. She also exhibited a variety of other distortions such as selective abstraction and jumping to conclusions. These distortions typically escalated her anxiety symptoms to panic proportions and also fueled her dysthymias [depressive episodes]. (1994, p. 84)

Further examples concern the underlying schemas that fuel anxious thoughts, feelings, and behaviors. Vulnerability is illustrated by statements such as, "Something terrible will happen to me at any moment, and I will lose control and go crazy." Dependence is illustrated by statements such as, "I am unable to cope on my own."

Studies have consistently shown that anxious adults disproportionately attend to emotionally threatening stimuli. The same is true of children with anxiety. One study found that in a sample (ages nine to 14) with primary diagnoses of anxiety disorder, there was an attentional bias toward threat words compared with carefully matched normal controls (Vasey et al. 1995). The researchers concluded that attentional processes may play an important part in the etiology and maintenance of childhood anxiety.

Overall, then, selective attention and selective recall can distort a person's view and lead to anxiety, and attention and memories can also distract one from tasks at hand. Distraction appears to be responsible for the poor cognitive performance often associated with anxiety (Holmes 1994). Anxious persons differ from normals in their processing of threat-related stimuli, showing a "mood congruent" attentional bias; anxiety is as anxiety perceives.

As with other disorders, there have been encouraging results with anxiety treated by CBT (Kendall and Panichelli 1995). This method of treatment shows promise in modifying the attentional bias that leads to misperception. For example, phobias have been studied in terms of cognition. There is evidence that many who develop agoraphobia, for example, expect to have a panic attack outside the home so they stay home to avoid the expected attack. One CBT method involves helping the individual to use fear-reduction self-statements that reflect coping and competency. This technique has been found to be effective in reducing anxiety and avoidance in phobic youngsters (Hussain and Kashani 1992).

Post-traumatic stress disorder. There is growing empirical support for the importance of cognitive appraisal in trauma. Attribution has been assigned a role in post-traumatic stress disorder (PTSD), specifically a psychological process of thinking about or perceiving causation. People have varying levels of attribution following disasters. At one end of the range, victims minimize or nullify human intervention. A victim who attributes the disaster to cosmic forces says, essentially, "Nature did it." At the other end of the attribution range are traumas stemming from perceived human malevolence. Following the April 1995 Oklahoma City bombing many victims were ready and willing to attribute this horrendous act to foreign terrorists. Other extreme attributions might refer to police brutality, rape, or torture.

The most important finding that has emerged from attribution theory relates to the actual human part in the trauma. It seems likely that the greater the role of human agency the greater will be the aftermath of anxiety (West and Coburn 1984). By this theory, we should expect the least misperception among those who have experienced a natural disaster and the most misperception among those who have experienced a disaster caused by other people.

PTSD also has been studied in terms of threat-related words. In one study (Cassiday, McNally, and Zeitlin 1992), PTSD rape victims and nonanxious women were shown threat-related words, including "penis" and "victim," as well as neutral words, such as "polite" and "typical," printed in different colors. When asked to name the colors in which the words were printed, rape victims took longer to respond to threat-related words, suggesting that they were attending to meanings rather than to colors. In addition, the rape victims took longer to respond to all words, suggesting that they suffered from general anxiety that interfered with cognitive processing.

One explanation of what is happening with rape victims, in particular, comes from Parson (1994), who noted that rape is probably the crime with the most damaging impact on the self-organization of the victim, that this impact is due not only to deprivation of control, manipulation, and injury to self but to violation of the inner space, the most sacred and private repository of the self. In this view, the victim's core, the inner sanctum of thoughts that glue the self together, is violated. Peterson, Prout, and Schwarz (1991) add that traumatic events are potent disrupters of basic assumptions about the self and the world, the basic assumptions being (1) belief in personal invulnerabilty, (2) perception of the world as meaningful and comprehensible, and (3) view of the self in a positive light (Janoff-Bulman 1986).

This may help explain the subsequent development of intense secrecy and privacy typically seen among those with PTSD, as well as the eating disorders that often accompany PTSD. There is an intense effort to control something, even if it is only one's eating habits. The development of PTSD and related disorders may represent the victim's effort to rebuild shattered basic assumptions. PTSD sufferers can be expected to benefit from CBT.

Disruptive behavior disorders. Aggression, often a component of disruptive behavior disorders, also has been the target of CBT efforts, and the results have been encouraging (Kendall and Panichelli 1995). Success likely relates to aggression's association with cognitive distortion. "One of the most common phenomena associated with aggressive attacks by behaviorally disturbed adolescents is the misperception that they have been insulted behind their backs, or that they have been looked at in a threatening way" (Lewis 1991, p. 299). Support for this perspective is the finding that highly aggressive delinquents are less able to perceive the viewpoints of other people than are their low-aggressive counterparts (Short and Simeonsson 1986).

The thinking of aggressives is fraught with poor judgment, faulty logic, and contradictory ideas. A student who uses poor judgment cannot assess situations in order to make appropriate responses; he either underestimates or overestimates their importance. A student who uses faulty logic reacts oddly to situations; reactions are nonsensical, curious, and puzzling. And a student whose ideas are contradictory shows an inability to monitor his own thinking so that it will be coherent. His verbalizations may contain facts that do not mesh. "How could Johnny have hit you when he was not even in the room at the time?" one teacher asked a student. In this student's thinking, even obvious facts are confused. If this youngster cannot deal with factual situations, he cannot begin to deal with contrary-to-fact situations and problem solving that involves alternative solutions.

Hendren (1991) adds that aggressive children have distinctive cognitive profiles characterized by immature logic. For example, highly aggressive boys were found to define social problems based on their perception that others were hostile adversaries. They found fewer effective solutions to problems and they foresaw fewer consequences for showing aggression than did low-aggression boys.

Misperception, which showed up in 11 cases in the primary sample, could be referred to as disordered thinking. Misperception often is referred to as "screwy thinking." One teacher commented, "They just don't think like the rest of us."

Misperception involves perceiving events differently than most people. A student may perceive that another student provoked him when the other student's intentions, in reality, were harmless. Unable to combine factors and see alternative explanations, a student may bend the truth or fail to perceive the truth.

Misperception could also be thought of as *social misperception*, an inability to read social cues. A student who misperceives nonverbal cues such as facial expressions or body gestures cannot interact appropriately because he or she has not received information that makes sense or that is socially functional. Misperception of social cues frequently is seen in students with learning disabilities. It is as if they cannot deal with a second symbol system: nonverbal symbols. (See Chapter 20 for a more detailed discussion of nonverbal communication problems.)

Misperception may be caused by overwhelming emotional concerns that impair efficient use of intellectual resources. It might also be viewed as an outcome of negative thinking. Whether misperception is an emotional distortion, a misreading of the social landscape, or negative thinking, it is integral with emotional and behavioral disorders.

Hassibi and Breuer (1980) concluded that indications of disorder and disorganization of children's thoughts are manifest in several ways, including verbal communication. This is the type of thought disorganization that arises after language has developed or in those children whose thought disorder has not been severe enough to interfere with language acquisition. This type of thought disorder is reflected in peculiarities of higher-level concepts and the content of verbal messages. Conceptual deviancy is most readily detectable in the individual's report of his own experiences, in his understanding of social reality, and in the dynamics of his interpersonal relationships. Both concepts of self as an object to others (the social self) and as a subject (the psychological self) are unstable and without clear boundaries. According to this view, there is no clear and consistent picture of the self or others that can be abstracted because emotions are undifferentiated and unregulated. Therefore, generalizations based on experience do not provide a cohesive and stable picture of reality. For these youngsters, a nonsignificant part of an object, situation, or event acquires vital importance because it has been observed simultaneously with the experience of an emotional state. So, the child makes unwarranted associations between the subjective and objective. Thinking, in other words, is extremely idiosyncratic.

While extremes of this type of thought disorder suggest a psychosis, there may be mild to moderate forms. The thought disorders seen in the present cases may not indicate psychosis, but they do indicate disabled thinking that interferes with the student's normal social and academic functioning.

Following Hassibi and Breuer (1980), we can summarize this disordered thinking as follows.

1. Thoughts are driven by affect. Consequently, the youngster develops an incomplete image of reality, which is of no help in building a solid self-concept, and the absence of an integrative core hinders further organization of affect, percepts, and concepts.

2. Interpretation of others' behavior and decoding of communication is disordered. The youngster attends to insignificant features (say, the tone of voice rather than the message) and cannot engage in communication that makes sense to others; the youngster misreads the intention, misses the point. Shared premises that allow for social discourse are lacking.

2. Ideas are based on underdeveloped or distorted social interactions and communication learning is hindered by deficiencies of interest, concentration, and objective evaluation.

4.   The youngster's tendency to withdraw is reinforced by
        the hesitation of others to interact with him. Interactional
        deprivation further impedes the construction of a sense
        of social reality and allows distorted concepts to go
        unchallenged.

5.   These youngsters cannot report on their own inner
        state, past or present.

6.   The youngster cannot detach sufficiently to be able to
        project into the future or to stand apart from others long
        enough to form an opinion about relationships with
        others. (See Chapter 24 discussion of detachment
        difficulty.)

Above all, the student with disordered thinking is guided by his own perceptions and conclusions rather than by shared standards. Thus, rather than individual thinking varying around a normal human theme, there is idiosyncratic thinking that varies from a normal human theme. That idiosyncratic thinking dictates the student's actions and reactions; maladaptive thinking leads to maladaptive behavior.

Within the primary sample, James, Jesse, Fred, Adam, Olivia, Laura, Chris, Joel, Rick, Sara, and Andy all show signs of misperception, or thought disorder. First, **Rick's** thinking is distorted by emotions. He perceives the playful teasing of peers as malevolent. Instead of teasing back or bantering with them, he becomes very angry. Also, Rick believes that his father's attempts to be a firm disciplinarian mean that his father hates him. Rick typically screams, slams doors, and stalks off into the night for long walks when his parents try to apply logical consequences to his behavior. Rick's thought pattern also is characterized by blaming others and misinterpreting what others say. Thus, when Rick's parents and resource teacher counseled him to make a good effort in his classes (i.e., show a work ethic), he immediately went to his English teacher to ask for makeup work, saying that he needed to get his grades up by the following week or he would be sent to another school. By filtering it through emotionally clouded thinking, Rick had twisted the original message.

Rick's thinking, too, is inflexible. He cannot see another's point of view. Students who show rigid mental patterns have difficulty dealing with contradictions to their own convictions about reality (Rhodes 1990). Rick becomes angry when someone disagrees with him or perceives an event differently. He shows faulty judgment and disorganized thinking under stress, wallowing in negativity, and his thinking is inconsisent and illogical. In short, reasoning with Rick is difficult.

Laura frequently is inconsistent in her thinking. For example, although she was able to perceive that stealing opposes an ethical code, she thought that by stealing less than her friend she was relatively guiltless; her thinking was twisted to justify her behavior. (Rob, in the secondary sample, cheated on a test and argued that because he gave, rather than received information, he was blameless. In his explanation, Rob neglected to account for the fact that he entered the test situation with information written on his arm.) There are significant deficits in perceptual accuracy that affect Laura's social perception. During psychological evaluation she was found to be deficient in her ability to perceive events as most people would. Also, Laura, like Rick, blames others for her own misbehavior. Somebody else "made me do it" is her refrain. Laura's thought disorder has created, in effect, an idiosyncratic moral code.

Sara's perception of her own body is out of synchrony with mirrors and with others' perceptions. She is a beautiful girl, by conventional standards, with a well-developed, athletic body; nevertheless, Sara perceives herself as fat and ugly. This misperception is closely linked with her poor self-esteem; how Sara feels about herself relates to how she perceives herself. Sara also misreads social cues, specifically others' intentions and behaviors. For example, when a teacher tried to be firm and realistic, Sara felt she was being attacked.

Joel denies the extent of his difficulties. He denies behaviors that are witnessed by classrooms full of students as well as by teachers. Joel's need to be like his peers leads him to draw a mental curtain over his behaviors that do not fit the norm. His teachers often have scratched their heads in disbelief. How could a student who so flagrantly misbehaves perceive that it does not happen? The answer is that this student so desperately needs to conform that he perceives his own behaviors in accordance with his emotions. Joel, clearly, shows a thought pattern in which pictures are incomplete and information deficient.

Andy tends to be very literal in his thinking, hence he misses nuances of communication. He has particular difficulty interacting with girls. While it is typical and normal for young adolescent boys and girls to pretend they do not like one another, to the point of teasing and exchanging verbal insults, Andy hangs onto and believes every word. He cannot integrate verbal information that says "I hate you" with nonverbal information such as smiling, physical proximity, laughter, and twinkling eyes. Consequently, Andy remains socially isolated. Interestingly, while often excluded by peers, Andy believes that he has friends. He not only misreads social cues but draws faulty conclusions; not only does he misperceive, but his own thoughts are contradictory.

Misperception also takes the form of obsessive thinking. **Jesse** and **Fred** exemplify this type of thought disorder. Both boys worry obsessively about world events to the exclusion of their immediate worlds. Their fears prevent them from rising above their own small worlds. For example, if Fred reads a newspaper article about an earthquake in Italy he will obsess about it for days, believing that it will affect him directly. Jesse, too, feels that every major world event demands his attention and involves him. For example, during the 1992 presidential election, Jesse spoke about Bill Clinton as if he knew him personally and knew what he was thinking on all issues.

James also shows thought problems. His emotions appear to affect his ability to interpret events and situations realistically. His thinking is narrow, and he cannot accept responsibility for his own behavior. Like other students with confused, distorted thinking, James blames others for his difficulties. So does **Adam**, who does not recognize his own part in conflict and blames others for his own behavior.

Olivia shows misperception of interpersonal relationships. She perceives threat in even the most benign relationships.

Chris has a tendency to distort events and situations, making it likely that he will act against the social code and experience interpersonal conflict. For example, Chris was apprehended for vandalism, but he did not understand that breaking into his neighbor's mailbox was a problem because there was no mail in the box at the time.

Within the secondary sample Justin, Brett, Andrew, and Alan also show thought disorders. Justin, who has a learning disability and attention deficit disorder, shows contradictory thinking. For example, he complained to one teacher that he did not have time to do her assignment because he had a test to make up for another class. Yet after the teacher had negotiated a way for him to accomplish both tasks, Justin spent a large chunk of time looking through the record of points earned in the course. His behavior contradicted his assertion that he needed more time to work.

Alan shows a lot of perceptual inaccuracy and mediational distortion. His emotions frequently distort his thinking, particularly his anger and negativistic orientation to the environment. His concepts of others seem to be based on imaginary features; his ideas are discontinuous; and thinking is often faulty. Serious errors in judgment have been made; for example, while leaving school grounds in his car without permission, Alan nearly ran into a staff member. Subsequently, Alan blamed the adult for getting in the way of his car, saying she must have had suicidal tendencies. He focused, too, on the principal, who removed Alan's permit to park on school grounds. Alan could not understand that his behavior, if it improved, would help him earn back his parking privilege. A quarter of the school year went by and Alan showed no improvement in self-control. He became so agitated and angry that he decided it was time to write the principal a list of 17 "grumbles," or reasons why he should no longer have to take the bus to school. One reason was that he should be able to drive his car to school "because I can't take a dump after seventh period and still make the bus," another "because I have to smell other students who pass gas." Alan could not see that such statements would hurt, rather than help, his cause. Alan is unable to see his areas of responsibility, to understand that the time he spends complaining about unfairness could be used to accomplish work and show self-control, and to fathom that nonstop obsessions, expressed fluidly and without coherence, and based on idiosyncratic, narcissistic interpretations, say more about his state of mind than about situations.

Andrew consistently blames others for his problems. He denies sexually abusing a seven-year-old cousin when he was 12. While he acknowledged that the abuse occurred, he becomes angry thinking about it and holds others who speak of the incident accountable for his feelings. Andrew's reaction to teachers who try to help him is hostile. He has told them to "shut up" and "get your butt out of my face." When Andrew was confronted by his parents for stealing, he denied responsibility and blamed them for not listening to him or caring. Andrew's thinking is befuddled and illogical.

Brett's thinking is askew, too. Recently transferred from a school in another state, he wants to fit in with peers but is too stuck in his thinking to act on this desire. He is full of excuses about why he cannot go to a teen center or a school dance, or initiate conversations with other students. Brett has developed an obsession about his appearance, which he tries to improve, albeit oddly. His reasoning is that other students will accept him if he dresses like them. He claims that students at his new school dress differently than those at his previous school, and he has become consumed by figuring out how to blend in through clothing. Objectively, the students in this school range from bum-like and punk styles to preppy styles, so Brett has set an unrealistic goal, particularly as he is a loner who has no association with any subgroup. His mother bought him shoes that Brett asserted are right, but Brett thought that the shoes should not look new. He filled the bath tub with dirt in order to break in the shoes without having to leave the house.

DEPRESSION

The mood disorder depression is seen in most of the students in the primary sample: **James**, **Andy**, **Jesse**, **Chris**, **Adam**, **Olivia**, **Joel**, **Sara**, **Michael**, and **Billy**. It is an important feature of emotional disturbance. (See Chapter 13.)

POOR BODY AWARENESS AND HYGIENE

For adolescents, the most important factor in self-esteem is physical appearance. Because of their desire to conform and their search for guidelines about how to behave, young adolescents may be especially susceptible to popular mass media stereotypes, particularly those images and values presented by the entertainment and fashion industries as vital elements of the "youth culture." It is abnormal for an adolescent to be oblivious to body image and hygiene.

Poor body awareness and hygiene are evident in the cases of Billy, James, Rick, Fred, and Michael. **Rick** is sloppy, has body odor, and is lax about brushing his teeth. Food accumulates around his braces. **James** is teased by peers because he smells. He has a history of soiling accidents. He wears the same clothes for days. **Michael** is overweight and unkempt. His hair looks like he combs it with a fan, his clothing is soiled, and his shoe laces often are untied. **Fred** smells. At times, as well, his hair spikes out in spots, and often his shoes are unlaced. **Billy** smells, too, and his hair looks unwashed. His jeans and shoes have gaping holes, and it appears that he sleeps in his clothes.

UNTRUSTWORTHINESS

In developmental theory (notably Erikson 1963), the first stage, and the foundation for all others, is learning to trust. Trust is an automatic response learned from repeated pairings of comfort and relief ministrations by friendly and loving caregivers when the infant is in distress. From such caring, responsive, and supportive treatment arises a general propensity to regard the world as safe and people as generally good.

Youngsters who cannot trust cannot themselves be trusted. A student who feels safe and good about the world tends to treat others in a trusting manner and, in turn, to behave in a trustworthy way. Feeling that he is trusted and supported, the student will expect continued trust and will fulfill the expectancy of trust by being worthy of it. On the other hand, students who are deceitful and dishonest are not trustworthy.

Trustworthiness is not characteristic of Laura and Adam. **Laura**, for example, cannot be trusted to bring home her grade reports. If she does not like the grades, she throws the reports away. Also, she cannot be trusted to take her medication at school. Once she forged a bus pass in order to visit with a friend after school.

Adam cannot be trusted to tell the truth about his school assignments. Often, he tells his mother that he has no homework so he can go outside to play. If a teacher asks him for his homework, Adam cannot be trusted to tell the truth about why he has not done it. He has created many interesting excuses for incomplete work.

PHYSICAL SYMPTOMS

Physical symptoms are integral with the existing federal definition of emotional disturbance. Anxiety may be associated with body aches; depression may translate into listlessness and fatigue; and other negative emotional states may be associated with somatic complaints. The understanding is that emotional distress creates somatic distress, and psychological wellness contributes to physical wellness.

Physical symptoms are shown by Rick, James, Jesse, Michael, Olivia, Billy, and Sara. These may range from covert signs such as fatigue and constipation to overt signs such as fecal soiling and skin sores.

Olivia is often sluggish because of poor sleeping patterns. Also, she has asthma and experiences stomachaches and headaches at school. **Michael** has asthma along with involuntary body movements (tics). Also, he experiences fatigue, headaches, falling, blurred vision, convulsions, and a persistent cough. **Billy** has asthma and often experiences headaches and fatigue. **Rick** develops psoriasis when under stress. His skin can be read like a stress gauge; the more sores that cover his body, the greater his internalized stress. **Sara's** primary physical symptom is weight loss, brought on by an eating disorder. In addition, she has spent a great deal of time in the school clinic because of headaches and stomachaches. **Jesse** is chronically tired. He says that this is due to morning medication, but the effect does not seem to wear off as the school day progresses. **James** has a history of soiling and constipation.

KEEN SENSITIVITY TO OTHERS

Some students with emotional and behavioral disorders have finely tuned emotional antennae. Their experiences may have taught them mistrust and fear, causing them to be vigilant. These students may test adults to determine whether or not trust is deserved. They seem keenly aware of adult hypocrisy and dishonesty, and they demand nothing less than complete fairness and honesty. Some students may be especially sensitive to adults because they are dependent on them, particularly if they are socially isolated from peers.

Andy, Joel, and Laura stand out as being keenly sensitive to others. **Andy** seems mature beyond his years because of his sensitivity. He has marginal peer relationships but is loved by all adults who know him because he shows interest in and sensitivity toward their needs and problems. Adults often feel that they can tell Andy their problems and that he will listen with concern. He always asks how his teachers feel, and he checks constantly to ensure that adults like him.

Joel is finely attuned to adult moods. He drives his mathematics teacher to distraction by uncannily tuning in to her bad days. On those days Joel invariably asks, "Why don't you like me?" She believes that he tunes in to her off days just to irritate her.

Laura hones in on others who have problems. However, given Laura's narcissistic tendencies, her form of sensitivity is self-serving. Rather than reaching out to others out of empathy, Laura uses them.

NARCISSISM

See Chapter 6 where the narcissism of **Jesse**, **Laura**, and **Adam** is discussed.

MOOD SWINGS

See Chapter 14 on bipolar disorder, which features **Rick** and **Laura**. Other primary sample cases show mood swings without having met diagnostic criteria for manic-depression. Mood swings that last and that interfere with a student's learning and relationships are serious.

Chris has mood swings that seem to coincide with custodial visits. While living with his mother, the custodial parent, he experiences bad moods, "real funks." When he visits his father, he feels free, rides his dirt bike, and does his homework. With his mother, on the other hand, Chris takes risks to try to escape the down feelings. When with his mother, Chris also keeps as busy as possible (fixing the car, mowing the lawn, and fixing anything electrical in the house), but he never relaxes and feels good. He cannot sit still at his mother's house; he is too busy finding ways to elevate his mood, even if the activities are illegal.

Adam, too, has interfering mood swings. Some weeks he seems to be on top of the world, other weeks he seems persistently sad. His moods seem to be affected by the quality of visits with his father. Adam desperately wants his mother and father to reunite, but each visit with his father reminds him that this dream is unattainable. His hopes start climbing as visits with his father near, and his mood plummets as he crashes to reality when he returns to his mother. Adam's teachers experience a happy, cooperative, conscientious student prior to visits with the father, and a hyperactive, sad, belligerent student after the visits.

LACK OF TOLERANCE FOR UNTROUBLED KIDS

Adolescents are engaged in an intensive identity search, and they care a lot about and are sensitive to what is normal. When adolescents have difficulty fitting into conventional roles, they may become intolerant of normal peers out of defensiveness. In effect, the troubled adolescent may opt for an identity that is unconventional, sometimes flagrantly so, to compensate for perceived identity failure.

Often, adolescents with disabilities lack compassion for their own and others' weaknesses (Elkind 1970). Not only do these youngsters deny the extent of their own problems, but they do not identify with other youngsters who are in synchrony with their environments. For example, **Sarah** felt isolated at her high school. She hated most of the other students, claiming that they did not understand her and that they were rich and cared only about clothes and cars. When she was placed in a public day school for ED students, Sarah blossomed. She called this school "cool."

One example of the adoption of an unconventional identity, with an implicit rejection of untroubled, conventional peers, is interest in witchcraft and Satanism. While the public perception seems to be that such interest and involvement is rare, in fact it is not as rare as anorexia nervosa or Tourette's syndrome (Burket et al. 1994). Bourget, Gagnon, and Bradford (1988) concluded that about 5 percent of the adolescents in a diverse population had such interest and involvement. Another study found, among a hospitalized group of adolescents, a significant identity disorder that rendered them vulnerable to the occult (Burket et al. 1994). These youths appeared to be vulnerable to the group identity, structure, and "specialness" of witchcraft or Satanism. Many of these youths may have gravitated to such unconventional involvement in search of acceptance. As the subjects of this study also identified with other fringe groups, including neo-Nazis, skinheads, and anarchists, the authors concluded that the predominant psychological issue was identity.

Along with intolerance, denial runs deep in troubled students who want to believe that they are normal. They seek company that affirms denial of their own abnormalcy. Like a form of codependency, troubled adolescents cluster together for solidarity. In the process, they may pick on more normal students in order to feel good about themselves.

James taunted a quiet student who got along well with the other students in a science class. James hid his notebook if he got up from his desk, wrote obscene notes on his papers, and generally made life miserable for him. Ironically, the student who was the brunt of the taunting was a part-time mainstreamer from a public day school for ED students, who was trying hard to fit in. He was so well behaved that he was a social isolate.

Laura mocks students she believes are "uncool." She associates with special education students and students who are in trouble with the law. Her best friend, who is failing school and is pregnant, is Laura's shoplifting buddy. Laura criticizes nonhandicapped and compliant students as "geeks," "preppies," and "goody-goodies."

SUMMARY

A comparison of the 10 practical characteristics of adolescents who have emotional and behavioral disorders with the federally defined ED criteria suggests several key conclusions. First, the practical characteristics evident in these cases validate the federal definition.

Second, the federal definition implies that ED is a serious impairment, but it is not until we look at practical characteristics, as presented in this book, that the word "serious" becomes meaningful. As we have seen in the primary sample cases, these students' difficulties are complex; all cases involve multiple characteristics along with chronicity. In fact, 12 out of 13 cases show four or more characteristics. This very complexity suggests seriousness.

Complexity also equates with interrelation of disabilities. Rick, Jesse, Billy, and Andy were eligible for special education services for both emotional and learning disabilities. Joel had been eligible for LD services in the past. In the past, too, Olivia had been eligible for LD services in addition to ED services. And Fred was eligible for autism, language, LD, and ED services at different times. (See Chapter 26 for an in-depth discussion of interrelated disorders.)

24

Taking Themselves
Too Seriously

A mountain in which no ease is ever found
Wallace Stevens

One overarching characteristic of all our primary sample cases, and a characteristic that has impressed those who work with students who have emotional-behavioral disorders, is a difficulty with *detachment:* an inability to be objective or to distance themselves from circumstances. They overpersonalize events; they complain that they are the brunt of insults, the butt of jokes, blamed, or targeted; or they believe that they are victims. Unable to prioritize, they react to everything in equal proportion; molehills become mountains.

To qualify, detachment, as used here, is not the same as *detachment disorder*, which is a serious difficulty often seen in autistic individuals, those who have spent long periods living in isolated conditions, or those with sensory deprivation. Detachment disorder is characterized by unfocused behavior in which the individual typically stares at others but does not really see them, as if responding to an internal dream world (Rimland 1964).

The detachment difficulty evident in students with emotional and behavior disorders does not involve such a pervasive quality of unreality. Their *detachment difficulty*, rather, is a process of selective perception. Thus, it is similar to a thought disorder, particularly cognitive distortion. These individuals can deal only with what relates to them; they cannot think beyond themselves; and they are unable to put order into their thoughts and behaviors, or prioritize.

The ability to distance oneself from circumstances and to prioritize relates to *metacognition*, the executive mental function that enables us to monitor our own behavior, feelings, and thinking. A higher order mental function, metacognition enables functional independence. One who cannot self-monitor is dependent on others for information and feedback. Normally, an adolescent needs to learn from his parents to distinguish between events that are merely unpleasant and annoying and those that are serious and tragic. He must learn a sense of proportion (Ginott 1969). A broken glass is not a broken arm, and a lost sweater should not lead to a lost temper.

This psychological ability, emergent in adolescence, typically to be deficient in adolescents with emotional and behavioral disorders. All of our primary sample cases show difficulty detaching from circumstances. These students are embroiled, entangled, and ensnared by events that worry them, draw their undivided attention, and, generally, prevent them from putting events in perspective. They lack the perspective that permits a sense of humor, a light heart, and the creation of a philosophy of life that involves a viewpoint beyond oneself. Because they are enmired in their own thoughts and feelings, they believe they are going the right way. It is, after all, their way.

For those who cannot rise above themselves and assume an objective perspective, mental health is compromised. The individual who regards every event as worthy of attention will become mentally crippled, unable to sort events out and to react to situations appropriately. This individual is trapped by events. At the extreme is the individual for whom every event is important, leaving him unable to make a decision; he is hopelessly adrift, unable to accomplish anything. This individual will probably need very structured and protective care. All the students described in this book may not exhibit such extreme dysfunction, but it remains to be seen how many of them will survive adulthood in an unstructured world where independent decisions are expected.

Interestingly, many of those who work in mental health programs show an extraordinary ability to use humor in their work with discordant youngsters. One psychiatric program teacher said, "If I don't laugh, I may cry." This talent, whether developed prior to or during their work with these youngsters, is invaluable. Their ability to use humor and lightness contrasts dramatically with the youngsters' inabilities to laugh and poke fun at the world around them, including themselves. Many a point is made or a lesson taught by these professionals using techniques that reflect and model detachment. They may be unaware of this skill and its necessity both for the youngsters and for their own mental health.

Detachment is essential for mental health. We cannot react to everything or we will react to nothing meaningfully. To wallow in subjectivity is to fail to perceive the boundaries between ourselves and other people or objects. The world, in such a state, is defined by the limits of the individual's perceptions. It is difficult for a mentally healthy person to imagine this kind of mental prison. A healthy individual takes for granted that there are choices; he monitors his own thinking, behavior, and feelings, and he sees himself as part of a bigger picture.

For students with emotional or behavioral disorders, life tends to be very serious and the choices limited. Theirs is a small world. They cannot enjoy life or understand Oscar Wilde's meaning when he said, "Life is too important to be taken seriously."

To understand detachment difficulty is to further understand students with emotional and behavioral disorders, who cannot attain healthy detachment because their specific difficulties contribute to the creation and maintenance of a constricted, acutely subjective world.

Let us reexamine the 10 practical characteristics in light of a detachment difficulty. They are listed below.

1. Students who are **depressed** are too pessimistic to see, feel, or hear beyond themselves. These students are too sad, pessimistic, preoccupied, and dissatisfied with themselves to try to rise above their circumstances.

2. Students who have **low self-esteem** do not believe they are worthy of being part of the world around them. They remain emotionally isolated even if they can play some socially functional role. Because they feel unimportant, others' opinions outweigh theirs. With their diminished perspective, they feel no right, or freedom, to question or test the limits that define social boundaries.

3. Students who are **narcissistic** feel that their needs are of supreme importance. They are too self-absorbed to incorporate the world beyond themselves. They are so absorbed in the minutia of their small world that they cannot separate the parts from the whole and put them back together in whole cloth.

4. Students who **misperceive** cannot put pieces of information together to make sense of reality. Their interpretation of life puts them constantly at odds with others. Emotions cloud their thinking; they cannot see clearly and objectively.

5. Students who have **physical symptoms** are wrapped up in their bodily functions. The symptoms, even when real and painful or at least annoying, absorb them. It is hard to adopt a broad view of life when nurturing one's own physical wounds, real or imagined. There is more interest in maintaining the symptoms than in processing life beyond themselves.

6. Students who have **poor body awareness and hygiene** are so mired in their own thoughts and feelings that they are unaware of the effect of their unkempt, soiled, or smelly bodies on other people. These students are out of synchrony in terms of social conventions regarding self-care. If they could be objective, they would perceive a need to adapt to social conventions of body awareness and hygiene.

7. Students who have **mood swings** are unable to stabilize emotionally in order to process objective information. These students are open to varying interpretations of the world as the information is received during varying emotional states. It must be very confusing to process information that is acquired under dissimilar conditions of receptivity. Objectivity is elusive; mood flux is constant.

8. Students who are **keenly sensitive to others** pick up information outside themselves, but the information is selectively chosen to satisfy their own

needs. They are uninterested in objective data. This student, essentially, is looking for confirmation of preexisting attitudes or beliefs, not new information that will help him or her grow, learn and, effectively, be free.

9. Students who **lack tolerance for untroubled kids** are, essentially, youngsters in misery seeking the company of other youngsters in misery. These students typically pick other troubled students for company, permitting no opportunity to learn about the realities or perceptions of untroubled students. Their narrow world is protected from the intrusion of normal ideas, behaviors, and emotions. Teachers have commented frequently about how quickly adolescents with problems find their own kind. It is as if there is a worldwide fraternity of adolescents with emotional or behavioral problems. Only the initiated seem to know the secret words and signals.

10. Students who are **untrustworthy** are, essentially, dishonest. Honest self-appraisal is impossible unless these students can incorporate objective data. Reactions, instead, are based upon subjective information. Lies, misrepresentations, fraudulent behavior, and dishonesty represent the personal style of the person who is untrustworthy.

Overall, students with emotional and behavioral disorders seem to be unable to detach from their constricted worlds to participate fully in the wider world. They are dependent on a defensive coping style that serves to protect the subjective worlds that they have carefully, painstakingly created.

For those who can detach and achieve a lightness of being to support growth and learning, this is incomprehensible. Why would anyone choose to live in an emotional closet? There is the rub. These students do not choose to live in emotionally constricted worlds. They are not free to choose. Consequently, these students resist change because their worlds, while mental prisons, are at least familiar. Change is not easy because the patterns have worked for them, at least in their own minds. To offer something different is to offer the unknown. A world that has been built over many years is not easily dismantled.

25

ED with or without SM?

In order to discuss emotional disturbance (ED) with or without social maladjustment (SM), it is necessary to clarify terminology. For present purposes, SM refers to both oppositional-defiant disorder (ODD) and conduct disorder (CD). Also, due to overlapping considerations, attention-deficit disorder with hyperactivity (ADHD) is included among the disruptive behavior disorders. For present purposes, then, SM refers collectively to the disruptive behavior disorders.

Disruptive behavior disorders currently are not covered by the guidelines of the Individuals with Disabilities Education Act (IDEA), either for ED or for any special education category. Because disruptive behavior disorders overlap in large measure (see Chapters 7 and 26), it is logical to subsume them under *social maladjustment.*

The responsibility of America's schools for providing special services to socially maladjusted students has been debated for many years (Nelson, Rutherford, and Walker 1991). Federal law provides a guideline for excluding SMs from special education, specifically in the ED category. This exclusionary clause has clouded the definition of ED and has galvanized the thinking of professionals in the field of education of youth with emotional and behavioral disorders.

A good example of the debate comes from a case of the U.S. Court of Appeals, 4th Circuit, which was decided in January 1998: *Edward P. Springer v. Fairfax County School Board* (No. 97-1482). At all points, this case was decided as an either-or issue (i.e., Edward was either ED or conduct disordered, not both). Edward had had a successful and unremarkable school experience in regular education until late in eleventh grade, when he developed significant behavioral problems. He was arrested for possessing burglary tools and automobile tampering; he snuck out of the house to stay out all night with friends; he stole from his parents; he abused alcohol and marijuana; he had a high rate of school absenteeism, including leaving school grounds without permission and cutting classes; he drove recklessly on school property; and he fought. The coup de grace was theft of a classmate's car, which Edward kept for a week of joy-riding. Despite above-average intelligence, Edward failed three of seven eleventh-grade courses. His parents enrolled him in a private residential school and asked the public school system to fund that placement because Edward was emotionally disabled, a qualifying disability under IDEA.

The school district denied funding, claiming that Edward was ineligible for special education services and tuition reimbursement because he had a conduct disorder. A local hearing officer decided that Edward was ED due to mild depression. The school system appealed. A state hearing officer, who reversed the local decision, stated that Edward did not meet state and federal ED criteria. The parents then appealed to the district court, which agreed with the state hearing officer. Finally, the parents took the case to the U.S. Court of Appeals, which affirmed the district court's decision, with comments that juvenile delinquency did not reflect emotional disturbance within the meaning of federal and state regulations implementing IDEA, and that Edward's truancy and substance abuse reflected a conduct disorder, defined as a persistent pattern of violating societal norms.

THE DEBATE

The debate about excluding students with SM will probably continue due to political, legal, and judgmental factors. Let us look at each factor.

Political factors. Political argument cites the expense of special education. Another part of the political picture is that SM often is considered to be less of a handicap and more of a threat, particularly to classroom teachers. Such a dangerous population, many teachers argue, should be excluded if it represents noncompliance, disruption, and aggressiveness. SM students, many educators believe, should be placed in alternative schools, detention centers, or reformatories. A current political reality is that some states are reclassifying ED students into non-special education categories (e.g., conduct disordered) in order to apply disciplinary sanctions without the constraints of due process (according to special education law) and to avoid legal penalties for expelling them from public schools (Center 1988).

Legal factors. Some argue that the SM exclusion clause cannot be willed away legally because Congress legislated it into the ED definition. One attorney commented that until someone can come up with a better definition of social maladjustment, currently defined by the courts and several states as conduct disordered and oppositional or defiant behavior, it appears these students need to be excluded from eligibility for SED (serious emotional disturbance) (Slenkovich 1992).

Judgmental factors. Finally, exclusion of SM in the ED definition creates a dualism for school psychologists in which professional and legal responsibilities are in constant conflict (Forness 1992). Those who must judge the severity of problems among troubled students are caught between legal imperatives and considerations for appropriate educational placement and programming.

The debate about ED with or without SM has taken on an either-or cast. To many educators, SM students should "either get with the program or get out." To legal analysts, it seems clear that social maladjustment has no place in special education because of the way in which the law is written. To many clinicians, SM equates with "bad" or delinquent, but not with mental illness. To many public school eligibility committees, SMs should clearly show eligibility in one of the federally defined special education categories other than ED or be excluded from services reserved for the disabled.

The arguments of advocates for inclusion of social maladjustment in the ED category include the following.

o   Most students served in the ED category are conduct or behavior disordered (Stephens et al. 1990).

o   About 88 percent of students classified as ED have been involved in the juvenile justice system for minor or major offenses (Bryant et al. 1995).

o   More than 40 percent of the states include SM in their ED definition (Forness 1992).

o   Conduct disorder, the most frequent reason for mental health referral, is the largest category under which ED students are placed (Phelps and McClintock 1994); behavior therapy and psychotherapy are usually necessary to help the youngster express and control anger appropriately.

o   Conduct disorder is one of the most serious and far-reaching disorders of childhood and adolescence (Phelps and McClintock 1994); treatment is rarely brief because establishing new attitudes and behavior patterns takes time.

o   Antisocial students experience more school failure and much greater exposure to special services and/or placements than other students (Walker et al. 1987).

Advocates for inclusion of SM in the ED category also point to the emotional and behavioral problems that are evident among students who are socially maladjusted. In terms of emotional disturbances, McManus argues for inclusion because there is a remarkable degree of agreement in the extensive literature on conduct disorder that aggressive, antisocial, and conduct disordered behavior in its more severe forms is an enduring symptom constellation, with clear-cut familial pattern of transmission and a highly predictable clinical course. In short, all the factors necessary to qualify conduct disorder as a psychiatric diagnosis are present. (1989, p. 271)

Robins (1966) noted that juvenile antisocial behavior is the single most powerful predictor of adult psychiatric status. Furthermore, we see affective disorders in many conduct disordered youngsters. For example, depression and aggression co-occur frequently in childhood.

In terms of behavioral disorder, inclusion advocates point to the constellation of behaviors that bring behaviorally disordered youngsters to the attention of the judicial system. The word *delinquent* is a legal term, but the offenses an adolescent commits to be labeled delinquent constitute a behavior disorder (Heward and Orlansky 1984). Social learning theorists also support the rationale that SM students merit inclusion in the ED category owing to a behavior disorder. They contend that learning of obnoxious behaviors usually results from the pattern of reinforcements children receive for being obnoxious. This orientation helps us understand how many parents reinforce obnoxious behavior even though they are irritated by the behavior (Turner and Dodd 1980).

Alternatively, there are those who believe that antisocial behavior is directly or indirectly influenced by physiological dysfunction. As many as 15 million American youngsters may suffer from physiological dysfunction that can increase the risk of antisocial or inappropriate behavior (Turner and Dodd 1980). Examples include the hyperactive child syndrome, allergic tension-fatigue syndrome, and the hypoglycemic aggressive reaction.

Inclusion advocates point out, furthermore, that behavior disorders often become more than just chronic social handicaps. Behavioral problems during childhood and adolescence often predict subsequent adult criminality. Nelson (1992) has argued that to refuse services to children with troubling behavior is to sentence them to treatment by the juvenile justice system. Those served by the juvenile justice system are likely to be served by the adult justice system, thereby making youthful behavior disorder a lifelong *social disability* (Wolf, Brauckman, and Ramp 1987), with risk of school failure, membership in deviant peer groups, school dropout, and eventual delinquency (Walker et al. 1987).

Kerr, Nelson, and Lambert (1987) argue that these students should also be considered educationally handicapped. By this reasoning, it is argued that if the antisocial and frequently illegal behavior of SM youth conforms to the standard of their deviant cultural or peer group, they should not be separated from the ED population simply because their behavior violates the norms of the larger social order and is intolerable to schools. Most SM youngsters show serious learning problems and most have not responded well to traditional school curricula and practices. Kerr and his colleagues believe that SMs need individualized educational experiences because they are handicapped.

Inclusion advocates also point to the similarity of educational interventions used for EDs and SMs (Nelson and Rutherford 1990): a continuum of public school treatment options (e.g., counseling, social work services, and such disciplinary procedures as in-school suspension). In addition, both groups have been subjected to such approaches as data-based decision making and behavioral contracts.

Nelson and Rutherford (1990) also found similar background factors in the cases of ED and SM students: school problems; low verbal intelligence; parents adjudicated (for criminal behavior) or alcoholic; family dependence on welfare, or poor income management; broken, crowded, chaotic homes; erratic parental supervision and discipline; parental and sibling indifference or hostility toward the youngster; and substance abuse.

Finally, advocates for inclusion point to weaknesses in the existing ED definition. "Adverse educational performance," for example, has been too narrowly interpreted as meaning only academic failure rather than a combination of academic, social, and behavioral problems (Forness and Knitzer 1992).

Advocates for excluding SM from ED point primarily to the law. Slenkovich (1992) noted that Congress expressly excluded SM students from the ED definition. Some individuals have advised school administrators and state policy makers to deny special education services to students identified as conduct disordered simply because such children are socially maladjusted, thus not emotionally disturbed (Kelly 1988). This argument is one that brooks no gray area.

A catch in this position is that there is no generally accepted definition of SM. Furthermore, SMs are assumed not to be ED because the behavior of SMs accords with the norms of their immediate reference group, assumed to be a deviant subculture. If it cannot be determined that the reference group's norms are deviant, SMs cannot with certainty be excluded from ED (Nelson and Rutherford 1990).

While the present discussion admittedly leans toward inclusion of SM within the ED category, let us focus less on labels and more on students. School personnel need to focus less on differential diagnosis (Nelson 1992) between and among categories. The wide use and acceptance of cross-categorical approaches in special education, and the abundant evidence of overlapping disorders, reflect a bigger picture, one of interest in *differentiated diagnosis* within categories, rather than *differential diagnosis* between and among categories.

Variation of ED severity receives little attention (Forness 1992), and subtypes within the ED population also receive little attention. Unlike other disability categories, students are determined to be eligible only if their problems are implicitly serious (pervasive, to a marked degree). Efforts should focus on establishing levels of differentiated behavioral or emotional responses (Forness and Knitzer 1992). The problem of delivering effective services for troubled youth supersedes that of differentially diagnosing an adolescent as ED or SM (Nelson and Rutherford, 1990).

Too much effort has been expended on defining the boundaries of ED in order to determine who qualifies for the ED classification. Applying strictly defined boundaries in the diagnostic process is inconsistent with the realities of human behavior and with the original intent of PL 94-142 (Skiba and Grizzle 1991). Reconceptualizing along intracategorical lines will help in the design and planning of appropriate services along a continuum. We have been focusing on an all-or-nothing boundary issue while ignoring the range of emotions and behaviors within the ED boundaries.

The learning disability (LD) category, in contrast to ED, has been studied in the pursuit of subtypes. Weller and colleagues (1990), for example, developed an assessment approach for diagnosis of LD subtypes. Their purpose in differentiating LD levels was to promote development of methods to identify LDs as a heterogeneous population.

Efforts have also been made to differentiate students within the SM boundaries. Clarizio (1992a), for example, argues for the exclusion of socialized and unsocialized aggressives and for the inclusion of SMs who are ED as a result of anxiety, withdrawal, or depression. While this reconceptualization assumes that there may be emotional disorders among only certain types of aggressive youngsters, and ignores the attendant social and educational handicaps likely to occur among all aggressive youngsters, it is, at least, a compromise position.

The identification of subtypes within ED has begun. One survey differentially analyzed primary emotional disabilities among 93,462 EDs in day and residential schools (Stephens et al. 1990). Research focusing on informal clustering, or formal statistical analysis, of behaviors to derive "syndromes" of behavior problems is exemplified by factor analysis of behavioral checklists (Von Isser, Quay, and Love 1980). That research, which yielded behavioral dimensions, replicated previous studies: conduct disorder, anxiety-withdrawal, immaturity, and socialized aggression.

This line of research has been very helpful in targeting clusters of intercorrelated behaviors, but some problems remain. One problem is that students with emotional and behavioral disorders frequently have difficulties across all dimensions. This is shown in the present primary sample. In order to structure a valid ED definition to include the range and multidimensionality of emotional-behavioral disorders, a different breakdown is needed (Kauffman 1985).

Even a more important point than the debate about including SM in the ED category is the need that educators have for more information about both ED and SM. SMs have been and will continue to be included within ED in many states. Even in states that adhere to the exclusionary clause, SMs slip through the holes in the eligibility net. One example is presented in the following discussion involving two cases.

DIFFERENTIATED ANALYSIS WITHIN ED

Two ED cases are used to illustrate one approach to differentiated analysis. These students, eligible for ED services, were enrolled in a large

Virginia public school system. One way to articulate two subtypes within ED (behaviorally disordered and emotionally disturbed) is to compare these students using predetermined criteria.

This approach has a precedent. Weller and colleagues (1990) developed, through field testing and vignettes, a practical approach to subtype LDs. These vignettes are intended to help clarify subtypes ED and BD (behaviorally disordered).

The cases of Brian and Zach, who have a lot in common, will be used to illustrate the suggested criteria (in addition to some material from two other cases). Brian and Zach live in the same neighborhood, are handsome and athletic, attend the same public middle school, and are latchkey children with mothers who, as single parents, are raising three or more children. Both boys have been removed from their homes for about a year because of aggressive behavior; Zach was sent to a military school, Brian went to live with a sympathetic teacher. Both students have been hospitalized for aggressive behaviors. Both mothers have been emotionally crippled by divorce and are severely lacking in parenting skills and in motivation to provide consistency for their sons. Both students have average intelligence and no sensory, health, or physical symptoms, or other noticeable problems, but they are in academic trouble and have social difficulties.

Conflict, also, is a defining characteristic of both students. Their teachers complain often that Brian and Zach spend a lot of time instigating problems. The boys are especially difficult to deal with when they are in the same classes. Despite every effort to separate them, their daily schedules allow them time together in science class, hallways, and lunch. At such times, Brian and Zach look for trouble or create it.

Both students were invited to join a special program for middle schoolers at risk for criminal careers. This program, designed to "turn boys into men," involves group support meetings, visits to prisons and detention centers, and individual attention. Brian and Zach were targeted as likely to end up in the juvenile justice system and were asked to join the program to prevent this.

What Brian and Zach do not share is unanimity about their eligibility for special education. The school-based eligibility committee was not unanimous in its decision to find both students eligible. One student was thought to be ED, the other SM.

Below is an examination of the cases of Brian and Zach using four analytical criteria that have emerged in clinical practice and that reflect the general literature. Literature validation of each criterion will be documented throughout the discussion. The criteria involve conscience, reality orientation, adaptive behavior, and psychological activity. Observable behaviors, both nonverbal and verbal, as well as case histories, will be used to detail and illustrate the criteria.

First, each of the four criteria for ED and BD subtypes will be presented. Following each criterion case information and observations about the actual students will be related.

As a caveat, the reader should not expect to find precisely differentiated emotions and behaviors relative to the presented criteria. While most criteria can be differentiated, the cases will show some overlap. Not only does this overlap reflect one of the themes of this book, but it reflects a reality in social science, which involves relatively more subjectivity than we find in hard science. The applied usefulness of such a differentiation more than makes up for its lack of precision, however.

Criterion 1: conscience. Professionals have often found that conscience differentiates EDs from BDs. Some EDs need help in loosening their moral grip so that they can feel better about themselves and enjoy life to a greater extent. Often EDs are burdened excessively by remorse, inadequacy, and guilt over their actual or perceived transgressions (Clarizio 1992b). ED students, typically, tend to criticize themselves and to experience guilt for wrongdoing. Often, EDs punish themselves for bad behavior or for failures, and self-punishment may look like anger toward others. They respond to caring, sympathetic approaches that unmask their defenses.

Professionals have found that many BDs, on the other hand, care little about the rights and feelings of others and experience little, if any, remorse or guilt when they break rules or hurt others. (See Chapter 8 for further discussion of absence of remorse and guilt among oppositional-defiant youngsters.) BDs are pleasure oriented. Furthermore, the BD student typically feels remorse for getting caught, not for wrongdoing. If he is caught, he will probably not accept responsibility for his behavior. BDs remain impassive and unresponsive to caring, sympathetic approaches. Rather, such approaches tend to bring out boastful stories and pride in misbehavior. Brian is a user. Brian appears to be BD by this criterion, Zach ED.

CONSCIENCE EXAMPLES. *Brian often is disruptive at home. He torments his younger brother until his brother reacts, and then Brian aggresses against him. When confronted, Brian usually says that his brother "started it," or "it's his fault." Brian believes that he is constantly blamed for family conflict. He has never apologized for fighting with his brother. When outbursts occur, Brian typically will break his own or others' possessions, kick objects, bang doors, damage walls, yell, swear, and cry. When the negative behavior ends, Brian does not want to discuss the incident or make amends. Brian likes school because he can socialize, get involved in conflicts, and find many ways to disrupt classes, all of which stimulates him. His behavior is no problem in his opinion, unless he gets caught. Brian backed out of a fight one day at school because he might be suspended, not because it was the right thing to do. Teachers say Brian has a "mean streak," which they believe accounts for his pleasure in aggressing toward other students. A sympathetic ear typically brings out Brian's delight in his adventures; he likes to have an audience. For example, he thought it was amusing that he pulled a male peer's pants down in school. He did not understand why he was promptly dismissed from that school. When counseled, Brian does not appear to register counselor feedback; he appears to be uncomfortable and asks when he can leave. However, he's happy to be in the counseling situation when he is scheduled to take a test in class, when he does not feel well, or when his class is doing something that he does not care to do.*

Zach does not like school. He intensely dislikes his math teacher, who confronts him for poor effort. Zach feels that he would rather not try to do schoolwork than experience failure. "That," he said, "will make me mad." Teachers do not refer to a mean streak when discussing Zach, but they believe that he takes out his sad feelings on others. Zach has been described as a caring, feeling, sensitive child who openly shows affection. When he has a sympathetic ear he may show tears. Zach is proud of himself when he goes for long periods of time without a referral to the crisis room. On the other hand, he is his own worst critic. Consequently, his self-image is more negative than positive. He seems to like counseling; he engages readily and uses it to talk openly about likes and dislikes. On the other hand, he did not care for therapy because he did not like his psychiatrist. Zach's eyes light up when talking about baseball, food, or mischief, particularly his counterreactions to adults whom he believes demean him. If he does not like an adult, he takes pleasure in offensive verbal remarks; the best defense is an offense.

Criterion 2: reality orientation: two differentiated facets of "if." Orientation to reality is another factor to consider in understanding subtypes of ED. EDs, who are prone to fantasy, often are naive and out of touch with practical issues. They are suggestible and easily influenced. EDs test the waters before wading in. ED students ask why something has to be, or they behave so as to discover to what extent adults and peers can be trusted. EDs also respond to behavioral contingencies ("if then" arrangements), particularly contingencies in which the consequences are positive; these students can be motivated by *positive reinforcement.*

BDs, on the other hand, readily read a system and quickly figure out how it works. They are able to hone in on others to get what they want. Also, they are more likely to tell adults why their rules or approaches are wrong, to defy behavioral boundaries, and to attempt to show that adults cannot be trusted. BD students ask "what if?" questions. For instance, what if they violate rules or boundaries? They want to know how far they can go before getting caught or before experiencing *negative reinforcement.* It is not a test to determine whether they can trust adults but, rather, a test for them to judge their own behavior and to determine whether they want to risk the negative consequences. In other words, is it worth the risk? BD students, then, seem to plan their behavior to avoid negative consequences. They are less likely to buy into contingency plans, even if there are attractive incentives. If they do buy into contingencies, they will push like courtroom attorneys for precise definition of what they need to do in order to get the rewards. Brian appears to be BD, Zach ED, by this criterion.

REALITY ORIENTATION EXAMPLES. *Brian is streetwise: bold and aggressive. He is at home on the suburban range and restless in school, where there is a narrower range of tolerated movement. He can read situations well and can manipulate other students. He believes that he can negotiate his way out of anything. A leader, he once planned a fight after school and was the only student who did not show. At the last minute he chose to go home and play video games. Apparently, the risk was not worth the effort. Brian does not trust most adults. He frequently asks "what if" questions, for example, "How many crisis referrals can I get before I get suspended?" "How many quizzes can I fail before I fail the course?" "Can I fail three quarters and still pass for the year if I pass one quarter?" "Exactly how many satisfactory marks do I need on my progress reports to earn lunch out?" He has figured out how much trouble he can get into in the community without being sent to detention. Assigned a probation officer after two court appearances for shoplifting and arson, he often asks his P.O. to define the law and limits so that he can know how far to go before getting caught again. Brian does not fantasize about life getting better because he does not believe it will. He lives, instead, for the moment.*

Zach often fantasizes about what life would be like if his father moved back home. While he presents himself with bravado, he often looks sad. He is more often the follower than the leader; he is unable to provoke class disruptions unless the other students are prone to distractibility. Zach has responded well to contingencies involving the reward of lunch at a restaurant, and his behavior improved under a contract involving weekly progress reports. He did not need to know exactly how many satisfactory marks were needed to earn rewards; he was satisfied to know that he needed more "S" than "U" marks. Zach is oriented to the past and the future; the present is not a place he likes. He fantasizes that life will get better and believes it can; after all, things were good when his father was at home.

Criterion 3: adaptive behavior. Adaptive behavior also helps us to understand ED and BD subtypes. ED students typically experience difficulties in adapting to varied settings. ED students are less able to blend into the social landscape. For example, their behavior may be eccentric or odd; their fears may cause them to withdraw; they may be too dependent upon adults to act in outrageous ways; and they may conflict openly because they cannot control themselves. They are in open conflict because they make an effort to adapt, but they do not know how to succeed. Whether they overreact or underreact, their behavior is not a good fit with the context.

While BD students may experience difficulties in adjusting to their settings, generally they are more self-reliant, adapting by moving through situations as if they are not a part of their surroundings. BDs are relatively more competent about adapting. They are able to blend into the social landscape; camouflaged, their protective coloration enables them to appear part of the social environment while they function apart from it and at odds with it. Antisocial types always seem to be participating in a game in which others exist as pieces to be manipulated and used (Sarason and Sarason 1993). The self-control of a BD student is the result of calculation and premeditation.

ADAPTIVE BEHAVIOR EXAMPLES. *Brian picks his battles. He watches carefully and moves stealthfully and guardedly. He has figured out just how much work to do to pass his courses. He is in academic trouble but may pass seventh grade, at least his English and mathematics courses, the two required for promotion. He is social but seems to stand apart. He has an aura of self-containment, as if he knows who he is and what he wants. His verbal statements are concise and to the point, and he has little tolerance for verbosity. In fact, Brian dislikes literary arts because the teacher requires that students express themselves with varied images, all of which is nonsense to Brian. While he is oriented primarily to the present, he has mentioned matter-of-factly that his future plans are to play high school football and become a veterinarian. However, as he is rooted to the present, Brian does not bother thinking about what he needs to do to reach his goals. He responded well to the structure provided by a former teacher and his wife, who took him in after his father left home when he was in third grade. While living in the teacher's home, Brian had no outbursts, did not curse, and did not lose control. Still, he was described as "a handful." When he returned home, the problems resumed. He showed that he could behave according to the expectations. Brian can adapt.*

Zach has no vocational, or any other, goals. He has enough to deal with now, and he is preoccupied with the past when his father lived at home. Often he has been in conflict at home and in school. In the community he has often gotten into mischief but has faced no serious legal charge. A big problem is his short fuse. Zach has aggressed against his younger sisters frequently, particularly after his father left home. During that time he shot one sister with a BB gun. She was not injured badly, but soon after the incident Zach was sent to military school because his mother could not control him. While Zach walks with a swagger and flashes some bravado, he is somewhat dependent and for the most part compliant. He likes to blend into a crowd and would like to succeed in school, but he does not know where to start. He fears failure so avoids exposing himself to criticism, even if it is constructive. When given a mathematics test Zach writes answers without doing the problems, or fills in blanks with arbitrary numbers. If he senses that a teacher disapproves of him or targets him for correction, he will counterattack, turning attention to the teacher's behavior. Zach likes to sit in the classroom and appear to be a part of everything even though he does not do any work. The more a teacher tries to engage him, the more Zach will counterattack or provoke disruption among other students in order to deflect attention from himself.

Criterion 4: psychological activity. Finally, we may differentially understand ED in terms of psychological activity: emotions, response styles, and thought processes. The ED and BD subtypes can be differentiated in terms of two types of emotional response styles. EDs, typically, internalize their feelings and suffer from painful affective disorders such as excessive anxiety, guilt, and depression. They acutely feel their difficulties. Their behavior causes them anxiety (Clarizio 1992b). To EDs, feelings are everything. Irrational thoughts and illogical thinking are frequently characteristic of EDs.

On the other hand, BDs appear to externalize their feelings by behaviors that violate norms and cause others pain. When BDs experience anxiety, it likely is a reaction to the threat of punishment or to such experiences as rejection, abandonment, disappointment, or to the perceived possibility of such negative experiences. Depression also may be quite real, but the expression is directed away from themselves (i.e., externalized). To BDs, feelings may be irrelevant or overwhelming. Their behavior may not cause them anxiety (Clarizio 1992b), or if their behavior leads to anxiety, other behaviors serve to deflect attention from their true feelings and provide an escape into externally oriented avenues. Without anxiety, BDs are unmotivated to change; with an investment in regulating their emotional thermostat in order to avoid pain, and with the attitude that they would rather be called "bad" than "nuts," it is difficult to help them change. Finally, the thinking of BDs often is very logical. Their arguments can be maddeningly insightful and rational; arguments and insults can cut to the bone. The problem is that their ideas serve only their own purposes and typically do not consider other points of view. By this criterion Brian seems to be BD, Zach ED.

PSYCHOLOGICAL ACTIVITY EXAMPLES. *Brian acts out his feelings. He stirs things up and tries to get everything out in the open except his feelings. His eyes open widely and some anxiety is apparent only when there is the possibility of a negative consequence. For example, when the assistant principal was calling students to his office for questioning regarding the presence of a knife in the building, Brian's eyes widened at this news. He presents himself as a boy's boy who avoids feelings. To Brian only girls have feelings. He leaves a path of broken feelings. His mother has more than sufficient reason to wring her hands in despair. She cannot manage her son, and Brian does not miss an opportunity to tell her what a bad parent she is. His teachers wonder what they have done wrong in view of all the extra help and care they have given him. Brian does not respect or trust most adults. His feelings of parental loss are projected onto other adults, who must jump through hoops to earn his respect. Little seems to lie dormant; Brian seems to be more comfortable parlaying his difficulties into overt, observable problems: a paper airplane flying by, a ripped up piece of artwork, a cutting remark to a teacher. It is not as if Brian has no feelings; it is what he does with his feelings that defines who he is. Brian was hospitalized twice during elementary school because of depression and disruptive behavior following his father's departure from home. Early in life Brian was described as a sensitive child. Brian's thinking seems to be clear. He says what he likes and dislikes, and he is quick to say what he wants. He is a boy of few words, but those few are to the point. His mathematics teacher confronts him routinely about missing assignments. Brian dismisses this teacher by saying that she cannot teach, so it is not his fault. He may not say this to her face because later he may need something from her. He figures it is better to lie low and play the game.*

Zach seems to feel his troubles. He expresses feelings of disappointment, dislike, and failure. He is preoccupied with anger and rage as well as with feelings of helplessness and abandonment. A major part of Zach's psychological functioning involves fear of abandonment. He has trouble connecting with people, particularly adults, because he does not trust them and does not share what he feels. It bothers him that he is failing school, but he prefers to protect himself by doing nothing, rather than showing teachers what he does not know and cannot do. Sometimes his depression spills out in the form of anger. At these times, Zach is overwhelmed by his feelings and needs an outlet. A teacher who responds in anger only perpetuates conflict. Zach calms down when teachers use humor and warmth, and when they ignore minor inappropriate behavior. Gum chewing has become his signature behavior. While the school rule prohibits gum, Zach chooses this low-level misbehavior to test adults. Teachers who confront him and make a big deal of it provoke worse behaviors; teachers who ignore it or deal with it in low-level ways do not provoke Zach to escalate negative behaviors. It is a matter of choosing one's battles with Zach. Zach's feelings about his abilities have formed a school phobic type reaction. He will come to school and blend in socially, but he refuses to try the work. He will not even do manual projects in teen living, preferring to sit beside the students who are working on their projects, chatting amiably. To say that Zach's behavioral style drives his teachers crazy is to describe exactly what he wants to do. He certainly does not want to shoulder his feelings alone. Zach is a woman's man. His enjoys being with his mother, with whom he confides and about whom he feels protective. He has been able to connect with his female resource teacher, sharing feelings with her. In terms of thought processes, Zach has many irrational thoughts. For example, he believes that his mathematics teacher hates him and that that is why he is failing. To Zach it has nothing to do with his lack of effort.

Another way to conceptualize the psychological activity of ED and BD subtypes is to analyze feelings of joy and pleasure consequent to misconduct. When antisocials beat the system, their pleasure and excitement comes not from the goods or money they get but from their successful efforts (Sarason and Sarason 1993). EDs may show oppositionality and what appears to be a conduct disorder but have overriding emotions that prevent them from taking pleasure from their misconduct. BDs, on the other hand, experience pleasure when they hurt others and misbehave.

EMOTIONS FOLLOWING PSYCHOLOGICAL ACTIVITY EXAMPLES. *Rob takes no pleasure from his oppositional behavior and noncompliance. He appears to be sad when relating tales of revenge on teachers. His stories of pushing teachers to react to him, and descriptions of his need for revenge, do not reflect happiness. Paxil, an antidepressant medication, freed him from his sadness, enabling him to comply and to feel pleasure in doing so. Importantly, the drug helped him to let go of his anger.*

On the other hand, John H, age 15, takes great pleasure from his misconduct. He lies baldly; even when witnessed stealing a teacher's keys or supplies, John smiles. His pleasure in misconduct is pervasive; he laughs at his cleverness in duping others, and he shrugs off acts that lack finesse. Teacher reports show a pattern of cheating and lying. For example, John stole another student's packet of research papers and altered them to submit for his own credit. Every page corner where the other student's name had been written was ripped, and John's name appeared beside it. The teacher noticed that the handwriting of his name and that of the paper content differed significantly. Her reply when John said that his dog chewed the paper corners was, "Your dog has an amazing ability to chew the same spot on 11 pages." John simply shrugged his shoulders and smiled, as if to say, "Oh well, it doesn't hurt to try."

DIFFERENTIATED ANALYSIS: PRACTICAL IMPLICATIONS

New definition. Practical implications follow from a differentiated analysis of ED into subtypes. One relates to policy decisions at both the state and local levels. For example, the National Association of School Psychologists has begun the process of endorsing a new definition of behavioral disorders (Skiba and Grizzle 1991). Understanding the subconditions of ED could promote substantive pursuit of a more differentiated definition for this heterogeneous population.

Programming. Analysis in terms of qualitative criteria also could help determine programs that are appropriate for subtypes. Skiba and Grizzle (1991) advise that attention be refocused on issues of instruction, classroom management, and program planning. Focusing on strategies holds "far more promise as equitable methods for containing special education referrals than does the use of an undefined and indefensible exclusion" factor (Skiba and Grizzle 1991, p. 593).

Among educational strategies, many relate to differentiated levels within ED. Clarizio (1992b), for example, notes that some EDs need behavioral control through explicit, concrete rules for behavior backed up by immediate rewards and punishments, while other EDs show increased anxiety and guilt when punished. Some EDs respond well to group approaches with a focus on development of interpersonal problem-solving skills, control over impulsivity, role-taking skills, and social-moral reasoning. Other EDs respond poorly to those approaches and better to approaches that aim to develop communication and self-esteem through relationship building and verbal communication. In addition, because of the power of peer pressure among antisocial students, efforts to change their behavior will likely be unsuccessful (Slavin 1990), compared with students whose problems are more internalized.

Time spent on important issues. Another practical implication is use of a model that promotes analysis of cases and observations in order to look for subconditions of ED, and ultimately to articulate levels of ED severity. Differentiated analysis can refocus eligibility decision making on existing criteria within the definition rather than on social maladjustment as the issue. "The current definition and its social maladjustment exclusion seems to delay services to children and youth" (Forness 1992, p. 32). In other words, much time is spent either trying to eliminate students by proving that their difficulties are attributable to social maladjustment or trying to force their problems to fit into an identifiable set of symptoms corresponding to the ED criteria in order to override the SM factor.

Promotion of an ED continuum. Finally, a specific practical implication involves a continuum of services. Clarizio (1992b) notes that both SM and ED students need a continuum of services. Both types vary in the severity of their emotions and behaviors, and their educational settings and interventions should vary accordingly.

CONCLUSION

It is time, then, to refocus the debate about ED with or without SM. The debate about the exclusionary clause in the federal definition continues as if the labels have lives of their own. Between the labels lies the reality of many overlapping emotions and behaviors. In a middle ground lies the possibility of responsible child study and educational planning using differentiated analysis of students on a case-by-case basis. Therefore, we should take stock of labels and classifications and their meanings in order to determine what purposes and injustices they are serving (Cromwell, Blashfield, and Strauss 1976).

Taking stock of labels can mean looking at them as referents in depth, within rather than between their boundaries. An inventory of what we have in all its variation within boundaries can provide more clarity about where we need to go in research and policy making than a debate that only confounds the practical problems of dealing with the students in the most appropriate ways. Taking stock of what we have could lead logically to needs-based services, which should be the underpinning for a special education delivery system.

The present differentiated, qualitative analysis of two cases into ED and BD subtypes suggests a model for clarifying the heterogeneous ED population, showing a range of severity. Four criteria are presented with case information and observations that relate to those criteria. Additional factors are suggested to further qualify differences. Research could help clarify other relevant factors and further validate those presented here.

When Quay (1979) presented the features of an ideal classification system, several criteria were articulated. First, the categories should be operationally defined (defined so that they can be measured). Second, the system should be reliable (defined in such a way that different observers would assign the same individuals to categories consistently). Third, the ideal classification system should be valid (comprehensive assessment would suggest the same assignment to a category from different perspectives). Finally, classification should have clear implications for education.

Recall the movement toward EBD terminology and defining features, presented in Chapter 23. Such a definition would include all students whose emotions and behaviors interfere with and disrupt their educational progress. The debate about inclusion or exclusion of students with SM in ED would, then, be irrelevant; the focus would be, instead, on their individualized educational needs. An ED framework, combined with criteria regarding subtypes and levels of severity, would contribute substantially to policy making and practice. The existing ED classification system functions to differentially diagnose (include or exclude) students. In the process, classification of ED students has taken on a meaningless life of its own.

26

Interrelatedness of Disorders

There is a cross-categorical movement in special education. Emergent terms are *interrelated* (Meyen 1990) and *noncategorical*. Specific evidence of this trend is the merging of special education programs, federal categorization, research, prevalence statistics, and psychiatric practice.

MERGING PROGRAMS

Increasingly, there is recognition that students with special needs are most appropriately served by combined programs. One indicator is that teacher preparation programs are combining specializations such as learning disabilities (LD) and emotional disturbance (ED). Other teacher preparation programs focus on the severity of disabilities (i.e., mild, moderate, severe, or profound) rather than on categories. Meyen (1990) noted a trend toward placing more emphasis in special education teacher training on noncategorical approaches.

Similarly, there has been an emergence of noncategorical special education programs in school systems around the nation. These programs are based on the assumption that there are common instructional needs for students among and between different handicapping conditions.

Another indicator of merging programs is the proposed ED definition (see Chapter 23). Specifically, part of that definition recognizes that ED can coexist with other handicapping conditions, as defined elsewhere in the Individuals with Disabilities Education Act (IDEA).

FEDERAL CATEGORIZATION

At the policy-making level, there are two federal indicators of a trend toward interrelatedness. One indicator is the emergence of the category, *multiple disabilities*, in IDEA.

A second indicator is the reauthorization of federal regulations. The U.S. Department of Education, in requesting public comment about the reauthorization of IDEA, issued a list of some of the topics that are of primary concern to parents, teachers, and state and local administrators. Included among these primary concerns was the question: Should there be changes to the current eligibility requirements, including the use of separate disability categories, that would promote the education of students in the least restrictive environment, or would noncategorical approaches better meet the needs of each child?

RESEARCH INDICATORS

Further support for interrelatedness comes from opinion research. Putnam, Spiegel, and Bruininks (1995) surveyed educators regarding future directions in education and made the following relevant findings:

o   About 91 percent of those surveyed desired that funding
           formulas support integration and nonlabeling.

o   About 61 percent of those surveyed said that it is undesirable
           to fund special education services according to
           categories of exceptionality.

o   About 94 percent of those surveyed, opining that labels have
           little instructional value and are unjustifiable in schools,
           did not favor categorical labels, particularly labels used
           to classify students with mild disabilities.

PREVALENCE STATISTICS

Large numbers of students receive special education services in public schools. From 12 to 15 percent of the school-age population can be considered exceptional according to U.S. government numbers (Ysseldyke and Algozzine 1984). This prevalence estimate accords with district special education budgets, which typically range from 9 to 14 percent.

The reader might become confused by the prevalence estimates presented in the previous chapters on particular disorders, which when totaled would appear to suggest that between 35 and 87 percent of the student population has the disorders featured in this book. A realistic interpretation of these prevalence statistics is that they reflect an interrelation between and among disorders. Magyary and Brandt (1996) support this interpretation when considering the feasibility of organizing community mental health care programs around diagnostic groupings: Because few youngsters are found in each category, it is more realistic to organize programs around functional issues (e.g., generic functional skills such as stress management and coping) rather than disorders.

PSYCHIATRIC PRACTICE

In psychiatry there appears to be a trend toward defining and articulating interrelated psychopathologies (Hussain and Kashani 1992). For example, sufficient data have been published on the similarities among attention-deficit disorder with hyperactivity (ADHD), conduct disorder, and oppositional-defiant disorder to merit the supradomain of "disruptive behavior disorders," as proposed by the American Psychiatric Association's *DSM-III-R* (1987). (See Chapter 7.) Anderson and colleagues (1987), the first to study the extent to which *DSM-III* disorders are interrelated, examined attention-deficit disorder, oppositional-defiant disorder, separation anxiety disorder, aggressive conduct disorder, overanxious disorder, simple phobia, depression, and social phobia. Of the 219 cases identified within their sample, 45 percent occurred as a single disorder, but 55 percent occurred as a combination of one or more other disorders.

Personality disorders also often represent different degrees of the same general disorder. In fact, about two-thirds of those who meet the criteria for one personality disorder also meet the criteria for at least one more (Sarason and Sarason 1993).

In this book it has been shown that students with emotional and behavioral disorders often exhibit a complexity of problems, many of which are interrelated conditions. This is not to say that all students with the described disorders would be found eligible for ED services or that all students with emotional and behavioral problems will have sufficiently serious problems to require ED services in addition to those they receive for their primary disorders. It has long been recognized that all exceptionality has a psychological component, but that does not mean that all exceptional students have serious psychological problems. For example, it is more likely that a student with Tourette's syndrome (TS) will have psychological problems than it is that a student with an emotional or behavioral disorder will have TS. Similarly, it is more likely that a student with a learning disability will have psychological problems than it is that a student with an emotional or behavioral disorder will have LD.

With that understanding, let us review the emotional and behavioral disorders presented in this book. Review will be clarified by some documented evidence of interrelationships.

Post-traumatic stress disorder. Clinicians have had difficulty separating PTSD from borderline personality disorder as well as from anxiety disorder. Interrelation has been suggested by Kroll.

The PTSD/borderline person suffers first and foremost from a disorder of the stream of consciousness. More specifically, the person suffers from the inability to turn off a stream of consciousness that has become its own enemy, comprised of actual memories of traumatic events, distorted and fragmented memories, intrusive imageries and flashbacks, dissociated memories, unwelcome somatic sensations, negative self-commentaries running like a tickertape through the mind, fantasied and feared elaborations from childhood of the abuse experiences, and concomitant strongly dysphoric moods of anxiety and anger. (1993, p. xv)

Furthermore, the irritability and depression of PTSD can be seen in cases of bipolar disorder, and fear and anxiety can be seen in both PTSD and school phobia. According to Pasnau, "Considerable overlap in the symptoms of anxiety states and depression does exist" (1984, p. 7). Finally, some adolescents may qualify for another diagnosis in addition to PTSD (Cantwell and Baker 1989).

Learning Disabilities. The rate of concurrent psychiatric disorder is high in LDs (Glosser and Koppell 1987). Issues of social-emotional development among LDs is a real concern of teachers, and this is predicted to be the next major area from which meaningful change will come (Bender 1994). Interrelation between LD and ED also is referenced by Feinstein and Aldershof (1991), who link the two disabilities through language processing, reasoning that because LDs, by definition, have a disorder in one or more of the basic psychological processes involved in understanding or in using language, there are implications for a negative emotional cycle, which may lead to poor self-esteem, anxiety, alienation, rebellion, and, generally, interference with school functioning. Further, Bender and Wall (1994) conclude that deficits in cognitive processing, which are sufficient to cause major learning problems in academic areas, are probably sufficient to also cause major learning problems in nonacademic areas. Sabornie (1994) also found that LDs felt unintegrated, victimized, and lonely. Finally, Zentall (1993) found that 53 percent of LDs were rated by their teachers as having impulsivity and inattention.

Tourette's syndrome. In TS, interrelation has been increasingly recognized and emphasized (Towbin 1995). Leckman and Cohen (1994) refer to a broad array of behavioral difficulties in individuals with tic disorders, including disinhibited speech or conduct, impulsivity, distractibility, and motor hyperactivity. As many as 50 percent of patients with TS meet criteria for attention-deficit disorder (Cohen, Riddle, and Leckman 1984; Golden 1977; Shapiro 1981). Nolan, Gadow, and Sverd (1994) also note a correlation between vocal tics and noncompliance. Difficulty with social adaptation at school has also been noted (Golden 1977; O'Quinn and Thompson 1980) as well as difficulty maintaining age-appropriate social skills (Leckman et al. 1994). Furthermore, substantial overlap has been seen between TS and anxiety in general, with test anxiety, stuttering, and rapid talking common features (Lemons and Barber 1991), and specific problems such as phobias (fear of public transportation, being alone, being in a crowd or water, animals, and public speaking), panic attacks (Comings and Comings 1987), and obsessive-compulsive disorder (OCD) (Leckman and Cohen 1994; March, Leonard, and Swedo 1995; Rapoport, Swedo, and Leonard 1994).

Obsessive-compulsive disorder. Rapoport, Swedo, and Leonard (1994) associate various disorders with severe primary childhood OCD: Tourette's syndrome, major depression, anxiety disorders, conduct/oppositional disorder, ADD/ADHD, and eating disorders. Towbin (1995) adds that depression is commonly associated with OCD. March, Leonard, and Swedo (1995) report various overlaps in one sample of children and adolescents with OCD: tic disorders (30 percent), depression (26 percent), simple phobias (17 percent), and disruptive behavior disorders (34 percent), which include ADD, oppositional-defiant disorder (ODD), and conduct disorder (CD).

Depression. Harrington (1994) notes that most children who meet the criteria for depression are given some other primary diagnosis. This interrelation has been one of the most consistent findings in research, where an association has been found with conditions as diverse as conduct disorder, anxiety states, learning problems, hyperactivity, anorexia nervosa, and school phobia. McCauley, Carolson, and Calderon (1991) report that 70 percent of the children with a diagnosis of depression have significant somatic complaints.

Communication disorders. There appears to be a high interrelation between language deficits and psychiatric disorders. A wide range of emotional and behavioral disorders often occur in adolescence when socialization skills are language based, including anxiety, withdrawal, aggressiveness, and rigidity (Feinstein and Aldershof 1991). The reported incidence of psychopathology in speech and language clinics is about 50 percent (Cantwell and Baker 1987).

ADHD. Overactivity has been observed in numerous disorders. Shaywitz and Shaywitz (1988) have proposed several subtypes of attention-deficit disorders, among which is *ADDPlus,* an attention-deficit disorder with any co-occurring condition. For example, overactivity has been observed in anxiety disorders and in childhood depression. As far back as 1962, Krakowski noted that overactivity is not exclusive for any one specific psychopathology. The interrelation between ADHD and LD is consistently reported in the literature (Riccio, Gonzalez, and Hynd 1994). Also, clinical studies have shown a high prevalence of anxiety disorders among youngsters with ADHD (Livingston, Dykman, and Ackerman 1990). Greenhill (1991) identified three subtypes of ADHD: with conduct disorder, with major depression, and with anxiety disorder. Barkley (1989) noted that low self-esteem, poor peer acceptance and depression are common in ADHDs. Finally, Towbin and his colleagues (1992) noted the interrelation between ADHD and Tourette's syndrome as a result of the common need to overcome bodily activity and impulsivity. At this point it is not known if symptoms of ADHD in TS patients are part of the TS etiology or if these symptoms are the expression of a separate disorder (Towbin et al. 1992).

Borderline personality disorder. Individuals with BPD may experience severe impulsivity and inattentiveness at a level necessary to fulfill some criteria of attention-deficit disorder (Greenhill 1991). BPD and eating disorders also seem to be interrelated; many BPD symptoms appear to be directly relevant to functional models of eating disorders (Waller 1994). Finally, half of BPDs could also be diagnosed as having mood disorders, and there is an overlap between BPD and narcissistic and antisocial personality disorders (Sarason and Sarason 1993).

Anorexia nervosa. Harrington (1994) comments that there is a melancholic subtype of depression in which major depressive episodes include loss of interest, lack of reactivity to pleasurable stimuli, and anorexia. Rapoport, Swedo, and Leonard (1994) associate eating disorders with severe primary childhood OCD.

Conduct/oppositional disorders. McMahon and Wells (1989) found that CD youngsters are at risk for other behavior disorders and adjustment problems:

ADHD, depression, and reading disabilities. Reeves, Werry, and Elkind (1987) found only six out of 108 cases of CD and ODD without co-occurring ADHD. McManus (1989) noted that, in childhood, ADD often coexists with conduct disorder. Hendren (1991) found that many adolescents who meet the criteria for CD have other psychiatric conditions. Lewis (1991) commented that CD youngsters conceal their underlying disturbances with a boastful, ostensibly callous, facade. The more paranoid the youngsters, the more likely they will reply, "I don't care," when asked about their negative behaviors. In a way, conduct disorder is often a transitional designation used when underlying causes for aberrant behaviors have not yet been identified; it is similar to a medical diagnosis of fever with unknown origin (Lewis 1991). Finaly, youngsters with Tourette's syndrome have exhibited disinhibition, violence, aggression, and increased sexual behavior (Towbin et al. 1992).

Bipolar disorder. The most obvious interrelation with bipolar disorder is depression. Anxiety and aggressiveness also are evident. Communication problems are evident in acute mania, with speech incoherency (Costello and Costello 1992). Finally, Spivack (1994) refers to dissociativeness and distractibility, implying an attention-deficit disorder, and Weiner (1983) refers to crossover with delinquency, anorexia, school refusal, learning problems, and antisocial behavior.

School phobia. The fears of school phobia (SP) overlap with the fears of the post-traumatic stress disorder. Hyde (1977) commented that, in many cases, SP is one of a number of indications of emotional disturbance in cases of PTSD. Bernstein and Garfinkel (1986) found that 50 percent of school refusers met the *DSM-III* criteria for both depressive and anxiety disorders.

Antisocial tendencies. The impulsivity, aggressiveness, irritability, and depression evident in youngsters with antisocial tendencies are also seen in other conditions, including bipolar disorder, ADHD, and PTSD. The most obvious relation between antisocial tendency and ODD and CD is the failure to conform with social norms. Psychiatrists who study the links between violence and juvenile delinquency characterize most offenders as emotionally scarred, angry, and impulsive. Another example is the interrelation among ADHD, ODD, and bipolar disorder; such problems as negativity and noncompliance are present in all three disorders.

Anxiety disorders. Anxiety disorders have been related to many other conditions. "Almost all mental disorders are accompanied by anxiety symptoms" (Wolman and Stricker 1994, p. xi). Specific research findings attest to the interrelation of anxiety disorders and nonanxiety disorders. For example, when Kashani and Orvaschel (1988) investigated anxiety disorders in a community sample of 150 adolescents, they found that the majority who had an anxiety disorder had at least one additional concurrent nonanxiety diagnosis.

27

Staying Hopeful and Attuned

Hope is the thing with feathers.
                    Emily Dickinson

A seventh-grade girl began to deteriorate in her physical appearance and to show other troubling signs. Her teachers became concerned. One day on a mathematics quiz paper she wrote in the margin, "If idiots could fly this place would be an airport." That night she was admitted on an emergency basis to a psychiatric hospital and diagnosed with depression. She had not been identified previously as in need of counseling or special attention, and her deterioration had occurred in just a few weeks.

One contribution of a book such as this is to provide information that will enable teachers and others who work with adolescents to reflect informatively on the behaviors they see daily. Troubled students may be more readily spotted.

Our knowledge about students who have emotional and behavioral disorders is fragile, even more fragile than they are, try as we may to acquire knowlege about them. There is so much that eludes our knowing. No matter how many facts, observations, and anecdotes we collect, there will always be questions. No sooner do we have an insight than something unpredictable or surprising happens. Adolescents who have emotional and behavioral disorders remain in some part a mystery. Likely, it will always be so.

In part, there is uncertainty because these individuals are still growing and changing. At this stage of life, some problems are subtle, others are overt, and often signs are a mixture of both. While we may capture some of the essence of their being, their becoming is even less clear. Numerous emotional and behavioral disorders are only beginning to be recognized in adolescence. This is no doubt due in part to the fact that this is a formative period. Adolescents are still evolving from childhood to adulthood. Development is rapid compared with the adult phase, and diagnoses often are made tentatively and conservatively.

Consequently, we need to monitor these students closely because some changes are rapid, certainly more rapid than adult changes. Problems may develop quickly, or so it seems. The emotional and behavioral signs can serve as working hypotheses.

A hypothesis can be forming when an adolescent tells a friend that the friend is on his "hit list"; when he shows cruelty toward animals; and when he brings a weapon to school. The Oregon high schooler who killed his parents and two students in May 1998, the day after being expelled for possessing a weapon on school grounds, was a candidate for a working hypothesis. Instead, those who knew him expressed surprise at the incident.

While we may reduce the element of surprise when troubled youngsters commit troubling acts and show obvious signs of disturbance, these youngsters, of course, are not completely knowable. They remain somewhat phantomlike, spirits that always elude us, no matter how hard we look.

Ancient Greek myth describes how Pandora, the first woman dispatched to Earth, bearing gifts from the gods and goddesses, brought a golden box that she was told never to open. However, Pandora's curiosity got the best of her, and she opened it. Terrible things flew out: some had wings, some slithered and crawled, and some had pointed ears, long tails, and sharp fangs. The creatures, personifying evil, envy, greed, sickness, and sorrow, were carried to every corner of the earth by the winds.

Many are curious about youngsters with emotional and behavioral disorders but are afraid to open the box, as it were, for fear that terrible things will fly out. Hope, though, is the thing with feathers.

Many people connote evil, envy, greed, sickness, and sorrow with the label of emotional disturbance (ED). This book was intended to dispel some of that fear. Within its pages are realistic facts about disorders and stories of real students who exemplify those disorders. They are, above all, youngsters with normal hopes and dreams, not terrible creatures who should be kept in a sealed box. They have challenges, and they are challenging, but typically they are not evil.

Learning more about adolescents with emotional and behavioral disorders will not unleash a torrent of emotional and behavioral mayhem. Clarification and understanding should serve, rather, to unleash competence and orderly thoughts to apply to their challenges, which are very much earth-bound.

The myth of Pandora also involved Hope, a creature from the box who stayed to help humans fight the evil that was unleashed. Hope stands for that part of us that needs something to push us forward. Students with emotional and behavioral disorders typically lack hope; they frequently show so much focus on the present that the future holds no meaning. Their inability to detach from the seriousness of the present denies them a future in which to believe and hope. Feedback from others about their disorderly behaviors leaves them feeling even more hopeless and powerless to change. We can build hope that their discord is not necessarily a life sentence.

Students in discord, as has been clear throughout this book, do not blend into the human symphony; they cannot keep a social tune. With ears attuned, educators who understand these disorders and the challenges that face discordant students will hear the missed notes and off-key notes and be able to teach these students to blend their sounds.

28

They Care If the Sun
Is on Fire

For she was the maker of the song she sang.
Wallace Stevens

Rick's poem, which set the tone for this book, called our attention to the sounds around us that make up our world. Rick's sounds, however, are intrusive, boring, angry, painful, oppositional, gossipy, mistaken, or swing too quickly from quiet to loud. There appears to be little harmony in Rick's perspective, as in his life.

Like all adolescents with emotional and behavioral disorders, Rick wants to blend in with the sounds of this world. For a complexity of reasons, internal and external, he, and they, cannot. Like all adolescents with emotional and behavioral disorders, Rick is caught up in the sounds of his own small world.

A high school student in Jones, Virginia wrote a poem that captures the essential difference between adolescents who can blend in and those who cannot. In that poem Hensley asked, "Who cares if the sun is on fire?" The poet answered her question by philosophizing that the sun is the only light we have (Hensley 1994).

Adolescents in discord cannot be philosophical; they cannot stand back and regard life lightly and with objectivity. They seem to care too much, and life is heavy on their shoulders. Normal adolescents, on the other hand, can regard life with a balanced perspective, with all its imperfections. They embrace a wider world.

Hensley's sentiments are echoed in the poem, "A Slant of Sun," by Stephen Crane, an intense man known for sensitivity toward children and for his extraordinary study of men amidst the turmoil and clamor of war. Crane's sentiments are those of an emotionally healthy person who can see that the sounds of our environment, both social and physical, are primarily beautiful, positive, and inspiring, even if cacophonous. For example: "The senseless babble of hens and wise men, a cluttered incoherency that says at the stars: O God, save us!" These images contrast with Rick's and portray in a few words the essential difference between one who is in discord and one who is in harmony with the world.

People in synchrony see the full spectrum of colors and hear the full range of sounds. Despite awareness of life's ups and downs, they can feel whole. They can stand back and scan the horizon, taking in everything in full measure without feeling small or diminished. People in synchrony see and hear, as Crane did, collisions and cries, rumbling wheels, hoofbeats, bells, welcomes, farewells, love calls, final moans, and voices of joy and despair. In short, people in accord hear all the sounds that make up life's song and feel that they blend.

Students in discord are, on the other hand, consumed by the sounds that most appropriately accompany their own emotions and behaviors. If their life is a film, the score is not harmoniousous; it is filled with harsh, unpleasant, abrupt, sluggish, extreme, painful, and annoying sounds. The adolescent in discord marches, as the saying goes, to a different drummer. These students are not viable parts of the human symphony. They hear discordant sounds, read discordant notes, and feel apart.

These students also see the world differently. They cannot perceive that the sun is the only true light we have and believe that the world is aglow, whether night or day, because of a positive outlook, belief, and hope, or an enduring light. Rather, for them there are shadows, dark places, and unevenly lit spots.

We do not have to tell them that they are not a part of the symphony. Their behaviors may appear to say otherwise, but they are acutely aware of their discord. They would like to blend in and indulge in their own specialness, that healthy, actualizing balance that those in accord show: "You pick out your own song from the uproar, line by line, and at last throw back your head and sing it" (Levertov 1965, p. 42).

If there is one thing to remember about adolescents with emotional and behavioral disorders, it is that they cannot throw their heads back and sing. They are too much with the world, too bogged down with their thoughts and feelings to detach and sing. More likely, their heads are down.

They care if the sun is on fire. Recall Fred, who worries obsessively about earthquakes 6,000 miles away. A star that is burning billions of miles from Earth might as well be at arm's length from such a youngster. If bipolar, a disturbed youngster will be touched by fire as he soars maniacally toward the star rather than waiting for the light to reach him.

With our understanding and help, such students can learn to play in tune. We can help them accustom to the normal sounds and sights and learn to read the music and sing with us. The discordant thoughts and feelings may never entirely relent and change, but the youngsters can be helped to join us. "But when their rhythms mesh then though the pain of living never lets up the singing begins" (Levertov 1965, p. 74).

Appendix

Primary Sample
Case Synopses

CASE SYNOPSIS: ADAM

Background: Positive Factors
> Father devoted to Adam; close relationship
> Normal growth and development with early speech
> Sensitive and caring nature
> Well-developed interests
> Cognitively, superior intelligence
> High-average to superior academic achievement

Background: Negative Factors
> Early temper tantrums
> Parental divorce
> Difficult relationships with stepsiblings
> Custodial battles over issue of medicating Adam for ADHD
> Mother frequently used physical means to discipline
> History of mental illness on maternal side
> Mother hospitalized at seventh month of pregnancy with severe
>   colitis, edema
> Difficult infancy: colic, milk allergy, sleeplessness
> Chronic ear infections until age five

Signs of Emotional-Behavioral Problems
> Poor self-control
> Angry, hostile behavior
> Poor interpersonal relationships
> Academic underachievement; inconsistent performance
> Inability to accept criticism; low frustration tolerance
> Distractibility
> Impulsivity
> Short attention span
> Hyperactivity
> Accident prone (e.g., at age four bit tongue in half)
> Low self-esteem
> Disorganized

Special Education Eligibility
> Emotional disability

Psychiatric Diagnosis
> Attention-deficit disorder with hyperactivity (age nine)

CASE SYNOPSIS: ANDY

Background: Positive Factors
> Highly educated parents
> Intact family with three children: Andy and two sisters
> Normal development overall
> Strong ability in music
> Gentle and sensitive nature
> Responsible about home chores
> Good relationships with adults

Background: Negative Factors
> Cognitively, low average intelligence (scores ranging from high
> > average to borderline retardation); very weak vocabulary, verbal
> > comprehension and social judgment
> Weak visual-motor integration
> Deficits in reading comprehension and mathematics reasoning
> Conflictual father-son relationship; both quick-tempered
> Early gross and fine motor skills in low-average range; slight
> > tremor in one hand
> Nighttime enuresis until age eleven years
> Ambiopia with five eye surgeries by age five years; chronic depth
> > imperception
> Dependence on adults

Signs of Emotional-Behavioral Problems
> Poor interpersonal relationships
> Verbal outbursts and physical aggression
> Distractibility
> Impulsivity
> Perseverative, fragmented thinking
> Poor concentration and attention
> Depression
> Bit other children during kindergarten
> Younger friends
> Restless

Special Education Eligibility
> Learning disability
> Emotional disability

Psychiatric Diagnosis
> Overanxious disorder of childhood

CASE SYNOPSIS: BILLY

Background: Positive Factors
Intact family with three sons; Billy is the oldest
Family united around religion
Rapid growth and development
Cognitively, average intelligence with above-average verbal
intelligence and reasoning

Background: Negative Factors
Chronic ear infections until the age of three years; hip surgery at
four years
Migraine headaches and episodes of blacking out
Mother grew up in an abusive situation
Continuous worldwide family relocations

Signs of Emotional-Behavioral Problem
Depression
Isolative and withdrawn
Academic underachievement
Flat affect and lack of enthusiasm
Passive approach to conversation and social interaction
Feels stressed
Easily frustrated and anxious about performance on schoolwork
Poor self-concept
Somatic complaints (fatigue, dizziness, aches and pains)

Special Education Eligibility
Emotional disability
Learning disability

Psychiatric Diagnosis
Attention-deficit disorder (without hyperactivity)

Psychological Diagnosis
Significant deficits in areas most susceptible to anxiety and
concentration difficulties as well as psychomotor
speed and efficiency; serious emotional concerns,
including symptoms of moderate to severe depression
and anxiety, perceptions that lead to a view of the world as
threatening and rejecting

CASE SYNOPSIS: CHRIS

Background: Positive Factors
  Highly educated parents
  Good relationship with older sister
  Normal growth and development
  Sociable with many friends
  Talented in electronics and construction; strong knowledge of
    science
  Cognitively, superior nonverbal intelligence; overall above-
    average intelligence

Background: Negative Factors
  Parental divorce
  Fragmented custody arrangement
  Sibling rivalry beteween Chris and younger brother
  Gestation complicated by placenta previa
  Mild jaundice and milk allergy in early infancy
  Body rocking and head banging from infancy to early childhood

Signs of Emotional-Behavioral Problems
  Apprended for vandalism, shoplifting, and driving without a
    license
  Academic underachievement, notably in written language and
    reading
  Substance abuse (marijuana, alcohol)
  Depression and mood swings
  Impaired reality testing
  Impulsivity and poor self-control
  Diminished capacity for stress tolerance
  Low self-esteem
  Restless

Special Education Eligibility
  Learning disability (second through fourth grades)
  Emotional disability

Psychiatric Diagnosis
  Attention-deficit disorder with hyperactivity (age eight)
  Depression
  Bipolar disorder

CASE SYNOPSIS: FRED

Background: Positive Factors
>Intact, stable family with two children: Fred and a younger sister
>Early growth and development uncertain due to mother's young
>>age and language barrier
>
>Family united religiously and socially through extended family
>Affectionate relationship between Fred and sister
>Well-developed interests: video games, TV sports programs
>Cognitively, strong visual-motor integration
>Relative strengths in reading and general knowledge

Background: Negative Factors
>Mother in last phase of pregnancy when parents emigrated from
>>Afghanistan; saw no physician during pregnancy
>
>Severe language delay and disruptive behavior exhibited in preschool
>Father worked long hours; both parents young
>In early childhood no interest in toys
>Sleep difficulty
>Mother had few parenting skills; Fred was toilet trained after age three
>Put on Ritalin at age four for uncontrollability, hyperactivity
>Lack of language stimulation
>Family isolation in neighborhood of residence
>Cognitively, low-average intelligence, with large discrepancy between
>>verbal and nonverbal abilities; auditory discrimination
>>weakness
>
>Poorly developed social perception
>Relatively weak mathematics and written language skills

Signs of Emotional-Behavioral Problems
>Peculiar interests such as reading and memorizing road maps
>Asked irrelevant questions; strange reactions to people
>Anxiety; preoccupation with fears
>Restless
>Inappropriate behaviors (for example, rocking, talking to self)
>Extreme communication problems; no eye contact
>No friends
>Limited insight into own or others' behaviors
>Sadness and pessimism
>Oversensitivity to situational variables
>Perseveration

Special Education Eligibility (singly or in combinations over time)

Autism	Emotional disability
Learning disability	Speech/language disorder

Psychological Diagnosis
>Central language processing disorder

CASE SYNOPSIS: JAMES

Background: Positive Factors
>   Normal and healthy development; rapid speech development
>   Cognitively, very superior intelligence
>   Mother provided model of a hard worker
>   Well-developed interests including Boy Scouts and 4-H Club
>   Creative thinker

Background: Negative Factors
>   Single parent with two jobs; absentee, irresponsible father
>   Enmeshed mother-son relationship
>   Early gestation complicated by toxemia
>   Premature baby needing incubation support; difficult delivery;
>   mother did not see physician until fifth month of pregnancy
>   Chronic constipation in infancy and early childhood, with
>   frequent soiling accidents
>   Ear infections and severe boil in early childhood
>   Weak short-term memory and visual-motor integration

Signs of Emotional-Behavioral Problems
>   Immature and silly behavior
>   Negative self-image
>   Depression and pessimism
>   Rigid thinking
>   Oppositional
>   Physical aggression
>   Distancing from others

Special Education Eligibility
>   Emotional disability

Psychiatric Diagnosis
>   None at the time data were collected

Psychological Diagnosis
>   Serious social and emotional concerns; symptoms of severe
>   depression

CASE SYNOPSIS: JESSE

Background: Positive Factors
>Intact family with two children: Jesse and a younger sister
>Normal development and growth
>Cognitively, average intelligence overall
>Strong verbal abstract reasoning

Background: Negative Factors
>Significant history of mental illness on maternal side
>Mother diagnosed as having a bipolar disorder
>Delayed fine and gross motor development; couldn't ride a bicycle
>>until age eight
>Numerous ear infections from infancy to age eight
>A bad fall and concussion at thirty months, followed by staring
>>spells; later EKG showed brain seizure activity
>Frequent moves due to father's military career
>Weak visual-motor integration and quantitative reasoning
>Underachievement in reading and written language

Signs of Emotional-Behavioral Problems
>Depression
>Distractibility
>Suicide attempt at age eleven
>Sleeplessness
>Social isolation
>Feelings of inadequacy and poor self-esteem
>Indecisiveness
>Easily upset and fearful
>Tactile, visual, and gustatory hallucinations

Special Education Eligibility
>Learning disability
>Emotional disability

Psychiatric and Psychological Diagnoses
>Major depression
>Possible bipolar disorder
>Possible thought disorder involving paranoid ideation

Neurological Diagnosis
>Chronic muscle contraction headaches

CASE SYNOPSIS: JOEL

Background: Positive Factors
>   Normal and healthy growth; rapid development
>   Good relationships with parents and much older brother
>   Family in U.S. and Portugal doted on Joel
>   High-average cognitive abilities, with superior memory
>   Well-developed interests: soccer, collecting baseball and football cards,
>   video games

Background: Negative Factors
>   Mother did not speak English
>   Parental discipline varied from soft (mother) to strict (father)
>   Parents indulged Joel; he had few responsibilities and many
>   possessions
>   Small physical stature
>   Below-average achievement in mathematics
>   Cognitively, weak auditory processing along with below-average
>   general information and numerical understanding, and nonverbal
>   abilities stronger than verbal abilities overall

Signs of Emotional-Behavioral Problems
>   Impulsivity
>   Poor concentration
>   Disorganized
>   Distractibility
>   Restless
>   Accident prone
>   Poor interpersonal relationships
>   Poor self-esteem
>   Oppositional
>   Unable to follow rules

Special Education Eligibility
>   Emotional disability
>   Learning disability

Psychiatric Diagnosis
>   Attention-deficit disorder with hyperactivity (age nine)

CASE SYNOPSIS: LAURA

Background: Positive Factors
> Normal and healthy growth; rapid development
> Intact family with three boys and Laura
> Highly educated parents
> Average cognitive abilities with superior general knowledge
> Above-grade level achievement in writing mechanics, science,
> > social studies, and humanities

Background: Negative Factors
> Parental discipline varied from passive (father) to inconsistent
> > (mother)
> Physical aggression among siblings
> Underachievement in mathematics and reading
> Deficient visual-motor integration
> Cognitively, large difference between verbal and nonverbal
> > abilities (verbal higher)

Signs of Emotional-Behavioral Problems
> Oppositional and defiant
> Conflictual relationships with family members
> Distancing from others
> Impulsivity
> Easily frustrated
> Mood swings
> Aggressive outbursts
> Unpredictability
> Shoplifting and stealing at home
> Vandalism
> Lying
> Vulgarity
> Sadistic treatment of animals
> Hallucinations (visual and auditory)
> Preoccupation with sexual matters

Special Education Eligibility
> Emotional disability

Psychiatric Diagnosis
> Bipolar disorder
> Antisocial tendencies

CASE SYNOPSIS: MICHAEL

Background: Positive Factors
> Intact family with four children; Michael is the youngest by many
> > years
> Family united around religion
> Normal growth and development
> Cognitively, high-average intelligence
> Average to high-average academic achievement

Background: Negative Factors
> Older parents who expressed feelings of impatience with
> > parenting duties
> Hospitalized for severe cough, tics, convulsion-like episodes,
> > and blurred vision; psychiatric hospitalization ensued
> Mother smoked during pregnancy
> Repeated kindergarten due to poor peer relationships
> Overweight
> Asthma
> Color blindness
> Cognitively, weak visual-motor integration

Signs of Emotional-Behavioral Problems
> Poor interpersonal relationships with peers and authority figures
> Fears and anxiety
> Frequent falling
> Poor personal hygiene
> Frequent complaints of fatigue and illness
> Auditory and visual hallucinations
> Low frustration tolerance
> Guarded and suspicious
> Idiosyncratic, inflexible thinking style; coherent but sometimes
> > bizarre ideas
> Depression
> Anger

Special Education Eligibility
> Emotional disability
> Physical disability

Psychiatric Diagnosis
> Tourette's syndrome (tentative)

Psychological Diagnosis
> Significant emotional concerns; symptoms of depression and
> > anxiety

CASE SYNOPSIS: OLIVIA

Background: Positive Factors
> Intact family with two children: Olivia and an older brother
> Father in recovery program for alcoholism
> Athletic, creative, and artistic
> Empathic nature
> Well-developed interests: soccer, track, piano, and jazz dancing
> Cognitively, high-average intelligence; strong fund of knowledge
> Sociable with numerous friends
> Conscientious; makes effort in school; is organized
> Strong oral communicator

Background: Negative Factors
> Father's alcoholism and drug abuse
> Father's physical abuse of son; verbal abuse of entire family
> Father's job instability
> Two parental separations
> Sexual abuse at age seven by brother's friend
> History of mental illness and substance abuse on both sides of the family
> Brother's physical abuse of Olivia
> Asthma and allergies
> Mother experienced vaginal bleeding and toxemia during last term of
>> pregnancy
> Eating difficulties in early childhood; vomiting whenever ill or stressed
> Tubes placed in ears at eighteen months and again at three years
> Psychiatric hospitalization at age ten due to refusal to get out of bed during
>> the day, sleeplessness, nightmares, and suicidal ideation
> Cognitively, below-average visual-motor integration
> Underachievement in reading

Signs of Emotional-Behavioral Problems
> Memory lapses
> Poor concentration and attention
> Anxious; episodes of blanking out
> Poor self-esteem
> Depression
> Feelings of hopelessness
> Impulsivity
> Insecure
> Slow academic progress

Special Education Eligibility
> Learning disability (grades three to five)
> Emotional disability

Psychiatric Diagnosis
> Major depression

CASE SYNOPSIS: RICK

Background: Positive Factors
> Normal growth and development except for delayed walking (sixteen
> > months)
>
> Intact family with two sons: Rick and an older brother
> Parents highly educated
> Cognitively, high-average intelligence
> Well-developed interests, including computers, music, coin
> > collecting

Background: Negative Factors
> Mother experienced chronic morning sickness during
> > pregnancy; she took over-the-counter medication without
> > consulting a physician
>
> History of mental illness on maternal side (mania)
> Severe sibling rivalry with violence and aggression
> Inconsistent parenting
> Early tantrums
> Allergies and chronic ear infections
> Cognitively, weak social reasoning, visual-motor integration, and
> > auditory processing
>
> Weak written language skills

Signs of Emotional-Behavioral Problems
> Stealing
> Impulsivity
> Poor interpersonal relationships
> Poor personal hygiene; body odor
> Feeling of hopelessness
> Physical aggression
> Low frustration tolerance
> Distractibility
> Psoriasis under stress
> Academic underachievement
> Sleeping in class
> Talking about killing people
> Hand tremor
> Distorted judgment
> Inflexible thinking style
> Low self-esteem

Special Education Eligibility
> Learning disability (grades four to six)
> Emotional disability

Psychiatric Diagnosis
> Bipolar disorder

CASE SYNOPSIS: SARA

Background Factors: Positive Factors
>   Normal and healthy growth; rapid development, with more female
>   hormones than usual
>   Average cognitive abilities overall
>   Good relationship with mother and younger brother
>   Average educational achievement, with superior reading skills
>   Motivated to learn, be successful, and to accept interventions
>   such as medication, counseling, and hospitalization when
>   needed

Background Factors: Negative Factors
>   Mother's surgery for endometriosis early in pregnancy; toxemia
>   late in pregnancy
>   Parental divorce
>   Relationship with stepfather confrontational
>   Biological father unavailable for the most part
>   Sexual abuse at age five by adult male; again at age five by nine-
>   year-old girl
>   Attended five different schools between preschool and grade six
>   Cognitively, a split between verbal and nonverbal abilities; weak
>   in visual processing and visual-motor integration

Signs of Emotional-Behavioral Problems
>   Mistrustful of others: adults or peers
>   Difficulty sleeping
>   Auditory and visual hallucinations
>   Depression
>   Poor concentration
>   Suicidal ideation
>   Headaches and stomachaches
>   Perfectionism
>   Extreme weight loss

Special Education Eligibility
>   Emotional disability

Psychiatric Diagnosis
>   Anorexia nervosa (age eleven)
>   Obsessive-compulsive disorder
>   Post-traumatic stress disorder

Bibliography

Adelson, J. 1975. The development of ideology in adolescence. In S. E. Dragastin and G. H. Elder, Jr. (Eds.), *Adolescence in the life cycle*. Washington, DC: Hemisphere.

Adelson, J., and O'Neill, R. 1966. The growth of political ideas in adolescence: The sense of community. *Journal of Personality and Social Psychology* 4: 295-306.

Alley, G., and Deshler, D. 1979. *Teaching the learning disabled adolescent: Strategies and methods*. Denver: Love.

American Psychiatric Association. 1994. *Diagnostic and statistical manual of mental disorders (DSM-IV)*. Washington, DC: APA.

Anderson, J. C., et al. 1987. DSM-III disorders in preadolescent children. *Archives of General Psychiatry* 44: 69-76.

Anhalt, K., McNeil, C. B., and Bahl, A. B. 1998. The ADHD classroom kit: A whole-classroom approach for managing disruptive behavior. *Psychology in the Schools* 35 (1): 67-79.

Anthony, E. J. 1975. Two contrasting types of adolescent depression and their treatment. In A. H. Esman (Ed.), *The psychology of adolescence*. New York: International Universities Press.

Argetsinger, A. 1995. Confronting a "quiet" problem. *Washington Post*. May 21: B1, B6.

Aseltine, R. H., Jr., Gore, S., and Colten, M. E. 1994. Depression and the social development context of adolescence. *Journal of Personality and Social Psychology* 67: 252-63.

August, G. J., and Garfinkel, B. D. 1989. Behavioral and cognitive subtypes of ADHD. *Journal of the American Academy of Child and Adolescent Psychiatry* 28: 739-48.

Ballard, M., Corman, L., Gottlieb, J., and Kaufman, M. 1977. Improving the social status of mainstreamed retarded children. *Journal of Educational Psychology* 69: 605-11.

Baller, W., and Charles, D. C. 1968. *The psychology of human growth and development.* New York: Holt, Rinehart, and Winston.

Barber, C. C., Rosenblatt, A., Harris, L-M., and Attkisson, C. C. 1992. Use of mental health services among severely emotionally disturbed children and adolescents in San Francisco. *Journal of Child and Family Studies* 1: 183-207.

Barkley, R. A. 1978. Recent developments in research on hyperactive children. *Journal of Pediatric Psychology* 3: 158-63.

———. 1981. Hyperactivity. In E. Mash and L. Terdal (Eds.), *Behavioral assessment of childhood disorders.* New York: Guilford.

———. 1989. Attention deficit-hyperactivity disorder. In E. J. Mash and R. A. Barkley (Eds.), *Treatment of childhood disorders.* New York: Guilford.

———. 1994. Foreword. In G. J. DuPaul and G. Stoner (Eds.), *ADHD in the schools: Assessment and intervention strategies.* New York: Guilford.

Barkley, R. A., Fischer, M., Edelbrock, C., and Smallish, L. 1990. The adolescent outcome of hyperactive children diagnosed by research criteria: I. An 8-year prospective follow-up study. *Journal of the American Academy of Child and Adolescent Psychiatry* 29: 546-57.

Beck, A. T. 1976. *Cognitive therapy and the emotional disorders.* New York: International Universities Press.

Beck, A. T., and Freeman, A. 1990. *Cognitive therapy for personality disorders.* New York: Guilford.

Beck, J. S. 1995. *Cognitive therapy: Basics and beyond.* New York: Guilford.

Bedrosian, J., and Prutting, C. 1978. Communicative performance of mentally retarded adults in four conversational settings. *Journal of Speech and Hearing Research* 21: 79-95.

Bell, A. P. 1969. Role modeling of fathers in adolescence and adulthood. *Journal of Counseling Psychology* 16: 30-35.

Bemis, K. M 1978. Current approaches to the etiology and treatment of anorexia nervosa. *Psychological Bulletin* 85: 593-617.

Bender, L., and Grugett, A. E. 1952. Incest: A synthesis of data. *American Journal of Orthopsychiatry* 12: 825-37.

Bender, W. N. 1994. Social-emotional development: The task and the challenge. *Learning Disability Quarterly* 17 (4): 250-52.

Bender, W. N., and Wall, M. E. 1994. Social-emotional development of students with learning disabilities. *Learning Disability Quarterly* 17 (4): 323-41.

Benditsky, H. 1978. *A psychosomatic approach to Gilles de la Tourette's syndrome.* Unpublished doctoral thesis, Yeshiva University.

Benedek, E. D. 1985. Children and disaster: Emerging issues. *Psychiatric Annals* 15: 168-72.

Benjamin, L. S., and Wonderlich, S. A. 1994. Social perceptions and borderline personality disorder: The relation to mood disorders. *Journal of Abnormal Psychology* 103 (4): 610-24.

Bernstein, G. A., and Garfinkel, B. B. 1986. School phobia: The overlap of affective and anxiety disorders. *Journal of the American Academy of Child Psychiatry* 25: 235-41.

Billingsley, B. B., and Cross, L. H. 1991. Predictors of commitment, job satisfaction, and intent to stay in teaching: A comparison of general and special education. *Journal of Special Education* 25: 453-71.

Bishop, D.V.M. 1994. Developmental disorders of speech and language. In M. Rutter, E. Taylor, and L. Hersov (Eds.), *Child and adolescent psychiatry* (3d ed.). London: Blackwell Scientific.

Blatt, B. 1994. The definition of mental retardation. *Mental Retardation* 32 (1): 71-72.

Bockner, S. 1959. Gilles de la Tourette's disease. *Journal of Mental Science* 105: 1078-81.

Bolger, H. 1965. The case method. In B. B. Wolman (Ed.), *Handbook of clinical psychology*. New York: McGraw-Hill.

Bos, C. S., and Tierney, R. J. 1984. Inferential reading abilities of mildly mentally retarded and nonretarded students. *American Journal of Mental Deficiency* 89: 75-82.

Boucher, C. R. 1984. Pragmatics: The verbal language of learning disabled and nondisabled boys. *Learning Disability Quarterly* 7 (3): 271-86.

_____ . 1986. Pragmatics: The meaning of verbal language in learning disabled and nondisabled boys. *Learning Disability Quarterly* 9 (4): 285-94.

Boudah, D. J., Schumacher, J. B., and Deshler, D. D. 1997. Collaborative instruction: Is it an effective option for inclusion in secondary classrooms? *Learning Disability Quarterly* 20 (4): 293-316.

Bourget, D., Gagnon, A., and Bradford, J.M.W. 1988. Satanism in a psychiatric adolescent population. *Canadian Journal of Psychiatry* 33: 197-202.

Bower, E. 1982. Defining emotional disturbance: Public policy and research. *Psychology in the Schools* 19: 55-60.

Bowlby, J. 1969. *Attachment*. New York: Basic Books.

Briere, J. 1984. The effects of childhood sexual abuse on later psychological functioning: Defining a "post-sexual-abuse syndrome." Washington, DC: Paper presented at the Third National Conference on Sexual Victimization of Children.

Briere, J., and Runtz, M. 1985. Symptomatology associated with prior sexual abuse in a nonclinical sample. Los Angeles: Paper presented at the annual meeting of the American Psychological Association.

Bronheim, S. 1991. An educator's guide to Tourette syndrome. *Journal of Learning Disabilities* 24 (1): 17-22.

Brooks-Gunn, J., and Reiter, E. O. 1990. The role of pubertal processes. In S. S. Feldman and G. R. Elliott (Eds.), *At the threshold: The developing adolescent*. Cambridge, MA: Harvard University.

Browne, A., and Finkelhor, D. 1986. Impact of child sexual abuse: A review of the research. *Psychological Bulletin* 99: 66-77.

Brozo, W. G. 1990. Hiding out in the secondary classroom: Coping strategies of unsuccessful readers. *Journal of Reading* 33: 324-28.

Bruch, H. 1966. Anorexia nervosa and its differential diagnosis. *Journal of Nervous and Mental Disease* 141: 555-66.

Bruininks, R. H., Rynders, J. E., and Gross, J. C. 1974. Social acceptance of mildly retarded pupils in resource rooms and regular classes. *American Journal of Mental Deficiency* 78: 377-83.

Bruininks, R. H., Warfield, G., and Stealey, D. S. 1982. The mentally retarded.

In E. L. Meyen (Ed.), *Exceptional children and youth in today's schools* (2nd ed.). Denver: Love.

Brumbach, R. A., Dietz-Schmidt, S., and Weinberg, W. 1977. Depression in children referred to an educational diagnostic center: Diagnosis and treatment and analysis of criteria and literature review. *Disorders of the Nervous System* 38: 529-35.

Brumbach, R. A., Staton, R. D., and Wilson, H. 1980. Neuropsychological study of children during and after remission of endogenous depressive episodes. *Perceptual and Motor Skills* 50: 1163-67.

Bruner, J. 1983. *Child's talk*. New York: W. W. Norton.

Bryan, R. H., and Bryan, J. H. 1975. *Understanding learning disabilities*. Sherman Oaks, CA: Alfred A. Knopf.

Bryan, T. 1974. Peer popularity of learning disabled children. *Journal of Learning Disabilities* 7: 261-68.

Bryant, E. S., et al. 1995. Correlates of major and minor offending among youth with severe emotional disturbance. *Journal of Emotional and Behavioral Disorders* 3 (2): 76-84.

Buhler, C. 1933; 1959. *The course of human life as a psychological problem*. Gottingen: Verlag fur Psychologie (2d ed.); Leipzig: S. Hirzel.

_____. 1968. The course of human life as a psychological problem. *Human Development* 11: 184-200.

Bullock, L. M., Ellis, L. L., and Wilson, M. J. 1994. Knowledge/skills needed by teachers who work with students with severe emotional/behavioral disorders: A revisitation. *Behavioral Disorders* 19 (2): 108-25.

Burcham, B., Carlson, L., and Milich, R. 1993. Promising school-based practices for students with attention deficit disorder. *Exceptional Children* 60 (2): 174-80.

Burd, L., et al. 1992. Tourette syndrome and learning disabilities. *Journal of Learning Disabilities* 25 (9): 598-604.

Burgess, A. W., Groth, A. N., and McCausland, M. 1981. Child sex initiation rings. *American Journal of Orthopsychiatry* 51: 110-19.

Burgess, A. W., Hartman, C. R., McCausland, M. P., and Powers, P. 1984. Response patterns in children and adolescents exploited through sex rings and pornography. *American Journal of Psychiatry* 141: 656-62.

Burket, R. C., Myers, W. C., Lyles, W. B., and Carrera, F., III. 1994. Adolescent involvement in witchcraft and Satanism. *Journal of Adolescence* 17: 41-52.

Burleson, B. R., and Keenkel, A. W. 1994. Socialization of emotional support skills in childhood: The influence of parents and peers. Indianapolis, IN: Poster presented at the biennial convention of the Society for Research in Child Development.

Burt, C. E. 1994. Diagnosing attention disorders. *Families Newspaper* 3 (10): 5-6.

Caldwell, B. 1996. Removing the noose. *Washington Post Magazine*. November 10: 14-19, 30-32.

Campbell, P., and Siperstein, G. N. 1994. *Improving social competence: A resource for elementary school teachers*. Boston: Allyn & Bacon.

Campbell, R. J. 1989. *Psychiatric dictionary*. New York: Oxford University Press.

Campbell, S. B. 1986. Developmental issues in childhood anxiety. In R.

Gittelman (Ed.), *Anxiety disorders of childhood.* New York: Guilford.

Cantwell, D. P., and Baker, L. 1987. *Developmental speech and language disorders.* New York: Guilford.

_____ . 1989. Anxiety disorders. In L.K.G. Hsu and M. Hersen (Eds.), *Recent developments in adolescent psychiatry.* New York: Wiley.

_____ . 1991. Manifestations of depressive affect in adolescence. *Journal of Youth and Adolescence* 20 (2): 121-33.

Cardell, C. D., and Parmar, R. S. 1988. Teacher perceptions of temperament characteristics of children classified as learning disabled. *Journal of Learning Disabilities* 21: 497-502.

Carlson, G. A., and Strober, M. 1983. Affective disorders in adolescence. In D. P. Cantwell and G. A. Carlson (Eds.), *Affective disorders in childhood.* New York: SP Medical and Scientific Books.

Carr, C. 1994. *The alienist.* New York: Random House.

Carr, E. G., and Durand, V. M. 1992. See me, help me. In K. Freiberg (Ed.), *Educating exceptional children.* Guilford, CT: Dushkin.

Carr, S. C., and Punzo, R. P. 1993. The effects of self-monitoring of academic accuracy and productivity on the performance of students with behavioral disorders. *Behavioral Disorders* 18 (4): 241-50.

Carter, A. S., Pauls, D. L., Leckman, J. F., and Cohen, D. J. 1994. A prospective longitudinal study of Gilles de la Tourette's syndrome. *Journal of the American Academy of Child and Adolescent Psychiatry* 33 (3): 377-85.

Cassiday, K. L., McNally, R. J., and Zeitlin, S. B. 1992. Cognitive processing of trauma cues in rape victims with post-traumatic stress disorder. *Cognitive Therapy and Research* 16: 283-95.

Center, D. B. 1988. *Curriculum and teaching strategies for students with behavioral disorders.* Englewood Cliffs, NJ: Prentice-Hall.

Challas, G., Chapel, J. L., and Jenkins, R. L. 1967. Tourette's disease: Control of symptoms and clinical course. *International Journal of Neuropsychiatry* 3 (1): 96-101.

Cheney, D., and Barringer, C. 1995. Teacher competence, student diversity, and staff training for the inclusion of middle school students with emotional and behavioral disorders. *Journal of Emotional and Behavioral Disorders* 3 (3): 174-82.

Clarizio, H. F. 1992a. Social maladjustment and emotional disturbance: Problems and positions I. *Psychology in the Schools* 29: 131-40.

_____ . 1992b. Social maladjustment and emotional disturbance: Problems and positions II. *Psychology in the Schools* 29: 331-41.

Cohen, D. J., Detlor, J., Young, J. G., and Shaywitz, B. A. 1980. Clonidine ameliorates Gilles de la Tourette's syndrome. *Archives of General Psychiatry* 37: 1350-57.

Cohen, D. J., Riddle, M. A., and Leckman, J. F. 1984. Tourette's syndrome. In D. V. Jeste and R. J. Wyatt (Eds.), *Neuropsychiatric movement disorders.* Washington, DC: American Psychiatric Press.

Cole, P. M., and Zahn-Waxler, C. 1992. Emotional dysregulation in disruptive behavior disorders. In D. Cicchetti and S. L. Toth (Eds.), *Rochester symposium on developmental psychopathology* (vol. 4). Rochester, NY: University of Rochester Press.

Comings, D. E., and Comings, B. G. 1987. A controlled study of Tourette syndrome.
    I. Attention-deficit disorder, learning disorders, and school problems.
    American Journal of Human Genetics 41: 701-41.
Conte, R., Kinsbourne, M., Swanson, J., Zirk, H., and Samuels, M. 1987.
    Presentation rate effects on paired associate learning by attention
    deficit disordered children. *Child Development* 57: 681-87.
Corbett, J. A., Matthews, A. M., Connell, P. H., and Shapiro, D. A. 1969. Tics
    and Gilles de la Tourette's syndrome: A follow-up study and critical
    review. *British Journal of Psychiatry* 115: 1229-41.
Corbett, J. A., and Turpin, G. 1985. Tics and Tourette's syndrome. In M. Rutter
    and M. Hersov (Eds.), *Child and Adolescent Psychiatry* (2d ed.).
    Oxford: Blackwell Scientific.
Costello, T. W., and Costello, J. T. 1992. *Abnormal psychology* (2d ed.). New
    York: Harper Collins.
Courtois, C. A., and Watts, D. L. 1982. Counseling adult women who had experienced
    incest in childhood or adolescence. *Personnel and Guidance Journal* 60:
    275-79.
Creak, M., and Guttmann, E. 1935. Chorea, tics and compulsive utterances.
    Journal of Mental Science 81: 834-39.
Cretekos, C.J.G. 1977. Some techniques in rehabilitating the school-phobic
    adolescent. *Adolescence* 12: 237-46.
Crisp, A. H., Kalucy, R. S., Lacey, J. H., and Hardig, B. 1977. The long-term
    prognosis in anorexia nervosa: Some factors predictive of outcome. In
    R. A. Vigersky (Ed.), *Anorexia nervosa.* New York: Raven.
Crnic, K. A., and Reid, M. 1989. Mental retardation. In E. J. Mash and R. A.
    Barkley (Eds.), *Treatment of childhood disorders.* New York: Guilford.
Cromwell, R. L., Blashfield, R. K., and Strauss, J. S. 1976. Criteria for
    classification systems. In N. Hobbs (Ed.), *Issues in the classification
    of children.* San Francisco: Jossey-Bass.
Cytryn, L., McKnew, D., Zahn-Waxler, C., and Gershon, E. 1986.
    Developmental issues in risk research: The offspring of affectively ill
    parents. In M. Rutter, C. E. Izard, and P. B. Read (Eds.), *Depression
    in young people: Developmental and clinical perspectives.* New York:
    Guilford.
Dalley, M. B., Bolocofsky, D. N., Alcorn, M. B., and Baker, C. 1992. Depressive
    symptomatology, attribution style, dysfunctional attitude, and social
    competency in adolescents with and without learning disabilities.
    Social Psychology Review 21: 444-58.
Dally, P. J. 1969. *Anorexia nervosa.* New York: Grune & Stratton.
Damasio, A. R., Tranel, D., and Damasio, H. C. 1991. Somatic markers and the
    guidance of behavior: Theory and preliminary testing. In H. S. Levin,
    H. M. Eisenberg, and A. L. Benton (Eds.), *Frontal lobe function and
    dysfunction.* New York: Oxford University Press.
Damon, W. 1995. *Greater expectations: Overcoming the culture of indulgence
    in America's homes and schools.* New York: The Free Press.
Davis, D. R. 1987. Anxiety. In R. L. Gregory (Ed.), *The Oxford companion to
    the mind.* New York: Oxford Press.
DeAvila, E. 1976. Mainstreaming ethnically and linguistically different children:

An exercise in paradox or a new approach? In R. L. Jones (Ed.), *Mainstreaming and the minority child.* Reston, VA: Council for Exceptional Children.

Deutsch, H. 1967. *Selected problems of adolescents.* New York: International Universities Press.

Dexter, L. A. 1994. On the politics and sociology of stupidity in our society. *Mental Retardation* 32 (2): 152-55.

Diamond, S. C. 1992. Working with disturbed adolescents. In K. L. Freiberg (Ed.), *Educating exceptional children.* Guilford, CT: Dushkin.

Dodd, D. H. 1980. Language development. In R. L. Ault (Ed.), *Developmental perspectives.* Santa Monica, CA: Goodyear.

Dorval, B., McKinney, J. D., and Feagans, L. 1982. Teacher interaction with learning disabled children and average achievers. *Journal of Pediatric Psychology* 7: 317-30.

Douvan, E., and Adelson, J. 1966. *The adolescence experience.* New York: Wiley.

Dykman, R. A., and Ackerman, P. T. 1993. Behavioral subtypes of attention deficit disorder. *Exceptional Children* 60 (2): 132-41.

Earls, F. 1994. Oppositional-defiant and conduct disorders. In M. Rutter, E. Taylor, and L. Hersov (Eds.), *Child and adolescent psychiatry* (3d ed.). London: Blackwell Scientific.

Egan, J. 1991. Oppositional defiant disorder. In J. M. Wiener (Ed.), *Textbook of child & adolescent psychiatry.* Washington, DC: American Psychiatric Press.

Eisenberg, L., Ascher, E. A., and Kanner, L. 1959. A clinical study of Gilles de la Tourette's disease (maladie des tics) in children. *American Journal of Psychiatry* 115: 715-26.

Eldridge, R., Sweet, R., Lake, C. R., Ziegler, M., and Shapiro, A. K. 1977. Gilles de la Tourette's syndrome: Clinical, genetic, psychologic and biochemical aspects of 21 selected families. *Neurology* 27: 115-24.

Elkind, D. 1970. *Children and adolescents.* New York: Oxford Universities Press.

Elliott, G. R., and Feldman, S. S. 1990. Capturing the adolescent experience. In S. S. Feldman and G. R. Elliott (Eds.), *At the Threshold: The developing adolescent.* Cambridge, MA: Harvard University Press.

Emmelkamp, P.M.G., and Scholing, A. 1994. Behavioral interpretations. In B. B. Wolman (Ed.) and G. Stricker (Co-Ed.), *Anxiety and related disorders.* New York: Wiley.

Enoch, M. D., and Trethowan, W. 1991. *Uncommon psychiatric syndromes* (3d ed.). Oxford: Butterworth-Heinemann.

Erickson, M. T. 1978. *Child psychopathology.* Englewood Cliffs, NJ: Prentice-Hall.

Erikson, E. 1950. *Childhood and society.* New York: W. W. Norton.

_____. 1963. *Childhood and society* (2d ed.). New York: W. W. Norton.

_____. 1968. *Identity, youth, and crisis.* New York: W. W. Norton.

Evans, D. W., Noam, G. G., Wertlieb, D., Paget, K. F., and Wolf, M. 1994. Self-perception and adolescent psychopathology: A clinical-developmental perspective. *American Journal of Orthopsychiatry* 64 (2): 293-300.

Eysenck, H. J. 1977. *Crime and personality.* London: Routledge & Kegan Paul.

Eysenck, N. W. 1991. Cognitive factors in clinical anxiety: Potential relevance to therapy. In M. Briley and S. E. File, *New concepts in anxiety.* Boca Raton, FL: CRC Press.

Faas, L. A. 1980. *Children with learning problems: A handbook for teachers.* Boston: Houghton Mifflin.

Faber, N. W. 1968. *The retarded child.* New York: Crown.

Fard, K., Hudgens, R., and Weiner, A. 1978. Undiagnosed psychiatric illness in adolescents: A prospective study and seven-year follow-up. *Archives of General Psychiatry* 35: 279-82.

Faux, E. J. 1966. Gilles de la Tourette's syndrome. *Archives of General Psychiatry* 14: 139-42.

Feighner, J. P. 1972. Diagnostic criteria for use in psychiatric research. *Archives of General Psychiatry* 26: 57-63.

Feinstein, C., and Aldershof, A. 1991. Developmental disorders of language and learning. In J. M. Wiener (Ed.), *Textbook of child & adolescent psychiatry.* Washington, DC: American Psychiatric Press.

Feldman, S. S., and Elliott, G. R. (Eds.). 1990. *At the threshold: The developing adolescent.* Cambridge, MA: Harvard University Press.

Fennell, M.J.V. 1997. Low self-esteem: A cognitive perspective. *Behavioural and Cognitive Psychotherapy* 25: 1-25.

Fergusson, D. M., Horwood, L. J., and Lynskey, M. T. 1995. The stability of disruptive childhood behaviors. *Journal of Abnormal Child Psychology* 23 (3): 379-96.

Fernando, S.J.M. 1976. Six cases of Gilles de la Tourette's syndrome. *British Journal of Psychiatry,* 128: 436-41.

Figley, C. R. (Ed.) 1986. *Trauma and its wake.* New York: Brunner/Mazel.

Fink, C. M. 1990. Special education students at risk. In P. E. Leone (Ed.), *Understanding troubled and troubling youth.* Newbury Park, CA: Sage.

Fiore, T. A., Becker, E. A., and Nero, R. C. 1993. Educational interventions for students with attention deficit disorder. *Exceptional Children* 60 (2): 163-73.

Flannigan, P. J., Baker, G. R., and LaFollette, L. G. 1970. *An orientation to mental retardation.* Springfield, IL: Charles C. Thomas.

Forness, S. R. 1992. Legalism versus professionalism in diagnosing SED in the public schools. *School Psychology Review* 21 (1): 29-34.

Forness, S. R., and Knitzer, J. 1992. A new proposed definition and terminology to replace "serious emotional disturbance" in Individuals with Disabilities Education Act. *School Psychology Review* 21 (1): 12-20.

Fowles, D.C. 1993. Electrodermal activity and antisocial behavior: Empirical findings and theoretical issues. In J. C. Roy, W. Boucsein, and D.C. Fowles (Eds.), *Progress in electroderman research.* London: Plenum, pp. 1-14.

Frank, S. M. 1978. Psycholinguistic findings in Gilles de la Tourette's syndrome. *Journal of Communication Disorders* 11: 349-63.

Freeman, A., and DiTomasso, R. A. 1994. The cognitive theory of anxiety. In B. B. Wolman (Ed.) and G. Stricker (Co-Ed.), *Anxiety and related disorders.* New York: Wiley.

Freiberg, K. L. (Ed.) 1992. *Educating exceptional children* (6th ed.). Guilford, CT: Dushkin.

Freud, A. 1958. *Adolescence.* Vol. 13. *Psychoanalytic study of the child.* New York: International Universities Press.

Fried, S. 1995. Creative tension. *Washington Post Magazine.* April 16: 10-13, 27-32.

Friedman, R. J., and Doyal, G. T. 1974. Depression in children: Some observations for the school psychologist. *Psychology in the Schools* 11 (1): 19-23.

Fromm, E. 1947. *Man for himself.* New York: Holt, Rinehart & Winston.

Fuchs, D., Fuchs, L. S., and Fernstrom, P. 1993. A conservative approach to special education reform: Mainstreaming through transenvironmental programming and curriculum-based measurement. *American Educational Research Journal* 30: 149-77.

Garelik, G. 1986. Exorcising a damnable disease. *Discover.* December: 74-84.

Garrison, K. C. 1973. Contemporary adolescents. In R. A. Magoon (Ed.), *Education and psychology.* Columbus, OH: Charles E. Merrill.

Gelfand, D. M., and Hartmann, D. P. 1980. The development of prosocial behavior and moral judgment. In R. L. Ault (Ed.), *Developmental perspectives.* Santa Monica, CA: Goodyear.

Gelfand, D. M., Jenson, W. R., and Drew, C. J. 1982. *Understanding child behavior disorders.* New York: Holt, Rinehart & Winston.

Ginott, H. G. 1969. *Between parent and teenager.* New York: Avon.

Gittelman, R. 1986. *Anxiety disorders of childhood.* New York: Guilford.

Glosser, B., and Koppell, S. 1987. Emotional-behavioral patterns in children with learning disabilities: Lateralized hemispheric differences. *Journal of Learning Disabilities* 20: 365-69.

Goforth, E. G. 1974. Gilles de la Tourette's syndrome: A 25-year follow-up study. *Journal of Nervous and Mental Disorders* 158: 306-9.

Gold, M. S., Pottash, A. L., Sweeney, A. R., Martin, D. M., and Davies, R. V. 1980. Further evidence of hypothalamic-pituitary dysfunction in anorexia nervosa. *American Journal of Psychiatry* 137: 101-2.

Goldbloom, D. S., and Garfinkel, P. E. 1989. Anorexia nervosa and bulimia nervosa. In C. G. Last and M. Hersen (Eds.), *Handbook of child psychiatric diagnosis.* New York: Wiley.

Golden, G. S. 1977. Tourette's syndrome: The pediatric perspective. *American Medical Journal of Diseases in Children* 131: 531-34.

Goldstein, S., and Goldstein, M. 1990. *Managing attention disorders in children.* New York: Wiley.

Goleman, D. 1995. Getting smart about emotions. *Washington Post.* Sunday, October 8: C1, C4.

_____. 1997. *Emotional intelligence.* New York: Bantam.

Gordon, M. J. 1963. *Wise sayings from the Orient.* Mt. Vernon, NY: Peter Pauper.

Gottlieb, J. 1975. Public, peer, and professional attitudes toward mentally retarded persons. In M. J. Begab and S. A. Richardson (Eds.), *The mentally retarded and society: A social science perspective.* Baltimore: University Park Press.

Gottlieb, J., and Budoff, M. 1973. Social acceptability of retarded children in nongraded schools differing in architecture. *American Journal of Mental Deficiency* 78: 15-19.

Gottlieb, J., Semmel, M., and Veldman, D. 1978. Correlates of social status
    among mainstreamed mentally retarded children. *Journal of
    Educational Psychology* 70: 396-405.
Graham, P. 1991. *Child psychiatry* (2d ed.). Oxford: Oxford University Press.
Graham, S., Harris, K. R., and Reid, R. 1990. Learning disabilities. In E. L. Meyen
    (Ed.), *Exceptional children in today's schools* (2d ed.). Denver: Love.
Gray, J. A. 1987. *The psychology of fear and stress.* Cambridge: Cambridge
    University Press.
Greenhill, L. L. 1991. Attention-deficit hyperactivity disorder. In J. M. Wiener
    (Ed.), *Textbook of child & adolescent psychiatry.* Washington, DC:
    American Psychiatric Press.
Gresham, F. M., and Reschly, D. J. 1986. Social skills deficits and low peer
    acceptance of mainstreamed learning disabled children. *Learning
    Disability Quarterly* 9: 23-32.
Grotevant, H. D., and Cooper, C. R. 1986. Individuation in family relationships.
    Human Development 29: 83-100.
Guetzloe, E. 1992. Suicide and depression: Special education's responsibility. In
    K. L. Freiberg (Ed.), *Educating exceptional children.* Guilford, CT:
    Dushkin.
Gunzburg, H. C. 1972. Mental deficiencies. In B. B. Wolman (Ed.), *Manual of
    child psychopathology.* New York: McGraw-Hill.
Gutsch, K. U. 1988. *Psychotherapeutic approaches to specific DSM-III-R
    categories.* Springfield, IL: Charles C. Thomas.
Hall, G. S. 1916. *Adolescence.* New York: Appleton.
Hallahan, D. P., and Kauffman, J. M. 1976. *Introduction to learning disabilities:
    A psycho-behavioral approach.* Englewood Cliffs, NJ: Prentice-Hall.
Halmi, K. A. 1974. Anorexia nervosa: Demographic and clinical features in 94
    cases. *Psychosomatic Medicine* 36: 18-25.
Harden, P. W., Pihl, R. O., Vitaro, F., Gendreau, P. L., and Tremblay, R. E. 1995.
    Stress response in anxious and nonanxious disruptive boys. *Journal
    of Emotional and Behavioral Disorders* 3 (3): 183-90.
Hare, R. D. 1991. *The Hare psychopathy checklist revised.* Toronto, Canada:
    Multi-Health Systems.
Harman, C. 1992. Selections and introduction to R. L. Stevenson, *The strange
    case of Dr. Jekyll and Mr. Hyde and other stories.* London: J. M.
    Dent & Sons.
Harrington, R. 1994. Affective disorders. In M. Rutter, E. Taylor, and L. Hersov
    (Eds.), *Child and adolescent psychiatry* (3d ed.). London: Blackwell
    Scientific.
Harris, J. R., and Liebert, R. M. 1984. *The child.* Englewood Cliffs, NJ:
    Prentice-Hall.
Hassibi, M., and Breuer, H. 1980. *Disordered thinking and communication in
    children.* New York: Plenum.
Hendren, R. L. 1991. Conduct disorder in childhood. In J. M. Wiener (Ed.),
    Textbook of child & adolescent psychiatry. Washington, DC: American
    Psychiatric Press.
Hensley, R. 1994. Untitled poem. *Virginia Writing* 8 (1): 41.

Hersen, M., and Barlow, D. H. 1976. *Single case experimental designs.* New York: Pergamon.

Hersov, L. 1985. School refusal. In M. Rutter and M. Hersov (Eds.), *Child and adolescent psychiatry* (2d ed.). Oxford: Blackwell Scientific.

Herzog, D. M., and Copeland, P. M. 1985. Eating disorders. *New England Journal of Medicine* 313: 294-303.

Heward, W. L., and Orlansky, M. D. 1984. *Exceptional children* (2d ed.). Columbus, OH: Charles E. Merrill.

Hewett, F. M. 1977. *Education of exceptional learners.* Boston: Allyn & Bacon.

Hickson, L., Blackman, L. S., and Reis, E. M. 1995. *Mental retardation.* Boston: Allyn & Bacon.

Hirshfield, R.M.A., et al. 1986. Personality of recovered patients with bipolar affective disorders. *Journal of Affective Disorders* 11: 81-89.

Holmes, D. S. 1994. *Abnormal psychology* (2d ed.). New York: Harper Collins.

Horner, R. H., and Carr, E. G. 1997. Behavioral support for students with severe disabilities: Functional assessment and comprehensive intervention. *Journal of Special Education* 31 (1): 84-104.

Howard, L. P. 1960. Identity conflicts in adolescent girls. *Smith College Studies in Social Work* 31: 1-21.

Howsam, R. B. 1980. The workplace: Does it hamper professionalization of pedagogy? *Phi Delta Kappan* 62: 93-96.

Hoyle, S. G., and Serifica, F. C. 1988. Peer status of children with and without learning disabilities--A multimethod study. *Learning Disability Quarterly* 11: 322-32.

Hussain, S. A., and Kashani, J. H. 1992. *Anxiety disorders in children and adolescents.* Washington, DC: American Psychiatric Press.

Hutt, M. L., and Gibby, R. G. 1965. *The mentally retarded child: Development, education and treatment* (2d ed.). Boston: Allyn & Bacon.

Hyde, M. O. 1977. *Fears and phobias.* New York: McGraw-Hill.

Irvin, T. 1978. The Education for All Handicapped Children Act of 1975: Public Law 94-142 regulations. In J. Smith (Ed.), *Personnel preparation and Public Law 94-142: The map, the mission and the mandate.* Boothwyn, PA: Educational Resources Center.

Jacobson, E. 1943. Depression: The Oedipus complex in the development of depressive mechanisms. *Psychoanalytic Quarterly* 12: 541-60.

Jacobson, J. W. 1982. Problem behavior and psychiatric impairment within a developmentally disabled population: I. Behavior frequency. *Applied Research in Mental Retardation* 3: 121-39.

Jagger, J., et al. 1982. The epidemiology of Tourette syndrome: A pilot study. *Schizophrenia Bulletin* 8: 267-77.

Jamison, K. R. 1993. *Touched with fire.* New York: Free Press.

Janoff-Bulman, R. 1986. The aftermath of victimization: Rebuilding shattered assumptions. In C. R. Figley (Ed.), *Trauma and its wake.* New York: Brunner/Mazel.

Johnson, A. M., Falstein, E. I., Szurek, S. A., and Svendsen, J. 1941. School phobia. *American Journal of Orthopsychiatry* 11: 702-11.

Johnstone, E. R. 1909-1910. The summer school for teachers of backward children. *Journal of Psycho-Asthenics* 14: 122-30.

Judd, L. L. 1965. Obsessive-compulsive neurosis in children. *Archives of General Psychiatry* 12: 136-43.

Kaplan, N. R., and Kaplan, M. L. 1978. The gestalt approach to stuttering. *Journal of Communication Disorders* 11: 1-9.

Kashani, J. H., and Eppright, T. D. 1991. Mood disorders in adolescents. In J. M. Wiener (Ed.), *Textbook of child & adolescent psychiatry*. Washington, DC: American Psychiatric Press.

Kashani, J. H., and Orvaschel, H. 1988. Anxiety disorders in mid-adolescence: A community sample. *American Journal of Psychiatry* 145: 960-64.

Kauffman, C., Grunebaum, H., Cohler, B., and Gamer, E. 1979. Superkids: Competent children of psychotic mothers. *American Journal of Psychiatry* 136: 1398-402.

Kauffman, J. M. 1983. Emotional disturbance. In S. G. Garwood (Ed.), *Educating young handicapped children*. Rockville, MD: Aspen Systems.

_____. 1985. *Characteristics of children's behavior disorders* (3d ed.). Columbus, OH: Charles E. Merrill.

_____. 1993a. *Characteristics of emotional and behavioral disorders of children and youth* (5th ed.). New York: Macmillan.

_____. 1993b. How we might achieve the radical reform of special education. *Exceptional Children* 60 (1): 6-16.

Kay, D.W.K., and Leigh, D. 1954. The natural history, treatment and prognosis of anorexia nervosa based on a study of 38 patients. *British Journal of Psychiatry* 100: 411-31.

Keller, M., and Baker, L. 1991. Bipolar disorder: Epidemiology, course, diagnosis, and treatment. *Bulletin of the Menninger Clinic* 55: 172-81.

Kelly, E. B. 1992. Learning disabilities. In K. L. Freiberg (Ed.), *Educating exceptional children* (6th ed.). Guilford, CT: Dushkin.

Kelly, E. J. 1988. Personality inventory for children: Selected scales in differentiating conduct disordered and emotionally disturbed students. *Psychological Reports* 63: 395-401.

Kendall, P. C. 1993. Cognitive-behavioral therapies with youth: Guiding theory, current status, and emerging developments. *Journal of Consulting and Clinical Psychology* 61: 235-47.

Kendall, P. C., and Panichelli, S. M. 1995. Cognitive-behavioral treatments. *Journal of Abnormal Child Psychology* 23 (1): 107-24.

Kennedy, W. A. 1965. School phobia: Rapid treatment of fifty cases. *Journal of Abnormal Psychology* 70: 285-89.

Kernberg, O. F. 1985. *Borderline conditions and pathological narcissism*. Northvale, NJ: Jason Aronson.

Kerr, M. M., Nelson, C. M., and Lambert, D. L. 1987. *Helping adolescents with learning and behavior problems*. Columbus, OH: Charles E. Merrill.

Kessler, J. W. 1972. Neurosis in childhood. In B. B. Wolman (Ed.), *Manual of child psychopathology*. New York: McGraw-Hill.

Klein, M. 1975. *The psychoanalysis of children*. New York: Dell.

Klove, H. 1989. The hypoarousal hypothesis: What is the evidence? In T. Sagvolden and T. Archer (Eds.), *Attention deficit disorder*. Hillsdale, NJ: Lawrence Erlbaum.

Krakowski, A. J. 1962. Neurosis of childhood: Its meaning, symptoms and psychodynamics. In A. J. Krakowski and D. A. Santora (Eds.), *Child psychiatry and the general practitioner.* Springfield, IL: Charles C. Thomas.

Krauss, H. H., and Krauss, B. J. 1994. Anxiety and the experience of time. In B. B. Wolman (Ed.) and G. Stricker (Co-Ed.), *Anxiety and related disorders.* New York: Wiley.

Kravas, K. J., and Kravas, C. H. 1974. Transactional analysis for classroom management. *Phi Delta Kappan* 56: 194-97.

Kreisman, J. J. 1989. *I hate you: Don't leave me.* New York: Avon.

Kroll, J. 1988. *The challenge of the borderline.* New York: W. W. Norton.

_____. 1993. *PTSD/borderlines in therapy.* New York: W. W. Norton.

Kronick, D. 1976. The importance of a sociological perspective toward learning disabilities. *Journal of Learning Disabilities* 9: 115-19.

Kube, J. B. Spring 1994. Hanging by a thread. *Parent Watch* (Richmond, VA: PACCT): 2, 4-5.

Lachenmeyer, J. R. 1982. Special disorders of childhood: Depression, school phobia and anorexia nervosa. In J. R. Lachenmeyer and M. S. Gibbs (Eds.), *Psychopathology in childhood.* New York: Gardner.

La Greca, A. M., and Stone, W. L. 1990. LD status and achievement: Confounding variables in the study of children's social status, self-esteem, and behavioral functioning. *Journal of Learning Disabilities* 23: 483-90.

Lambert, N. M., Sandoval, J., and Sassone, D. 1978. Prevalence of hyperactivity in elementary school children as a function of social system definers. *American Journal of Orthopsychiatry* 48: 446-63.

Landau, E. D., Epstein, S. L., and Stone, A. P. (Eds.) 1972. *Child development through literature.* Englewood Cliffs, NJ: Prentice-Hall.

Landrum, T. J., Singh, N. N., Nemil, M. S., Ellis, C. R., and Best, A. M. 1995. Characteristics of children and adolescents with serious emotional disturbance in systems of care. Part II: Community-based services. *Journal of Emotional and Behavioral Disorders* 3 (3): 141-49.

Larson, R., and Ham, M. 1993. Stress and "storm and stress" in early adolescence: The relationship of negative events with dysphoric affect. *Developmental Psychology* 29: 130-40.

Lasch, C. 1978. *The culture of narcissism.* New York: W. W. Norton.

Last, C. G., et al. 1987. Separation anxiety and school phobia: A comparison using DSM-III criteria. *American Journal of Psychiatry* 144: 653-57.

Lauritzen, P. 1990. How critical is the special education teacher shortage? Toronto: Paper presented at the annual meeting of The Council for Exceptional Children.

Leckman, J. F., and Cohen, D. J. 1994. Tic disorders. In M. Rutter, E. Taylor, and L. Hersov (Eds.), *Child and adolescent psychiatry* (3d ed.). London: Blackwell Scientific.

Leckman, J. F., Walker, D. E., Goodman, W. K., and Pauls, D. L. 1994. "Just right" perceptions associated with compulsive behavior in Tourette's syndrome. *American Journal of Psychiatry* 151 (5): 675-80.

Lemons, L. A., and Barber, W. H. 1991. Gilles de la Tourette syndrome: A review and implications for educators. *British Columbia Journal of Special Education* 15 (2): 146-58.

Leon, G. R., and Dinklage, D. 1983. Childhood obesity and anorexia nervosa. In

T. H. Ollendick and M. Hersen (Eds.), *Handbook of child psychopathology.*
New York: Plenum.

Leone, P. E. 1990. *Understanding troubled and troubling youth.* Newbury Park,
CA: Sage.

Lerner, J., Lowenthal, B., and Lerner, S. R. 1995. *Attention deficit disorders.*
Pacific Grove, CA: Brooks/Cole.

Lerner, J. W. 1976. *Children with learning disabilities* (2d ed.). Boston:
Houghton Mifflin.

Lester, G., and Kelman, M. 1997. State disparities in the diagnosis and
placement of pupils with learning disabilities. *Journal of Learning
Disabilities* 30 (6): 599-607.

Levertov, D. 1965. *To stay alive.* New York: New Directions.

Levine, M. 1990. *Keeping a head in school.* Cambridge, MA: Educators
Publishing Service.

Lewinsohn, P. M., et al. 1994. Adolescent psychopathology: II. Psychosocial risk
factors for depression. *Journal of Abnormal Psychology* 103 (2): 302-15.

Lewis, D. O. 1991. Adolescent conduct and antisocial disorders. In J. M.
Wiener (Ed.), *Textbook of child & adolescent psychiatry.* Washington,
DC: American Psychiatric Press.

Lilly, M. S. (Ed.) 1979. *Children with exceptional needs.* New York: Holt,
Rinehart & Winston.

Lincoln, D. F. 1903. Special classes for feeble-minded children in the Boston
public schools. *Journal of Psycho-Asthenics* 7: 83-93.

Lindemann, C. 1994. Phobias. In B. B. Wolman (Ed.) and G. Stricker (Co-Ed.),
Anxiety and related disorders. New York: Wiley.

Livingston, R. L., Dykman, R. A., and Ackerman, P. T. 1990. The frequency and
significance of additional self-reported psychiatric diagnoses in
children with attention deficit disorder. *Journal of Abnormal
Child Psychology* 18 (5): 465-78.

Lochman, J. E. 1984. Psychological characteristics and assessment of
aggressive adolescents. In C. R. Keith (Ed.), *The aggressive
adolescent.* New York: Free Press.

Loeber, R., and Schmaling, K. B. 1985. Empirical evidence for overt and covert
patterns of antisocial conduct problems: A meta-analysis. *Journal of
Abnormal Child Psychology* 13: 337-52.

Logan, K. R., Bakeman, R., and Keefe, E. B. 1997. Effects of instructional
variables on engaged behavior of students with disabilities in general
education classrooms. *Exceptional Children* 63 (4): 481-97.

Lohr, J. B., and Wisniewski, A. A. 1987. *Movement disorders.* New York: Guilford.

Looft, W. R. 1972. *Developmental psychology.* Hinsdale, IL: The Dryden
Press.

Lowen, A. 1985. *Narcissism: Denial of the true self.* New York: Collier.

Luckasson, R., et al. 1992. *Mental retardation: Definition, classification, and
systems of supports.* Washington, DC: American Association on Mental
Retardation.

Ludlow, C., Polinsky, R. J., Caine, E. D., Bassich, C. J., and Ebert, M. H. 1982.
Language and speech abnormalities in Tourette's syndrome (TS). In A.
J. Freidhoff and T. Chase (Eds.), *Tourette syndrome.* New York: Raven.

MacFarlane, K. 1978. Sexual abuse of children. In J. R. Chapman and M. Gates (Eds.), *Victimization of women.* Beverly Hills, CA: Sage.

Magyary, D., and Brandt, P. 1996. School-based mental health programs: Issues for implementation and evaluation. Tampa, FL: Proceedings of the 9th Annual Research Conference: A System of Care for Children's Mental Health. Chapter 9: Expanding the Research Base, February 26-28.

Malmquist, C. P. 1972. Depressive phenomena in children. In B. B. Wolman (Ed.), *Manual of child psychopathology.* New York: McGraw-Hill.

_____. 1991. Conduct disorder: Conceptual and diagnostic issues. In J. M. Wiener (Ed.), *Textbook of child & adolescent psychiatry.* Washington, DC: American Psychiatric Press.

Manuck, S. B., Kaplan, J. R., Clarkson, T. B., Adams, M. R., and Shively, C. A. 1992. Behavioral influences on coronary artery disease: A nonhuman primate model. In H. S. Friedman (Ed.), *Hostility, coping and health.* Washington, DC: American Psychological Association.

March, J. S., Leonard, H. L., and Swedo, S. E. 1995. Obsessive-compulsive disorder. In J. S. March (Ed.), *Anxiety disorders in children and adolescents.* New York: Guilford.

Marin, P. 1971. The open truth and fiery vehemence of youth. In R. Gross and P. Osterman (Eds.), *High school.* New York: Simon & Schuster.

Marshall, R. M., Hynd, G. W., Handwick, M. J., and Hall, J. 1997. Academic underachievement in ADHD subtypes. *Journal of Learning Disabilities* 30 (6): 635-42.

Martindale, C. 1976. The grammar of the tic in Gilles de la Tourette's syndrome. *Language and Speech* 19: 266-75.

Masson, J. M. 1984. *The assault on truth: Freud's suppression of the seduction theory.* New York: Farrar, Straus, & Giroux.

Mayer, M. 1964. The schools. In B. Johnston (Ed.), *Issues in education.* Boston: Houghton Mifflin.

McBride, H.E.A., and Siegel, L. S. 1997. Learning disabilities and adolescent suicide. *Journal of Learning Disabilities* 30 (6): 652-59.

McBurnett, K., et al. 1991. Anxiety, inhibition, and conduct disorder in children: II. Relation to salivary cortisol. *Journal of the American Academy of Child and Adolescent Psychiatry* 30: 192-96.

McCarney, S. B., and McCain, B. R. 1995. *Behavior dimensions intervention manual.* Columbia, MO: Hawthorne Educational Services.

McCauley, E., Carolson, G. A., and Calderon, R. 1991. The role of somatic complaints in the diagnosis of depression in children and adolescents. *Journal of the American Academy of Child Psychiatry* 30: 631-35.

McDonald, J. E., and Sheperd, G. 1976. School phobia: An overview. *Journal of School Psychology* 14: 291-306.

McDougall, D., and Brady, M. P. 1998. Initiating and fading self-management interventions to increase math fluency in general education classes. *Exceptional Children* 64 (2): 151-66.

McGuire, W. H. 1979. Teacher burnout. *Today's Education* 68: 5.

McIntosh, R., Vaughn, S., Schumm, J. S., Haager, D., and Lee, O. 1994. Observations of students with learning disabilities in general education classrooms. *Exceptional Children* 60 (3): 249-61.

McKinney, J. D., Montague, M., and Hocutt, A. M. 1993. Educational assessment of
    students with attention deficit disorder. *Exceptional Children* 60 (2): 125-
    31.
McMahon, R. J., and Wells, K. C. 1989. Conduct disorders. In E. J. Mash and R. A.
    Barkley (Eds.), *Treatment of childhood disorders.* New York: Guilford.
McManus, M. 1989. Conduct disorder. In L.K.G. Hsu and M. Hersen (Eds.),
    Recent developments in adolescent psychiatry. New York: Wiley.
Mehrabian, A. 1968. Communication without words. *Psychology Today* 24: 52-55.
Meiselman, K. C. 1978. *Incest: A psychological study of causes and effects
    with treatment recommendations.* San Francisco: Jossey-Bass.
Mellin, L. 1983. *Shapedown.* San Francisco: Balboa.
Mercer, C. D. 1979. *Children and adolescents with learning disabilities.*
    Columbus, OH: Charles E. Merrill.
_____. 1987. *Students with learning disabilities* (3d ed.). Columbus, OH: Charles
    E. Merrill.
Meyen, E. L. 1990. *Exceptional children in today's schools* (2d ed.). Denver: Love.
Miller, L. 1978. Pragmatics and early childhood language disorders:
    Communicative interactions in a half-hour sample. *Journal of
    Speech and Hearing Disorders* 43: 419-36.
Miller, M. W. 1994. Survey sketches new portrait of the mentally ill. *Wall
    Street Journal.* January 14: B1.
Miller-Perrin, C. L., and Wurtele, S. K. 1990. Reactions to childhood sexual abuse:
    Implications for post-traumatic stress disorder. In C. L. Meek (Ed.),
    Posttraumatic stress disorder. Sarasota, FL: Professional Resource
    Exchange.
Millman, H. L., Schaefer, C. E., and Cohen, J. J. 1980. *Therapies for school
    behavior problems.* San Francisco: Jossey-Bass.
Millstein, S. G., and Litt, I. F. 1990. Adolescent health. In S. S. Feldman and G.
    R. Elliott (Eds.), *At the threshold: The developing adolescent.*
    Cambridge, MA: Harvard University Press.
Modell, J., and Goodman, M. 1990. Historical perspectives. In S. S. Feldman
    and G. R. Elliott (Eds.), *At the threshold: The developing adolescent.*
    Cambridge, MA: Harvard University Press.
Morris, W. (Ed.) 1973. *The American heritage dictionary of the English
    language.* Boston: Houghton Mifflin.
Morse, W. C. 1971. Worksheet on life space interviewing for teachers. In N. J.
    Long, W. C. Morse, and R. G. Newman (Eds.). *Conflict in the classroom*
    (2d ed.). Belmont, CA: Wadsworth.
Munk, D. D., and Repp. A. C. 1994. The relationship between instructional
    variables and problem behavior: A review. *Exceptional Children* 60
    (5): 390-401.
Murphy, L. 1956. *Personality in young children.* Vol. 2. New York: Basic Books.
Muus, R. E. 1988. *Theories of adolescence.* New York: Random House.
Nee, L. E., Caine, E. D., Polinsky, R. J., Eldridge, R., and Ebert, M. H. 1980.
    Gilles de la Tourette's syndrome: Clinical and family study of 50 cases.
    Annals of Neurology 7: 41-49.
Neel, R. S., and Cessna, K. K. 1993. *Instructionally differentiated programming:
    A needs-based approach.* Denver: Colorado Department of Education.

Nelson, C. M. 1992. Searching for meaning in the behavior of antisocial pupils, public school educators, and lawmakers. *School Psychology Review* 21 (1): 35-39.

Nelson, C. M., and Rutherford, R. B. 1990. Troubled youth in the public schools: Emotionally disturbed or socially maladjusted? In P. E. Leone (Ed.), *Understanding troubled and troubling youth.* Newbury Park, CA: Sage.

Nelson, C. M., Rutherford, R. B., and Walker, H. M. 1991. Do public schools have an obligation to serve troubled children and youth? *Exceptional Children* (March/April): 406-15.

Nelson, J. R., Johnson, A., and Marchand-Martella, N. 1996. Effects of direct instruction, cooperative learning, and independent learning practices on the classroom behavior of students with behavioral disorders: A comparative analysis. *Journal of Emotional and Behavioral Disorders* 4 (1): 53-62.

Nevid, J. S., Rathus, S. A., and Greene, B. 1994. *Abnormal psychology* (2d ed.). Englewood Cliffs, NJ: Prentice-Hall.

Newcomer, P. L., Barenbaum, E., and Pearson, N. 1995. Depression and anxiety in children and adolescents with learning disabilities, conduct disorders, and no disabilities. *Journal of Emotional and Behavioral Disorders* 3 (1): 27-39.

New York Times. 1983. Chemical clue in anorexia. Sunday, May 15.

Nolan, E. E., Gadow, K. D., and Sverd, J. 1994. Observations and ratings of tics in school settings. *Journal of Abnormal Child Psychology* 22 (5): 579-93.

Norton, G. R., Cox, B. J., Asmundson, G.J.G., and Maser, J. D. 1995. The growth of anxiety disorders in the 1980s. *Journal of Anxiety Disorders* 9 (1): 75-85.

Nowicki, S., and Duke, M. P. 1992. *Helping the child who doesn't fit in.* Atlanta: Peachtree.

Oppenheimer, R., Palmer, R. L., and Brandon, S. 1984. *A clinical evaluation of early abusive experiences in adult anorexic and bulimic females: Implications for preventive work in childhood.* Montreal, Canada: Paper presented at the Fifth International Congress on Child Abuse and Neglect.

Oquendo, M. A. 1994. Differential diagnosis of ataque de nervous. *American Journal of Orthopsychiatry* 65 (1): 60-65.

O'Quinn, A. N., and Thompson, R. J., Jr. 1980. Tourette's syndrome: An expanded view. *Pediatrics* 66: 420-24.

Oster, G. D., and Caro, J. E. 1990. *Understanding and treating depressed adolescents and their families.* New York: Wiley.

Packard, V. 1983. *Our endangered children.* Boston: Little, Brown.

Palla, B., and Litt, I. F. 1988. Medical complications of eating disorders in adolescents. *Pediatrics* 81: 613-23.

Paris, J., Zweig-Frank., H., and Guzder, J. 1994. Risk factors for borderline personality in male outpatients. *Journal of Nervous and Mental Disease* 182 (7): 375-80.

Parmar, R. S., Cawley, J. F., and Miller, J. H. 1994. Differences in mathematics performance between students with learning disabilities and students with mild retardation. *Exceptional Children* 60 (6): 549-63.

Parson, E. R. 1994. Post-traumatic stress disorder (PTSD): Its biopsychobehavioral aspects and management. In B. B. Wolman (Ed.) and G. Stricker (Co-Ed.),

Anxiety and related disorders. New York: Wiley.

Pasnau, R. O. 1984. The anxiety disorders. In R. O. Pasnau (Ed.), *Diagnosis and treatment of anxiety disorders.* Washington, DC: American Psychiatric Press.

Peck, M. S. 1978. *The road less traveled.* New York: Simon & Schuster.

Pelham, W. E., and Bender, M. E. 1982. Peer relationships and hyperactive children: Description and treatment. In K. Gadow and I. Bailer (Eds.), *Advances in learning and behavioral disabilities.* Vol. 1. Greenwich, CT: JAI Press.

Peterson, K. C., Prout, M. F., and Schwarz, R. A. 1991. *Post-traumatic stress disorder.* New York: Plenum.

Petti, T. A. 1981. Active treatment of childhood depression. In J. F. Clarkin and H. I. Glazer (Eds.), *Depression.* New York: Garland STPM Press.

Pfiffner, L. J., and Barkley, R. A. 1990. Educational placement and classroom management. In R. A. Barkley (Ed.), *Attention deficit hyperactivity disorder: A handbook for diagnosis and treatment.* New York: Guilford.

Phelps, L., and McClintock, K. 1994. Papa and peers: A biosocial approach to conduct disorder. *Journal of Psychopathology and Behavioral Assessment* 16 (1): 53-67.

Pickar, D. B., and Tori, C. D. 1986. The learning disabled adolescent: Ericksonian psychosocial development, self-concept, and delinquent behavior. *Journal of Youth and Adolescence* 15: 429-40.

Pine, F. 1982. On the concept "borderline" in children: A clinical essay. In S. I. Harrison and J. F. McDermott (Eds.), *New directions in childhood psychopathology.* New York: International Universities Press.

Pishkin, H. 1967. Pubertal onset and ego functioning. *Journal of Abnormal Psychology* 72 (1): 1-15.

Poissonet, C. M., La Valle, M., and Burdi, A. R. 1988. Growth and development of adipose tissue. *Journal of Pediatrics* 113: 1-9.

Proctor, J. T. 1958. Hysteria in childhood. *American Journal of Orthopsychiatry* 28: 394-406.

Prout, H. T., and Harvey, J. R. 1978. Applications of desensitization procedures for school-related problems: A review. *Psychology in the Schools* 13: 533-40.

Putnam, J. W., Spiegel, A. N., and Bruininks, R. H. 1995. Future directions in education and inclusion of students with disabilities: A Delphi investigation. *Exceptional Children* 61 (6): 553-76.

Quay, H. C. 1979. Classification. In H. C. Quay and S. Werry (Eds.), *Psychopathological disorders of childhood* (2d ed.). New York: Wiley.

Quay, H. C., and La Greca, A. M. 1986. Disorders of anxiety, withdrawal, and dysphoria. In H. C. Quay (Ed.), *Psychopathological disorders of childhood.* New York: Wiley.

Raine, A. 1994. *The psychopathology of crime: Criminal behavior as a clinical disorder.* San Diego: Academic Press.

Rapoport, J. 1959. Maladie des tics in children. *American Journal of Psychiatry* 116: 177-78.

Rapoport, J. L. 1991. *The boy who couldn't stop washing.* New York: Signet.

Rapoport, J. L., Swedo, S., and Leonard, H. 1994. Obsessive-compulsive disorder. In M. Rutter, E. Taylor, and L. Hersov (Eds.), *Child and adolescent psychiatry* (3d ed.). London: Blackwell Scientific.

Reeves, J. C., et al. 1987. Attention deficit, conduct, oppositional and anxiety disorders in children, II: Clinical characteristics. *Journal of the American Academy of Child and Adolescent Psychiatry* 26: 144-55.

Reid, R., Maag, J. W., Vasa, S. F., and Wright, G. 1994. Who are the children with attention deficit-hyperactivity disorder? A school-based survey. *Journal of Special Education* 28 (2): 117-36.

Reynolds, W. M. 1990a. Introduction to the nature and study of internalizing disorders in children and adolescents. *School Psychology Review* 19 (2): 137-41.

_____. 1990b. Depression in children and adolescents: Nature, diagnoses, assessment, and treatment. *School Psychology Review* 19 (2): 158-73.

Rhodes, W. C. 1990. From classic to holistic paradigm. In P. E. Leone (Ed.), *Understanding troubled and troubling youth*. Newbury Park, CA: Sage.

Riccio, C. A., Gonzalez, J. J., and Hynd, G. W. 1994. Attention-deficit hyperactivity disorder (ADHD) and learning disabilities. *Learning Disability Quarterly* 17 (4): 311-22.

Riccio, C. A., Hynd, G. W., Cohen, M. J., and Gonzalez, J. J. 1993. Neurological basis of attention deficit hyperactivity disorder. *Exceptional Children* 60 (2): 118-24.

Rice, M. L. 1986. Mismatched premises of competence and intervention. In R. L. Schiefelbusch (Ed.), *Language competence: Assessment and intervention*. San Diego: College Hill Press, pp. 261-80.

Richman, N., Stevenson, J., and Graham, P. 1982. *Pre-school to school: A behavioural study*. London: Academic Press.

Richman, P. C. 1995. Life's just a bowl of chutney. *Washington Post*. July 16: C5.

Rimland, B. 1964. *Infantile autism*. New York: Appleton-Century-Crofts.

Rincover, A., Newsom, C. D., and Carr, E. G. 1979. Using sensory extinction procedures in the treatment of compulsive-like behavior of developmentally disabled children. *Journal of Consulting and Clinical Psychology* 47: 695-701.

Robins, L. N. 1966. *Deviant children grown up*. Baltimore: Williams & Wilkins.

Robins, L. N., et al. 1984. Life-time prevalence of specific psychiatric disorders in three sites. *Archives of General Psychiatry* 41: 949-58.

Ross, D. M., and Ross, S. A. 1982. *Hyperactivity: Current issues, research and theory* (2d ed.). New York: Wiley.

Rothstein, J. H. 1971. *Mental retardation: Readings and resources* (2d ed.). New York: Holt, Rinehart & Winston.

Routh, D. K., and Daugherty, T. K. 1992. Conduct disorder. In S. R. Hooper, G. W. Hynd, and R. E. Mattison (Eds.), *Child psychopathology*. Hillsdale, NJ: Lawrence Erlbaum.

Rudolph, K. D., Hammen, C., and Burge, D. 1994. Interpersonal functioning and depressive symptoms in childhood: Addressing the issues of specificity and comorbidity. *Journal of Abnormal Child Psychology* 22 (3): 355-71.

Rule, A. 1992. *Everything she ever wanted: A true story of obsessive love, murder, and betrayal*. New York: Simon & Schuster.

Russell, G.F.M. 1985. Anorexia and bulimia nervosa. In M. Rutter and M. Hersov (Eds.), *Child and adolescent psychiatry* (2d ed.). Oxford: Blackwell Scientific.

Rutter, M. 1979. Protective factors in children's responses to stress and disadvantage. In M. W. Kent and J. E. Rolf (Eds.), *Primary prevention of psychopathology*. Vol. 3. *Social competence in children*. Hanover, NH: University Press of New England.

———. 1985. The developmental psychopathology of depression: Issues and perspectives. In M. Rutter, C. E. Izard, and P. B. Read (Eds.), *Depression in young people*. New York: Guilford.

———. 1987. Psychosocial resilience and protective mechanisms. *American Journal of Orthopsychiatry* 57: 47-61.

Rutter, M., Maughan, B., Mortimore, P., and Ouston, J. 1979. *Fifteen thousand hours*. Cambridge, MA: Harvard University Press.

Rutter, M., Tizard, J., and Whitmore, K. 1970. *Education, health and behaviour*. London: Longman.

Rynders, J. E., Johnson, R. T., Johnson, D. W., and Schmidt, B. 1980. Producing positive interaction among Down's syndrome and nonhandicapped teenagers through cooperative goal structuring. *American Journal of Mental Deficiency* 85: 268-73.

Sabornie, E. J. 1994. Social-affective characteristics in early adolescents identified as learning disabled and nondisabled. *Learning Disability Quarterly* 17 (4): 268-79.

Sarason, I. G., and Sarason, B. R. 1993. *Abnormal psychology* (7th ed.). Englewood Cliffs, NJ: Prentice-Hall.

Sarason, S. B., Davidson, K., and Blatt, B. 1962. *The preparation of teachers: An unstudied problem in education*. New York: Wiley.

Schalock, R. L., et al. 1994. The changing conception of mental retardation: Implications for the field. *Mental Retardation* 32 (3): 181-93.

Schechter, M. D., Toussieng, P. W., and Sternlof, R. E. 1972. Normal development in adolescence. In B. B. Wolman (Ed.), *Manual of child psychopathology*. New York: McGraw-Hill.

Scheerenberger, R. C. 1971. Mental retardation: Definition, classification, and prevalence. In J. H. Rothstein (Ed.), *Mental retardation*. New York: Holt, Rinehart & Winston.

Schwartz, S., and Johnson, J. H. 1981. *Psychopathology of childhood*. New York: Pergamon Press.

Sebald, H. 1968. *Adolescence: A sociological analysis*. New York: Appleton-Century-Crofts.

Seligman, L., and Moore, B. M. 1995. Diagnosis of mood disorders. *Journal of Counseling and Development* 74 (1): 65-69.

Shaffer, D. 1985. Depression, mania and suicidal acts. In M. Rutter and M. Hersov (Eds.), *Child and adolescent psychiatry* (2d ed.). Oxford: Blackwell Scientific.

Shapiro, A. K., Shapiro, E. S., Bruun, R. D., and Sweet, T.R.D. 1978. *Gilles de la Tourette syndrome*. New York: Raven Press.

Shapiro, E.A.K. 1981. Tic disorders. *Journal of the American Medical Association* 245: 1583-85.

Shaywitz, S. E., and Shaywitz, B. A. 1988. Attention deficit disorder: Current perspectives. In J. F. Kavanaugh and T. J. Truss, Jr. (Eds.), *Learning disabilities: Proceedings of the national conference*. Parkton, MD: York.

Short, R. J., and Simeonsson, R. J. 1986. Social cognition and aggression in
    delinquent adolescent males. *Adolescence* 21: 159-76.
Siantz, J., and Moore, E. 1978. Inservice programming and preservice priorities.
    In J. Smith (Ed.), *Personnel preparation and Public Law 94-142: The map,
    the mission and the mandate* (2d ed.). Boothwyn, PA: Educational Resources
    Center.
Simon, W., and Gagnon, J. H. 1972. On psychosexual development. In W. R. Looft
    (Ed.), *Developmental psychology*. Hinsdale, IL: Dryden.
Singer, J. 1993. Once is not enough: Former special educators who return to
    teaching. *Exceptional Children* 60 (1): 58-72.
Siperstein, G. N., and Goding, M. J. 1985. Teachers' behavior toward learning
    disabled and non-learning disabled children: A strategy for change.
    Journal of Learning Disabilities 18: 139-44.
Skiba, R., and Grizzle, K. 1991. The social maladjustment exclusion: Issues of defin-
    ition and assessment. *School Psychology Review* 20 (4): 580-98.
Slate, J. R., and Saudargas, R. A. 1986. Differences in learning disabled and average
    students' classroom behaviors. *Learning Disability Quarterly* 9: 61-67.
Slavin, R. 1990. *Educational psychology*. Englewood Cliffs, NJ: Prentice-Hall.
Slenkovich, J. E. 1992. Can the language "social maladjustment" in the SED
    definition be ignored? *School Psychology Review* 21 (1): 21-22.
Slomkowski, C., Klein, R. G., and Mannuzza, S. 1995. Is self-esteem an
    important outcome in hyperactive children? *Journal of Abnormal Child
    Psychology* 23 (3): 303-16.
Smith, B. O. 1980. Pedagogical education: How about reform? *Phi Delta Kappan*
    62: 87-91.
Smith, C. R. 1983. *Learning disabilities*. Boston: Little, Brown.
Smith, D. C., and Street, S. 1980. The professional component in selected
    professions. *Phi Delta Kappan* 62: 103-7.
Smith, R. M., and Neisworth, J. T. 1975. *The exceptional child: A functional
    approach.* New York: McGraw-Hill.
Snyder, J., and Huntley, D. 1990. Troubled families and troubled youth: The
    development of antisocial   behavior and depression in children. In P. E.
    Leone (Ed.), *Understanding troubled and troubling youth*. Newbury Park, CA:
    Sage.
Snyder, L. 1975. *Pragmatics in language disabled children: Their prelinguistic
    and early verbal performatives and presuppositions.* Unpublished
    doctoral dissertation, University of Colorado.
Sontag, L. W. 1972. Contributions of biological and organic viewpoints. In B. B.
    Wolman (Ed.), *Manual of child psychopathology*. New York: McGraw-Hill.
Spivack, G. R. 1994. When ADHD is not ADHD. *Families Newspaper* 3 (10): 8.
Stein, P., and Hoover, J. 1989. Manifest anxiety in children with learning
    disabilities. *Journal of Learning Disabilities* 22: 66-67.
Steinberg, D. 1983. *The clinical psychiatry of adolescence*. New York: Wiley.
Steinhausen, H. 1994. Anorexia and bulimia nervosa. In M. Rutter, E. Taylor,
    and L. Hersov (Eds.), *Child and adolescent psychiatry* (3d ed.). London:
    Blackwell Scientific.
Stephens, S. A., Lakin, K. C., Brauen, M., and O'Reilly, F. 1990. *The study of
    programs of instruction for handicapped children and youth in day and*

residential facilities (3 vols.). Washington, DC: U. S. Department of Education and Mathematics Policy Research.

Stephenson, W. 1953. *The study of behavior: Q technique and its methodology.* Chicago: University of Chicago Press.

Stevens, T. M. 1977. *Teaching skills to children with learning and behavior disorders.* Columbus, OH: Charles E. Merrill.

Stevenson, R. L. 1886; 1992. The strange case of Dr. Jekyll and Mr. Hyde. In C. Harman (Eds.), *The strange case of Dr. Jekyll and Mr. Hyde and other stories.* London: J. M. Dent & Sons.

Stone, L. J., and Church, J. 1968. *Childhood and adolescence* (2d ed.). New York: Random House.

Swedo, S. E., et al. 1989. Obsessive-compulsive disorder in children and adolescents: Clinical phenomenology of 70 consecutive cases. *Archives of General Psychiatry* 46 (4): 335-41.

Szymanski, L. S. 1988. Integrative approach to diagnosis of mental disorders in retarded persons. In J. A. Stark et al. (Eds.), *Mental retardation and mental health.* New York: Springer-Verlag.

Szymanski, L. S., and Kaplan, L. C. 1991. Mental retardation. In J. M. Wiener (Ed.), *Textbook of child & adolescent psychiatry.* Washington, DC: American Psychiatric Press.

Taylor, A. R., Asher, S. R., and Williams, G. A. 1987. The social adaptation of mainstreamed mildly retarded children. *Child Development* 58: 1321-34.

Taylor, E. 1985. Syndromes of overactivity and attention deficit. In M. Rutter and M. Hersov (Eds.), *Child and adolescent psychiatry* (2d ed.). Oxford: Blackwell Scientific.

Tharinger, D. J., Laurent, J., and Best, L. R. 1986. Classification of children referred for emotional and behavioral problems: A comparison of the PL 94-142 SED criteria, DSM III, and the CBCL system. *Journal of School Psychology* 24: 111-21.

Thompson, R. 1986. Behavior problems in children with developmental and learning disabilities. *International Academy of Research in Learning Disabilities Monograph Series* 3: 1-125.

Thompson, T. 1995. Shadow on the brain. *Washington Post Magazine.* July 9: 8-13, 22-27.

Torgeson, J. K. 1982. The learning disabled child as an inactive learner: Educational implications. *Topics in Learning and Learning Disabilities* 5: 45-52.

Tourette, G. de la. 1885. Etude sur une affection nerveuse caracterisee par l'incoordination motrice accompagnee d'echolalie et de copralalie. *Archives of Neurology* 9: 19-42, 158-200.

_____. 1899. La maladie des tics convulsifs. *La Semaine Medicale* 19: 153-56.

Tourette Syndrome Association. 1994. *Questions and answers about Tourette Syndrome.* Bayside, NY: TSA.

Towbin, K. 1995. Presentation to the Greater Washington Tourette Syndrome Association. May 21. Silver Spring, MD.

Towbin, K. E., Riddle, M. A., Leckman, J. F., and Cohen, D. J. 1992. The diagnosis and assessment of tic disorders. In S. R. Hooper, G. W.

Hynd, and R. E. Mattison (Eds.), *Child psychopathology*. Hillsdale, NJ: Lawrence Erlbaum, pp. 343-77.

Trammel, D. L., Schloss, P. T., and Alper, S. 1994. Using self-recording, evaluation, and graphing to increase completion of homework assignments. *Journal of Learning Disabilities* 27 (2): 75-81.

Turner, C. W., and Dodd, D. K. 1980. The development of antisocial behavior. In R. L. Ault (Ed.), *Developmental perspectives*. Santa Monica, CA: Goodyear.

U.S. Department of Education, Office of Special Education and Rehabilitative Services (OSERS). 1991. *Thirteenth annual report to Congress on the implementation of PL 94-142*. Washington, DC: U.S. Government Printing Office.

_____. 1993. *Fifteenth annual report to Congress on the implementation of the Individuals with Disabilities Act*. Washington, DC: U.S. Government Printing Office.

_____.1996. *Eighteenth annual report to Congress on the implementation of the Individuals with Disabilities Act*. Washington, DC: U.S. Government Printing Office.

Van Buskirk, S. S. 1977. A two-phase perspective in the treatment of anorexia nervosa. *Psychological Bulletin* 84: 529-38.

Vasey, M. W., Daleiden, E. L., Williams, L. L., and Brown, L. M. 1995. Biased attention in childhood anxiety disorders: A preliminary study. *Journal of Abnormal Child Psychology* 23 (2): 267-79.

Vincent, L. M. 1979. *Competing with the sylph: Dancers and the pursuit of the ideal body form*. New York: Andrews and McMeel.

Voeller, K.K.S. 1991. Toward a neurobiologic nosology of attention deficit hyperactivity disorder. *Journal of Clinical Neurology* 6 (S): S2-S8.

Volavka, J. 1995. *Neurobiology of violence*. Washington, DC: American Psychiatric Association Press.

Von Isser, A., Quay, H. C., and Love, C. T. 1980. Interrelationships among three measures of deviant behavior. *Exceptional Children* 46: 272-76.

Waldron, S., Shier, D. K., Stone, B., and Tobin, F. 1975. School phobia and other childhood neuroses: A systematic study of children and their families. *American Journal of Psychiatry* 132: 802-5.

Walker, H. M., Shinn, M. R., O'Neill, R. E., and Ramsey, E. 1987. A longitudinal assessment of the development of antisocial behavior in boys: Rationale, methodology, and first year results. *Remedial and Special Education* 8 (4): 7-16.

Walker, J. L., et al. 1991. Anxiety, inhibition, and conduct disorder in children: I. Relation to social impairment. *Journal of the American Academy of Child and Adolescent Psychiatry* 30: 187-91.

Waller, G. 1994. Borderline personality disorder and perceived family dysfunction in the eating disorders. *Journal of Nervous and Mental Disease* 182 (10): 541-46.

Waller, J. V., Kaufman, M. R., and Deutsch, F. 1975. Anorexia nervosa: A psychosomatic entity. In A. H. Esman (Ed.), *The psychology of adolescence*. New York: International Universities Press.

Walsh, P.J.F. 1962. Compulsive shouting and Gilles de la Tourette's disease.

British Journal of Clinical Practice 16: 652-55.

Warren, M. P. 1985. When weight loss accompanies amenorrhea. *Contemporary Obstetrics and Gynecology* 28 (3): 588-97.

Weill, M. P. 1992. Gifted/learning disabled students. In K. L. Freiberg (Ed.), *Educating exceptional children.* Guilford, CT: Dushkin.

Weinberg, W., Rutman, J., Sullivan, L., Penick, E., and Deitz, B. 1973. Depression in children referred to an educational diagnostic center. *Journal of Pediatrics* 83: 1065-72.

Weiner, A. S. 1983. Emotional problems of adolescence: A review of affective disorders and schizophrenia. In C. E. Walker and C. Roberts (Eds.), *Handbook of clinical child psychology.* New York: Wiley.

Weller, C., Strawser, S., Callahan, J. S., Pugh, L. A., and Watanabe, A. K. 1990. Assessment of sub-types of learning disabilities: A practical approach to diagnosis and intervention. *Special Services in the Schools* 6 (1/2): 100-114.

Weller, E., and Weller, R. A. 1991. Mood disorders in children. In J. M. Wiener (Ed.), *Textbook of child & adolescent psychiatry.* Washington, DC: American Psychiatric Press.

Wenar, C. 1990. *Developmental psychopathology: From infancy through adolescence.* New York: McGraw-Hill.

Wender, P. H. 1975. The minimal brain dysfunction syndrome. *Annual Review of Medicine* 26: 45-62.

Wenz-Gross, M., and Siperstein, G. N. 1997. Importance of social support in the adjustment of children with learning problems. *Exceptional Children* 63 (2): 183-93.

West, L. J., and Coburn, K. 1984. Posttraumatic anxiety. In R. O. Pasnau (Ed.), *Diagnosis and treatment of anxiety disorders.* Washington, DC: American Psychiatric Press.

Whalen, C. K., Henker, B., Collins, B. E., Finck, D., and Dotemoto, S. 1979. A social ecology of hyperactive boys: Medication effects in structured classroom environments. *Journal of Applied Behavior Analysis* 12: 65-81.

White, B. L. 1975. *The first three years of life.* Englewood Cliffs, NJ: Prentice-Hall.

Whybrow, P. C., Akiskal, H. S., and McKinney, W. T. 1984. *Mood disorders.* New York: Plenum.

Wiig, E. H., and Harris, S. P. 1974. Perception and interpretation of nonverbally expressed emotions by adolescents with learning disabilities. *Perceptual and Motor Skills* 38: 239-45.

Winn, M. 1984. *Children without childhood.* New York: Penguin Books.

Wolf, M. M., Brauckman, C. J., and Ramp, K. A. 1987. Serious delinquent behavior as part of a significantly handicapping condition: Cures and supportive environments. *Journal of Applied Behavior Analysis* 20: 347-59.

Wolman, B. B. (Ed.), and Stricker, G. (Co-Ed.) 1994. *Anxiety and related disorders.* New York: Wiley.

Woodrow, K. M. 1974. Gilles de la Tourette's disease: A review. *American Journal of Psychiatry* 131: 1000-1003.

Worell, J., and Stilwell, W. E. 1981. *Psychology for teachers and students.* New York: McGraw-Hill.

World Health Organization. 1980, 1990. *The international classification of diseases* (ICD-9, ICD-10). Geneva: WHO.

Wurtzel, E. 1994. *Prozac nation: Young and depressed in America.* New York: Houghton Mifflin.

Wyne, M. D., and O'Connor, P. D. 1979. *Exceptional children: A developmental view.* Lexington, MA: D. C. Heath.

Yaryura-Tobias, J. A. 1982. Clinical and laboratory data on Gilles de la Tourette syndrome. In A. J. Friedhoff and T. Chase (Eds.), *Tourette syndrome.* New York: Raven.

Yates, A. 1978. *Sex without shame: Encouraging the child's healthy sexual development.* New York: William Morrow.

Yorukoglu, A., and Kemph, J. P. 1966. Children not severely damaged by incest with a parent. *Journal of the American Academy of Child Psychiatry* 5: 111.

Ysseldyke, J. E., and Algozzine, B. 1982. *Critical issues in special and remedial education.* Boston: Houghton Mifflin.

_____. 1984. *Introduction to special education.* Boston: Houghton Mifflin.

Yule, W. 1994. Posttraumatic stress disorders. In M. Rutter, E. Taylor, and L. Hersov (Eds.), *Child and adolescent psychiatry* (3d ed.). London: Blackwell Scientific.

Zarcone, V., Thorpe, B., and Dement, W. 1972. Sleep parameters in two patients with Gilles de la Tourette syndrome. *Sleep Research* 1: 155-57.

Zausmer, D. M. 1954. Treatment of tics in childhood. *Archives of the Disabled Child* 29: 537-42.

Zentall, S. 1993. Research on the educational implications of attention deficit hyperactivity disorder. *Exceptional Children* 60 (2): 143-53.

Zentall, S. S. 1977. Environmental stimulation model. *Exceptional Children* 44: 502-10

Zentall, S. S., and Gohs, D. E. 1984. Hyperactive and comparison children's response to detailed vs. global cues in communication tasks. *Learning Disability Quarterly* 7: 77-87.

Zentall, S. S., and Meyer, M. J. 1987. Self-regulation of stimulation for ADD-H children during reading and vigilance task performance. *Journal of Abnormal Child Psychology* 15: 519-36.

Index

About the Author

C. ROBIN BOUCHER, Ph.D. is an impartial hearing officer for the Washington, D.C. Public Schools and resource specialist (emotional disabilities) for the Fairfax, Virginia Public Schools. She has thirteen years of experience as a teacher of students with autism, emotional and behavioral disorders, and learning disabilities.